The Age of Titans

Onassis Series in Hellenic Culture

The Age of Titans: The Rise and Fall of the Great Hellenistic Navies
William M. Murray

Onassis
Foundation (USA)

The Age of Titans

The Rise and Fall of the Great Hellenistic Navies

WILLIAM M. MURRAY

OXFORD
UNIVERSITY PRESS

OXFORD
UNIVERSITY PRESS

Oxford University Press is a department of the University of Oxford.
It furthers the University's objective of excellence in research, scholarship,
and education by publishing worldwide.

Oxford   New York
Auckland   Cape Town   Dar es Salaam   Hong Kong   Karachi
Kuala Lumpur   Madrid   Melbourne   Mexico City   Nairobi
New Delhi   Shanghai   Taipei   Toronto

With offices in
Argentina   Austria   Brazil   Chile   Czech Republic   France   Greece
Guatemala   Hungary   Italy   Japan   Poland   Portugal   Singapore
South Korea   Switzerland   Thailand   Turkey   Ukraine   Vietnam

Published in the United States of America by
Oxford University Press
198 Madison Avenue, New York, NY 10016

Library of Congress Cataloging-in-Publication Data
Murray, William M.
The age of titans : the rise and fall of the great Hellenistic navies / William M. Murray.
    p.   cm. — (The Onassis series in Hellenic culture)
Includes bibliographical references and index.
ISBN 978-0-19-538864-0 (hardcover); 978-0-19-938225-5 (paperback)
1. Naval history, Ancient. 2. Greece—History, Naval.
3. Naval art and science—Greece—History. I. Title.
V37.M87   2012
359.00938—dc22   2011010647

9 8 7 6 5 4 3 2 1

Printed in the United States of America
on acid-free paper

For Mom and Dad

Contents

List of Figures

(All photographs are by the author unless indicated otherwise. Relevant publications not mentioned in the text are placed in square brackets at the end of select entries.)

(A): *Columna rostrata* of Octavian depicted on a denarius, 29–27 BCE. Courtesy of the American Numismatic Society. [Sutherland 1984, 60, #271, and Pl. 5.]

(B): Equestrian statue of Octavian (?) *in rostris* depicted on a denarius minted by Cossus Cornelius Lentulus in 12 BCE. Courtesy of the American Numismatic Society. [Sutherland 1984, 73, #412, and Pl. 7.]

(C): "Antonian Rostra" depicted on a denarius minted by Lollius Palicanus in 45 BCE. Courtesy of the American Numismatic Society. [Crawford 1974, Vol. 1, 482–483, #473/1.]

(D): *Rostra Aedis Divi Iulii* on the *Anaglypha Traiani* (detail from left panel). Early second century CE. Forum Romanum, Rome. [Torelli 1982, 98, and Pls. IV.1, IV.5–6.]

(E): *Rostra Augusti* on the *Anaglypha Traiani* (detail from right panel). Early second century CE. Forum Romanum, Rome. [Torelli 1982, 98, and IV.2, IV.11.]

(F): Rostrate altar (Augustan period?) with the inscription *Ara Neptuni*. One of four such altars dredged from a small harbor at Antium by Innocent XII. Stanza del Fauno, Palazzo dei Conservatori, Rome. [Jones 1912, 327, 23a with Pl. 80; the other altars are depicted as follows: 330, Fig. 26a; 331, Fig. 27a.]

Belgammel Ram (Fitzwilliam Ram): Museum of Libya, Tripoli. Image adapted from Nichols 1970–71, 85, Fig. 14.

Bremerhaven Ram: Deutsches Schiffahrtsmuseum, Bremerhaven. Photo by René Mueller, courtesy of the Römisch-Germanisches Zentralmuseum, Mainz. By permission of the Deutsches Schiffahrtsmuseum, Bremerhaven.

Piraeus Ram: Piraeus Archaeological Museum. By permission of
the 26th Ephorate of Prehistoric and Classical Antiquities,
Greek Ministry of Culture.

Acqualadroni Ram: Currently undergoing conservation and study
by the Soprintendenza del Mare of Sicily. Image adapted from
photo by "Odisseo" posted 2/16/2009 to the following URL
(http://www.betasom.it/forum/index.php?showtopic=26840&p
id=264615&mode=threaded&;start).

Egadi 1 (Trapani) Ram: Currently undergoing study by the
Soprintendenza del Mare of Sicily. Photo courtesy of Claire
Calcagno.

Egadi 2 (Catherine D) Ram: Currently undergoing conservation and
study by the Soprintendenza del Mare of Sicily. Photo courtesy
of Jeff Royal.

Athlit Ram: National Maritime Museum, Haifa.

List of Maps

List of Tables

Acknowledgments

THE IDEAS EXPRESSED in this book have evolved slowly over a long period of time, originating in my studies of the Athlit ram and Augustus's Victory Monument at Nikopolis. These ideas further coalesced during the academic year of 1995–96 when, as Whitehead Professor at the American School of Classical Studies at Athens, I led a seminar titled "Ancient Navies" for interested members of the School community. A year later, I was invited by Professor Avner Raban to visit the University of Haifa as Maurice Hatter Visiting Scholar and to present this seminar to the faculty and students of the Maritime Civilizations Department. This book owes its genesis to these two fertile experiences, to the faculty, students, staff, and libraries of these two institutions.

Books of this sort are not written without specialized publications, without time to think and reflect, and without travel stipends to visit museums and sites. In this regard, I owe a debt of gratitude to my institutional library at the University of South Florida, who managed to purchase, borrow, or grant me Internet access to most of the items listed in my bibliography, and to my Chair, Fraser Ottanelli, who enabled my partial release from teaching at critical times. In like manner, I owe much to the generosity of Gus and Mary Stathis, whose professorship I hold at USF, and whose research stipend has made possible my repeated travel to sites, libraries and museums. I am also indebted to the American Foundation for Greek Language and Culture for their support of my university. I thank the USF Humanities Institute for a grant that allowed me, in 2009, to visit certain important sites and museums where I recorded images appearing in this book. This trip would have been impossible without the logistical and linguistic talents of my colleagues Suzanne Murray and Giovanna Benadusi, both of whom I thank here.

Trips to sites and museums would have been fruitless without the generous help of many archaeologists and museum curators in Greece, Israel, and Italy and, although they are too numerous to mention individually, I wish to thank them here for their permission to study and photograph the artifacts appearing in this book. A few, like Elisha Linder and Photios Petsas, require special mention because they started me on the journey resulting in this book. In regard to Actium, special thanks must go to Konstantinos L. Zachos, who continues to encourage my study of Augustus's Victory Monument, to Nikos D. Karabelas, President of the Actia Nicopolis Foundation, and to Lorne Thyssen for funding my attempts to recreate the rams once displayed on Augustus's monument. John McK. Camp II, William D. E. Coulson and Maria Pilali helped at critical moments and provided sound advice when it was most needed. Lionel Casson encouraged me to pursue ideas that often conflicted with his own published views and unknowingly provided a model of behavior I still try to follow. J. Richard Steffy also served as a scholarly role model and patiently introduced me to the intricacies of the Athlit ram, as did Shlomo Eisenberg and, later, Çemal Pulak and Asaf Oron. I thank them all for their willingness to share their thoughts and insights.

As regards the book itself, I received help from numerous people whom I now wish to acknowledge. Jon Mikalson kindly clarified numerous issues related to Philo's Greek, Michael Decker introduced me to various Byzantine military writers and then he, Jeff Royal, John Grainger, and Kurt Raaflaub commented on specific chapters, catching mistakes and omissions in the process. Andrea Johnson Pittard helped prepare the final manuscript by fact checking, tending to formatting changes, and compiling various lists, working at times with Andrew J. Bird, who helped with Appendix B. Both helped with final proofing and index creation. I thank the press for helping me to improve this book in many ways and by working closely with me to produce the maps to my specifications. The press's anonymous reader added useful comments as well as my editor Stefan Vranka, copyeditor Lynn Kauppi, and production editor Maria Pucci. Their assistance greatly improved the book's content, consistency, clarity and presentation. And last, but not least, I thank the Onassis Foundation (USA) for selecting my work for their new Onassis Series in Hellenic Culture and for the enriching opportunity to participate in their University Seminars Program as both a host and a lecturer.

At last, we come to my family whose support makes everything possible. I thank my wife Suzanne who has encouraged and helped me in ways too complex and numerous to describe adequately. Without her help, both at home and in the field, this book would have never been written. She alone understands the depth of my gratitude. My son Alex may not know it, but he helped tremendously by enduring with good humor a life filled with summer trips to archaeological sites and museums since he was a little boy. And finally, I must acknowledge my parents Robert and Evelyn Murray for providing the right support throughout my life whenever I most needed it. For these reasons and a host of others that defy reduction into words, I dedicate this book to them. I finish with the oft repeated phrase that none of those who helped and supported me should share the blame for errors or misstatements remaining in my text. For these, I am alone responsible.

Abbreviations

Barrington Atlas: Richard A. Talbert, ed., *Barrington Atlas of the Greek and Roman World* (Princeton: Princeton University Press, 2000).

FGrH: Felix Jacoby, *Die Fragmente der griechischen Historiker* (Leiden: Brill, 1954). My references stem from Brill's CD-Rom Edition (2005).

IG II²: Johannes Kirchner, *Inscriptiones Atticae Euclidis anno posteriores, Inscriptiones Graecae, consilio et auctoritate Academiae Litterarum Borussicae editae,* Editio minor, vols. 2–3, pars 2, fasc. posterior (Berlin: de Gruyter, 1931).

Loeb Dio: Cassius Dio Cocceianus, Earnest Cary and Herbert Baldwin Foster, *Dio's Roman History,* 9 vols. (London: W. Heinemann, 1914–27).

Loeb *Select Papyri*: Arthur S. Hunt and C. C. Edgar, *Select Papyri,* 2 vols. (Cambridge: Harvard University Press, 1932–33).

LSJ⁹: H. G. Liddell, and R. Scott, eds., *A Greek-English Lexicon,* rev. H. S. Jones, R. McKenzie, E. A. Barber, 9th ed. (Oxford: Clarendon, 1976).

OGIS: Wilhelmus Dittenberger, *Orientis Graeci Inscriptiones Selectae. Supplementum Sylloges Inscriptionum Graecarum,* 2 vols. (Leipzig: S. Hirzel, 1903–1905).

OLD: P. G. W. Glare, ed., *Oxford Latin Dictionary,* corrected ed. (Oxford: Clarendon, 1996).

TLG: *Thesaurus Linguae Graecae: A Digital Library of Greek*
                               Literature. Available online at http://www.tlg.uci.
                               edu/. Published by the TLG Project, University of
                               California, Irvine, California, 2001–. Precise details
                               for texts coded into this online database can be
                               found in Berkowitz and Squitier 1990. Texts cited
                               with a *TLG* reference placed within parentheses can
                               be found under the author and work cited in the
                               primary reference.

For standard abbreviations referring to collections of inscriptions, papyri,
ancient authors and their works, etc., see those appearing in LSJ[9] and
OLD. Notable exceptions or particularly obscure authors are abbreviated
as follows (Anglicized names used in the text appear in parentheses):

Arr. *Anab.*	Arrianus (Arrian), *Anabasis*
Athen. *Deip.*	Athenaeus, *Deipnosophistai*
Athen. Mech.	Athenaeus Mechanicus, *Peri Mechanematon*
Caes. *BC*	Caesar, *de Bello Civile*
BG	Caesar, *de Bello Gallico*
Callixenus in Athen. *Deip.*	Callixenus as quoted by Athenaeus, *Deipnosophistai*
Dio	Dio Cassius, *Historiae Romanae*
Dion. Geogr. *Per Bosp.*	Dionysius Byzantius Geographicus, *Per Bosporum navigatio*
Jos. *AJ*	Josephus, *Antiquitates Judaicae*
Lucian *Dial. mort.*	Lucianus (Lucian), *Dialogi mortuorum*
Luc. *BC*	Lucanus (Lucan), *Bellum Civile*
Moschion in Athen. *Deip.*	Moschion as quoted by Athenaeus, *Deipnosophistai*
Philo *Polior.*	Philo Byzantius (= Philo Mechanicus in LSJ[9] and *TLG*), *Poliorketika*
Bel.	Philo Byzantius, *Belopoiika*
Pliny *NH*	Pliny the Elder, *Naturalis Historia*
Plut. *Demetr.*	Plutarchus (Plutarch), *Demetrius*
Mor.	Plutarchus (Plutarch), *Moralia*
Pelop.	Plutarchus (Plutarch), *Pelopidas*
Mar.	Plutarchus (Plutarch), *Marcellus*

Quaest. conv.	Plutarchus (Plutarch), *Quaestiones convivales*
Sen. *Ira*	Seneca, *de Ira*
St. Byz.	Stephanus Byzantius, *Ethnikon*
Syr. *Srat.*	Syrianus Magister, *Peri Strategias*
Naum.	Syrianus Magister, *Naumachiai*
Theophr. *Hist. pl.*	Theophrastus, *Historia Plantarum*
Veg. *Mil.*	Vegetius *Epitoma Rei Militaris*

The Age of Titans

Introduction

Understanding the Big Ship Phenomenon

[Ptolemy II] Philadelphus stood apart from all other kings in wealth and strove so zealously in regard to all his constructions that he surpassed everyone even in the number of his ships. Indeed, the largest of his ships included two "thirties," one "twenty," four "thirteens," two "twelves," 14 "elevens," 30 "nines," 37 "sevens," five "sixes," and 17 "fives." He had twice as many ships as these from "fours" to *triemioliai*; and the ships sent to the islands and to the other cities he ruled and to Libya numbered more than 4000.

—ATHEN. *DEIP.* 5.203D (*TLG*, 5.36.11–21)

THE GENERAL SUBJECT of this book concerns the genesis and evolution of a distinctly Macedonian model of naval power during the last four centuries BCE. At the core of my investigation lies a unique period dubbed "The Age of Titans" by Lionel Casson, when an intense arms race developed among the most powerful successors of Alexander the Great.[1] In the space of a single generation, we detect a burst of naval development that produced warships of increasingly large size. The term we traditionally apply to warships larger than triremes ("threes"), the standard warship in major fleets during the fifth and fourth centuries BCE, is "polyremes," from the Greek *polyereis*, but such a term—which translates roughly as "many fitted"— never existed in antiquity.[2] The ancients either called these ships by their class name (a number plus the *-eres* root) or by a descriptive term "cata-phract" (*kataphraktos*) which means something like "armored" or "fenced" in the sense of having reinforced decks and sides to protect the oarcrew

---

1. See Casson 1991, 127–42, who uses the term as a chapter title.

2. While this term reflects the root *-eres* found in names applied to these large ships, e.g. *tetreres* ("four") or *dekeres* ("ten"), it does not appear until the 6th century (Agathias 5.22 = *TLG*, 192.23), well after the big ship phenomenon had run its course, and is applied to small skiffs (*epaktridas . . . polyereis*, "many-oared skiffs") of a completely different build. Modern practice applies the term polyreme to ships rated as "fours" or larger.

from missiles and deck fighting. Because "The Age of Titans" involved galleys whose signature feature was their larger than normal size, and because cataphract galleys could comprise small ships that were protected by extra planking, I frequently employ another term to describe these ships, namely, "big" or "large," from the Greek *megala skaphe* and its variants *megalai nees* ("big ships) and *megista skaphe* ("biggest ships").

Surprisingly, this simple-sounding term has a respectable pedigree. We find the expression in the text of Athenaeus's "The Learned Banqueters" (*Deipnosophistai*) quoted above; we find it in Appian's history of the Roman civil wars (*BC* 2.12.84 and 5.11.108); and we find it in the siegecraft manual of Philo the Byzantine (*Polior.* D 22, 29). The Latin language had an equivalent, which we can see in Livy's expression *naves maioris/maximae formae* or "ships of larger/largest size" (37.23.5, 30.2). While the adjectives "big" or "large" were used to describe merchant ships as well, the simple concept of size has a straightforward quality appropriate to our investigation, and so I have chosen to use it throughout this book.[3]

Was bigger better? The obvious answer was "yes," but exactly why this was the case is more difficult to discern than one might suspect. According to most naval historians, the driving force behind this big ship phenomenon was a move from "maneuver-and-ram" battle tactics, popular with the Athenian navy in the Classical period, to "grapple-and-board" tactics, preferred by the Romans in their struggle with Carthage. Each new increase in size produced wider and more stable fighting decks that afforded more space for soldiers and for artillery, a new invention that was perfected during the time these big ships were built. Grappling hooks and harpoons were shot or thrown into enemy vessels so they could be dragged alongside for boarding by increasingly large gangs of deck soldiers. Eventually, so one argument goes, catapults were powerful enough to shoot large arrows through the decks of opposing ships, disrupting the oarcrews and thereby negating the use of ramming tactics in battle.[4] Battles between big ships came to resemble fights between floating fortresses.[5] Eventually, Roman excellence in this kind of grapple-and-board warfare revealed the useless expense involved with big ships that proved

---

3. For "big" merchant ships, see Strabo 3.2.4, 3.1; 5.2.10.

4. Foley and Soedel 1981, 148–63, especially 154, 160–62.

5. Garlan 1984, 361.

increasingly vulnerable to fleets of properly managed "fives" and smaller vessels. The final proof is seen at Actium, where Antony and Cleopatra opposed Octavian with a fleet that included a number of Hellenistic big ships in their front line. The results are well known: Octavian's lighter galleys ran rings around Antony's and Cleopatra's heavier ships, which they attacked in groups and set afire with incendiary missiles. Following this decisive victory, Octavian decommissioned the biggest ships that fell into his hands and the details of their use and construction were thereafter quickly forgotten.

This basic argument, with slight variations of degree and detail, can be found in most general treatments of naval power during the Hellenistic period.[6] Its fullest expression, at least in modern English, can be traced to a small book published by W. W. Tarn in 1930 titled "Hellenistic Military and Naval Developments."[7] The influence of this book is quite impressive, and extends through all modern scholarship on the subject of Hellenistic naval power.[8] I first began to question the basic conclusions reached by Tarn in this book when I encountered some new archaeological evidence that came to light in the 1980s. By this I mean the Athlit ram, an intact bronze warship ram from the late third or early second century, and Augustus's Victory Monument for the Actian War, where traces of large warship rams are still preserved in stone. This evidence suggested to me that ramming warfare had not fallen from favor, that big ships carried big rams at their bows, that great care and expense were lavished on the design and fabrication of these very large weapons, and that ramming tactics must have formed an integral part of the combat roles played by the big ships of the Hellenistic Age.

If Tarn's basic premise about these big ships was wrong, then what were the reasons for their introduction and rapid development? In order to understand the phenomenon of Hellenistic big ships, we must start

---

6. For a selection of authors who present this argument or reflect its influence on them, see: Köster 1923, 222–23, 232–34; Tarn (1930) 1960, 144–52; Casson 1995, 103; Rougé 1981, 98–99; Meijer 1986, 134, 207; Basch 1987, 345; Casson 1991, 134–36 (who notes that despite the emphasis on boarding, ramming was still utilized); and J. Coates in Morrison and Coates 1996, 309–10.

7. Tarn (1930) 1960, 101–52.

8. Only recently are scholars starting to question some of the basic premises stated as fact by Tarn in this little book. A good example can be found in the discussion by de Souza 2007, 357–61.

from what we know, or at least, from what we think we know. Naval architecture, like architecture in general, builds on previous developments, and we should expect to see an evolutionary process of some sort behind the development of these big ships.[9] Our best chance to determine what is going on involves returning to the period of Athens' Classical trireme navy, which is comprised of smaller warships called "threes," for which the sources are more plentiful, and from which we may detect the evolutionary trend that helps to explain the big ship phenomenon of the late fourth and third centuries. But first, I need to make clear the terms and definitions that will structure our discussion.

The Problem of Ship Classes

Each warship, big or small, forms a class with others of like build that follow a similar design and adhere to a particular set of uniform characteristics and dimensions. During the fifth century BCE, the major fleets of the Mediterranean powers were comprised of oared galleys called *triereis* in Greek (singular = *trieres*) or "triremes" to use the more familiar English form. Triremes, or "threes" (another common way to refer to these vessels), comprise the lower end of a series of warship classes named according to the number of oarsmen seated fore-and-aft along the hull in repeatable groupings. The size of this grouping is determined by the so-called *interscalmium*, mentioned by Vitruvius (1.2.4) as important for a ship's symmetry. Properly speaking, the *interscalmium* represents the linear distance between thole pins (*skalmoi*)—the vertical pins against which the oars were worked—at the same level.[10] This unit of measure, like the foot of a Greek temple, determined the basic proportions of its ship, and, along with the ship's beam, or width, limited the number of oarsmen that could be placed in the space between thole pins on each side of the ship. In the "three," we know that three oarsmen occupied this space. During the fourth and third centuries, a series of classes larger than "threes" were developed that ranged from "fours" (*tetrereis*), "fives" (*pentereis*), "sixes" (*hexereis*), "sevens" (*heptereis*), "eights" (*oktereis*), "nines" (*ennereis*), and so forth up to a gargantuan *tesserakonteres*, or "forty," the largest class on record.

---

9. This premise is also stated by Tarn 1910, 209: "I shall suppose . . . that the advances made in building, dimly as we can distinguish them, were due, not to this or that chance or whim, but to a linked process of development."

10. See further Morrison, Coates, and Rankov 2000, 133.

Because the determining factor of these big ships seems to have been the groupings of oarsmen along the side of the hull, scholars have argued for centuries about the precise nature of these arrangements and how they are reflected in written texts and preserved images of ancient warships.[11] Much ink has already been spilled on this topic and I do not intend to add any more. Still, we need to understand the basic elements involved in the debate because it will increase our confidence in the current *communis opinio* and influence our general understanding of how these warships worked and what their capabilities were.

Two different theories have been put forward to explain the *-eres* series of ship classes. The first grouped the oarsmen together at the same horizontal level, while the second placed the oarsmen in vertical levels, one above the other (sometimes in echelon, sometimes directly above). Each approach has its advocates, although the second solution is the one generally accepted today by most scholars for the "three." The first horizontal theory drew its inspiration from the *alla sensile* system of rowing attested on Mediterranean galleys of the thirteenth to sixteenth centuries.[12] Its adherents held firm until the late 1960s, when J. S. Morrison and R. T. Williams gathered an overwhelming body of textual and iconographic evidence to support the vertical theory.[13] Most scholars now accept that among Athenian oarsmen on a "three," each pulled his own oar and sat at one of three levels along the starboard and port sides of the hull. General acceptance of this idea has been bolstered by the successful launch of *Olympias*, a full-scale working model that demonstrates the feasibility of the vertical solution to the so-called "trireme question."[14]

Although the vertical theory works well for a "three," it cannot account for the larger classes, since there were practical limits to the levels one could build. There must be another way to explain classes larger than

---

11. See Casson 1995, 78–80, for a brief synopsis; Lehmann 1995 provides a detailed and often amusing view of some of the more obscure bibliography stretching back to the sixteenth century.

12. The *alla sensile* ("in the simple fashion") system of rowing was the earlier of the two used in Mediterranean fleets of the thirteenth to sixteenth centuries. It involved three to five oarsmen each pulling his own oar but sitting together on a single slanted bench. See Anderson 1976, 52–60 and Alertz 1995, 142–62.

13. Morrison and Williams 1968; see also Morrison 1941 for his initial argument.

14. The full story behind this impressive feat of experimental archaeology is described in Morrison, Coates, and Rankov 2000.

"threes" than by piling up levels of oarsmen atop one another.[15] The answer must involve combining the two theories. Variations are possible, but a "four" could be defined either by four men pulling a single heavy oar at one level, or by two men pulling a lighter oar at two different levels. Indeed, as we shall see, evidence from various periods reveals the "four" as a two level galley with significantly fewer oars than a "three."[16] If this approach is valid, then a "ten" might be defined by five men pulling a single large oar at two different levels, and a "sixteen" by eight men per oar at two different levels.

Multiple manned sweeps, as they are called, involved their own set of problems, but fortunately we can rely on recorded evidence from the sixteenth to eighteenth centuries to guide us. At this time, galleys were built with long oars or sweeps pulled by up to seven men. The oarsmen sat or stood side-by-side on long benches and pulled immense oars fitted with secondary handles called battens. They employed a system of rowing termed *al scaloccio* ("on the staircase") in which the inboard oarsmen ascended a step when dipping the oar in the water.[17] This standing/seated stroke apparently became necessary when more than two men were placed on an oar, and could be performed by unskilled oarsmen except for the inboard man, the *vogavante*, who was essentially the foreman of the gang.[18] All this, of course, required changes in the ship's design to accommodate more oarsmen and this new system of rowing. We may assume that the increases in size and weight brought about by these additional oarsmen, longer benches, steps, heavier oars, etc., were considerable. And while we may lack the precise details of these increases, we may be sure that they occurred.

There is one final aspect to consider. If the known condition of the *vogavante* is an indicator of ancient practice, then another benefit realized by the introduction of big ships involved a labor issue. Throughout the

---

15. An increase in height would result in an increase in oar length or in the angle at which the uppermost oar entered the water, and both conditions would increase the difficulty for oarsmen on the upper benches to coordinate their stroke with those below them. Furthermore, no ancient warship image shows more than three levels of oars.

16. See Appendix A (pp. 251–59).

17. See Anderson 1976, 67–73. In general on the problems involved in the different kinds of rowing, see M. Bondioli, R. Burlet and A. Zysberg in Gardiner and Morrison 1995, 172–205.

18. Anderson 1976, 69.

fourth century we have indications at Athens that it became increasingly difficult to find skilled oarcrews to row the "threes" of Athenian fleets.[19] Perhaps, so the argument goes, the big ships reduced drastically the number of trained men needed to row them, and this, along with the other factors of grapple-and-board warfare, made them more and more attractive. As incomplete a picture as this forms, it represents in brief our current understanding of big ships. There were exceptions and variations of course, and we will deal with these as they occur in subsequent sections.

The Main Questions

If what we think we know is even partially correct, then the advance in class size increased the number of oarsmen in the so-called *interscalmium* and forced the architects to enlarge the ship's beam and corresponding support structure. Thus, each increase in class seems to have resulted in heavier, broader-beamed warships with a corresponding increase in ramming power, and a corresponding decrease in speed and maneuverability—an observation substantiated by a number of testimonia describing these larger classes in action.[20] The next obvious question is this: "Why would one desire to increase ramming power at the expense of speed and maneuverability?" Why, for example, were "fours" and "fives" invented at the end of the fifth and beginning of the fourth centuries? And once they were built, why did Athens avoid adding these new classes to her own fleet for some 70 years?[21] If Athens thought these new classes were undesirable for some reason, what drove others to introduce a succession of classes from "sixes" to "sixteens" in the space of 35 years following Alexander's death (323–288 BCE)? Finally, how do we make sense of the special "eight" called *Leontophoros* (*Lion Bearer*) built by Lysimachus, or the "twenty" and

---

19. Casson 1991, 112.

20. For a different view, see Foley and Soedel 1981, 155, who argue that the increase in oar power from a "three" to a "five" was to gain an increase in speed. While this may be possible in theory, surviving descriptions of these classes in action do not support this view. See Appendices A and B.

21. In 330, Athens had 18 "fours" in her fleet, but no "fives" (*IG* II² 1627.275–78); seven "fives" appear for the first time in 324 (*IG* II² 1629.808–11). This situation is reflected in the text of Arist. *Ath.* 46.1, which lists among the tasks of the Boule the building of new "fours" and "threes," but not "fives." The latest secure date for authorship derives from a reference to the archon of 329/8 in Arist. *Ath.* 54.7.

two "thirties" built by Ptolemy II (not to mention the monster "forty" built by Ptolemy IV)?

Last but not least, how do we interpret the quote (presented at the beginning of this introduction) describing the navy of Ptolemy II during the mid-third century? His fleet included 112 big ships from "thirties" to "fives," and an equal number of "fours" to *triemioliai* (smaller variants of "threes") plus 4000 additional ships in service throughout the empire. Can we believe these numbers? The author Athenaeus clearly wrote to impress, but how do we place what he tells us in proper perspective? Was Ptolemy's fleet intended mainly as a display of royal power like the magnificent processions he was known to stage in Alexandria, or was it required to achieve specific strategic objectives?[22] And if he had certain objectives in mind when he gathered this collection of warships, what could possibly justify the crushing expenses needed to build, man, and maintain such a fleet?

In order to address these questions and others, I will trace the development of these big ships in a generally chronological fashion from the latter phases of the Peloponnesian War to the Battle of Actium. I say "generally" because the nature of our evidence demands that we look at different classes of historical data in turn and this will require occasional backtracking. Furthermore, the incomplete nature of our sources forces us to piece together our picture by drawing details from different geographical areas over the span of many years. We must not assume that details of a particular class applied uniformly from region to region or remained unchanged over time simply because our evidence is incomplete. We are reasonably certain, for example, that Phoenician "threes" differed from Athenian "threes" as did Roman from Carthaginian "fives."[23] We also suspect that Athenian "threes" from the fourth century were lighter in build than Roman cataphract "threes" from a few centuries later. We must therefore recognize the limitations of our data. On the other hand, it is reasonable to suspect that something basic in design and performance separated one class from another in the same fleet, like "fives" from "sixes," or "sixes"

---

22. For a detailed discussion of these displays, see Rice 1983.

23. For the suspected differences between Phoenician and Athenian "threes," see Basch 1987, 328–36. During the early phases of the First Punic War, a Carthaginian "five" differed so much from a Roman "five," that the Romans used a captured Punic vessel to improve their own inferior design (Polyb. 1.59.8).

from "sevens."[24] This much, at any rate, is indicated by preserved descriptions of these classes in action.

We will begin our investigation by attempting to place into its proper historical perspective the introduction of the earliest big ships for which we have reliable evidence. In so doing, I will avoid following blind leads as much as possible. By this, I mean I will not fret over unsubstantiated lists of "firsts." There was a genre of literature during the Hellenistic period that produced lists such as the first inventors of various machines, lists of tallest mountains, biggest seas, and so forth. Pliny the Elder (*NH* 7.207–208) preserves such a list in his *Natural History* regarding the inventors of different kinds of warships. According to Pliny's list, Aristotle ascribed the "four" to Carthage; Mnesigiton ascribed the "five" to Cyprian Salamis; Xenagoras the "six" to Syracuse; Mnesigiton the sizes from "seven" to "ten" to Alexander the Great; Philostephanus the "eleven" and "twelve" to Ptolemy I, the "fifteen" to Demetrius Poliorcetes, the "thirty" to Ptolemy II Philadelphus, and the "forty" to Ptolemy IV Philopator. While this list provides a tantalizing glimpse of the literature we have lost, where the attributions remain unsubstantiated by other, surviving authors, it does us no good to fret over this loss.[25] If we are to understand why a particular ship class is developed at a particular time and place, I feel we must work from established historical contexts. In this regard, I consider it more important to explore the introduction of the "five" at Syracuse by Dionysius, where we know the historical context, than to hypothesize what Mnesigiton knew about the introduction of the "five" at Cyprian Salamis, where we do not. The same holds true for the other classes.

---

24. I am unconvinced by the argument of Basch 1987, 342, (based on the seventeenth century French practice of utilizing a variable number of oarsmen in transverse section on the same galley) that a two-level "seven" could serve as a two-level "eight" by simply squeezing an additional man on the oars normally worked by three men.

25. Beyond the list's problems (Thuc. 1.13.2 says only that the first triremes built *in Greece* were built by Ameinocles of Corinth; the Salaminian invention of the "five," if true, should be mentioned by Isocrates in his *Panegyricus* or his *Euagoras*, but is not; Plutarch credits Demetrius with warships up to "sixteens" in size), it provides little to help us reconstruct the evolution of naval power during the Hellenistic period. What we should most like to know is not mentioned, namely, the objectives for which these new vessels were built. See Morrison and Coates 1996, xiv, for a brief characterization of the sources behind this list, and for the astute observation (xiv–xv) that the list *is* useful for showing how Pliny, an admiral of the Misenum fleet, used the Latin word *ordines* ("files") to define the different classes and thus demonstrates the principle by which *-eres* classes received their names.

In what follows, my text is divided into seven chapters. Chapter 1 traces the origin of the big ship concept back to the Peloponnesian War (431–404) and explores the reasons for the introduction of "fours" and "fives" by Carthage and Syracuse at the turn of the fourth century. In chapter 2, we examine new physical evidence that was unavailable to Tarn and others when they developed the currently prevailing models of Hellenistic naval warfare. The evidence explains the importance of frontal ramming in Hellenistic naval warfare, both in individual combat between ships and in attacks on harbor defenses. Chapter 3 traces the origin and development of naval siege warfare from the fifth century to the death of Demetrius Poliorcetes (283). In the following chapter, we turn to a set of siegecraft instructions, written during the third century, that explain in detail how to use a naval siege unit to either attack or defend a coastal city. Chapter 5 next considers naval artillery and boarding tactics to challenge the theory that these two factors drove the big ship phenomenon. The height of the big ship phenomenon is examined in chapter 6, when the largest of the big ships were built, as are the reasons why Ptolemy II Philadelphus amassed the largest fleet of polyremes ever constructed. The seventh and final chapter brings the story of big ships down to Actium, by analyzing the attested performance of midsized polyremes ("sixes" to "tens") in battle, including Actium. Appended to the text is a collection of testimonia from ancient texts informing us about warship classes from "fours" to the "forty," plus the use of naval artillery. While many of the references in this collection are noted in the book's main text, it seemed useful to have them grouped into lists for easy reference.

1

Frontal Ramming and the Development of "Fours" and "Fives"

The Athenian "Three" during the Peloponnesian War

Because of its extreme popularity and long period of use, the ship class about which we know the most is the "three" (Fig. 1.1). Of all the states who built these vessels, we know the most about the Athenian version of the fifth and fourth centuries BCE. Our evidence comes from an array of sources, from literary descriptions of fleets in action to depictions of "threes" on pottery, stone, or coins, to foundations for shipsheds (covered slipways) where the ships were stored, to detailed inventories of state owned property associated with the fleet between 377 and 323/22 BCE.[1]

Much of what we know has been summarized in an excellent book by J. S. Morrison and his colleagues titled *The Athenian Trireme*.[2] I do not mean to imply that all the questions have been answered. Indeed, there is a long history of scholarly interest in solving the so-called "trireme question" and the debate has sometimes become quite heated.[3] Nevertheless, we have reached a point where there is enough agreement on basic details for us to sketch the physical outlines of the class. To judge from the preserved slipways and known oarcrew (170) the galley was long and narrow—roughly 37 m. × 5 m. (at the outrigger)—with a beam to length ratio of roughly 1:7.[4] A full crew numbered 200 men, and this included

---

1. On this evidence, see Gabrielsen 1995, 234–40 and Gabrielsen 1994, 13–15.

2. Morrison, Coates, and Rankov 2000.

3. Casson 1995, 77–96 provides an excellent introduction to the matter.

4. Morrison, Coates, and Rankov 2000, 131–33; and Morrison in Gardiner and Morrison 1995, 62–63.

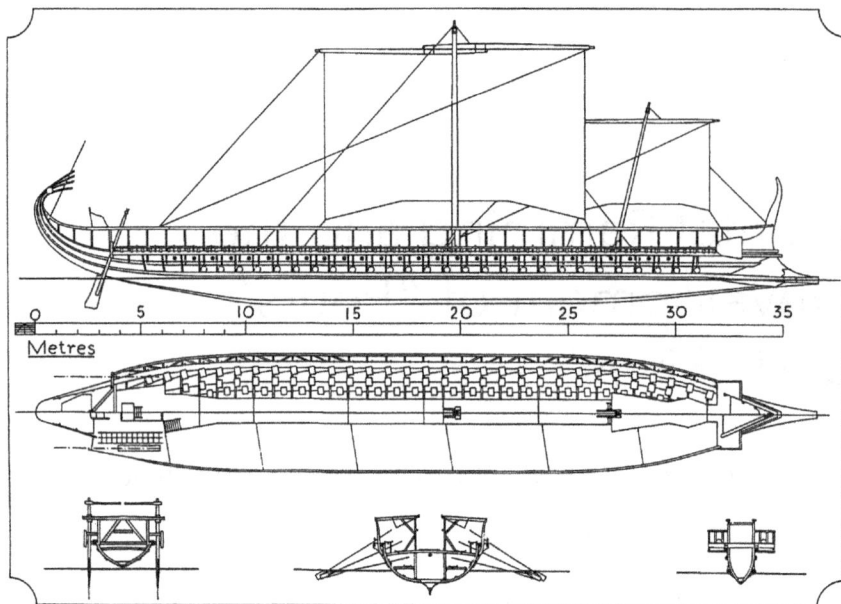

FIGURE 1.1 Line drawing of Athenian "three" by J. F. Coates. Copyright © 2000, Cambridge University Press.

170 oarsmen, a complement of 10 marines (*epibatai*) who were carried on the deck, four archers (*toxotai*), and 16 officers and sailors. Among the officers, there was a trierarch or captain and six petty officers: a helmsman (*kybernetes*), a rowing master or boatswain (*keleustes*), a purser (*pentekontarchos*), a bow officer (*prorates*), a shipwright (*naupegos*) and a time keeper (*auletes*). The remaining crew members were included under the term "support staff" (*hyperesia*) and must have handled the ship's lines, sails and anchors.[5]

We may learn something of its performance under oar by a number of ancient authors who describe the vessel in action. By far, the best authority is the historian Thucydides, a trireme commander in his own right until he was exiled from Athens in 424 during the war he chronicles. According to his account, an Athenian "three" was able to accelerate quickly, turn sharply, reverse direction smartly, and deliver a ram blow of sufficient strength to shatter steering oars from the rear or splinter an enemy hull. Numerous accounts make it clear that attacks had to be carried out

5. Morrison, Coates, and Rankov 2000, 113; for a full description of the crew and definition of the term *hyperesia*, see 108–18.

carefully to prevent the ram from becoming entangled or, worse yet, from being carried along in the struck ship and wrenched from the attacker's bow. For this reason, ram strikes were best made from oblique angles to a ship's side or stern in such a way that the target ship's momentum allowed your own ram to safely withdraw from the hole it created. Since groups of warships relied upon one another for protection, "threes" worked well in fast moving squadrons of 10 to 30 ships.

A classic example that demonstrates these characteristics can be found in a speech attributed to the general Phormio by Thucydides (2.89.1–11). At the time of this speech (429), an Athenian squadron of 20 "threes" lay just outside the entrance to the Corinthian Gulf on its north shore. A Peloponnesian fleet of 77 "threes" anchored nearby on the Peloponnesian side of the Gulf.[6]

> Now, as for the battle, if I can help it, I shall not fight it in the gulf, nor shall I sail into the gulf. I fully realize that lack of sea room is a disadvantage for a small, experienced and fast squadron fighting with a lot of badly managed ships. One cannot sail up in the proper way to make an attack by ramming, unless one has a good long view of the enemy ahead, nor can one back away at the right moment if one is hard pressed oneself; it is impossible also to execute the *diekplous* and *anastrophe* maneuvers [i.e., to sail through the enemy's line and then wheel back on him]—which are the right tactics for a fleet which has the superior seamanship. Instead of all this, one would be compelled to fight a naval action as though it were a battle on land, and under those circumstances the side with the greater number of ships has the advantage.

(Thuc. 2.89.8)[7]

Thucydides felt the Athenians had developed an expert knowledge of naval warfare that stood in contrast to their adversaries' old fashioned tactics. He states this clearly in his description of the sea battle off the Sybota

---

6. Largely owing to their discipline and superior ship handling skills, the Athenians managed to turn an initial setback into victory. For the account of the battle see Thuc. 2.90–92.

7. Trans. Warner 1972, 182–83. I have replaced Warner's phrase "it is impossible also to sail through the enemy's line and then wheel back on him" with "it is impossible to execute the *diekplous* and *anastrophe* maneuvers" to preserve the original Greek terms in the text.

islands (off the mainland opposite the southern end of Corcyra) between the forces of Corinth and Corcyra in 433 (Thuc. 1.49.1–4):

> Then, after the signals had been hoisted on both sides, they joined battle. The fighting was of a somewhat old fashioned kind, since they were still behindhand in naval matters, both sides having numbers of hoplites [i.e., heavily armed infantrymen] aboard their ships, together with archers and javelin throwers. . . . Indeed, it was more like a battle on land than a naval engagement. When the ships came into collision it was difficult for them to break away clear, because of the number engaged and of their close formation. In fact, both sides relied more for victory on their hoplites, who were on the decks and who fought a regular pitched battle while the ships remained motionless. No one attempted the *diekplous* maneuver; in fact, it was a battle where courage and sheer strength played a greater part than scientific methods. Everywhere in the battle confusion reigned, and there was shouting on all sides.[8]

Both accounts tend to reinforce the same impression. The principal maneuvers are described by terms like *diekplous* and *anastrophe*, (sailing through the enemy line and turning back to attack the enemy in the rear), *periplous* (sailing around the enemy's wings) and a defensive tactic called the *kyklos* where ships form a circle, bows outward, and at a signal sprint forward to attack the enemy.[9] Although scholars may debate the precise definitions of these maneuvers, the general impression remains the same: Athenian "threes" were formidable weapons when they fought together in squadrons and had adequate sea room to maneuver. At the close of the first 10 years of the Peloponnesian War, the Athenians and Spartans agreed to make peace, largely on the *status quo*. The Athenians had demonstrated repeatedly that they were virtually unbeatable at sea, if the fight involved maneuver-and-ram warfare.

---

8. Trans. Warner 1972, 63–64; I have replaced Warner's incorrect phrase "no one attempted the manoeuvre of encirclement" with "no one attempted the *diekplous* maneuver." The encirclement maneuver (*periplous*) involves sailing around the end of the enemy's line, while the *diekplous* involves cutting through the line, i.e., passing through the gaps between individual ships in the line.

9. A scholarly debate has developed in recent years over the precise meaning of these terms. The issue turns on whether these maneuvers are completed by single ships, or by squadrons operating in line-ahead formation. For the relevant literature, see Strauss 2007, 230–31 with n. 180.

Frontal Ramming as a Battle Tactic

Frontal ramming, or the deliberate head-on collision between two warships, is a well attested maneuver practiced by fleets and individual warships as early as the fifth century BCE. During the generation following Alexander the Great, and then frequently thereafter, we find this maneuver used at the start of many pitched naval battles.[10] So long as fleets were composed of warships that were roughly the same size and mass, no commander could be sure his vessel would survive a head-on collision with the enemy and the *antiproiros* or "prow-opposed" maneuver was used as a defensive stance. Ships would adopt this position, for example, when they found themselves overtaken by faster pursuers. We might assume that this defensive maneuver dates back to the beginnings of ramming warfare, although our first clear reference to it as a battle tactic does not occur until the invasion of Xerxes in 480, when Herodotus describes the Greek fleet in this posture at Artemision.[11]

During the course of the fifth century, the Athenians developed and refined their ability to initiate offensive attacks from a prow-opposed position. This unexpected action clearly intimidated their enemies; so much so, that in 425 when the Athenians charged the prows of the Spartan fleet at Pylos, arrayed in the standard prow-opposed defensive position, the Spartans flinched first and fled.[12] Thucydides does not provide the details of this encounter, but presumably the Spartans so feared the Athenian ability to accelerate and maneuver out of this prow-opposed formation that they

---

10. Prow-to-prow charges opened the battles off Salamis in 306 (Diod. 20.51.1–3), Mylae in 260 (Polyb. 1.23.3), Chios in 201 (Polyb. 16.4.7), Side and Myonnesus in 190 (Livy 37.24.2 and 30.3–5), and off Mylae and Naulochus in 36 (App. *BC* 5.11.106, and 12.119). Antony hoped to use the prow-to-prow charge at Actium in 31, except that Octavian's men were told to stay clear of Antony's prows (Plut. *Ant.* 65.4).

11. Effective ramming required that bronze-casting technology be advanced enough to produce a ram that would routinely survive the impact of deliberate ramming strikes. According to this essential criterion, *routine* ramming in naval warfare (and this is what is important for our purposes) should not predate the latter half of the sixth century BCE. The action at Artemision described by Herodotus (8.11.2) must have been a defensive maneuver which did not involve deliberate head-on collisions with the Persian vessels: "At the first signal for action, the Greeks formed into a close circle—bows outward toward the Persians, sterns toward the center; then at the second signal, with little room to maneuver, and lying, as they were, bows-on to the enemy, they set to work and succeeded in capturing thirty Persian ships." Morrison, Coates, and Rankov 2000, 54, think that the Greek circle "exploded in all directions," and so captured the Persian ships.

12. Thuc. 4.14.1: ". . . and falling on the major portion of the Spartan ships which were already at sea and lined up, prows opposed, they drove them away in flight. . . ."

withdrew rather than wait to receive the attacks of the enemy on their flanks and sterns (Thuc. 7.36.3–4).[13]

Until advances in technology allowed for the manufacture of bronze rams that would routinely withstand the force of a head-on collision between warships, intentional prow-to-prow ramming strikes were reserved for extreme situations or were limited to attacks on the forward lateral ends of the outriggers, the catheads (*epotides*), which were strengthened for this purpose. These collisions, when carried out in a deliberate, purposeful manner could be quite violent. In a battle off Naulochus in 36, Agrippa struck the enemy flagship with a prow-to-prow strike and the force ejected men from the enemy deck towers into the sea (App. *BC* 5.11.107). In 306, off Cyprian Salamis, we are told that deck soldiers crouched down just before the collision, presumably to hold on for dear life (Diod. 20.51.2).[14] The sounds of bow hitting bow were so loud that they drowned out the commands of the combatants. The jolt was likened to the force of a 55.5 meter-long battering ram striking a stone city wall (Diod. 20.95.1). The considerable forces generated by such collisions would cause all but the most solid of rams to fail unless they were made with great care. This is because the process of bronze casting leaves weak spots and cracks when gas bubbles are not released from the melt and the metal is allowed to cool and thus shrink too rapidly.[15] It is likely that the first step involved strengthening the timbers forming the ends of the outriggers. This beefed-up bow structure then became a weapon in its own right for those wishing to attack from a prow-opposed stance.

The sheer audacity involved in carrying out the threat to attack an enemy's prow lies behind the advice given to the Syracusans by Hermocrates in 413 (Thuc. 7.21.3): "What daring people like the Athenians find most awkward is to be confronted with equal daring on the other side; Athens, sometimes without any real superiority in strength, was in the habit of terrorizing her neighbors by the very audacity of her attacks; the same

---

13. It seems that no ships actually collided at the prow in this engagement; Athenians considered a helmsman who actually collided prow-to-prow to be $\dot{\alpha}\mu\alpha\theta\eta\varsigma$ or unskilled in his craft (Thuc. 7.36.5).

14. See also App. *BC* 5.12.119: (off Naulochus, 36 BCE): "Then the ships dashed against each other, some striking amidships, others on the catheads, others on the rams, where the blows are especially violent in shaking the marines and in rendering the ship useless."

15. We still do not have a collection of securely dated rams that allows us to see these changes in manufacturing techniques, but we can safely presume that the earliest rams would have cracked from their prows when subjected to the force of a prow-to-prow strike.

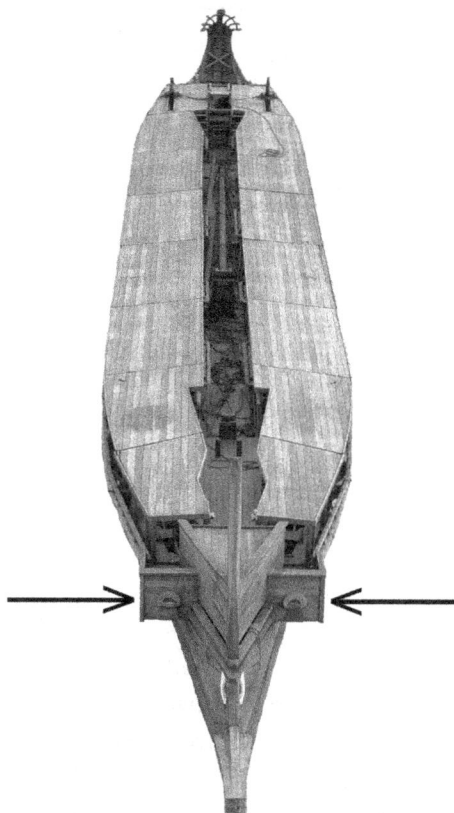

FIGURE I.2 *Olympias,* view from the bow showing catheads (marked with arrows).

method might now be used by Syracuse against Athens."[16] The rules of engagement were about to change.

The Sicilian Expedition and Frontal Ramming

During the period between 415 and 413, the Athenians sent an expeditionary force to Sicily in hopes of adding Syracuse and the cities of the island to her empire. The force departed Athens with much fanfare in the spring of 415 but experienced no major gains until the spring of 414 when they moved to Syracuse, began to circumvallate the community, and established a naval base in the Great Harbor next to the city. The Corinthians, meanwhile, responded to an appeal from their colonists in Syracuse by

---

16. Trans. Warner 1972, 489–90.

MAP 1.1 Greece, Sicily and Southern Italy.

agreeing, during the winter of 415/14, to send aid. Their first ships were dispatched during the summer of 414 about the same time as the Spartans sent a general named Gylippus to organize the city's defenses. In fact, the Corinthian commander Gongylus arrived just before Gylippus and prevented the Syracusans from holding an assembly to discuss their surrender. Soon thereafter, 12 ships arrived from Corinth and her western Greek colonies at Ambracia and Leucas (Thuc. 7.7).

Once they saw for themselves the extent of the Athenian counter wall around the city, envoys were dispatched back to Sparta and Corinth to gather reinforcements, a process that continued through the winter of 414/13. Finally, during the summer of 413, the reinforcements were ready and the Peloponnesians sent a fleet of roughly 30 ships to prevent the Athenians at Naupactus from hindering the departure of the transports. Knowing that they would face the Athenians in a constricted area, the Corinthians had strengthened the bows of their "threes" with additional timbers at the *epotides* or catheads, which formed the forward end of the outrigger. In a battle fought near Achaean Erineus, they deliberately collided with their enemies' unreinforced *epotides*. According to Thucydides (7.34.5), "the Corinthians lost three ships, and although they did not completely swamp any of the Athenian ships, they disabled some seven of the enemy, which were struck prow-to-prow and had their outriggers broken open by the Corinthian vessels, whose catheads had been thickened for this very purpose."

The Corinthians were heartened by this outcome, which was essentially a draw. Their attitude is partly explained by the Athenians' inability to hinder the convoy's departure, but also partly because they had hit upon a strategy that negated the superior skill of their enemies. The Athenians seemed to recognize this fact because they did not immediately claim victory, although they had managed to destroy the greater number of warships and managed to gain control of the wrecks (Thuc. 7.34.6–8). It is worth stressing again that the Corinthians did not rely on ram-to-ram strikes but rather on collisions at their strengthened *epotides*, which dislocated the Athenians' outriggers. And this would have affected the working of their foremost oars on the top-most level.

News of this success was immediately relayed to Syracuse, where the Syracusans began to alter the bows of their own "threes" in preparation for an all-out confrontation with the Athenians in their harbor.[17] Thucydides' account of the episode (7.36.2–5) is revealing for the detail that it provides:

> (2) In the equipment of their fleet, [the Syracusans] made various changes, which, on the basis of their experience in the previous naval battle, were calculated to give them some advantages;[18] in particular, they cut down the length of the prows to make them more solid, put extra material into the sides by the catheads, and from the catheads themselves they built in stays of timber which went through to the ships' sides, a distance of about six cubits (2.64 m.), and projected outwards to about the same distance.[19] They were thus following the same method as the Corinthians, who had strengthened their ships at the prows before fighting with the Athenians [who were stationed] at Naupactus. (3) The Syracusans thought that in this way they would have an advantage over the

---

17. The Peloponnesian troop ships would have brought with them the news that the Corinthian modifications had been effective.

18. Gylippus and Hermocrates had urged the Syracusans to become more bold and daring in their attacks on the Athenians, particularly in their naval battles (Thuc. 7.21.3–4). As a result of this new daring, they managed to capture the Athenian base on the promontory called Plemmyrium (Thuc. 7.22–24). Attacking the prows of the Athenian triremes was clearly perceived as being in this same vein, i.e., as a bold and unexpected tactic.

19. In "cutting down" their prows, the Syracusans must have reduced the fore and aft distance between the tip of the ram and the port and starboard catheads. In order to do this, they would have had to remove the rams, reduce the lengths of the port and starboard wales by cutting off their forward ends, and then refit the rams. The result would have been a more squared off, less elongated, bow that would have reduced the speed of the vessel through the water. Speed, however, was not the main consideration here.

Athenian ships, which, instead of being constructed like theirs, were light in the prow. [They felt this way] because the usual Athenian tactics were not to meet the enemy head on, but to row around and ram him amidships. The fact that the battle would be in the Great Harbor, where there would be many ships in a small space, was also in their favor, since, charging prow-to-prow and striking with stout solid rams against hollow and weak ones, they would stave in the enemy's forward sections. (4) It would not be possible for the Athenians, in that narrow space, to sail around the line or to break through it (*oute periploun oute diekploun*), maneuvering skills on which their confidence was based. For the Syracusans would do their best to prevent them from breaking through the line, and lack of space would prevent them from trying the encircling maneuver. (5) In fact, this system of colliding prow-to-prow, which previously was thought to show a steersman's lack of skill, was now going to be the chief method employed by the Syracusans, since it would give them the greatest advantages.[20]

As expected, in the confined space of their harbor, the Syracusan plan worked well against the Athenians. Not only did they crush the Athenians' outriggers at the *epotides*, but they also wounded their enemy with javelin fire and with attacks on the oarsmen (*nautai*) from small boats that slipped in beside the enemy ships (Thuc. 7.40.5). As early as 413, therefore, we see the essential elements that would come to dominate naval warfare of the Hellenistic Age: frontal ramming attacks, the discharge of long-range projectiles, and the use of small boats to slip into gaps between ships of the line. The particular effectiveness of these tactics at Syracuse is best explained by the reduced maneuvering room inside the harbor in which the combatants were forced to fight.

As we shall see, fighting in this manner, just inside or at the mouth of a harbor, becomes a standard feature of naval warfare during the Hellenistic Age in the eastern Mediterranean. Indeed, two other features of Hellenistic naval warfare also appear in subsequent battles fought in the Great Harbor. First, we see the use of fire to destroy an enemy fleet from a distance. The delivery system was an old cargo ship, which the Syracusans filled with brushwood, set ablaze, and released upwind from the Athenian fleet station (Thuc. 7.53.4). Secondly, the Syracusans built a

---

20. Translation adapted from Warner 1972, 500–501.

pontoon barrier of linked vessels to block the entrance of the harbor and thus prevented the Athenians from escaping (Thuc. 7.56.1, 59.3). When compared to the basic tactics and hardware used a century later, the only elements missing are warships larger than "threes" that could break through the barrier, and naval artillery that could inflict serious damage on the marines and deliver blazing projectiles from a much further distance. When, during the late fourth and third centuries, attacks on harbor installations became a major objective in naval warfare, the elements that we see so clearly at Syracuse in 413 determined how new classes of larger warships were built and utilized.

I began this historical digression to provide a context for the Syracusan introduction of a new class in the -*eres* series at the beginning of the fourth century. As we consider the reasons for their invention of the "five," we should keep in mind the Syracusans' close brush with disaster in 413, the overwhelming success of their modified "threes," and the impact this must have had on subsequent ship construction. Additionally, the Syracusans had every reason to perfect their new design in the decade following their unexpected success. Additional pressures, this time from the Carthaginians, should have urged them to continue their experimentation with reinforced warship bows capable of fighting in and around harbor entrances. The evidence, however, is not as consistent as we might like.

Carthage, Sicily and the Introduction of "Fours" and "Fives"

Pliny *NH* 7.208: . . . according to Aristotle, the Carthaginians, [were the first to build] "fours" . . .

Diod. 14.41.3 (under the year 399): At once, therefore, [Dionysius] gathered skilled workmen, commandeering them from the cities under his control and attracting them by high wages from Italy and Greece as well as Carthaginian territory. For his purpose was to make weapons in great numbers and every kind of missile, and also "fours"[21] and "fives," no "fives" having been built before.

---

21. Although the manuscripts of Diodorus list "threes" instead of "fours" in both this passage and the next, P. Wesseling (Diodorus 1746), an early editor of the text, substituted *tetrereis* ("fours") for *te triereis* (and "threes") in both passages, presumably because of the clear mention of "fours" at Diod. 2.5.6, and his emendations have been accepted by subsequent editors.

Diod. 14.42.2: [Dionysius] also began the construction of "fours" and "fives," being the first to think of the construction of such ships.[22]

Apparently, both Aristotle and the sources on whom Diodorus relied (probably Timaeus or Ephorus) felt that the Sicilian tyrant Dionysius I was the first to invent "fives," and the Carthaginians the first to invent "fours." Pliny, who does not date the invention, includes his reference to the "four" in a list of naval inventors. Since our earliest dateable reference to the "four" stems from Alexander's siege of Tyre in 332, J. S. Morrison has argued that the two-level "four" developed from a fifty-oared galley (pentecontor) and thus stems from a different tradition of shipbuilding.[23] As a result, the introduction of the "four" and "five" are not connected with the same historical events. While this view is certainly possible, I believe it more likely that "fours" and "fives" were built to answer new demands placed on a naval force by the introduction of siege warfare directed against maritime cities. Since this impetus can clearly be seen driving the introduction of new classes later in the century, it may be worthwhile to see if the argument applies at the beginning of the century as well. I think it does.

Sicily, during the late fifth century, saw a period of alternating aggression between Carthage and Syracuse that began within years of the destruction of the Athenian fleet in 413. Two major Carthaginian invasions occurred between 409 and 406, followed by a brief peace in 405, and then by a period of renewed conflict. The cities of Selinus and Himera fell to Carthaginian siegecraft in 409 and were followed by Acragas, Gela and Camarina in 406. The main provisions of the treaty that concluded hostilities between Carthage and Syracuse are recorded by Diodorus (13.114.1) and list Selinus, Acragas, Himera, Gela, and Camarina as *poleis* that must remain unfortified and pay tribute to Carthage. Leontini, Messene, and the Sicels were to be autonomous and the Syracusans were to be under Dionysius.[24]

---

22. Translations of this and the preceding passage were adapted from Oldfather 1954, 127–31.

23. See, for example, Morrison's arguments in Gardiner and Morrison 1995, 66–71; and in Morrison and Coates 1996, 267–69.

24. Lewis 1994, 120–35. For these events and those of the following paragraph, see also chapter 3.

The next few years saw Dionysius struggling to consolidate his power in Syracuse and at the same time secure a sphere of influence in eastern Sicily.[25] Ultimately, he planned to capitalize on a plague that had weakened the Carthaginian homeland, break the treaty of 405, and drive the Carthaginians from the island (Diod. 14.18.1, 41.1), or at least limit their influence to its western end. He therefore resolved to build up his defensive and offensive capabilities by making additions to the city's walls (Diod. 14.18.1–8), by repairing old shipsheds, by building new ones (Diod. 14.42.5), and by luring engineers and weapons manufacturers from Greece, Italy, and Carthaginian territories with promises of high pay (Diod. 14.41.3). It is during this period of preparation that Diodorus dates the invention of catapults as well as the introduction of "fives."

The first "five" was apparently launched in spring 397, when she was sent on a state mission to fetch a young Locrian woman named Doris, daughter of Xenetos, whose marriage to Dionysius was to cement an alliance with Locri (Diod. 14.44.7). This episode and one other, in 390, when his flagship limped into port after a storm (Diod. 14.100.5), demonstrate clearly how Dionysius used his larger, more impressive galleys for prestige missions and flagships. Numerous examples from subsequent periods demonstrate how such prestige duties were often assigned to the largest galleys in the fleet.[26] Still, the invention and quick popularity of "fives" should originate in some perceived tactical advantage over smaller galleys likes "threes" and "fours" with whom they competed in battle. While this may be so, we search in vain for "fives" in the naval actions of these years to learn how these new warships were utilized and precisely why they were adopted. In the past, a few scholars assumed that Dionysius introduced "fives" to carry catapults for the siege of Motya in 397, but Diodorus's account makes it clear that the Syracusan warships were initially dragged up on land (Diod. 14.48.3).[27] When we see catapults in use, they are not placed on the ships' decks, which are loaded with archers and slingers, but rather on the land (Diod. 14.50.4). Later, in 396, we may catch a hint of "fours" and "fives" when Dionysius massed 180 warships near Taurus (later Tauromenium), "of which only a few were 'threes'" (Diod.

---

25. Lewis 1994, 135–42.

26. See Appendices B–D.

27. See, for example: Rodgers 1964, 197; and Meijer 1986, 120.

14.58.2).[28] But in the sea battle that followed, no specific mention of "fives" or "fours" can be found. The commander Leptines placed 30 of his best ships (*nausi tais aristais*—were they "fives"?) far in front of the rest of the fleet and sank "not a few of the 'threes'" they first encountered. Here we should expect examples of frontal ramming, and the use of "fours" against "fives," but of this, not a word. When the rest of the Carthaginians arrived and surrounded these 30 ships of Leptines, the battle devolved into an infantry contest, and the Syracusan force was eventually defeated by their enemy's superior numbers (Diod. 14.60.1–6). All this accords well with the use of "fives," but again, not a word about ship classes, especially when the Carthaginians took their captured prizes in tow (Diod. 14.60.7). If "fives" were new, the capture of one should have caused a stir.

Soon thereafter, when Himilco reached Syracuse and set up his camp in the Great Harbor like the Athenians before him, we find no "fives" in the few skirmishes that followed (Diod. 14.64.1–2), or in the final sea battle fought in the harbor (Diod. 14.72.1, 4–6; 73.1–74.5). And yet, we can probably see the effects of their presence. On two separate occasions, major battles were fought inside the harbor, and on both, the Syracusan navy prevailed over their enemies. In the first encounter, the Syracusans captured the Carthaginian flagship and destroyed 24 others, certainly by ramming.[29] In the second encounter, Dionysius used the fleet as part of a coordinated land and sea attack on the Carthaginian camp, as he had tried to do at Gela in 405. Again the navy performed well, ramming the enemy's moored ships with powerful blows (Diod. 14.72.4). The infantry attacked from the land and torched a number of beached vessels, from which fire spread to the merchant ships moored close to shore. The victory was so crushing that Himilco delivered to Dionysius the remaining 300 talents of his war chest, negotiated the withdrawal of his citizen troops, and left his mercenaries to the mercy of the Syracusans and their allies. Unfortunately, we are not given sufficient details to determine if "fives" or "fours" played a role in the victory, but it is likely that these vessels, with their greater capacity for carrying deck soldiers and heavier build, were foremost in the ramming attacks at the Carthaginian camp.

---

28. Morrison 1990, 37–39 believes that this passage is corrupt and should read something like "of which only a few were ['fives', and many] 'threes'".

29. Had they boarded the 24 vessels, they would have presumably captured them. The authenticity of this battle is doubted by Caven 1990, 115–16.

So where were they?—a good question, for which there is no easy answer. There are two possibilities that are not mutually exclusive. First, we might explain this lack of "fives" by the fact that Dionysius only built a small number of them during the program that produced 200 new warships (Diod. 14.42.5). We have a few indirect indicators on which to rely for this view. In the fleet of 396, we are told that Dionysius freed 10,000 slaves in order to man 60 ships (Diod. 14.58.1); at an average crew size of 167 men per ship, these must have been "threes."[30] And again, in 390, when seven of Dionysius's ships were driven ashore near Rhegium, they too were apparently "threes," considering that roughly 1500 men were lost (Diod. 14.100.4) on all seven vessels (ca. 214 per ship). There is a financial consideration as well. Being new designs, these "fives" would have cost more than "threes" to construct, to man, and to maintain, and at the time they were built, Dionysius did not possess unlimited resources.[31] If I am correct in detecting the reasons behind their construction, the new "fives" were intended to outclass "threes" in conditions where frontal attacks were important. Beyond this, their ability to maneuver was largely untested. Dionysius was not a fool, and until the design of this new class was perfected, we should not expect to see large numbers of them in his fleet. This is the same impression we get from the small numbers of "fours" and "fives" at Athens, shortly after their introduction.[32]

There is another possible factor, and this involves a general disinterest on the part of either Diodorus or his source in the details of frontal ramming. Drawing conclusions from negative evidence is always risky, but we can detect the level of disinterest when we compare the accounts of Diodorus and Thucydides for the events of 413 in the Great Harbor of Syracuse. Our focus now is on the Syracusan adoption of the new prow-to-prow ramming maneuver that Thucydides credits for enabling the Syracusans to defeat the Athenians in these final battles.

---

30. Presumably these manumitted slaves served as oarsmen, which numbered 170 on an Athenian "three" of this same period.

31. See Lewis 1994, 141–43; and Caven 1990, 160–66.

32. See Appendices A–B.

Version According to Diodorus (synopsis unless indicated by quotation marks)

Diod. 13.10.2–3: Ariston, the Corinthian pilot, advised the Syracusans to make the bows of their "threes" shorter and lower (*tas proras . . . brachyteras kai tapeinoteras*). The Athenians' prows were weaker and higher (*asthenesteras . . . tas proras kai meteorous*) and, for this reason, only damaged the parts above the water in ram strikes. The Syracusans, with the area about the prow strong and low (*ton peri ten proran topon ischyron . . . kai tapeinon*) would often, as they delivered their ramming blows, sink with one strike the "threes" of the Athenians.

Diod. 13.10.4–6: In the sea battle that follows, there is no reference to prow-to-prow attacks. The Athenians had no opportunity to maneuver in the narrow confines of the harbor, to back away and to turn and, as a result, the Syracusans primarily relied on getting close to their enemies and fighting from their decks. The Athenians, being pressed upon from all sides, turned to flight; and the Syracusans, in pursuit, sank seven "threes" and rendered a large number unfit for use.

Version According to Thucydides (synopsis unless indicated by quotation marks)

Thuc. 7.36.2–6: The Syracusans cut down their prows to a smaller compass to make them more solid, and they reinforced their catheads with timbers both inside the hull and out in the same way the Corinthians had done for the fight off Erineus. This fight would not be in open water, but in the confines of the harbor, and here they would damage their enemies' weaker bows in prow-to-prow strikes. Although this tactic had been considered a lack of skill in the past, it would now become the Syracusans' chief maneuver.

Thuc. 7.40.5, 41.4: The Syracusans received them, and charging prow-to-prow as they had intended, stove in a great part of the Athenian outriggers by the strength of their rams; the javelin throwers on the decks also did great damage to the Athenians; but still greater damage was done by the Syracusans in small boats who ran in upon the oars of the Athenian "threes," sailed in against their sides and threw javelins at the oarsmen. The Syracusans sank seven Athenian vessels and disabled many.

(continued)

Diod. 13.15.1–2: Diodorus describes how, just before the final sea battle in the Great Harbor, Nicias delivered his remarks to the men from a small boat that passed along the line of Athenian ships. Nicias called each captain by name, stretching forth his hands, imploring all to grasp the only hope left to them. He urged them to remember sons and fathers, to remember the trophies at Salamis and to fight like Athenians should.

Thuc. 7.62.1–3: Thucydides assigns a fully developed speech in direct discourse to Nicias, in which he reviews the tactical situation. He tells his men that he has met with the helmsmen to consider how best to offset the crush of vessels in such a narrow harbor. As for the force upon the decks of the enemy, they will take archers and javelin men aboard their own vessels. "We have also discovered the changes in construction that we must make to meet theirs; and against the thickness of their *epotides*, which did us the greatest mischief, we have provided grappling irons, which will prevent an assailant backing water after charging . . ."

What can be made of these differing accounts? Either Diodorus rewrote what he found in Thucydides' text, leaving out all references to prow-to-prow (*antiproiros*) ramming, or he relied on a source who did not understand (or care about) the importance of the structural changes involved.[33] How else do we explain his misleading description of the changes made in the "three's" bow structure (Diod. 13.10.2–3)? And how else do we explain his omission of the battle tactics resulting from these structural changes, something stressed so clearly by Thucydides? Considering Diodorus's careful attention to the details of prow-to-prow ramming on at least one other occasion, I slightly incline toward a view that traces the difference to Diodorus's source (Ephorus?), but either way, the results are the same.[34] In this way, we can more readily explain how Diodorus could mention the introduction of "fives" and "fours" and then ignore the effects on subsequent events in his narrative.

Faced with such evidence, we are left to hypothesize why the first warships larger than "threes" were developed at this time. I suggest that the demonstrable success of frontal ramming in constricted places, where maneuver-and-ram tactics were impossible, spurred the development of both "fours" and "fives." The desire, on the part of the builders, was to design a warship that could both deliver and withstand the jolt of deliberate collisions at the bow. I also propose that the builders desired a warship that could be relied

33. For examples of Diodorus's ability to rewrite Thucydides, see Green 2006, 28–29. Diodorus admits (20.1.1–2.3) that he prefers to avoid lengthy speeches in his text.

34. Diod. 20.51.1–3 includes an excellent description of prow-to-prow ramming at the battle off Salamis in 306 between Demetrius Poliorcetes and Ptolemy.

upon to support and defend against harbor attacks. The new vessels would have been more heavily constructed than "threes" and would have had heavier bows with larger rams and wider decks for the transport of more men and equipment. In addition, they could be counted on to survive prow strikes with "threes" in frontal ramming contests without serious damage. This structural feature became increasingly important when the fleet was asked to convoy transports, and when naval contests occurred in the constricted areas both inside and outside a harbor where maneuverability was restricted. Furthermore, a new kind of warfare developed in Sicily during these years, which involved the reliance on siege machinery and the ability to support the armies engaged in siege warfare. As a result, harbors increasingly became a focus for hostile action because the goal of the invasion was the capture of coastal cities and because attacks on a city's harbors diverted the besieged's attention from areas where land forces could operate with less opposition.

In naval terms, the "five" proved more powerful than the "four," although both excelled at prow-to-prow encounters with "threes." "Fives," however, were higher out of the water than both "threes" and "fours" and this enhanced the effectiveness of missiles thrown or shot from their decks.[35] As for prow-to-prow ramming, we should note that, thus far, our evidence extends to frontal attacks focused on a warship's outriggers; we do not yet hear that prow-to-prow ramming involved targeting the enemy's ram. This is not to say that ram-to-ram strikes did not occur, simply that such collisions were still as likely to cause damage to one's own ram as to the enemy's. Until rams could be manufactured to routinely withstand the impact of such bone-jarring collisions, prow-to-prow ramming still involved a level of danger that made the tactic risky. And for this reason, the most successful "fours" and "fives" had expert helmsmen who knew precisely where to attack the enemy, skilled crews able to accelerate and back water smartly, and deck soldiers who knew how to fight at sea.[36] In time, however, technological advances in bronze-casting reduced these risks by producing casts of high quality and great integrity. We can see these results in the Athlit ram and gauge what was happening by the increasing regularity with which frontal ramming maneuvers began naval battles. We can also gauge the resulting effect on warship design in the massive timbers that were inside the rams of Antony's largest warships at Actium. These are subjects to which we must now turn.

---

35. See Appendices A–B.

36. Philo (*Polior.* D 103) defines marines who knew how to fight at sea as ones who resisted the urge to board enemy vessels.

2

Frontal Ramming

STRUCTURAL CONSIDERATIONS

The Evidence of the Athlit Ram

On November 11, 1980, Yehoshua Ramon spotted the exposed corner of a large bronze warship ram while snorkeling near Athlit castle, just south of Haifa, after a storm. Although he suspected his find was important, Ramon could not foresee how important his discovery would become. In time, the Athlit ram would teach us how ancient galleys functioned as ramming machines. Two weeks after its discovery, however, when the ram was finally pulled from the sea, the main concerns were more pragmatic and focused on issues like the artifact's protection and conservation. It would be some time before the secrets of the Athlit ram were fully revealed.

Now, some three decades later, it is far easier to see how much we have learned. For example, symbols on the weapon suggest that it was cast on Cyprus for the Ptolemaic fleet at the end of the third century or during the first generation of the second century.[1] The ram, which is completely intact, measures 2.26 m. in length, 95 cm. in height, and 76 cm. in width from starboard to port trough ear (for the terms, see Fig. 2.1). It weighs 465 kg. and is made of resilient, high grade bronze with a copper to tin ratio of roughly 9:1.[2] Although it was initially thought to belong to a heavy galley, much larger

---

1. For a full discussion of the Athlit ram, see Casson and Steffy 1991. Coin evidence suggests the ram was cast on Cyprus at Kition or Paphos between 204 and 164 BCE, that is, during the reign of Ptolemy V Epiphanes or Ptolemy VI Philometor; see Murray 1991.

2. According to Oron 2006, 69, the alloy exhibits "a major element distribution with mean values of 90.4% copper and 9.78% tin, with virtually no lead." A 9:1 copper to tin ratio is most suitable for a weapon like a warship ram due to the alloy's high resistance to wear, high hardness, and moderate strength; see Eisenberg 1991, 41.

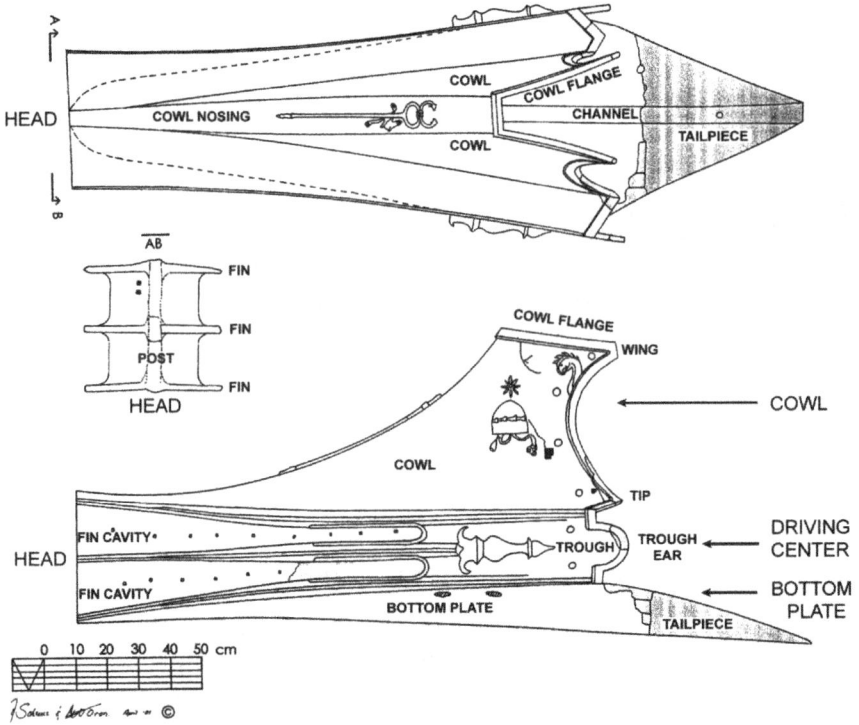

FIGURE 2.1 The Athlit ram. Adapted from line drawing by A. Oron and A. Shreur.

than a "three," the ram's size and weight now suggest that it came from a relatively small capital ship, by Hellenistic standards, most likely from a "four."[3] The ram was cast with a hollow interior that fit closely around the bow timbers of its warship. Fortunately for us, a thick layer of sediment covered this weapon soon after its loss and preserved the wood inside from decay, so that when the weapon was found, it still contained all 16 bow timbers in their original configurations. Subsequent study of this amazing artifact has revealed the extreme care with which it was made and fitted to its warship.

The Wood Inside the Ram

When the ram was pulled from the sea, it was a 600 kilo unit of water-logged wood and metal that was extremely difficult to manipulate. Because the wood had become concreted to the sides of the bronze

---

3. For early estimates of its class, see Basch 1982; Frost 1982; Pomey 1983; and Morrison 1984, 217.

casting, the process of extraction proceeded slowly and carefully over a period of more than 18 months. The work was carried out by J. Richard Steffy and a team of Israeli conservators who carefully measured, sectioned, and removed the structural timbers that made up the ram's interior.[4] Ultimately, in 1991, Steffy published a full set of drawings plus a meticulous description of the ram's structure, the step-by-step process by which the ship's bow was constructed, and the reasons behind its careful design.[5]

Since the ram marks the locus of the collision between attacking and attacked vessels, the weapon must be designed to withstand the force that it generates. This was partly achieved by the support timbers inside the weapon and partly by the integrity of the ram's cast. When both worked in harmony, an attacking vessel was able to deliver a damaging blow and yet remain undamaged in the process. The architects of the Athlit ship accomplished this tricky feat by utilizing the entire bottom of the vessel as much as the ram, which served to disperse the intense forces generated at the ram's head to the ship's hull. The surface designed to withstand the collision was an area that measured less than half a square meter and was comprised of three horizontal fins, each 2 cm. thick, 44 cm. wide, and connected at their midpoints by a vertical post that was 41 cm. high (Fig. 2.1). The real power was generated by the momentum of the heavy hull, which transferred its force to the ram "by a pair of thick wales and bottom planking, reinforced at their junction by a ramming timber."[6] The shock from the blow was first relayed to the main waterline wales and through them to the ramming timber—made from a great log specially shaped into five different faces that was squeezed between both wales and notched to touch the keel and bottom planks. These bottom timbers were all rigidly interconnected by mortise and tenon joinery secured by thick oak pegs through which long copper nails were driven (Fig. 2.2). This careful construction insured that the forces of the collision were transferred from the ram—literally the ship's warhead—to the entire bottom of the ship's hull where they were absorbed harmlessly. With such a design, the Athlit ship was able to deliver powerful ramming blows and survive the collisions undamaged.

---

4. For the process of wood removal, see Steffy 1991, 6–11.

5. Steffy 1991, 6–39; see also Steffy 1994, 59–62.

6. Steffy 1994, 59, compared the ram to the head of a hammer.

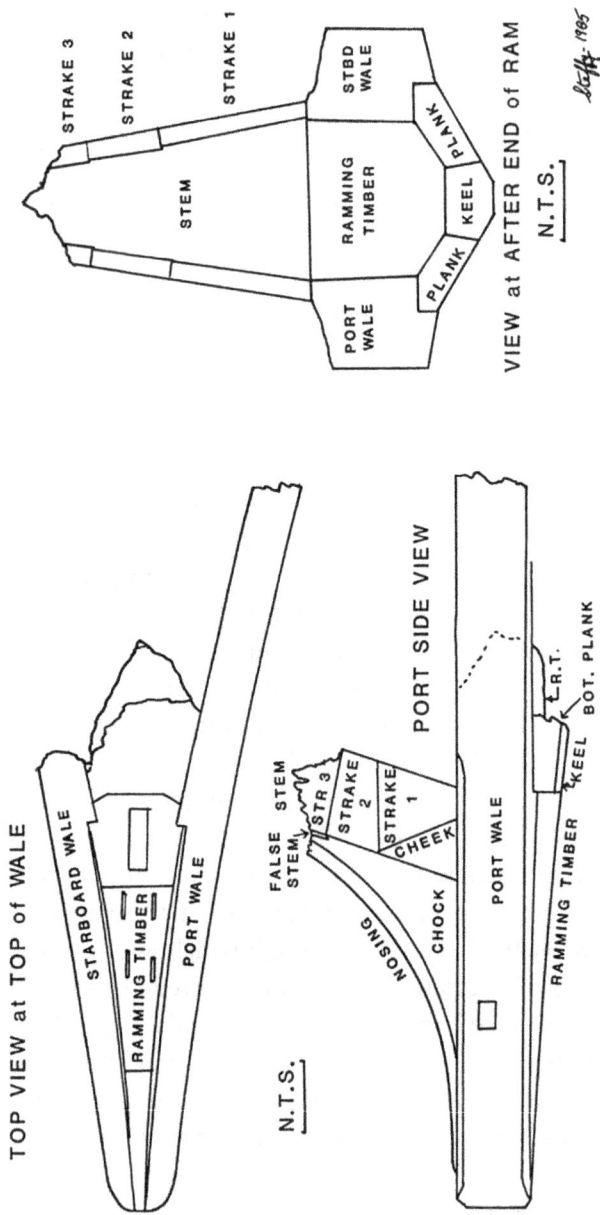

TOP VIEW at TOP of WALE

STARBOARD WALE

RAMMING TIMBER

PORT WALE

N.T.S.

FALSE STEM

STEM

STR 3

STRAKE 2

STRAKE 1

CHEEK

NOOSING

CHOCK

PORT WALE

RAMMING TIMBER

R.T.

KEEL

BOT. PLANK

PORT SIDE VIEW

STRAKE 3

STRAKE 2

STRAKE 1

STEM

STBD WALE

RAMMING TIMBER

PLANK

KEEL

PLANK

PORT WALE

VIEW at AFTER END of RAM

N.T.S.

FIGURE 2.2 Bow structure inside the Athlit ram. Line drawing by J. Richard Steffy. Copyright © 1991, Texas A & M University Press.

The Ram's Casting

While Steffy and his colleagues struggled with the wood inside the ram, Elisha Linder, the director of the research team, asked Shlomo Eisenberg to x-ray the casting and look for internal fasteners. Following two unsuccessful attempts, the ram was transported to the Soreq Nuclear Research Center in Yavne, Israel, where a successful series of radiographs were finally recorded.[7] Although no fasteners were found, Eisenberg was unprepared for what the images revealed about the structure of the ram's bronze. At first, he was surprised to see no obvious joins, except for a small section of the bottom plate (see Fig. 2.1, "tailpiece"). Most of what we know about large-scale Greek and Roman casting derives from sculptural bronzes, that is, from statues. Generally speaking, these statues are cast in pieces and then joined together by solder or by mechanical joins hidden behind drapery, belts, straps, or other kinds of modeled flanges.[8] The Athlit ram, on the other hand, was apparently cast in a single pour, which represents a considerable technological achievement. According to Eisenberg, "Even today, casting the ram in such a manner would be considered a unique accomplishment."[9]

The images also revealed the cast to be extremely sound, particularly at the ramming head and along the driving center (Fig. 2.1), where the radiographs revealed no porosity flaws, gas holes, or fractures caused by shrinkage of the cooling metal after it was poured into the mold. Eisenberg, a professional metallurgist trained in failure analysis, described the metal's quality at the ramming head as "aircraft grade" when he showed me the radiographs in 1997.[10] Since then, Israeli conservator Asaf Oron has demonstrated convincingly that the ram was cast according to the lost wax process, a well-attested technique for producing hollow bronzes during the Classical and Hellenistic periods.[11]

---

7. See Linder 1991, 5; and Breitman et al. 1991, 83.

8. See Mattusch 1996, 24.

9. Eisenberg 1991, 40.

10. Cf. Eisenberg 1991, esp. 43–44. Eisenberg proposed that the weapon was cast horizontally on its side in a two-part sandbox, a technique previously undocumented before the late Medieval period; see Maryon and Penderleith 1954, 628; Maryon 1957, 475; and Oron 2006, 63, 71–72.

11. Oron 2006. Oron's full reassessment of the ram, conducted in 2001, formed the basis for his master's thesis (= Oron 2001) available online by courtesy of the Nautical Archaeology Program at Texas A&M University (http://nautarch.tamu.edu/pdf-files/Oron-MA2001.pdf). For a basic treatment of metal casting, see Maryon and Penderleith 1954, Vol. 1, 623–35 and Vol. 2, 475–81. An excellent discussion of the lost wax technique can be found in Cavanagh 1990, 145–60.

Although the general technique was well known from other kinds of casts like bronze statuary, Oron argued that its precise application to the ram was somewhat different. This was because the ram needed to fit snugly onto the bow of its warship which bore slight irregularities on its port and starboard sides. Since the ship's bow was not symmetrical, the ram had to be custom-made to match its asymmetry. This required the makers to build up a wax model of the final ram directly on the bow of the warship for which it was intended. Oron reconstructs the process as follows: once the ship's wooden bow was completed, workers coated with pitch the timbers to be inserted into the ram in order to make them slightly oversized. This was done to compensate for a known shrinkage coefficient that affects all bronze casts. After the pitch had hardened sufficiently, they brushed it with olive oil to keep the wax from sticking, and then built up a 1:1 wax model of the ram using a combination of wax slabs and paste. Once the model was finished and the surface decoration added, they removed it from the ship, inserted a core specially made of clay and organic material into the cavity left by the ship's bow timbers, and drove long iron rods, called chaplets, through the side walls of the wax model into its core. Next they added, in wax, a complex system of tubing that would admit metal into the mold through "gates" and allow gasses to escape via "vents." Finally, they invested or coated the model with refractory clay, insuring that the chaplets held together the entire package or mold, consisting of the exterior clay invest-ment, the wax model with its gates and vents, and interior core.

The workmen next placed the mold into the casting pit head down, baked it to melt out the wax and, while the mold was still hot, poured mol-ten bronze into it through the gating system (Fig. 2.3). As the metal flowed into the mold, it filled the ramming head first, then progressively filled the driving center, bottom plate, port and starboard cowls, wings, tips and trough ears, and reached all the vents (for the terms, see Fig. 2.1). Once the cast had cooled, workmen broke the mold, freed the ram, and lifted it from the pit using lifting lugs cast onto the weapon's sides. At this point, the workmen trimmed off excess metal, plugged the hole left in the head by the main inlet gate, trimmed the chaplets still protruding from the sides of the weapon, covered any resulting holes with bronze patches, and added the triangular tailpiece to the bottom plate. Cracks and imperfections were repaired with patches before the weapon was released to the shipwrights.[12]

---

12. See Oron 2006, 75.

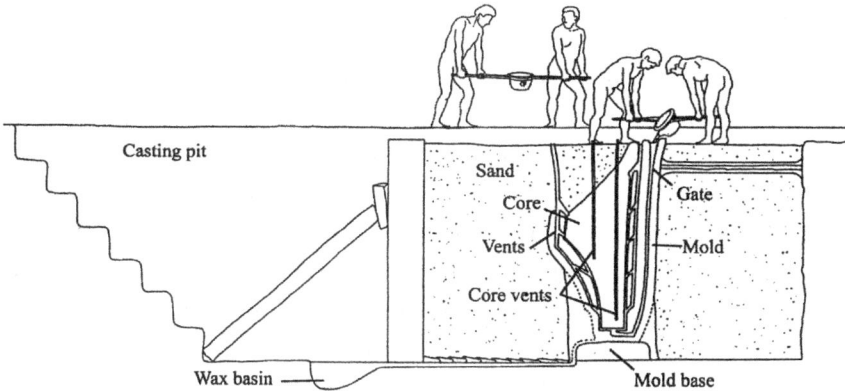

FIGURE 2.3 Ram casting pit in operation. Line drawing by A. Oron.

These men had already prepared the warship to receive its ram by re-moving the pitch used to oversize the ship's bow when the wax model was made. If the calculations were correct, the ram fit snugly when it was slid onto the bow, but if not, the workmen removed the ram and trimmed any necessary surfaces. After insuring a snug fit, they once again coated the bow and ram's interior with pitch, seated the weapon firmly into place, and then nailed it to the bow with long copper spikes driven through the cowl and troughs.

The process may look straight-forward when printed on a page, but the devil was in the details. Success resulted only when an elaborate set of linked techniques were executed perfectly: when the core, wax model, mold, gates, and vents were prepared in precisely the correct manner, when the mold was correctly positioned in the casting pit, and when it was carefully heated and the wax completely extracted. Before the pour, the copper and tin alloy had to be meticulously purified so that no inclusions made the final cast unsound. What is more, the foundry workers had to carefully control the temperatures of the melt, the pouring, and the cool-down phase, all of which became increasingly difficult with the large volume of metal required for filling the mold.

I say large, because the Athlit ram is much larger than most sculptural bronzes and, as a result, its manufacture required additional care. The Greeks seem to have learned how to cast large-scale bronzes by the last quarter of the sixth century, when statues like the Piraeus Apollo suggest that craftsmen were able to produce casts weighing as much as 300 kg. in a single pour.[13] Over the next century, when sculptural bronzes became thinner, less massive, and were cast in smaller sections, they obviously continued to refine the "old" techniques of large scale casting in the naval yards' foundries.[14]

Considering the ram's resilient cast and its solidly built support structure, we are fully justified in picturing the Athlit ship as a ramming machine capable of delivering and withstanding powerful blows at the bow. Everything about the ram's design and construction bespeaks brute force. Not surprisingly, when the ram was found, most scholars felt it came from a large class like a "nine" or a "ten," but this now seems not to be the case. In order to understand the reasons why, we must now consider some unique archaeological evidence that allows us to place this ram in a sequence with other ram sizes.

The Evidence from Augustus's Victory Monument for the Actian War

There is a hill near the modern city of Preveza on the west coast of Greece where one can still see the outlines of warship rams that fought in the Battle of Actium. The ghostly shapes appear on a monument built by Octavian ("Augustus" after 16 January 27 BCE) to glorify his victory over Antony and Cleopatra and to provide an important religious center for the victory city called Nikopolis built in the plain below. The monument was large and impressive, consisting of a large central altar flanked by a three-sided portico that was built on a hillside at the site of Octavian's personal camp. The entire complex was anchored in place by a massive retaining wall that bore

---

13. For the Piraeus Apollo, see Mattusch 1988, 74–75; for the weight of this and other casts, see Oron 2001, 39–45, esp. 41. Large scale bronzes from the first half of the fifth century include the Serpent Column from Istanbul (c. 479 BCE) and the Riace Bronzes (c. 460 BCE). The Serpent Column is demonstrably larger than the Athlit weapon (height = 5.35 m; max. diameter = approx. 60 cm.), but despite its easy accessibility in the ancient hippodrome area, no one has yet determined if it was joined together from separate pieces, or cast in a single pour; see Mattusch 1988, 96–97. This column was originally part of a famous memorial erected at Delphi to commemorate the Greek victory over Xerxes in 479 BCE; it was removed to Istanbul in the fourth century of our era.; see Mattusch 1988, 204. Both examples from Riace were cast in a number of pieces, the largest of which included the torso and the legs. Each statue must have weighed close to 375 kg.; see Oron 2001, 41.

14. Such a view supports the conclusions reached by S. Mark that warships fitted with cast rams (not reinforced cutwaters or forefeet) were developed during the sixth century; Mark 2008, 18–19.

FIGURE 2.4 Actian Victory Monument, restored view. Line drawing by N. Vagenas.

a long inscription and held, imbedded in its face, the back ends of some 36–37 warship rams of at least six different sizes (Figs. 2.4 and 2.6).[15]

Over the years, the rams were removed, broken up, and recycled, statues were carted off to Constantinople, the site was abandoned to the weeds, and eventually forgotten. Relocated in 1913 when this region became part of modern Greece, the ruins were initially pronounced a temple of Apollo, but over the decades that followed, excavations progressively uncovered the long and massive retaining wall that originally held the rams. The rams themselves were displayed at ground level on a 5

---

15. For a general description of the monument up to 1987, see Murray and Petsas 1989. Since that time, the monument has been extensively excavated by the 12th Ephorate of Prehistoric and Classical Antiquities under the direction of K. L. Zachos. Annual reports of the work in Greek can be found in the "Chronika" of the *Archaologikon Deltion* of the Greek Archaeological Service from 1996 to 2002 (some are still in press); for a synopsis in English of the excavations from 1996 to 2002, see Zachos 2001a and 2003 (which is an English translation of Zachos 2001b with additions from the 2002 season), and also Zachos et al. 2008, 57–71. For a small, 6 kg. ram fragment found at the site, see Varoufakis 2007 with illustrations in Vol. 2, 343–45. The precise number of rams, 36 or 37, is difficult to determine because of the retaining wall's broken condition at its extremities.

FIGURE 2.5 Actian Victory Monument, ram terrace, western end.

meter-wide terrace that was supported by a second, lower retaining wall. Bases, still preserved in front of many sockets, held bronze brackets that supported each weapon's ramming head and suggest the weapons' original lengths were no more than 2.5 m. (Fig. 2.5).

The Ram Sockets

Today, one can see the remains of 27 sockets, generally arranged in a progression from large to small beginning on the west and continuing to the east, or from left to right as you look at the wall (Fig. 2.6). While some are preserved better than others, each represents a complex cavity, 25 to 50 cm. in depth, that originally held the back end of a warship ram. As a result, these cuttings faithfully reproduce the weapons' cross-sectional dimensions for a distance of up to 50 cm. at a point beginning about 2 m. aft of the ramming head. These dimensions include the thickness and height of the main timbers that were removed from each ram to allow it to slide into its socket.[16]

---

16. For a complete presentation of the evidence, see Murray and Petsas 1989, 22–61; and also Murray 1996, 335–50.

4   **6**   **8**

11   **13**   **18**

FIGURE 2.6 Actian Victory Monument, different sizes of sockets.

In order to "read" this information from each cutting, one needs to understand how the rams were fit into their respective sockets. A comparison of the Athlit ram's casting with a well-preserved socket like #13 shows what was involved. First, the timbers inside each ram were either trimmed back or removed to reveal the casting's hollow interior (Fig. 2.7). Next, the ram's tailpiece was cut off, if one existed. In this state, the ram was positioned next to the wall, which was constructed to the level of the second course blocks. At this point, the masons prepared to carve the grooves of the sockets' bottoms in the blocks of the second course.

How they next proceeded was determined by the degree to which the ram's exterior width increased from front to back. You can see from the top view in Figure 2.8 that the width of the Athlit ram is greater at "B" than it is at "A." Because the ram is inserted into the socket from the wall's front side, the exterior edge of the socket's groove (Fig. 2.9 at B) must be as wide as the ram's exterior dimension at Section B. But because the

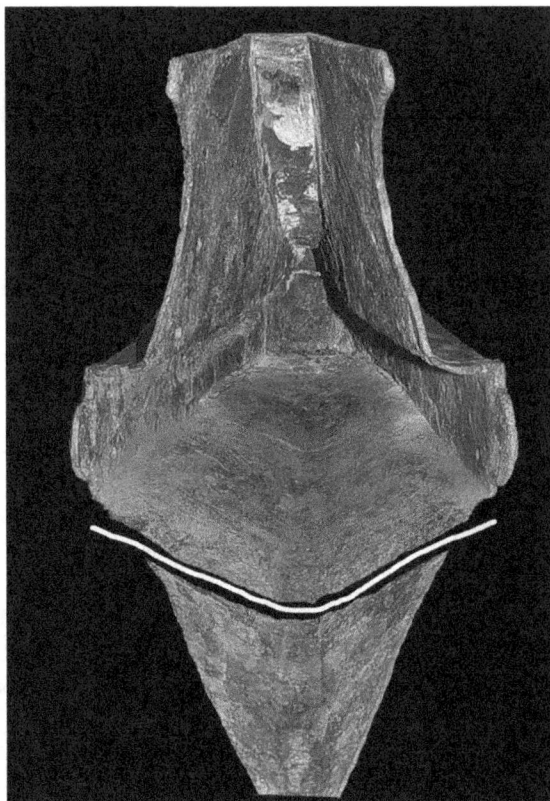

FIGURE 2.7 Athlit ram, rear view.

bronze of the ram-casting angles inward from the trough ears toward the weapon's head, the interior edge of the socket's groove (which will be *inside* the ram-casting; Fig. 2.9 at A) must accommodate the interior dimensions of Section A. The width of the cut groove in each socket is defined by the difference between the *exterior* width of the casting at Section B and the *interior* width of the casting at Section A.

Once these dimensions were transferred to the wall, the lower portion of each socket was then cut into the appropriate blocks of the second course. The rams were then pushed back into place with their bottom plates and troughs sliding into the carved grooves in the second course. Because the blocks of the third course were cut with backward flaring grooves (Fig. 2.10, arrows indicate backward flare), they must have been cut away from the monument and then carefully maneuvered over the rams' cowls and down onto the top of the second course.[17] This was done, presumably, to match

17. See Murray and Petsas 1989, 57–59 for the details.

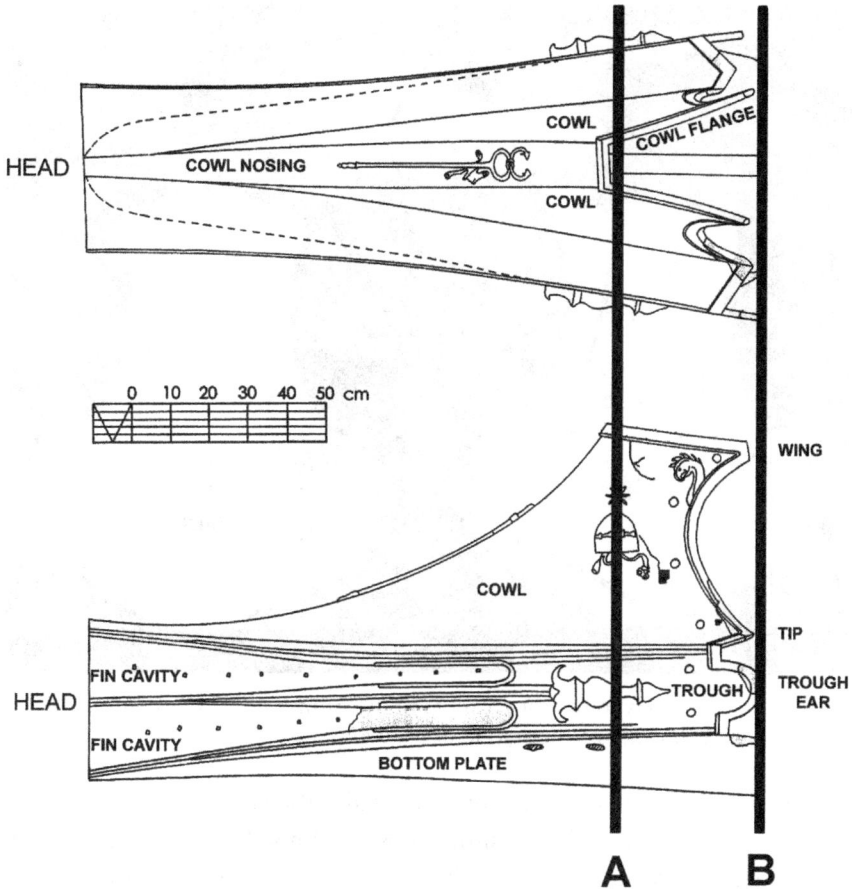

FIGURE 2.8 Athlit ram, area imbedded in hypothetical socket. Image adapted from line drawing by A. Oron.

the flare of the rams' cowls while reducing the width of the side grooves as much as possible. Even though such special care was taken to improve the "fit" of each ram in its socket, gaps still remained to the left and right of each ram. Whether these were left visible, or were concealed by a filler of some sort remains unknown, although a poem from the time of Nero mentions bee hives full of honey inside the rams, implying the existence of gaps between bronze and stone (Philippus in *Anth. Pal.* 6.236).[18]

---

18. For the date, see Cameron 1993, 56–65. At one time, I concluded from a few small fragments of marble revetment (0.011 m. thick) found on the ram terrace that these gaps may have been covered with a thin veneer of gray-white marble (Murray 1996, 437). Since no other traces of revetment have been found anywhere along the wall, I have since abandoned this view.

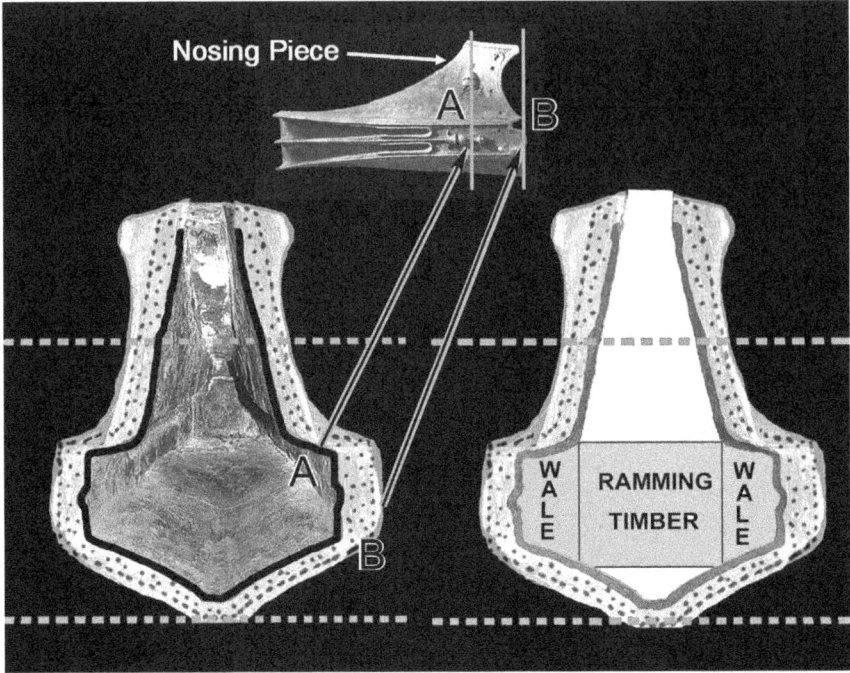

FIGURE 2.9 (Left): Hypothetical socket to fit the Athlit ram. (Right): Core of hypothetical socket showing configuration of timbers.

Since we are now in a position to consider the shapes and sizes of the sockets, let us begin with two simple observations. First, the sockets' outlines clearly show that rams similar in shape to the Athlit example were mounted here. And second, the Athlit ram is too small to fit any of the visible sockets still preserved *in situ* (Fig. 2.6).[19] The similarity in shape between the sockets and the Athlit ram is important for a number of reasons. First, it demonstrates beyond any doubt that both the Athlit and Actian warships were constructed following a similar design at the bow, with rams that sheathed both port and starboard wales along with a ramming timber squeezed in between. Second, it allows for an easy comparison between the sizes of Antony's warship bows and the timbers inside the Athlit ram. Finally, if we can determine the range of classes displayed on the monument, we might determine the class of the Athlit ship. On this final point, our evidence is reasonably clear.

---

19. The recent excavations of K. L. Zachos have recovered a number of socket blocks dislodged from the monument's eastern end, one of which (AM 153) seems to have held a weapon the size of the Athlit ram.

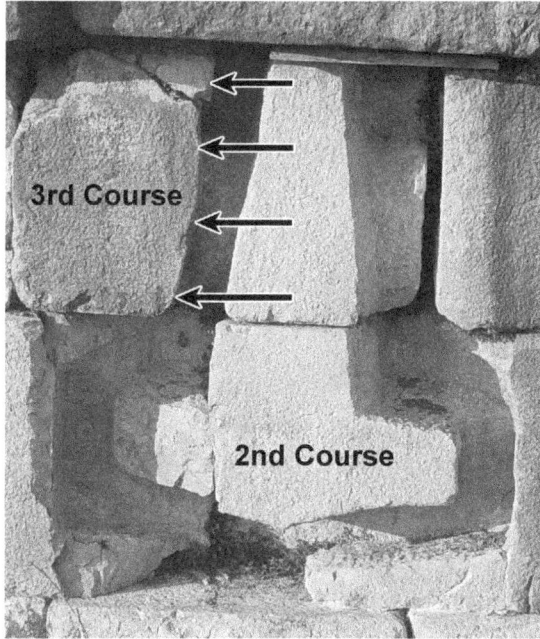

FIGURE 2.10 Socket #13, flare at third course (indicated by arrows).

The nature of the monument, a victory dedication to Neptune and Mars, plus the number of rams included in the display (36–37) make it likely that Octavian dedicated a *dekate* or one-tenth dedication from the more than 300 rams that fell into his hands during the Actian War.[20] Second, because of the special nature of this dedication—the official victory monument of the new Victory City—the future Augustus dedicated the most impressive display he was able to assemble; in other words, he displayed here the largest rams in his possession.

Now, what sizes were these? Again, the evidence is reasonably clear. Strabo (7.7.6) tells us that Octavian dedicated a set of complete warships at the nearby sanctuary of Apollo Actius—one from each of the ten different classes that had fought in the war—a "one," a "two," a "three," and so forth up to a "ten."[21] Unless Antony possessed only one "ten,"

---

20. For the evidence, see Murray and Petsas 1989, 137–41.

21. For the different traditions concerning the sizes of Antony's ships and the reason for preferring Strabo's account, see Murray and Petsas 1989, 99n25.

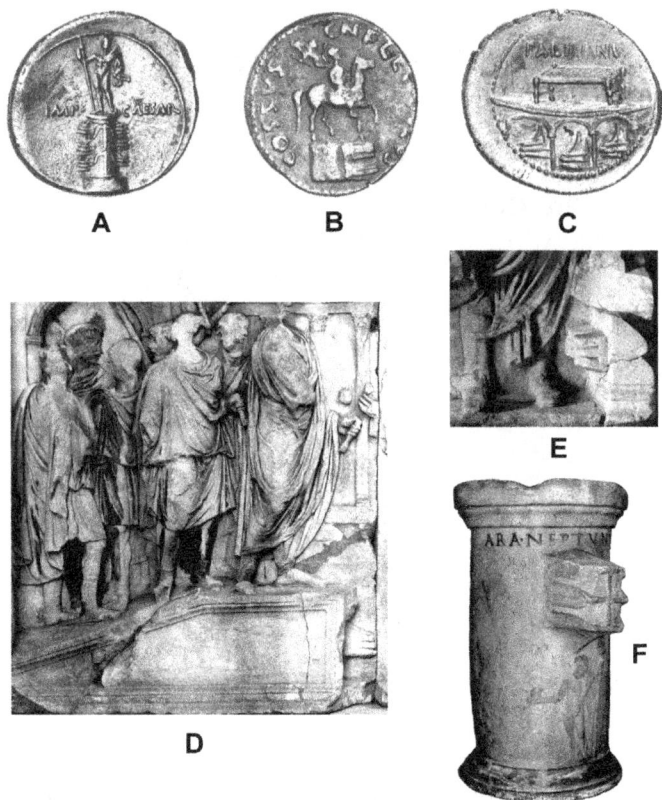

FIGURE 2.11 Examples of suspended rams. (A): *Columna rostrata* of Octavian depicted on a denarius, 29–27 BCE. Courtesy of the American Numismatic Society. (B): Equestrian statue of Octavian (?) *in rostris* depicted on a denarius minted by Cossus Cornelius Lentulus in 12 BCE. Courtesy of the American Numismatic Society. (C): "Antonian Rostra" depicted on a denarius minted by Lollius Palicanus in 45 BCE. Courtesy of the American Numismatic Society. (D): *Rostra Aedis Divi Iulii* on the *Anaglypha Traiani* (detail from left panel). Early second century CE. (E): *Rostra Augusti* on the *Anaglypha Traiani* (detail from right panel). Early second century CE. (F): Rostrate altar (Augustan period?) with the inscription *Ara Neptuni*.

and our sources imply otherwise, we are faced with the unavoidable conclusion that rams up to the size of "tens" were displayed on this monument. Surely the largest sockets held rams from "tens," "nines," "eights," and so forth. The lower limit is a bit more difficult to determine and depends upon how many sizes one discerns in the preserved sockets. Initially I thought I could detect five or six different sizes, and concluded that surely "sixes" and perhaps "fives" were included in the display.[22] It now seems certain (see note 19) that at least one socket was smaller yet than those still *in situ* and thus increases the different sizes to six or seven. Because the visual boundaries between sizes are subject to personal opinion and render certainty impossible, we must consider other ways to assess the size of the smallest ram preserved on the monument.

One possible indicator is in the peculiar Roman tendency to suspend warship rams from statue bases, podia (like the Rostra in the Forum Romanum), and columns. The half-ton Athlit ram is simply too heavy and too elongated in shape to be easily suspended off the ground on a wall or column like we find in numerous preserved images of such monuments (Fig. 2.11). Furthermore, when the literary record provides details for rostral monuments with suspended rams, we find no secure evidence for rams from classes larger than "threes."[23] Although this evidence is suggestive rather than conclusive, it implies that the class of the Athlit ram must be larger than a "three." A similar impression emerges from the analysis of authentic three-bladed waterline rams and from images of warships that survive from the Hellenistic period through the first century CE.

Ships of Larger and Smaller Build: Differences in Ram Design

When describing the fleets that clashed off Anatolian Side in 190 BCE, the Roman historian Livy characterized the warships as follows: " . . . the royal fleet (of Antiochus III) was made up of 37 ships of larger size (*maioris formae*), among which were three 'sevens' and four 'sixes'; aside from these, there were 10 'threes'" (Livy 37.23.4–5). The curious expression "of larger size" recalls another passage where Livy referred to small, open vessels as being "of smaller size" (34.26.11: *minoris formae*).[24] For Livy, and presumably for others as well, this difference made it sensible to group "fours" with "sixes" and "sevens" as somehow *larger* and *heavier,* and "threes" with

---

22. Murray and Petsas 1989, 113–14.

23. For the evidence, see Murray and Petsas 1989, 105–13.

24. Although Livy 37.30.2 refers to "sixes" and "sevens" as being "of the largest size" (*maximae formae*), his basic framework seems to be derived from the comparative terminology of smaller and larger, rather than from small, large, and largest.

lemboi and other open warships as somehow *smaller* and *lighter*.[25] Further-more, a comparison of warship rams—authentic examples, as well as detailed depictions in stone or paint—reveals two clearly defined groups. Because these groups may help to define the differences between "threes" and "fours," it is useful to consider this evidence now.

We should begin with the best evidence we possess, that is, authentic three-bladed waterline rams that survive from antiquity. With the recent discovery of two rams in the summer of 2008, we possessed seven authentic examples to analyze at the time this chapter was written (Table 2.1).[26] The smallest example, the Belgammel ram (formerly, Fitzwilliam ram, Fig. 2.12), exhibits a different design than the others and, because it adds little to our understanding of rams from "larger ships," will be omitted from our discussion.[27] The remaining six examples, however, possess the five basic elements that define the Athlit ram: a ramming head, driving center, troughs, cowl, and bottom plate.[28] They also divide naturally into two distinct sizes and seemingly correspond to Livy's evidence that "threes" fall among the smaller classes and "fours" among the larger ones. While such a conclusion might not seem immediately obvious, it results from a consideration of "fours" and their performance characteristics in relation to "threes."

---

25. We have already seen that Philo (*Polior.* D 29 with C 59) and Appian (*BC* 2.12.84 and 5.11.108) use adjectives such as "bigger" or "big" when speaking of warships. Appian (*BC* 5.11.99, 106) also utilizes the adjectives "heavy" (*bareiai*) and "lighter" (*kouphoterai*) to signify these differences. See also chapter 7.

26. Since writing this chapter, three more rams have been found by the Soprintendenza per i Beni Culturali e Ambientali del Mare and RPM Nautical Foundation off the Egadi (ancient Aegates) Islands of northwestern Sicily. One (called the Vincenzo T ram = Egade 3 ram) was found during the summer of 2010, and two more (the Claude D and Rachael R rams = Egade 4 and 5 rams) were found by mid-June 2011 along with two bronze helmets. Initial photographs of the weapons published on the website of the RPM Nautical Foundation reveal them to be roughly the same size as the Egade 2 (Catherine D) ram found nearby by the same team in 2008; see http://rpmnautical.org/index.html; and http://rpmnautical.org/egadi2010.htm. The team promises a full report after conservation and analysis have been completed.

27. Sleeswyk 1996, 431–32 suggests a way in which the Belgammel (Fitzwilliam) ram might be viewed as a *proembolion*, or subsidiary ram, by turning it upside-down. Although ingenious (Sleeswyk 1996, 448, Fig. 5), this position causes the bird's head on the ring above the ram (as it appears in my Fig. 2.11) to be oriented upside down and is therefore unlikely to be correct; see Nichols 1970–71, 85; and Pridemore 1996, 85. Despite its orientation, it is still possible that this small ram represents a *proembolion*. Most recently, a team of British researchers has arrived at a similar conclusion. For the results of their extensive research into the ram's function, date and metallurgy, see Adams et al. forthcoming.

28. Both the Piraeus and Egade 2 (Catherine D) rams have been damaged as a result of a violent blow to the head of the ram. The cowls have been largely sheared away, and in the case of the Egade 2 (Catherine D) ram, its upper fin is largely missing.

Table 2.1 Authentic Three-Bladed Waterline Rams (listed according to date of discovery, recovery or purchase; dimensions appear in Table 2.2).

Belgammel (Fitzwilliam) Ram

Discovery: Discovered in 1964 by a group of British recreational divers (Derek Schofield, Mick Lally, and Ken Oliver) at a depth of 25 m. off Wadi Belgammel, west of Tobruk, Libya.

Additional information: Originally named after the museum that displayed it; now named "Belgammel" from its find spot: see Adams et al. forthcoming; correspondence regarding the ram's original discovery is posted at http://www.don-simmonds.co.uk/ram.html (accessed June 13, 2011); Nichols 1970–71, 85 with fig. 14; Göttlicher 1978, no. 491a; Basch 1987, 407 with ill. 866; and Pridemore 1996, 74–98. This ram is not only extremely light (19.7 kg.), it lacks a bottom plate and is mounted on the bow of its ship in a way that differs from the others.

Athlit Ram

Discovery: Found on Nov. 11, 1980 by Yehoshua Ramon just to the north of Athlit, Israel.

Additional information: Casson and Steffy 1991. See text below.

Bremerhaven Ram

Discovery: Unknown. Purchased by the Deutsches Schiffahrtsmuseum, Bremerhaven, from Galeria Nefer, Zurich, in 1988.

Additional information: R. Bockius is currently preparing a full technical publication of the weapon that will be published by the Römisch-Germanisches Zentralmuseum.

Piraeus Ram

Discovery: Reportedly found near Cape Artemision in northern Euboea; donated to the Piraeus Archaeological Museum by Vasilis Kallios in 1996.

Additional information: Steinhauer 2002.

Egadi 1 (Trapani) Ram

Discovery: Precise findspot unknown. Recovered from an antiquities smuggler on June 15, 2004, in Trapani by the Commando Tutela Patrimonio Culturale of Rome in concert with the Nucleo Tutela Patrimonio Culturale of Palermo.

Additional information: Originally named 'Trapani' for the place of its recovery; now named 'Egadi 1' following the recovery of numerous rams of similar type off the nearby Egadi islands.
Unpublished. The ram is currently in the care of Dr. Sebastiano Tusa, Director of the Soprintendenza per i Beni Culturali e Ambientali del Mare (Department for Archaeological Heritage and the Environment of the Sea, hereafter Soprintendenza del Mare), Trapani, Sicily, who is undertaking its publication. I saw the ram at an exhibition in Rome in June 2008.

(continued)

EGADI 2 (CATHERINE D) RAM

Discovery: Found on June 26, 2008, during the Egadi Islands Survey off northwestern Sicily by RPM Nautical Foundation and the Soprintendenza del Mare of Sicily (codirectors Sebastiano Tusa and Jeff Royal).

Additional information: Unpublished. The dual nomenclature results from the directors' decision to name the rams after deceased loved ones while still preserving an indication of sequential numbering. Thus, the ram found in 2010 is named Egadi 3 (Vincenzo T) and the ones found by mid-June, 2011, are named Egadi 4 (Claude D) and Egadi 5 (Rachael R). Specific details and photos are presented on the website of RPM Nautical Foundation. Photos and measurements kindly provided by J. Royal.

ACQUALADRONI RAM

Discovery: Found in the sea by Alfonsa Moscato in the bay of Acqualadroni (Acquarone), Messina, on September 7, 2008.

Additional information: Unpublished. The ram is currently in the care of Dr. Sebastiano Tusa (see Egadi 1 ram), who is undertaking its publication. A notice of the find appeared in Modica 2008. From photographs published on the internet, the ram appears to be similar in size to the Egadi 1 and 2 examples and smaller than the Athlit ram. The ram was found with timbers still preserved inside.

How are "Fours" Larger than "Threes"?

As the smallest of the larger ship classes, "fours" help us more than any other class to understand the important differences between larger and smaller warships. In recent years, J. S. Morrison has published perhaps the most thorough treatment of the class, although the picture he presents is somewhat confusing. According to him, "'fours' were regularly cataphract and among the bigger ships." Despite this fact, when compared with a "three," the "four" was "a smaller two-level ship, cheaper to build and with double-manning and a smaller crew more economical to run."[29] In Morrison's view, "fours" are somehow smaller than "threes," perhaps in their freeboard (distance from waterline to deck) or overall length. He therefore provides no help with the question confronting us now, namely, in what way did authors like Livy and Appian consider "fours" to be "large" and "threes" small? The evidence from which we build our answer falls into two general

29. Morrison and Coates 1996, 257, 269; see also 267–69 for a description of the "four's" general characteristics.

Table 2.2 Authentic Three-Bladed Waterline Rams—Dimensions (in cm.) and Weights (in kg.).[1]

(max = maximum; H = height; L = length; W = width; est = estimated dimension)

Dimensions	Belgammel	Bremer-haven	Piraeus	Egadi 1	Egadi 2	Acquala-droni	Athlit
max H of ram	44.1	62.6	NA	80 (est)	NA	?	95
max L of ram	64	66.9	74	89 (display label)	76.5	?	226
H, ramming head	13.1	27.5	35	23 (est)	25 (est)	?	41.1
W, upper fin, ramming head	12.6	26	36 (est)	40 (est)	31.8 (est	?	44.2
H of trough, after end interior:	?	21 (est)	21 (est)	?	?	?	23
max. H of trough, after end exterior	9.4	22	23.5 (est)	20 (est)	17.4	?	24.5
H of preserved wale at after end of ram	NA	NA	NA	NA	NA	?	20
max L of driving center	64	43.5	59	57 (display label)	67	?	168
W of ram, rear, starboard to port trough	18 (est)	23.5	33-35 (est)	32 (est)	38.5	?	76
weight of ram casting in kg. (* = with wood)	19.7	53	80 (est.)	100–125 ?? (est)	?	200? *300?	465 *600
area (cm²), wale-ramming timber unit	169.2	517.00	822.50	656.00 (est)	670.00	?	1824.00
H/L ratio: (L of driving center) ÷ (H of trough)	6.8	1.98	2.51	2.78	3.85	4.62	7

1. The weights and dimensions of the Belgammel (Fitzwilliam), Piraeus, and Athlit rams can be found in the literature cited in Table 2.1. Information for the Bremerhaven ram was kindly supplied by D. Ellmers (personal communication, 1988) and R. Bockius (personal communication, 2008); and for the Egadi 2 (Catherine D) ram by J. Royal (personal communication, 2009). Dimensions for the Egadi 1 (Trapani) ram have been secured from an exhibition display label and estimated from published photographs that included scales, so they represent estimates only. The same is true for the Acqualadroni ram. These weapons, plus those recently discovered during the Egadi Islands Survey, will add considerably to our knowledge of smaller rams when they are fully published; see n. 26.

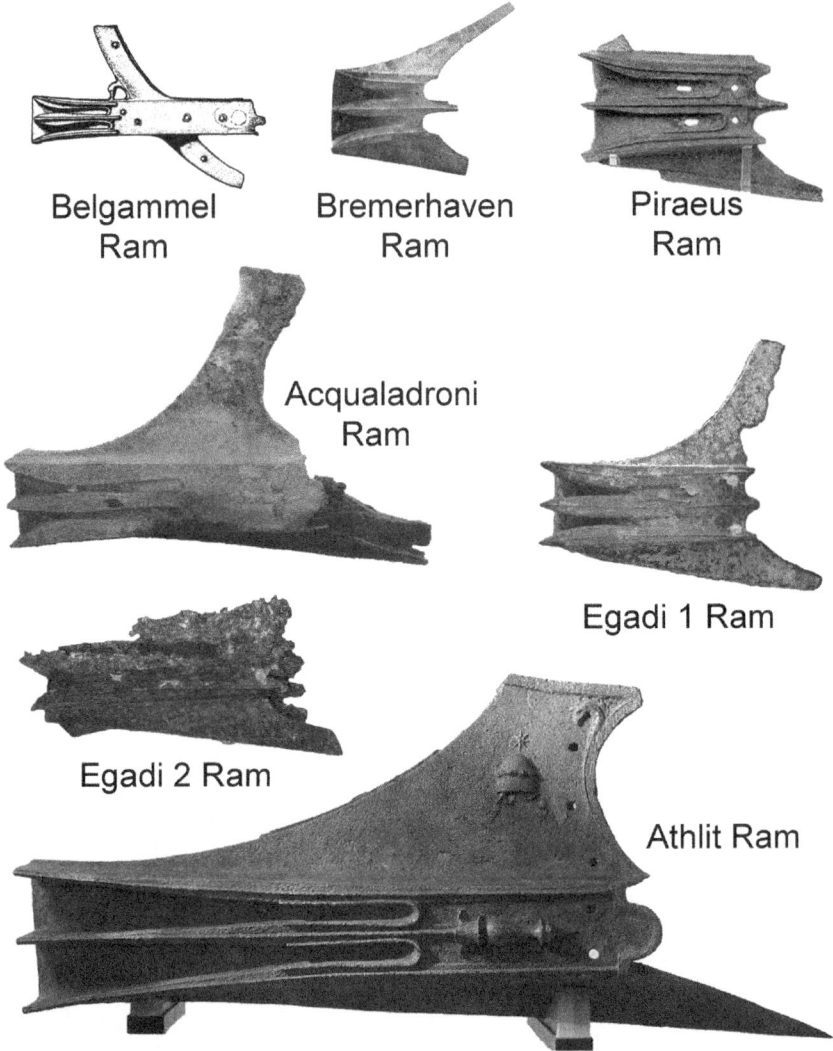

FIGURE 2.12 Authentic three-bladed waterline rams (cf. Table 2.1). *Belgammel Ram (Fitzwilliam Ram)*: Museum of Libya, Tripoli. *Bremerhaven Ram*: Deutsches Schiffahrtsmuseum, Bremerhaven. *Piraeus Ram*: Piraeus Archaeological Museum. *Acqualadroni Ram*: Currently undergoing conservation and study by the Soprintendenza del Mare of Sicily. *Egadi 1 (Trapani) Ram*: Currently undergoing study by the Soprintendenza del Mare of Sicily. *Egadi 2 (Catherine D) Ram*: Currently undergoing conservation and study by the Soprintendenza del Mare of Sicily. *Athlit Ram*: National Maritime Museum, Haifa.

categories: written (ancient texts and inscriptions) and artifactual (authentic rams and Actian sockets). As we consider the written evidence, the reader might also refer to Appendix A, where I have collected the relevant testimonia.

Written Evidence

Because "fours" were utilized in most of the major fleets, a fair amount of evidence survives regarding their chronological development, performance characteristics, and use by various naval commanders. Although we might logically expect "fours" to be the least expensive of the "larger" classes to build and deploy, there is no evidence to support Morrison's claim that "fours" were cheaper to build and man than were "threes." Athenian inscriptions that published the city's naval assets during the fourth century show clearly that when trierarchs of "fours" reimbursed the state for ship's gear, they paid 50% more than did trierarchs of "threes." Surely this reflects the greater costs associated with "fours," at least in fourth century Athens.[30]

From values preserved in these same lists, one can also see that this class had double-manned oars. Morrison was the first to notice this fact, although I believe we can refine his calculations slightly.[31] In 325/4 BCE, the *Epimeletai ton Neorion*, or board of ten who oversaw the naval yards, received 415 drachmai for a set of oars from a "four" that were characterized as "unfinished" or "rough" (*tarrou argou*). Many years earlier during the Peloponnesian War (in 411), a rough-hewn spar for a trireme oar (*kopeus*) was apparently worth 5 drachmai. Although we must use prices that are separated by almost nine decades for two different commodities (oar spars for "threes" and for "fours"), we can still get a general idea of the relative numbers involved. The money received for the unfinished oars of a "four" would purchase roughly 83 units if they cost 5 drachmai a piece. Even if we are off by a variance of 25% to account for the imprecise nature of our evidence, our calculations still indicate a relatively low number of oars for a "four" (roughly 40 to 50 per side) when compared to a "three," whose *tarros*, or full set, numbered 170 (85 per side). Since a full set of oars for a "four" must have numbered between 80 and 100 units, and since we know the ship could keep pace with "fives" and "threes" in fleet maneuvers, the oars must have been double manned.[32] If so, the oarcrew of an Athenian

---

30. See Appendix A: "Physical Characteristics. Ship's Gear" (pp. 256–57) for the evidence. Gabrielsen 1994, 139–45 argues that payments from trierarchs for the replacement of hulls and gear represent averaged values resulting from all replacement costs charged to a particular group. Since "fours" were less numerous than "threes" and are listed with unique costs, perhaps the values associated with their gear more closely represent actual (i.e., non-averaged) values.

31. See Appendix A: "Physical Characteristics. Oarsystem" (pp. 255–56) for the evidence behind the statements in the text.

32. See Appendix A: "Physical Characteristics. Speed" (pp. 254–55).

"four," at 160–200 men, would have roughly equaled that on a "three" of the same period (170 men). It seems likely, then, that a "four" cost as much to man as did a "three." No savings here. And finally, since we suspect that "fours" normally carried more deck soldiers than did "threes" among the full crew, Morrison's conclusion that this class was more economical to run than "threes" must be incorrect.

In general, ancient references to "fours" imply they were heavier than "threes" and were considered to be an upgrade in size. Both "fours" and "fives" were expected to defeat "threes" in prow-to-prow ramming attacks, but when "fours" challenged "fives" in a similar way, "fours" were normally expected to lose. This is why Rhodian "fours" rigged fire pots at their prows to deter attacks on their bows from larger vessels.[33]

Artifactual Evidence

Let us return, for a moment, to my earlier statement that authentic three-bladed waterline rams divide visually into smaller and larger sizes (Fig. 2.12 and Table 2.2). If we consider the "smaller" rams to include the Bremerhaven, Piraeus, Egade 1 (Trapani), Egade 2 (Catherine D), and Acqualadroni examples (Tables 2.1–2 and Fig. 2.12), we see that, in general, they exhibit:

1) a shorter overall length than do the "larger" examples;
2) a "driving center" with height to length values between 1.8 and 4.62;[34]
3) the existence of short or shallow troughs with wale pockets that serve to envelope only the last half-meter of the wales (or less); and finally,
4) a shallow cowl or no cowl at all.

Among the "larger" examples of authentic rams, I include the Athlit weapon along with the Actian rams that were displayed on Augustus's Victory Monument at Nikopolis. Although the Actian rams may seem difficult to assess because they have physically disappeared, the monument's sockets preserve clear impressions of their cowls, the heights of their troughs, and their approximate lengths from the cuttings and bases preserved at the site. Enough detail survives to indicate the general shapes

---

33. See Appendix A: "Physical Characteristics. Ramming Characteristics" (pp. 257–58); for the Rhodian fire pots, see Livy 37.11, 30.3–5; Polyb. 21.7.1–4; App. *Syr.* 24; and Walbank 1999, Vol. 3, 97–99.

34. The height to length value represents how many trough heights "x" equal the driving center's length "y" (see Fig. 2.12).

FIGURE 2.13 Hypothetical ram for socket #4. Model created by W. M. Murray and the Institute for the Visualization of History under the supervision of K. L. Zachos.

and sizes of many weapons once displayed along the wall. For example, Figure 2.13 attempts to visualize the weapon originally placed in socket #4.[35] Although we see a wide range of shapes and sizes in the sockets (Fig. 2.6), their characteristics include the following similarities with the Athlit ram:

1) a much larger size, weight and overall length than the smaller examples;
2) a "driving center" with height to length values between 3 and 7;
3) the existence of long or deep trough pockets that serve to envelope the ship's wales for a meter or more; and finally,
4) a deep cowl that envelopes the ship's hull timbers above the wales.

In sum, significant differences between the two groups involve: 1) the length of the driving center and corresponding depth of the wale pockets; 2) the height of the wales and corresponding height of the troughs; and 3) the existence or non-existence of a deep cowl.

---

35. For a brief explanation of the evidence and methodology employed to create the first model, see Murray 2007. Fig. 2.13 represents a series of further refinements made to the model in 2010.

Ships of Larger and Smaller Build: Pictorial Evidence

Because pictorial evidence from large or detailed ship representations often display the same characteristics observed in authentic rams, we might try to look for clues in these images regarding their classes. Before discussing this evidence, however, I must stress that such pictorial evidence was never intended to preserve the accuracy found in modern architectural plans. Ancient warships were complex machines whose long and narrow proportions challenged the skills of those who sculpted, painted, or drew them. In order to portray them effectively, artists often chose to shorten their originals, compress their curves, and omit certain details. Clearly, some artists were more skilled than were others in producing their models faithfully, while others purposefully ignored certain features in order to accentuate specific details for effect. Still others may have mixed elements from different sized galleys into a single image, thus blurring for us the original differences between closely related classes. As a result, an unexpected feature (or lack of one) might represent something meaningful or simply the inability or disinterest on the part of the artist to reproduce the original faithfully. Despite the difficulties, however, we would be foolish to ignore this evidence, although we must be mindful of its limitations and potential problems.

"Threes"

If we start with the earliest of the "smaller" examples (Fig. 2.14, A), we can see that a weapon like the Piraeus ram or Egade 1 (Trapani) ram would have fit the warship bow sculpted on the Democleides stele from the National Museum in Athens (Inv. # 752), dating to the early fourth century BCE. Although the original details of the ram's shape, once highlighted in paint, are now faded, the weapon's relative size is indicated by the blades represented at its head. Since "threes" dominated the navy in Athens during the time this relief was created, we can be fairly certain that the image represents a "three."

A similar sized weapon must be envisioned on the bow of a warship (ostensibly the *Argo*) sculpted on a third century honorific stele from Boeotia now in the Boston Museum of Fine Arts (Fig. 2.14, B). The class of warship serving as the model for this image is uncertain, although it displays similarities in scale to the vessel depicted on the Democleides stele and might reasonably be considered a "three." Explicit examples of "threes" can be seen in examples of warships from Nymphaion (Fig. 2.15, A and B) and

A   B

FIGURE 2.14 (A): Democleides Stele. Early fourth century BCE. National Archaeological Museum, Athens. (B): Warship Depicted on a Boeotian Stele. Third century
BCE. Museum of Fine Arts, Boston. Photo © 2011 Museum of Fine Arts, Boston.

Pozzuoli (2.15, F) where they clearly display three levels of oars or oarports
and bear apparently small rams. Similar examples appear in a number
of warships modeled in plaster relief from Sicilian Soluntum (Solunto).
Although in fragments, the models depict oarboxes with oarports set at
three levels (Fig. 2.15, D) and small rams (C, E). It would seem, on this
evidence, that the Piraeus and Egade 1 (Trapani) weapons correspond reasonably well to "threes" or to other warships that Livy would classify as
"smaller" in size. We might say the same about the Egade 1 (Trapani) ram
and the larger Acqualadroni weapon, which seem remarkably similar to
rams depicted on a fresco from Pompeii showing a number of warships
inside a series of arched openings interpreted as *navalia* or shipsheds (Fig.
2.16).[36] The composition of the original painting (which is now cut into
three panels) is unrecorded. Since two of the vessels clearly show oarboxes
with ports arranged in a diagonal line at three different levels (Fig. 2.16, A,
left vessel), the ships are most likely "threes."

Before passing to the larger examples, I should note the well known,
but sometimes ignored fact that "threes" from different cities and centuries
displayed different oarsystems, and presumably other characteristics as
well. For this reason, I do not mean to imply by my previous remarks that
"threes" were similar over time and thus had similar rams. We possess
ample written and pictorial evidence to demonstrate substantial variations

36. The paintings were found November 7–14, 1763, in Regio VI, 17 (Insula Occidentalis), 10;
see Bragantini and Sampaolo 2009, 196–97 and Basch 1979, 291–94. They appear on three
separate panels now in the Naples Museum (Inv. 8603, 8604, 1172).

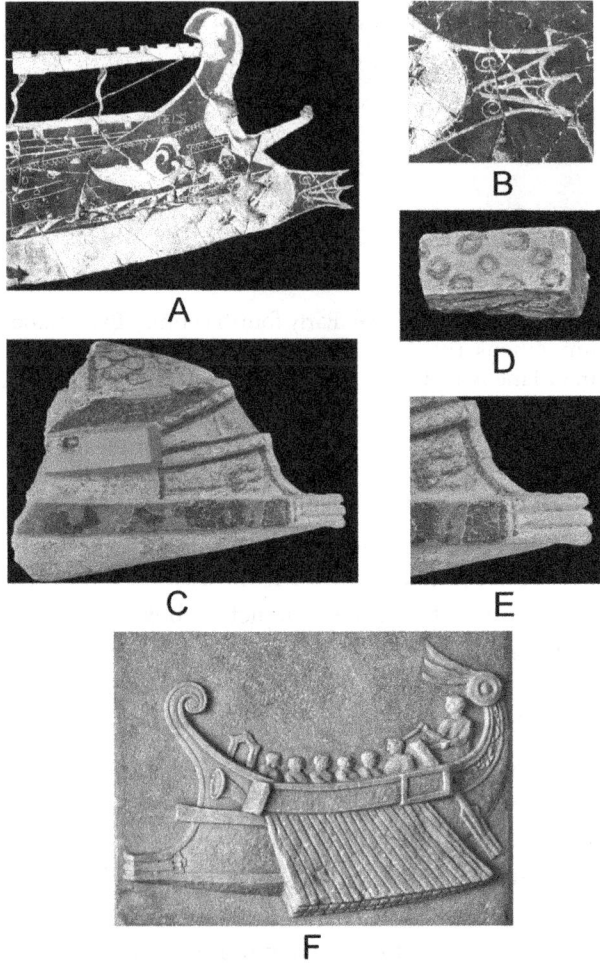

FIGURE 2.15 Warships from Nymphaion (Ukraine), Solunto (Sicily) and "Pozzuoli" (Italy) showing three levels of oars or oarports. (A, B): Warship prow from a scraffito at Nymphaion, Ukraine. Mid-third century BCE. (C, E): Plaster relief of warship prow from Soluntum (modern Solunto). (D): Plaster fragment of an oarbox found with the warship prow illustrated in C and E. (F): One of two marble reliefs depicting warships (frequently called the Pozzuoli Reliefs) found at Lago Fusaro, near Misenum, Italy. Augustan period.

in the design of the class.[37] And this surely explains the variations in the sizes and shapes of individual rams, such as the Egade 1 (Trapani) and Acqualadroni examples. Still, I think it reasonable, though I cannot prove it, to expect that these differences in design produced variations in ram

---

37. In an important article published in 1979 (Basch 1979), L. Basch emphatically argued against the notion of a single design for a trireme (i.e., the "Greek" one) and pointed out the

FIGURE 2.16 (A): Fresco, originally from Pompeii, depicting warship prows inside *navalia* (shipsheds). Second half of first century CE. (B): Ram on a warship prow depicted inside *navalia*, originally from Pompeii. Second half of 1st century CE.

sizes that were less pronounced than the differences between rams of different classes.

"Fours" and "Fives"

Among the larger group of rams, the Athlit weapon commands our attention first (Fig. 2.17, A). While it clearly derives from one of the "larger" classes, the question remains: which one? The answer, a "four," may be suggested by the following evidence. The first item is a large sculpted

different oar systems that are indicated by representations of Roman and Phoenician "threes." Although "threes" are normally classed among the "open" galleys in a fleet, we know from certain authors that "cataphract" versions existed as well: see App. *Mith.* 17 and 92; Memnon of Herakleia, *FGrH* 434, F1, 21, (= *FGrH*, Dritter Teil, Text, 24. Herakleia am Pontos, p. 351); Caes. *BC* 2.23. Casson 1995, 123–24 is no doubt correct that both versions of "threes" were built at the same time.

monument, built of six courses of travertine blocks, depicting a warship prow on the downstream end of the Tiber Island in Rome.[38] Fortunately, this monument caught the eye of the Venetian architect Giovanni-Battista Piranesi who drew a number of detailed views and plans of it in the mid-eighteenth century.[39] At that time, the warship exhibited both port and starboard sides, at least at its preserved end, but had already lost its ram (Fig. 2.18, B). Piranesi records the width of the bow just behind the missing ram as slightly more than 4 palms, or about 90 cm. from port to starboard wale (Fig. 2.18, A). In subsequent years, the ship was enveloped in a stair-case leading up to the church of San Bartolomeo, but was still accessible enough for Friedrich Krauss to publish a series of detailed profile draw-ings in 1944.[40] He records the height of the port wale as roughly 38 cm. and this corresponds perfectly with Piranesi's plan (1.75 palms = 38 cm.). The monument alludes to the galley sent by Rome to Epidaurus to fetch the healing cult of Asclepius following a plague in the early third century BCE.[41] Although one cannot be certain of the ship's class, if the model is sculpted at full scale, or follows its original in every detail, it is clear from the size of its waterline wale that the original warship was larger than the "threes" we have just identified.[42] Such a conclusion also corresponds to the fact that Romans normally sent larger galleys, usually "fives," on mis-

---

38. The monument, located on the south end of the Tiber Island, was built in the first cen-tury BCE if we may judge from the stone used in its construction. See Göttlicher 1978, 81, no. 484, for bibliography not mentioned in my text and notes.

39. For Piranesi's plans and views, see Piranesi 1762, Tab. XI, XIIa-b, XIII; the best detailed view of the monument's prow appears in Vol. 4 of Piranesi's *Le Antichità Romane* (1756), Tab. XV. Piranesi used the late antique *palmus maior* roughly equal to 22.19 cm. These eigh-teenth-century works are now online as part of Brown University's Center for Digital Initia-tives (http://dl.lib.brown.edu/index.html).

40. Krauss 1944, 159–72 with Beilagen I–VI. Piranesi's measurement of the monument's width (90 cm.) just behind the lost ram (see my Fig. 2.18, A) should be more accurate than the 120 cm. width Krauss calculates from traces and presents in his Section F. Krauss records the height of the port wale as roughly 37–38 cm. (Beilage VI, sections D′ = 37 cm.; E′ = 38 cm.; and F = 37 cm.).

41. For the details, see Richardson 1992, 3–4 (Aesculapius, Aedes) and 209–10 (Insula Tiberina). Basch 1987, 366, believes that the monument follows a Greek, not Roman, design.

42. Krauss 1944, 160, notes that the ship's width or beam is "greatly exaggerated" because it was built to conform to the island's topography. According to his analysis, the hull was wid-ened without altering the ship's important characteristics or its overall appearance. While some features of the hull were deformed more than others, the height of vertical features like the wale remained unaffected.

sions involving prestige or ceremony.[43] Despite the uncertainty that such evidence frequently possesses, we will see from the next piece of evidence good reasons for identifying this warship with a "five."[44]

The second piece of evidence that helps to define the Athlit ship's class is a large marble ram found at Ostia just outside the Marina Gate near a funerary monument to honor one Gaius Cartilius Poplicola.[45] Since Poplicola's monument includes a sculpted frieze bearing at least two warships, it was thought by those who published the remains that a large marble ram, found some 68 meters to the north, was originally part of Poplicola's structure.[46] More recently, L. B. van der Meer has suggested that the ram belongs with a second funerary monument which he identifies with another Ostian notable, Publius Lucilius Gamala. Gamala is known from an inscription (*CIL* XIV, 375) to have donated money for a *bellum navale*, "naval war"—perhaps the war against Sextus Pompey in 38–36 BCE—which may explain the presence of the ram on this monument.[47] The ram in question is currently comprised of two blocks. The upper block, which seems to represent the ram's cowl with a lion's head protome, or decorative element, was found at the crossroads of the *decumanus* (the central N-S road) and the Via Epagathiana, about 350 m. to the northeast. The lower block was found where it is currently displayed, just to the north of the funerary monument at Regio III, Insula VII, Building 2.[48] The ram formed by these two blocks lacks certain "finished" elements like a bottom plate or indication of casting edges at the trough, and the cowl's forward edge does not match the nosing width on the top surface of the lower block (Fig. 2.19, B).

---

43. See Appendix B: Physical Characteristics. Additional Characteristics of Usage.

44. J. F. Coates admits that the vessel can be reconstructed at a 1:1 scale as a two level "five," but dismisses this possibility because he feels that the resulting vessel would not be maximized for speed; see Coates in Morrison and Coates 1996, 296; Morrison (Morrison and Coates 1996, 229) suggests that the warship represents a "six." If "fives" were built primarily for their ramming characteristics and secondarily for speed, then Coates' objection is not a serious problem.

45. For this monument and its decorative relief, see Squarciapino et al. 1958, 171–81, 191–207; for the identity of Cartilius Poplicola, see Squarciapino et al. 1958, 209–19.

46. Such is the view expressed in the full publication of the monument: Squarciapino et al. 1958, 194–95, with Pls. 30–32, 39–43.

47. See Meer 2005, 101–102; he also argues (92, 101) that the funerary monument he identifies with Gamala is likely to be slightly earlier (ca. 30–20 BCE) than the monument of Poplicola (22–20 BCE).

48. See Squarciapino et al. 1958, 179, 194.

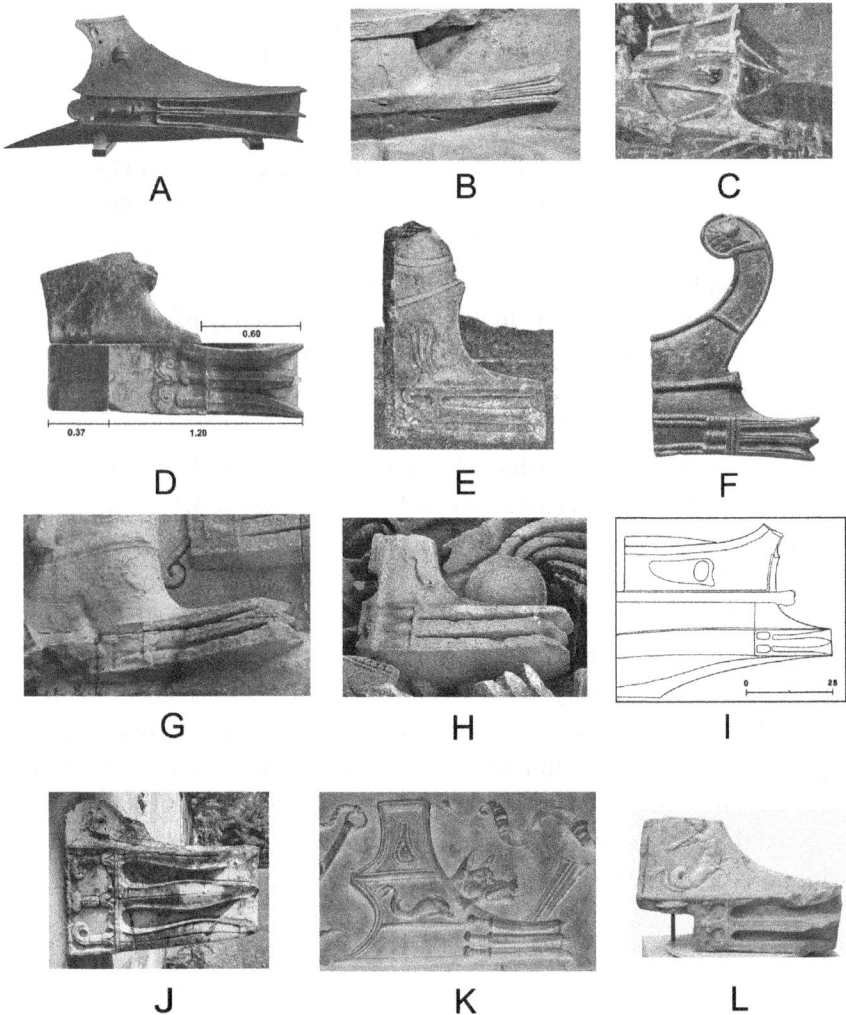

FIGURE 2.17 Rams from "warships of larger build." (A): Athlit ram (see Table 2.1; image mirrored). (B): Ram depicted on a warship relief from the Palatine. Augustan period. (C): Detail from a fresco panel showing paired warships, Temple of Isis, Pompeii. First century CE. (D): Marble ram, Ostia. Second half of first century BCE. (E): Marble ram, Nikopolis, Greece (now lost). Image (mirrored) from Papademetriou 1941, 30, Fig. 6. By permission of the Archaeological Society at Athens. (F): Bronze model of a ship's prow, formerly in the Altes Museum, Berlin (now lost). (G, H): Warship rams sculpted in relief on a triumphal arch at Orange (ancient Arausio), France. Reign of Tiberius. (I): Marble ship prow from Aquileia, Italy. First century CE. After a line drawing by A. L. Ermeti. (J): Marble ram, presumably from Rome or its environs (findpot unrecorded). Augustan period. Federico Zeri Collection, Mentana, Italy. (K): Ram on relief panel showing naval trophies and priests' emblems from Rome (precise findspot unrecorded). Augustan period. Palazzo dei Conservatori, Rome. (L): Marble ram, findspot unrecorded. Augustan period. Antikenmuseum, University of Leipzig.

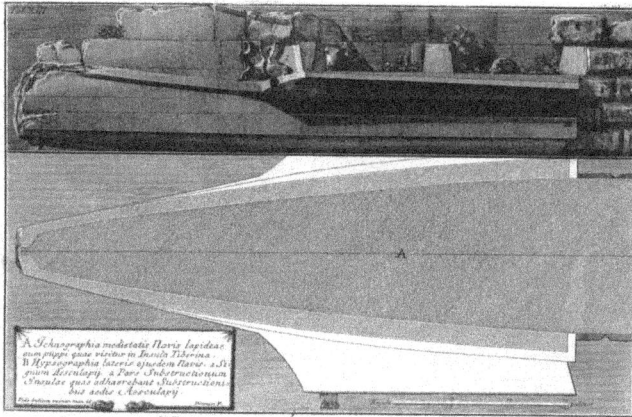

A

B

FIGURE 2.18 (A): Tiber Island Warship, side view and top plan by Giovanni-Battista Piranesi (1762). Vincent Buonanno Collection. (B): Tiber Island Warship, view from the ship's forward end by Piranesi (1756). Vincent Buonanno Collection.

Presumably, the ram's constituent blocks were placed in their current position because the clamp cuttings on the after ends of each block appeared to match (Fig. 2.19, C). This is unlikely, however, for the cuttings are carved to different depths, indicating they are not a matched pair.[49] If the blocks were precisely aligned according to the cuttings, the mismatch between the lower and upper block would become even more pronounced. Apart from the problems with the nosing contours, the blocks' current alignment produces a ram that is too stumpy in its proportions

---

49. The depth of the channel in the upper block is 0.014 m., while that of the lower block is 0.019 m.

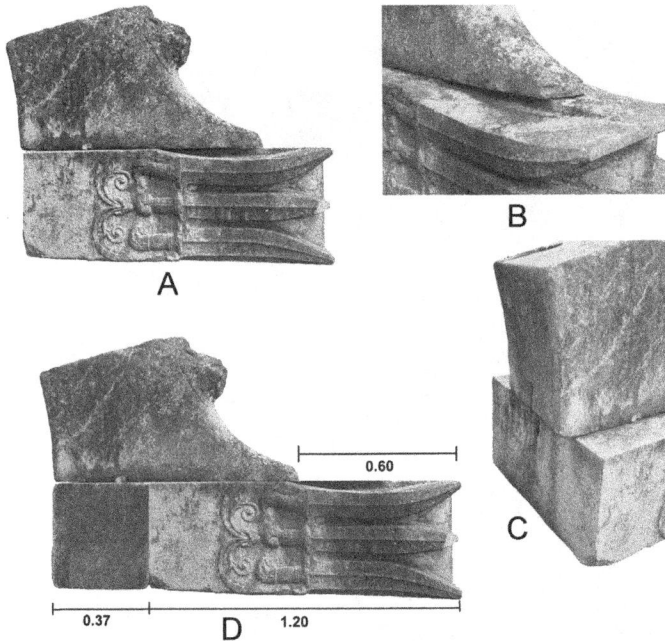

FIGURE 2.19 Marble ram, Ostia. Second half of first century BCE.

(Fig. 2.19, A). I suspect, therefore, that other blocks are missing from the original ensemble, and that the missing elements, if present, would alter the overall proportions of the ram's length, width, and height. For example, by repositioning the upper block to a point where its nosing contours seem to match the lower block, the ram's length, height, and width from trough to trough at its after end increase substantially (Fig. 2.19, D). If we cannot gain a sure sense of the ram's original size from its overall dimensions, we might still gauge its size from the height of its port and starboard troughs that measure 41.5 cm. This dimension is appropriate to receive wales equal in height to the one sculpted on the Tiber Island warship (Table 2.3).

A simple similarity in wale heights cannot be considered conclusive evidence, but it suggests that the scale of the Ostia weapon corresponds with the Tiber Island warship whose original model makes best sense as a "five." Furthermore, the Ostia ram's wale height corresponds to more than one of the smaller sockets (but not the smallest one) on the Actian Victory Monument at Nikopolis (Table 2.3). While these dimensions still require further refinement, they produce the following conditions:

1) The Ostia ram and Tiber Island warship seem to represent bow structures of roughly the same scale.

2) The wale height of this scale is almost twice that represented in the Athlit ram.

3) This scale corresponds to more than one of the *smaller* sockets on the Actian Victory Monument.

4) The Athlit ram corresponds to the *smallest* socket identified at the Victory Monument.

5) "Threes" seem to correspond to a set of rams smaller than the Athlit weapon.

Considering these five conditions and allowing for variances in size among different vessels of the same class, I believe it reasonable to conclude that the Athlit ram comes from a Hellenistic "four" and the Ostia ram and Tiber Island ship were modeled after the dimensions of a Roman "five." A more detailed analysis of the measurements from these monuments will be required to confirm this hypothesis fully, but I am hopeful we are close to resolving the issue.

Warships of "Larger" Size

Before concluding this discussion of pictorial images, we should note a few examples whose rams correspond to the characteristics of "larger"

Table 2.3 Trough Dimensions from Tiber Island Ship, Ostia Ram, and Sockets #13 and #15.

Ram / Ship / Socket	Width from port to starboard trough ears	Height of port trough	Height of starboard trough
Tiber Island Ship	90–120 cm.[1]	approx. 42 cm.[2]	–
Ostia Ram	approx. 90–100 cm.	41.5 cm.	41.5 cm.
Socket #13	103 cm.	37 cm.	40 cm.
Socket #15	100.5 cm.	44 cm.	40 cm.

1. Piranesi's measurement (1857) = 90 cm.; Krauss's measurement (1944) = 120 cm. from traces.

2. Since a 4 cm. difference exists between the height of the wale inside the Athlit ram and its trough height, I have estimated the total height of the trough for the Tiber island ship as roughly 42 cm.

weapons, but whose precise class cannot yet be determined. These include a sculpted ram that was found at Nikopolis in 1940 (Fig. 2.17, E, now lost), a sculpted warship of Augustan date in the Palatine Museum (B), a series of rams depicted on a relief from an Augustan building, now in the Capitoline Museum (K), a marble ram in the collection of the Archaeological Museum at the University of Leipzig (L), a marble ship's prow at Aquileia, Italy (I), and a detailed series of rams and prows sculpted on the first century CE triumphal arch at Orange in southern France (G, H). I might also add to this collection a sculpted warship ram, currently in the collection of the Villa Zeri outside Rome at Mentana (J), and the warships painted on a series of frescoes in the Temple of Isis at Pompeii (C). Although made by different artists at different times and for different purposes, each image (with one or two exceptions) displays the characteristic features of larger rams, including sizeable wales, deep trough pockets, and deep cowls.[50]

Of all these large examples, however, I wish to single out the warship rams from Orange because I feel they were modeled after the rams cut from Antony's prows at Actium. I say this because their rear profiles match perfectly the contours of the sockets at Nikopolis and because Actian rams would have provided natural models for the builders of this arch.[51] What is more, a few of these examples are shown on the bows of their warships (Fig. 2.20) and thus give the viewer an excellent sense of scale of rams from midsized polyremes ("sixes" to "tens") in relationship to their prows.

Conclusions

Our currently available evidence from authentic three-bladed waterline rams indicates the existence of two basic physical designs: one that corresponds to smaller warships and another that corresponds to larger ones. The dividing line seems to occur, just as Livy indicates, between the "threes" and "fours." The division between the two types involves significant differences in physical characteristics, namely, the length of the ram, the size of the wales, and the existence or non-existence of an enveloping cowl. These characteristics inform us about the main difference in performance between larger and

---

50. Certain problems can be seen in the Mentana ram (small scale, small cowl, and large wales), the Palatine Warship ram (which resembles the Athlit ram, but appears on the bow of a single-level warship), and Capitoline rams (which display an odd mix of characteristics). Each of these examples, however, resembles larger rams rather than smaller ones.

51. For the arch at Orange, see Amy et al. 1962; and Murray and Petsas 1989, 100–103 for the similarity between the profiles of the sockets and the rams depicted on this arch.

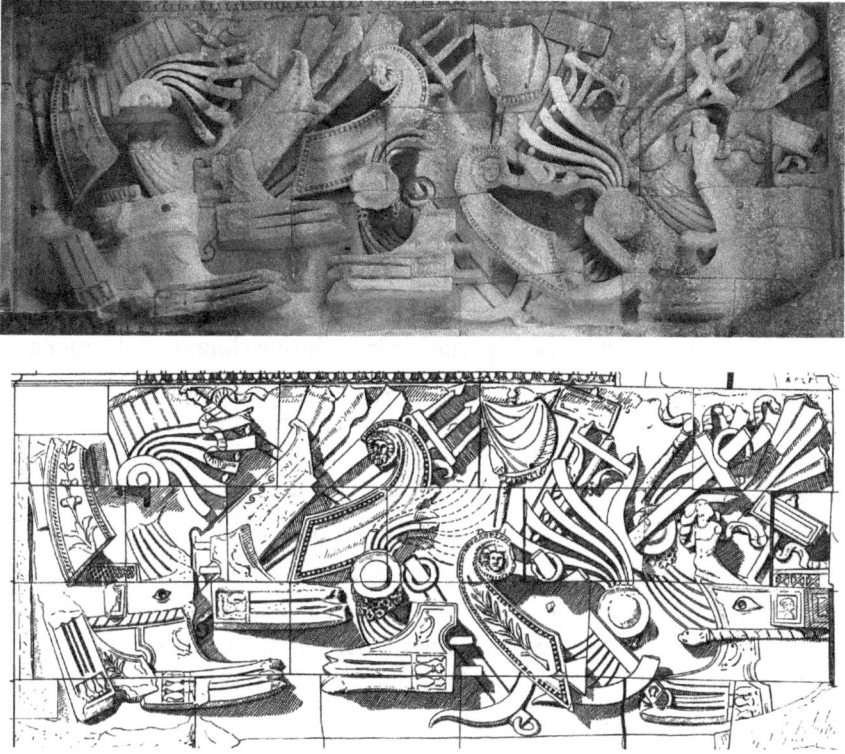

FIGURE 2.20 Panel showing naval spoils on a triumphal arch at Orange (ancient Arausio), France. Reign of Tiberius. Lower image from Amy et al. 1962, Plate 24.

smaller warships. Smaller warships were designed for speed and maneuverability and they tended to avoid prow-to-prow ramming attacks. These performance characteristics are indicated by their smaller rams, smaller wales, and lack of cowls. Larger warships were designed with heavier wales that required longer rams with deeper trough pockets and cowls to help distribute the shock of the ramming maneuver to the ship's structure, both below and above the waterline. These features correspond to the numerous references describing the use of frontal ramming techniques during this period. The evidence we possess for "fives" indicates that their wales are much heavier than those of "fours." This, too, is reflected in testimonia from the Hellenistic and Augustan periods that reveal the superiority of "fives" over "threes" and "fours" in frontal ramming encounters. As for ship representations, particularly those executed in large scale, one can see clear distinctions between smaller and larger rams as they are depicted on monuments from the fourth century BCE to the first century CE. The main differences parallel what we observe in authentic rams.

Until quite recently, our ability to visualize these changes in warship design depended entirely upon ancient texts and the power of our imaginations. We now know that the ram of a relatively small "cataphract" like the Athlit ship weighed more than one-half ton, and that it was so carefully manufactured that a modern metallurgist rates the quality of the cast at its ramming head as "aircraft grade." The intention was not to resist the vibrations produced by thousands of rpms but, rather, to withstand the crushing impact of head-to-head collisions with other warships of similar and larger mass. This simple quality—the need to resist failure in purposeful head-on collisions—must have played an important role in the development of larger and larger classes during the fourth and third centuries BCE. Driven by intense political rivalries, Alexander's successors drew from their stores of Persian treasure to build larger and heavier warships, one after another in quick succession. Because of the speed with which the new classes appeared, the driving force behind this "arms race," as it has been called, should have been something quite simple, like a desire to increase the warship's mass in order to increase the destructive power of its frontal ramming blow. When the Athlit ram was first discovered, many scholars wondered if it came from a large vessel like a "nine" or "ten."[52] We now know that the Athlit weapon was dwarfed by rams of this size that weighed perhaps four times as much and sheathed timbers four times more massive. As a result of this increase in mass, we can see how the new designs excelled in the kind of warfare that navies of this age were increasingly asked to perform—attacks on cities and their harbor defenses. Let us now turn to the subject of naval siege warfare.

---

52. See Morrison 1984, 216–17. It was once thought, incorrectly, that the weight of trireme rams could be calculated from an entry in the Athenian inventory lists. For the confusion this has caused in evaluating the class of the Athlit ram, see Murray 1985, 141 with notes.

3

The Development of
Naval Siege Warfare

THE COMPOSITION OF the traditional trireme navy underwent profound
changes during the fourth century. The reasons for this transformation
involved a new set of naval objectives developed in response to certain
advances in siege warfare. In chapter 1, we saw how frontal ramming
developed from the success of the Syracusans in countering the superior
seamanship skills of the Athenians. This tactic, which was so effective in
the confined space of a harbor mouth, became increasingly important as
improved artillery weapons increased the ability of an armed force, supported by a navy, to force entry into a besieged city.

Since the days of the *Iliad*'s composition, Greeks had understood that
their navies could be used to project power onto their enemy's cities, but
this force was expressed primarily through soldiers conveyed in ships to
the target city's environs. Considering the size limitations of ancient galleys and the fact that oarcrews were neither trained nor armed to fight in
the hoplite phalanx, the fleet was used mainly to establish and maintain
naval superiority in the region under attack. Once this was accomplished,
usually through a decisive sea battle, hoplites were landed, camps were
built, and fortifications were constructed to cut off the attacked city from
its land.[1] The army, it seems, was responsible for building these fortifications, although in hauling stones and timber, the oarcrews could be
useful.[2] During the course of the siege, the fleet was used mainly to prevent the enemy from sending or receiving supplies by sea (Thuc. 1.64–65

---

1. Clear examples of this four-step process can be seen at Thasos in 465 (Thuc. 1.100.2,
101.1–3), at Samos in 440 (Thuc. 1.116–117), and at Mytilene in 407 (Diod. 13.78.4–7).

2. Normally, our sources ignore the activities of the oarcrews once the battle for naval supremacy had been won. Although we might expect that the rowers participated in the construction of the stockade that protected their fleet station (Thuc. 6.66.2), crews were not
immediately assigned to wall building duties if fleet actions were contemplated. When the

and 1.117), to protect the attackers' convoys of men and supplies (Thuc. 7.13.1), to convey messengers by sea (Thuc. 7.8.1, 11.1), and to oppose the arrival of a relieving force (Thuc. 7.34.1). As for aiding the attack on a city's fortifications, the men and vessels of the fleet were utilized very little, or not at all.

The Fifth Century BCE

This reluctance to use one's fleet to attack the enemy's harbor stems mainly from the inadequacy of contemporary assault weapons, a feature of siege warfare that would not change until the invention of torsion catapults. Although certain pieces of siege machinery—the "ram" (*krios*) and "tortoise" (*chelone*)—were used by the Athenians at Samos in 440 BCE, the mounting of such machines on ships does not occur until much later (see Diodorus 12.28.2–3). This said, we can see the early signs of things to come in three episodes from the Peloponnesian war—the Athenian sieges of Syracuse (414–13) and Byzantium (409), and the Peloponnesian siege of Mytilene (407). Details of these events show clearly the benefits of using one's navy to facilitate and hinder offensive attacks on a city's harbor. More than this, we can see certain defensive tactics already in use at the harbor *before* the invention of artillery, a fact that explains the quickness with which siege warfare was adapted to a naval setting and incorporated into the major fleets of the Greek world.

The Siege of Syracuse (414–13)

We can observe, in the siege of Syracuse, the appearance of numerous techniques that would become standard operating procedure for attacking cities during the Hellenistic period. We see, for example, that the

---

Athenian force rushed to build a wall around Syracuse, the men of the fleet seem not to have been a part of the available labor force until they moved their fleet station inside the Great Harbor (Thuc. 6.99.2–4; 102.1–4). In a few cases, we are told (or can assume) that the oarcrews were assigned to building crews. For example, the crews of 12 Corinthian, Leucadian, and Ambraciot ships, who slipped into Syracuse in 413, helped the Syracusans complete their counter wall (Thuc. 7.7.1). Although Thucydides says that the idea of building a wall occurred to the "soldiers" (τοῖς στρατιώταις), the oarcrews must have participated in the building of the fort at Pylos (4.4.1–3), because there was nothing else for them to do at the time. In general, on the subject of manpower in building such fortifications, see Garlan 1974, 112–13; and now Kern 1999, 114–16, who believes that hoplites comprised most wall building crews.

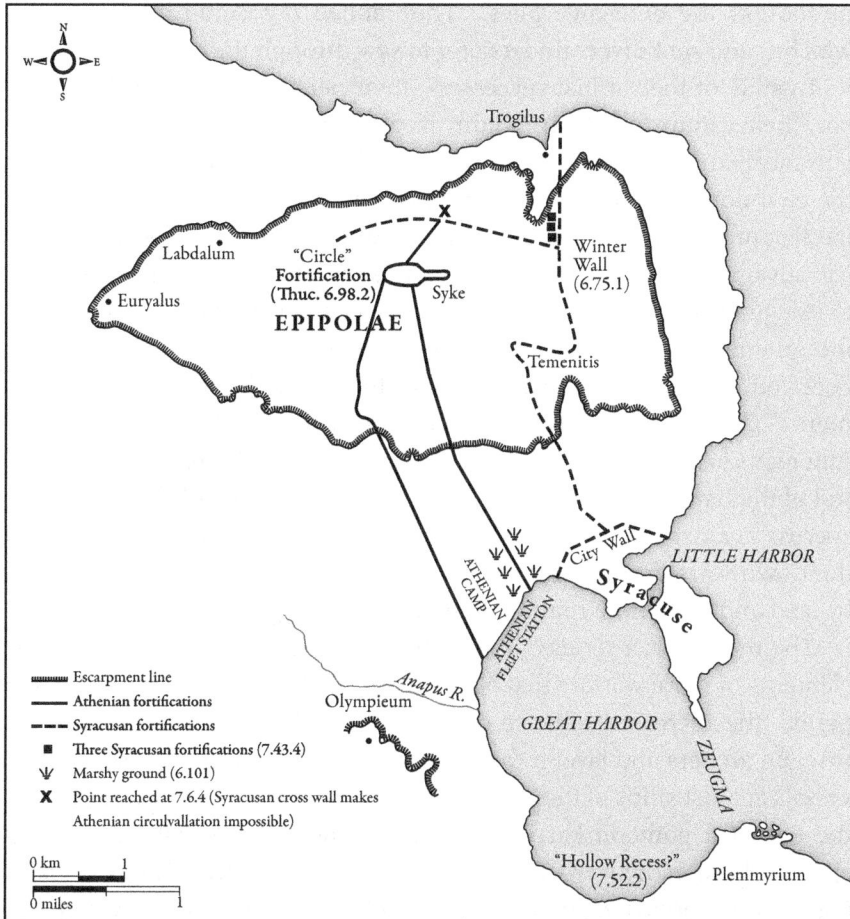

MAP 3.1 Syracuse at the time of the Athenian siege. Map adapted (with alterations) from Hornblower 2008, Vol. 3, 490 Map 5; and Kern 1999, 125 Map 1.

Syracusans drove in stakes and piles to close off potential landing places (Thuc. 6.75.1) and to protect their old shipsheds from attack (7.25.5).[3] The Athenians initially avoided the barriers by landing their troops away from the city (6.97.1), but eventually faced them when they moved into the harbor. At the Syracusans' old shipsheds they used a large cargo vessel, fitted with wooden towers and leather side screens, as a fortified work platform

---

3. Throughout the remainder of this section, all in-text references are from Thucydides unless otherwise noted.

to address the defensive piles.[4] They pulled out some by cables and winches and sent divers underwater to saw through the others (7.25.6–9).

In spite of their initial successes—their penetration of the Great Harbor, their capture of Plemmyrium (a promontory flanking its southern entrance), and the completion of a wall from Epipolae (the heights above the city) down to the sea—the Athenians were unable to maintain their naval supremacy.[5] By the end of 414, the Athenian fleet had lost its numerical advantage (7.12.4) and was forced to keep constantly vigilant in order to safeguard their own supplies and protect against attack (7.13.1). Nicias, the Athenian commander, fretted over the deteriorating efficiency of his fleet and crews (7.12.3–5, 13.2) and sent to Athens for massive reinforcements. The following spring, matters went from bad to worse when the Athenians lost Plemmyrium to the Syracusans, who thereby regained control of the harbor mouth (7.23–24). Then, after learning of the Corinthian success against the Athenians with frontal ramming, they strengthened their own warships' bows (7.36) and resolved to challenge the Athenians by land and sea before reinforcements arrived (7.37–38).

The result was a series of engagements in which we can see the basic elements of naval warfare that became so prevalent during the Hellenistic period: the increased reliance on long-range offensive weapons (in this case, on archers and javelin throwers), frontal ramming, the use of small vessels against ships of the line, fire, grappling irons and boarding tactics, the use of a pontoon barrier or *zeugma*, and fighting within confined spaces where maneuver-and-ram warfare is less effective. The first major engagement occurred in front of the Athenian fleet station, where the Athenians had anchored a line of cargo ships. These had been spaced "two *plethra*" apart (approx. 200 feet) and their yardarms fitted with weights, called dolphins, that could be dropped on enemy vessels that approached too closely (7.38.3, 41.1–2). Forced by their circumstances to adopt a defensive posture, the Athenians found themselves vulnerable to the frontal attacks of their enemies (7.40.5). They were also seriously affected by javelin

---

4. Thucydides describes the ship as a μυριοφόρος, i.e., "a 10,000 carrier." Although we do not know to what unit the 10,000 refers, the ship was clearly a big one; see Gomme et al. 1970, 398–99. The wooden towers would have held sharpshooters and the sidescreens would have protected the deck personnel, both soldiers and workmen.

5. Part of the Athenians' problems involved their inability to maintain an effective blockade of Syracuse's main harbor. On the day after Gylippus (the Spartan officer who led the resistance) arrived, the Athenians ominously lost a moored ship to the enemy (Thuc. 7.3.5). And shortly thereafter, 12 ships from western Greece slipped past the Athenian blockade (Thuc. 7.7.1).

fire and by in-close attacks against their oarcrews by men in small boats (7.40.5). In the end, the Syracusans drove the Athenians back behind their barrier, having destroyed seven ships and disabling many others (7.41.1–4).

Although the Syracusans had demonstrated their clear naval superiority in this battle, the subsequent arrival of Demosthenes and his reinforcements from Athens tipped the balance once again in the Athenians' favor (7.42), but only for a brief time. Demosthenes led a night attack on the heights above the city, but when this failed, he advised the Athenians to immediately abandon the siege and to withdraw all forces from Syracuse. Nicias was afraid of the Athenian reaction at home and so he waffled and prevented an immediate withdrawal, but eventually relented when Gylippus arrived with additional reinforcements (7.50). At this point, a lunar eclipse further alarmed the Athenian army, whose soothsayers advised Nicias to postpone their departure for another month. This lengthy delay allowed the Syracusans sufficient time to challenge and eventually to destroy the Athenian naval forces in their harbor.

In the last two sea battles that concluded the naval war at Syracuse, the Athenians did not fare well, in spite of the 73 new warships that had arrived with Demosthenes. Their problems stemmed partly from their warships' bows, which remained vulnerable to the Syracusans' frontal ramming attacks, and partly from the location in which they found themselves—inside a harbor (albeit a large one) with its natural constraints on maneuverability. The first battle witnessed the defeat of their center and left wing, presumably by frontal ramming and deck fighting, while their right was destroyed trying to effect an encircling maneuver, for which there was insufficient room. Eurymedon and his entire wing were caught in a hollow recess of the harbor and destroyed (7.52.2). The remainder of the fleet was driven backwards onto the shore where a fight developed between both sides' land forces for control of the vessels (7.53).

In this fight, the Syracusans managed to capture 18 ships before the Athenians gained control of the rest and dragged them back to their camp. Then, hoping to burn what they could not capture outright, the Syracusans loaded an old cargo ship with brushwood, pine, and pitch, set it afire, and let it drift downwind onto the Athenian position (7.53.4).[6] Although the fire did not destroy the Athenians' ships, the attack demon-

---

6. Diod. 13.13.6 adds the detail about the pitch; considering the nearby presence of their naval shipyards and the general use of pitch in naval shipbuilding and repair, this seems likely enough. Other details of Diodorus's account are less convincing; cf. n. 7.

strates a clear understanding, on the part of the Syracusans, of a principle of war that becomes increasingly important after the invention of catapults. It was generally safer to damage one's enemy from a distance, because the alternative—direct physical contact—exposed one's own troops to danger. Before the appearance of long-range artillery, one was forced to do this in ingenious ways, and the use of a fire ship was one such technique.

Thucydides' account of the last battle between the Athenian and Syracusan navies reveals a few additional techniques that defenders commonly employed during the Hellenistic period.[7] The Syracusans, for example, built a *zeugma*, or pontoon barrier, across the entrance to the Great Harbor.[8] To my knowledge it is the first time that we encounter such a defensive construction, which was normally built to keep an enemy *out*, not *in*, as we see it used here. Thucydides says (7.59.3, 69.4) that they moored a line of triremes, merchant ships, and smaller oared vessels, side-by-side across the mile-wide entrance, leaving a gap in the middle for the passage of ships. Diodorus adds (13.14.2) that the vessels were joined

---

7. Diodorus also presents an account of the Athenian naval war at Syracuse which derives from sources other than Thucydides; we may suppose, from Diod. 13.60.5, that he used both Timaeus and Ephorus for these years. When his details conflict with Thucydides' account, I generally prefer the latter over the former. For example, when he writes that the Athenians manned their triremes with "the officers and choicest troops from the whole army" (Diod. 13.14.3–4), this accords well with Hellenistic practice (see Philo *Polior.* D 103), but conflicts starkly with Thucydides' statement (7.60.3) that the Athenians put "everyone on board who was of an age to be of any use at all." Additionally, among these "choice" troops were large numbers of archers and javelineers who were totally unused to fighting at sea (Thuc. 7.67.2–3). On another occasion, Diodorus writes that "many leaped on the prows of the hostile ships" (Diod. 13.16.1), while Thucydides observed that the Athenians fixed leather hides on their prows to prevent this from occurring (Thuc. 7.65.2). Because warships did not normally sink, we might also doubt statements made by Diodorus (13.16.3) that refer to struck warships being "swallowed together with the entire crew beneath the sea." When he writes of the great noise caused by collisions and the "sweeping off of oars" (Diod. 13.16.5: παρασυρομένων τῶν ταρσῶν) it is thus difficult to know what to believe. The tactic is well known from Polybius (1.50.3; 16.4.14) who explains clearly how one ship broke the oars of another with a glancing blow along its hull from the front or rear. Since Diodorus uses the expression once more at 13.78.1 (τοὺς ταρσοὺς παρασύρων), and perhaps again at 13.99.3 (where the context has led editors of the text to supply it—see Oldfather 1950, 403n6), he seems to provide evidence for another tactic employed at Syracuse that we see during the Hellenistic period when frontal ramming became more common.

8. Cf. Philo *Polior.* C 54–55. The word ζεῦγμα was also used as a synonym for γέφυρα or "pontoon bridge" by Hellenistic and Roman period writers. Diodorus (11.19.6) and Plutarch (*Them.* 16.2 and *Arist.* 9.6) both use ζεῦγμα to describe the pontoon bridge Xerxes built for his invasion of Greece in 480. Herodotus, however, refers to such bridges only by the noun γέφυρα (cf. 1.205.2; 3.134.4; 7.37.1; etc.).

together by iron chains, that planking was added from vessel-to-vessel, and that the construction took three days to complete. Since the sole objective was to keep the Athenian fleet from escaping, by building this barrier, the Syracusans began in a real sense to besiege the besiegers.

Not surprisingly, the Athenians viewed the closing of the harbor with alarm. They abandoned their position on the upper walls of the city, built a new cross wall close to their ships, and prepared to fight for the control of the harbor entrance—not for victory, but for the chance to withdraw their forces in safety. As Thucydides writes (7.60.3) "They came down from the upper walls and manned all their ships, forcing everyone to go on board who was of an age to be of any use at all. Altogether they manned about 110 ships and put on board them large numbers of archers and javelin-throwers. . . ."

In order to defend against the frontal attacks of their enemies, they decided to use grappling irons, which could be thrown at the moment of impact and then pulled tight to prevent the enemy from backing away (7.62.3). Bound to their enemies at the bow, the Athenians hoped that their own "mass" (*ochlos*) of deck soldiers including archers, javelineers, and hoplites, would be able to clear the enemy decks of hoplites (7.62.2–63.3). Alerted to this plan, the Syracusans stretched hides over their bows and topsides to reduce the places where the grappling irons might catch hold (7.65.2). Knowing that the Athenians would try to break out, they stationed a part of their fleet in front of the barrier at the passageway. The Syracusans then sent the remainder of their ships around the harbor in order to charge their enemy from all sides when the Athenians finally sailed out from their base (7.70.1).

As expected, the Athenians headed immediately for the *zeugma* and, in the first charge, overpowered the Syracusan ships stationed there, and tried to break through the bindings. Diodorus (13.15.3, 18.1) writes that they actually succeeded in breaking the barrier, but Thucydides is less explicit, saying only that they attempted to do so (7.70.2). Whatever the short-term outcome, the Athenians were unable to get past or hold the barrier and were eventually driven back into the harbor where their ships came under attack from all sides.

The struggle that followed not only sealed the fate of the expedition, it also demonstrated, in a spectacular manner, how to beat a trireme force that possessed superior ship-handling skills. The main tactics emerge clearly from Thucydides' description of the action (7.70.4–7):

(4) Many ships crowded in upon each other in a small area (indeed, never before had so many ships fought together in so narrow a space; there were almost 200 of them on the two sides). Consequently, there were not many attacks made with the ram amidships, since there was no backing water and no chance of executing the *diekplous* maneuver [passing through the enemy line to attack from the rear]; collisions were much more frequent, ship crashing into ship in their efforts to escape from or to attack some other vessel. (5) All the time that one ship was bearing down upon another, javelins, arrows, and stones were shot or hurled onto it without cessation by the men on the decks; and once the ships met, the soldiers fought hand-to-hand, each trying to board the enemy. (6) Because of the narrowness of the space, it often happened that a ship was ramming and being rammed at the same time, and that two, or sometimes more, ships found themselves jammed against one, so that the steersmen had to think of defense on one side and attack on the other and, instead of being able to give their attention to one point at a time, had to deal with many different things in all directions; and the great din of all these ships crashing together was not only frightening in itself, but also made it impossible to hear the orders given by the boatswains (*keleustai*). (7) And indeed, in the ordinary course of duty and in the present excitement of battle, plenty of instructions were given and plenty of shouting was done by the boatswains on either side.[9]

In the end, the Athenians gave way, fled to their camp, and abandoned all thought of transporting their forces from Syracuse by sea. Their defeat was not yet complete, but without a fleet to insure the continued import of food and other supplies, the expedition was doomed. Forced to abandon their ships and retreat overland, the once great force from Athens was eventually either captured or killed.

The Sieges of Byzantium (409) and Mytilene (407)

During the final years of the Peloponnesian War, when the naval war had shifted to the eastern Aegean and the coast of Asia Minor, we find two other sieges that display early signs of naval siege warfare. The first

---

9. Translation adapted from Warner 1972, 523–24.

episode occurred during the Athenian siege of Byzantium, in 409, and involved an attack on the Byzantines' harbor.[10] After having made a prior arrangement with traitors inside the city, the Athenians withdrew their forces as if they were abandoning the siege. On the night of this sham withdrawal, the Athenians attacked the harbor with their "threes" to cause a diversion for the army, which waited outside the walls. Their attack focused on the ships in the harbor, some of which they rammed while others they towed off with grappling irons. Aroused by the commotion of the attack, the Byzantines and their Lacedaemonian garrison rushed to the harbor to give aid, and thereby neglected certain sectors of the wall where the Athenian army was able to enter the city.[11] In this case, we see clearly that an attack at the harbor was sufficiently unexpected to cause the force inside the city to neglect portions of the circuit wall. The harbor was apparently unprotected by a barrier, and the attack was a simple one, limited to the vessels moored there. Nevertheless, with help from partisans inside the city who indicated where the defenses were unguarded, the attackers were able to cut short the lengthy procedure of starving the city into surrender.[12]

The second episode occurred a few years later and involved the Athenian general Conon, who had taken refuge in Mytilene on the island of Lesbos after losing 30 "threes" to the Spartan admiral Callicratidas. Because Conon knew he would be attacked immediately, he quickly constructed a makeshift barrier at the city's harbor mouth. First, he sank small boats filled with stones in the shallows in order to constrict the entrance, then, in deeper water, he anchored merchant ships with stones suspended from their yardarms (Diod. 13.78.4). This line of defenses, which continued from the harbor's breakwaters to the underwater obstructions and merchant ships, formed a sort of defensive barrier, or *diaphragma*, across the harbor mouth (Diod. 13.78.5).[13] Conon placed some of his soldiers on his "threes," which he stationed "prows-opposed"

---

10. For the siege, see Diod. 13.66.3–67.7 and Xen. *Hell.* 1.3.14–22. According to Xenophon, the attack occurred while the Spartan commander was away from the city trying to organize a naval force to challenge Athenian control of the sea. He does not mention the attack on the harbor.

11. Xenophon (*Hell.* 1.3.20) says that certain gates were opened for them by their allies in the city, while Diodorus (13.67.3) says they climbed over the wall.

12. For this siege's dire effects on the Byzantines, see Xen. *Hell.* 1.3.19.

13. I should mention that when speaking of this barrier, Diodorus uses language that implies the *diaphragma* was constructed with bindings that could be broken or loosened in

along the gap in the *diaphragma*; others he placed on the merchantmen and still others he placed on the harbor breakwaters to oppose enemy landings (Diod. 13.78.6).

In the battle that followed, the Lacedaemonians attacked frontally in a close-packed formation (Diod. 13.79.1), showering the Athenians with missiles (Diod. 13.79.3) and boarding their prows, presumably after becoming entangled following prow strikes (Diod. 13.79.1). The Athenians fought back with their own missiles and dropped stones from their merchant ships on those who approached too closely. After a brief withdrawal, Callicratidas made a second attack and eventually thrust back the Athenians "by means of the superior number of his ships and the strength of the marines . . ." (Diod. 13.79.5). He then led his forces past the obstructions and into the harbor, surrounded the city with his army, and "launched assaults upon it from every side" (Diod. 13.79.7).[14]

Conclusions from Fifth Century Evidence

From this evidence, it seems that Greek fleets were expected to play a role in siege warfare—a form of fighting that became an increasingly important part of Greek foreign policy and consequent military strategy during the second half of the fifth century. Beginning with the siege of Samos in 440, the Athenians and then others began to use special machinery like battering rams and covered sheds to aid their attacks on their enemies' fortifications. These machines, however, were never adapted for use on naval vessels, presumably because most harbors were still located outside the main city circuit.[15] The primary role of the navy, therefore, remained

---

some way (λῦσαι τὸ διάφραγμα τῶν πολεμίων, "to break the enemy's diaphragma"). In spite of the verb λῦσαι ("to loosen" or "take apart"), he describes the defensive arrangement of breakwater, obstructions, and merchant ships with a verbal construction related to *diaphragma* (ὅπως πανταχόθεν ᾖ πεφραγμένος καὶ κατὰ γῆν καὶ κατὰ θάλατταν, "so that the harbor might be fenced from all sides, both by land and by sea"). Mainly for this reason, I presume that the so-called *diaphragma* was the name he gave to the line of defenses that protected the harbor entrance.

14. In both this case and the one at Byzantium, it is clear that the harbors were located outside the city circuit; see further, n. 15. The siege was eventually unsuccessful as a result of the Athenian victory at Arginusae and the death of Callicratidas (Diod. 13.100.5).

15. Many Greek cities did not include a harbor within the city's fortification circuit (called a *limen kleistos* or "closed harbor") until the fifth or fourth centuries, or even later; see Lehmann-Hartleben 1923, 65–74.

unchanged from what it had been for centuries, namely, to secure and maintain control of the seas so that the army's equipment, supplies, and communications could be safeguarded. In contrast to the static nature of the attacker's navy, those under siege, first at Syracuse and then elsewhere, introduced a number of successful new techniques and devices aimed at challenging the naval supremacy of their attackers. The unexpected magnitude of their successes served to emphasize the serious limitations of "threes" in certain situations related to siege warfare.

For example, the "select" triremes that accelerated so quickly and maneuvered so superbly may have been the pride of the fleet, but within the confines of a harbor, they were surprisingly vulnerable to vessels with reinforced bows. Furthermore, two new criteria became important considerations for those intending to fight in or around the besieged city's harbor. The first involved an increased number of hoplites, archers, and javelineers who were placed on the triremes' decks. These deck soldiers were introduced by the Athenians to keep the Syracusans from backing away following a prow strike, and in this regard they were considered offensive weapons. But to navies with superior bows, the best tactic was to make repeated bow strikes, backing away from the enemy following each blow. The deck soldiers, initially drawn from the army without regard to their training, required specialized skills and formed a more effective force if they were experienced in fighting at sea (cf. Thuc. 7.67.2–3). The second new criterion involved an increased need for effective long-range weapons among the soldiers on deck. Simply stated, the side able to inflict the most damage from afar, i.e., before closing with their enemy, had a clear advantage in the fight.

To some, including Thucydides (cf. 1.49.1), this must have seemed like a return to the "old style" of fighting naval battles and, in a sense, it was. But new weapons would soon be invented that would make this old style of fighting more appropriate for achieving the new objectives that navies were increasingly asked to achieve. Even though navies were not yet used to attack the city itself, by the end of the fifth century, we see the development of certain devices and techniques that will figure prominently in defending against naval siege attacks in future years. This included various kinds of harbor barriers, often constructed from vessels chained side by side, harbor entrances blocked with sunken ships, pointed stakes used as landing obstacles, and cargo vessels employed as workboats, floating barriers, fortified platforms, and fire ships.

When effective field artillery was finally introduced during the first half of the next century, it completely revolutionized the army's ability to carry out a siege. No longer must an attacker wait for the defenders to run out of food. Commanders now felt with justification that they could control the siege's pace by the ferocity of their offensive attacks. Following these developments, it was only a matter of time before the fleet was recognized as a means to pressure the city's harbor defenses, which were often inferior in strength to the city's landward defenses. And naval powers like the Athenians, who clung steadfastly to their traditional ways, were eventually outclassed by the new fleets built to aid their land forces in taking coastal cities by force.

Dionysius I of Syracuse (405–367)

We can rightly say that events at Syracuse during the end of the fifth and beginning of the fourth centuries gave birth to a new form of naval warfare. Three new elements herald the beginning of this transformation and all three appear at Syracuse during the tyranny of Dionysius I: the invention of artillery, the development of warships larger than "threes," and the decision to use a fleet in conjunction with one's army when attacking a fortified position on land.

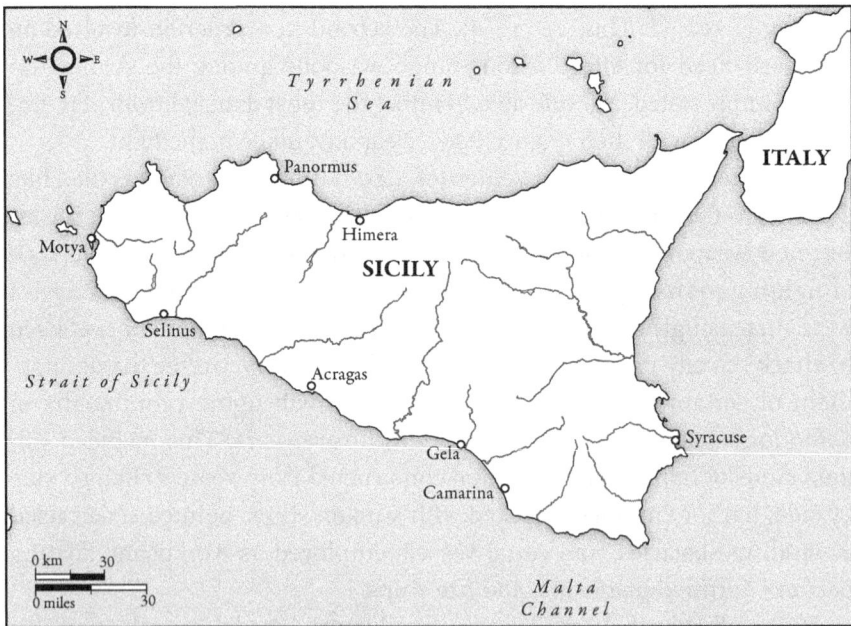

MAP 3.2 Sicily.

The dual inventions of artillery and *pentereis* or "fives" occurred in response to a series of Carthaginian attacks (410–409 and 406–405) that destroyed the Sicilian cities of Selinus, Himera, Acragas, Gela, and Camarina, mostly through energetic sieges. A Carthaginian named Hannibal, who was both "king" and general at the time (Diod. 13.43.5) led the first invasion (410–409) and displayed a practical knowledge of siege warfare not yet seen by the Greeks. For his siege of Selinus, he built six tall siege towers from which his archers and slingers cleared the walls of defenders so that he could batter away at its base with his iron-plated rams (Diod. 13.54.7). The city fell in nine days (Diod. 13.56.5). At Himera, the next victim, he undermined the walls and then burned out the props before eventually taking the place (Diod. 13.59.8–61).

During the second invasion, led by the same Hannibal and another general named Himilco, the Carthaginians besieged Acragas by surrounding it with a deep trench and palisade and by attacking the walls from two tall siege towers. When these were burned by the Acragantines during a night raid, the attackers built siege mounds up to the city walls, but faltered in their attacks when a plague swept through their camp and carried away Hannibal, a man advanced in age (Diod. 13.85–86; cf. 13.80.2). The Syracusans, who were heading the allied resistance, organized a force that prevented food and supplies from reaching the Carthaginian camp. When the remaining general Himilco found himself besieged in his own camp, he summoned 40 triremes from Panormus and Motya, caught a Syracusan grain convoy off guard, sank eight warships, drove the rest ashore, and captured the entire cargo of grain intended for the city (Diod. 13.88.3–5). Faced with a dwindling food supply, and with no hope of additional help, the bulk of the Acragantines evacuated their city, which fell to Himilco shortly after their departure (Diod. 13.88.8).

The following year (405), Himilco besieged Gela while Dionysius led the relieving force from Syracuse. He planned to use his fleet to support his land force in a coordinated attack on the Carthaginian camp by land and by sea (Diod. 13.109.4–5). In a plan that recalls the Athenian attack on Byzantium in 409, the fleet was ordered to attack the camp from the sea. Their attacks along the unfortified sea side were not directed at vessels in the harbor, as they had been at Byzantium, but involved a landing of marines whose diversionary presence helped the Italian Greeks break into the camp elsewhere along its perimeter (Diod. 13.109.5–110.3). Eventually, however, the Italiots were forced to retreat back to the city and, during this retreat, archers from the ships provided covering fire and hindered the attacks of their pursuers (Diod. 13.110.5).

Six years later (399), when Dionysius set about preparing for war against the Carthaginians in western Sicily, he drew from the lessons he had learned during the past 15 years. Having seen firsthand the skills of the Carthaginians in siege warfare, he strengthened his own city's defensive circuit by fortifying Epipolae with a massive new wall, built to withstand the best siege techniques of the enemy (Diod. 14.18.2–8). He also collected a corps of engineers, architects, and craftsmen from his own cities and enticed others to Syracuse from Italy, Greece, and even Carthage by the promise of high wages (Diod. 14.41.3). He asked these men not only to outfit his army with conventional weapons, but also to produce a bigger bow that would shoot farther and with greater force than the conventional weapons used by the enemy. The result was the *gastraphetes* or "belly bow," a crossbow-like weapon that one cocked by pushing his stomach against the stock (Fig. 3.1). The weapon shot an arrow some 50 yards further than the contemporary composite bow, and at closer ranges could propel its missile through a shield (thus the name *katapeltes*).[16]

Knowing that his war would require attacks on the Carthaginian bases at Panormus and Motya, Dionysius instructed his naval architects to develop a new warship design that could best a "three" in prow-to-prow ramming and yet remain maneuverable enough to be useful outside the confines of a harbor. They responded, most likely, by increasing the size and weight of the "three," and by double manning the top two oars, thus producing a *penteres* or "five."[17] Mindful of the Corinthian traditions behind his design (Diod. 14.42.2–3), he surely developed the reinforced bow concept that had been so instrumental in defeating a trireme navy with superior ship-handling skills. The prototype vessel was completed by 397, when she was sent on a diplomatic mission to Locri in southern Italy (Diod. 14.44.7).[18]

Although Diodorus claims that Dionysius built many of these new vessels, we have already seen in chapter 1 that he probably did not do so at first.

---

16. Marsden 1969, 12–13, estimates that it could have shot an arrow approximately 200–250 yards as opposed to the 150–200 yards of a composite bow. A winch pull-back system and base were added soon after its introduction.

17. Although the matter is far from settled, I have followed the interpretation of J. F. Coates in Morrison and Coates 1996, 285–91 with Ill. 57.

18. The vessel was sent to fetch Dionysius's new bride, Doris, from Epizephyrian Locri.

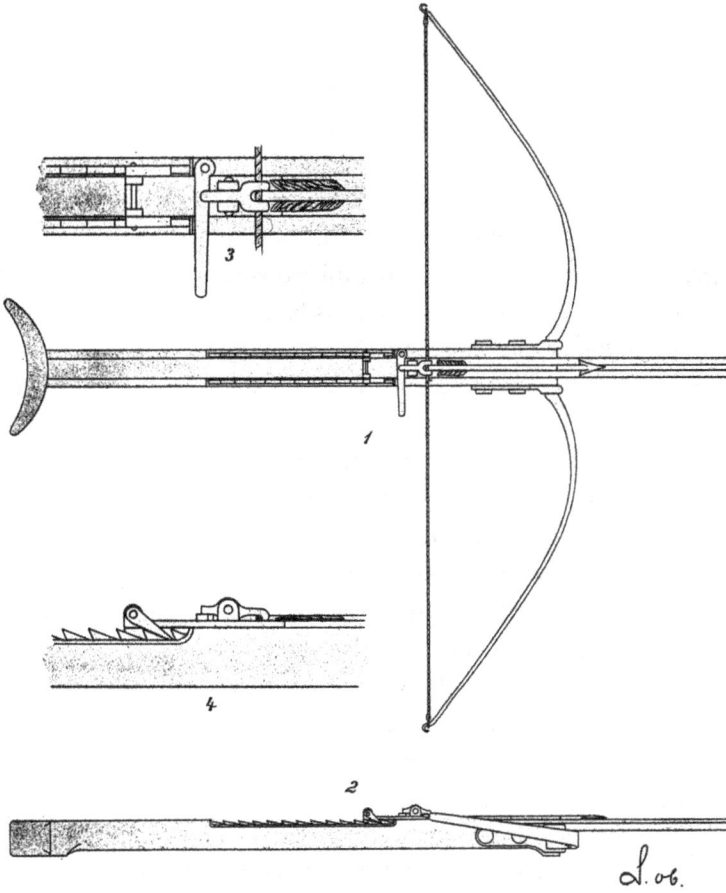

Bauchspanner nach Heron

1 Ansicht von Oben , 2 Ansicht von der Seite . 3 u.4 Spannvorrichtung 1:5

Maßstab 1:10

FIGURE 3.1 *Gastraphetes.* Line drawing by E. Schramm.

The "fives" required more men to operate, cost more money to build and maintain, and were untested in battle. In the record of historical events that followed the introduction of these weapons, we learn that Dionysius's catapults and siege towers worked well when he besieged Motya in 397, but thereafter we do not hear of them. As for his "fives," we see them definitely on only two occasions: when the prototype was sent to pick up his bride in 397 (Diod. 14.44.7), and when his flagship limped into port after a storm in

390 (Diod. 14.100.5). On this evidence, we may safely conclude that his "fives" did not prove to be devastatingly effective. Even so, if we may judge from the overall performance of the Syracusan navy during the rule of Dionysius, it excelled in fighting within the confines of its own harbor. This can be seen clearly in 396, when the Carthaginians sailed into the Great Harbor and besieged Syracuse in much the same way the Athenians had done in 414. They not only found the city's new defensive circuit impregnable to their attacks, they also suffered severely from the unhealthy region in which they made their camp. As bad as this was, they also found, like the Athenians before them, that it was impossible to maintain naval superiority within the Syracusans' harbor. Himilco eventually negotiated a withdrawal of his citizen troops, and left his mercenaries to the mercy of the Syracusans and their allies. Although Dionysius's "fives" figure nowhere in our accounts of the fighting, their greater capacity for carrying deck soldiers and heavier build made them useful in their ramming attacks on the fleet moored at the Carthaginian camp.[19]

Considering the volatile nature of Dionysius's fortunes, many of his engineers and craftsmen would not have remained long in his employ and would have looked for work elsewhere. From Syracuse, the knowledge of these new weapons would have spread to those dynasts willing and able to pay for their manufacture. We might look for another avenue of diffusion through the Carthaginians, who were the first victims of these new weapons systems. The record from which we must work allows for little more than a skeletal outline of the process, and even this is fragmentary. I have already referred to Aristotle's belief that the "four" was first built by the Carthaginians, and this makes sense in the years following their defeat in the Great Harbor at Syracuse.[20] Working, perhaps, from vessels captured during the war with Dionysius, they may have adapted the design to their own tradition of "threes" for their own "fives" or tried to produce a cheaper or more maneuverable warship in their "fours" that would still prevail in prow-to-prow contests with "threes." In a process similar to the mechanism by which the Corinthian Ameinocles built ships for the Samians (Thuc. 1.13.3), the design of the "five" would have spread with its builders from Syracuse to Carthage and to Phoenicia, where we hear that the king of Sidon possessed "fives" in his fleet in 351/50 BCE (Diod. 16.44.6).

---

19. For details of the naval actions fought against the Carthaginians, see chapter 1.

20. See Pliny NH 7.207–208 for the full list; also the introduction and chapter 1.

Philip II (359–36) and Alexander III (336–23)

During the reigns of Philip II and his son Alexander the Great, we can trace the slow, continual development of the first serious naval siege unit. By this, I mean the development of a naval force equipped with specialized gear to facilitate besieging a coastal city. When Philip came to the throne in 359, no one could have predicted that he would lay the foundations for this new kind of naval force. The process cannot be sketched in great detail because of the inadequacies of our sources, but the general outline of the process seems clear enough. Shortly after the start of his reign, Philip resolved to build and maintain a small navy. He seems to have established a trierarchic class by grants of land to nobles who were thereafter expected to help build and maintain the fleet. He built a modest number of ships, dockyards, and shipsheds, and by the 340s was able to use his small fleet for various tasks in support of his foreign policy objectives.[21]

The Sieges of Perinthus, Selymbria, and Byzantium (340)

Although Athens complained about Philip's naval aspirations, his navy never posed a serious threat until the summer of 340 when he decided to attack the Propontine coastal cities of Perinthus, Selymbria, and Byzantium. Diodorus provides a detailed account of the attack on Perinthus, presumably because his source Ephorus did so, but ignores Selymbria altogether and reduces his description of events at Byzantium to a misleading synopsis.[22] As a result, we must piece together from other fragmentary sources the outlines of what happened, the uses to which the fleet was put, and why Philip's attacks eventually failed.[23]

It seems that, initially, the fleet did not accompany the army to Perinthus, but was sent to Peparethus to punish the islanders for their unauthorized occupation of nearby Halonessus.[24] Only after the king saw reinforcements

---

21. For the evidence behind these statements, see Murray 2008, 35–36.

22. Diod. 16.74.2–76.4; he remarks (16.76.5) that Ephorus concluded his history with this siege. Evidence for the siege of Selymbria is discussed by Griffith 1979, 574. Diodorus's brief synopsis of events at Byzantium is found at 16.77.2–3.

23. For attempts to reconstruct these events see, for example, Schaeffer 1885–87, 499–517; Ellis 1986, 174–85; and Griffith 1979, 566–81.

24. Peparethus and Halonessus are the modern Greek islands of Skopelos and Alonessos. Ellis 1986, 175, suggests that the action might have also been intended to discourage the Athenians from sending a force northward along the normal route past Peparethus.

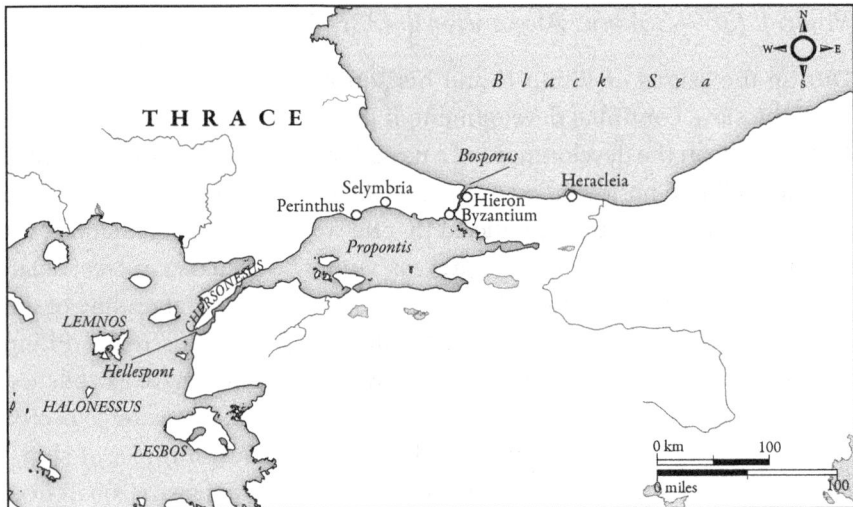

MAP 3.3 Propontis Region.

and supplies streaming into Perinthus through its open harbor (cf. Diod. 16.75.2) did he summon his fleet. By this time, the Athenians had a force of 40 warships in the region under their general Chares and this compelled Philip to march an armed force to secure the shore along the route of his fleet's approach.[25] Even after the fleet had arrived, it largely remained quiet, being outclassed by the Athenian warships and by some others from Rhodes, Chios, and Persia, whose western satraps had become alarmed by Philip's aggressive actions.[26] Chares, to be sure, was not in the region to fight with Philip, but rather to escort the grain fleet on its annual voyage from the Black Sea region to Athens. When the king learned that the Athenian commander had sailed off to confer with the Persian king's generals, he unexpectedly seized the grain transports that had gathered at a port called Hieron, just south of the northern entrance to the Bosporus.[27]

How he did this is not explicitly recorded by our source, but this single act netted a huge amount of booty (worth 700 talents), including hides

25. This is the context for the letter sent to Athens by Philip that appears in the Demosthenic corpus as no. 12; see especially [Dem] 12.16. See also Ellis 1986, 176–78; and Griffith 1979, 570–71, who argue that the army's action would have served to protect the fleet from Athenian colonists in the region as well as to discourage Chares from initiating a sea battle.

26. See Ellis 1986, 178–79, for the details.

27. For Hieron's location, see Harding 2006, 213: "It was situated on the Asiatic side of the Bosporus (cf. Polybios, 4.50.2), north of Khalkedon, about seven miles from the entrance to the Black Sea. . . . It can be found at E2 on map 53 in the Barrington Atlas."

and ship timber, which he subsequently used for his siege engines at Byzantium, and shows that his siege had not yet seriously started prior to the month of October 340.[28] The Athenians responded to this act of war by sending a superior naval force into the region under a general named Phocion and dashed Philip's hopes for cutting off the city from outside help.[29] Despite the best efforts of his engineer Polyidus, who constructed the earliest known *helepolis* or large mobile siege tower for this siege, Philip was forced to admit defeat and break off his attacks toward the end of winter/early spring, 339.[30] The main reason for his failure was easy to discern: he lacked control of the sea.[31]

When Philip was forced to abandon his Propontine sieges in 339, this must have initiated a serious process of analysis regarding how best to avoid a similar failure in the future. I say "must have" because we have no direct evidence to suggest that Philip or his engineers conducted any sort of debriefing following their withdrawal from the Propontis. That such a debriefing occurred seems likely considering the nature of Philip's corps of engineers who were charged with enhancing his ability to besiege and defend fortified positions.[32] The corps was led by a Thessalian named Polyidus, about whom we know a little from a patchwork of sources.[33] He was the man behind Philip's development of powerful torsion catapults that relied on twisted skeins of sinew-rope to increase the force with

---

28. Philochorus, *FGrH* 328, F 162 (= *FGrH*, Dritter Teil, Text, XI. Athen, p. 145); for the details, see Murray 2008, 37–38 with notes.

29. Plut. *Phoc.* 14; Hesychius Frag. 1.26–32 [- *FGrH* 390 F 1.26–32]; and Fron. *Str.* 1.4.13. Although Ellis 1986, 181–83 makes an attempt to reconstruct the outlines of a connected narrative, Griffith 1979, 578–79 is more defensible: "We hear of Philip's siege-train, of damage to the walls, of a surprise assault on a very wet night when dogs of the city gave the alarm, of a naval defeat for Philip's squadron, of Chares with forty ships based on the coast opposite near Chalcedon, of the popular and trusted Phocion arriving with reinforcements and of the Athenians thereafter based on the city and harbour itself." As he says (578), "only isolated details" survive which enable us to see that the siege was "a full-scale affair lasting some months at least, from about October of 340 to probably spring of 339."

30. *Helepolis*, or "city taker," was the Greek name for a large offensive siege tower mounted on wheels. For the *helepolis* of Polyidus, see below, n. 36. Fron. *Str.* 1.4.13 preserves a stratagem associated with Philip's extrication of the fleet from the region.

31. For other contributing factors, see Marsden 1969, 101.

32. Marsden 1971, 58.

33. See especially Athen. Mech. 10.5–10; and Vitr. 10.13.3. Both Athenaeus and Vitruvius produced very similar texts and are now thought to have been contemporaries working from similar sources; Whitehead and Blyth 2004, 14–31.

which a stone or arrow was launched (see chapter 5).[34] In addition to designing a fortification system that maximized a defender's use of this new technology, Polyidus also seems to have experimented with different types of covered siege machinery like rams.[35] A Hellenistic "book of lists" includes him among the seven best engineers of all time and, as we have just seen, credits him with building a *helepolis* for Philip's siege of Byzantium in 340.[36] We also learn from Vitruvius (10.13.3), Augustus's chief of artillery, that Polyidus developed many new simplified designs for this same siege.

Men like this, who advanced their knowledge through trial and error observations, would surely have deconstructed the events of 340–39 with an eye toward fixing problems. If they did engage in such a task (and it is hard to imagine otherwise), we might guess the substance of their conclusions. Philip's lack of naval power resulted in a number of direct consequences. First, he was unable to close off the harbors of those under siege and thereby stop direct shipments of aid from outside allies. Second, he failed to establish a zone of naval dominance in the region of his siege and, thus, he could not prevent the besieged from receiving aid through indirect routes nor could he safely import his own supplies by sea. And finally, he still lacked the raw firepower to force the city's defenses in areas that were open to attack. He and his men would have to rectify these problems if they hoped to reduce a coastal city by siege in the future. The last problem involved an engineering solution and we might imagine that

---

34. On Philip's probable development of torsion catapults, see Marsden 1971, 58–60. Marsden argues (59) that Philip's keen interest in catapult technology may go back to a defeat he suffered in Thessaly at the hands of a Phocian force aided by stone-throwing field artillery. The incident, dating to the year 354 BCE, is mentioned by Polyaenus (2.38.2).

35. See Philo *Poliorketika* A 44 (= 83.7–14) with Garlan 1974, 245–46; and Whitehead and Blyth 2004, 84 with n. 13, for the fortification system; for the covered rams, see Athen. Mech. 10.8-10 (which mentions Polyidus), and 8.14-14.2 (for the full discussion).

36. See Diels 1904, 8 (col. 8, lines 5–8); and M. Huys and collaborators, "Catalog of Paraliterary Papyri," Record 0273 = http://cpp.arts.kuleuven.be/index.php?page=closeup&id=0273, Col. 8.5–8: Πολύιδος ὁ τὴν ἑλόπολιν ἐν Βυζαντίωι καὶ τὴν ἐν Ῥόδωι τετ[ρά]κυκλον (i.e., ποιήσας) = "Polyidus, the one who built the *helopolis* [sic] at Byzantium and the four-wheeler at Rhodes. . . ." This list of seven engineers occurs before a list of "Seven Wonders" (τὰ ἑπτὰ θ[αύματα) and stems from a second or first century BCE papyrus whose text presented shorthand lists of important facts like highest mountains, longest rivers, most famous lawgivers, sculptors, architects, engineers, etc. The papyrus presumably formed part of a school library; cf. Zhmud 2006, 283. If Polyidus's *helepolis* served as the model for later versions of this device, it was a large wooden tower mounted on wheels from which the besiegers attacked the city walls. How precisely they carried out their attacks at Byzantium is not recorded. The "four-wheeler" is otherwise unknown.

Philip directed Polyidus and his pupils, Diades and Charias, to analyze the problems, theorize solutions, and carry out experiments in the years that followed.[37] Since it was generally known that a city's harbor defenses were among the weakest sectors of the wall, one might expect their discussions also involved methods of attacking a city's harbor defenses where vigorous attacks might have the greatest effect.

Such a conclusion seems to be confirmed by Diades' subsequent naval inventions and the ability he demonstrated at Tyre, a few years later, to fit catapults, landing bridges, ladders, and assault towers to the decks of warships.[38] In the years between 339 and 334, Philip's engineers must have refined the designs of their siege machinery, calculated the centers of gravity, and worked out the problems involved in fitting these devices on warships.[39] At this same time, no doubt, they redesigned and simplified certain machines to include modular sections for easier transport and deployment once the ships had reached their stations (see below).[40] The limiting factor, however, was money because a serious naval siege unit would require a large conventional navy to protect it. Since the combined cost would be staggering, Philip (and Alexander after him) decided he could not yet afford the expense, but I suspect that he and his staff theorized what would be required.

A simple review of the failed sieges must have also underscored the crucial role a naval force, even an inferior one, could play in the siege of a coastal city. Successful siege warfare involved *perceptions* of power as much as its possession. In other words, the besieged gauged their chances according to their perceptions of the attacker's power and their own ability to withstand his attacks. If the attacker gave the impression of being able to enforce a naval blockade, this might tip the balance in the attacker's favor and bring about a speedy resolution to the siege. Even an inferior

---

37. For the pupils of Polyidus, see Murray 2008, 34–35. We know from Philo *Bel.* 3 [50.20–51.37] that scientific advances were achieved through trial and error: "[In the old days] it was impossible to obtain [this measurement] except by experimentally increasing and diminishing the perimeter of the hole. . . . Later engineers drew conclusions from former mistakes." If a practicing engineer like Philo learned through "much association with the craftsmen engaged in such matters [at Alexandria] and through intercourse with many master craftsmen in Rhodes" (Philo *Bel.* 5 [51.15–19]), surely others did as well. Translations of Philo are adapted from Marsden 1971, 107 and 109.

38. On Diades and his role at Tyre see Murray 2008, 35, 45.

39. For the evidence, see Murray 2008, 52n49.

40. Whitehead and Blyth 2004, 180–81, suggest these developments occurred early in Alexander's reign, but it makes better sense for these innovations to start *in Philip's reign*, immediately following 339.

force, if deployed skillfully, could allow the attackers to make a show of enforcing a blockade. In the absence of a navy, however, the besieged could hope for aid and ignore those who argued for quick submission. There was also the matter of transport. Siege machinery was heavy and transport by sea was generally preferable to transport by land. It seems clear from Vitruvius (10.13.3) that Diades recognized this fact and built siege towers in sections that could be disassembled and thus moved more easily by sea to the region of the siege, offloaded onto carts, and then taken to the attack site.[41] Transport by sea involved certain risks associated with shipwreck, but it also brought a degree of protection since the vessels supervising the transport could insure the safe import of machinery and supplies to staging areas near the targeted city. It might also provide the attacker with a means to strike quickly and accomplish the unexpected, as Philip had done when he seized the grain fleet in the Bosporus. If anything, the failed sieges of 340–39 would have affirmed in Philip's mind the need to continue building and maintaining a viable naval force.

Alexander III (336–23) and the Development of the Naval Siege Unit

Following the assassination of Philip in 336, Alexander inherited intact the assets of his father's military forces: the army, the cavalry, the fleet, and the engineering corps. We should also remember that Alexander began his campaign into Asia a mere five years after the failures in the Propontis with engineers who had participated in all three sieges. By this time, Polyidus was either dead or otherwise unavailable, but his two pupils Diades and Charias continued their service with Alexander, with Diades succeeding his master as chief engineer, presumably by the start of the campaign.[42] In addition to these two, we know the names of two additional engineers on his staff—Posidonius and Philippus—and there must have been others.[43] The fleet gathered by Alexander at Amphipolis in 334 was much larger than anything Philip ever commanded, being

---

41. Although Whitehead and Blyth 2004, 181, suggest that Diades' main purpose was to facilitate transport by cart, shipment by sea *and* cart may have been Diades' primary consideration when he first theorized his design. Only later, after Alexander decided to march into Mesopotamia, did he contemplate moving these towers over long distances by cart alone.

42. Marsden 1977, 220.

43. Posidonius built a famous *helepolis* for Alexander; see Biton 52.1–56.7 with Marsden 1971, 70–73, and 84–90. We know nothing about Philippus "the engineer" beyond the fact he was a

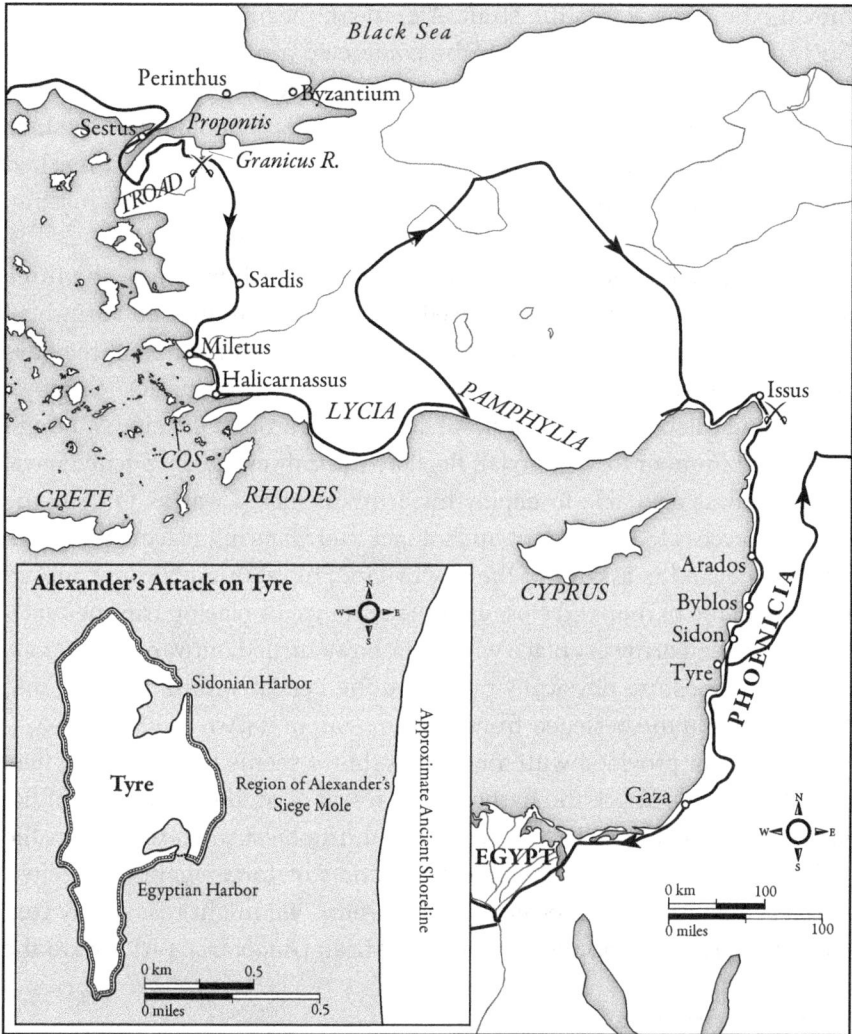

MAP 3.4 Eastern Mediterranean with inset of Tyre at the time of Alexander's siege. Inset map adapted (with alterations) from Romm 2010, 92, Map 2.23; and Marriner and Morhange 2005, Fig. 2.

drawn primarily from his Greek allies.[44] At Sestus in the Hellespont, 160 "threes" and numerous merchantmen assisted his general Parmenio in

guest at Alexander's last symposion before he died: Ps. Call. 3.31.8; and Berve (1926) 1988, Vol. 2, 389 = #789. Griffith 1979, 447, argues that we should "guard against overestimating" the numbers in the engineering corps and cautions that most of the work was carried out by the infantry or by teams of local labor. Nevertheless, I suspect there were many master craftsmen and apprentices, founders, smiths, and carpenters whose names have gone unrecorded.

44. For the nature of this fleet, see Hauben 1976a, 80–81.

moving the army across the strait. Alexander, meanwhile, took a force of 60 warships to the Troad where he conducted a number of ceremonial acts.[45] J. S. Morrison sees in this force a separate Macedonian squadron apart from the 160 units in the allied fleet, but this cannot be correct since Arrian gives the same total (i.e., 160) for the entire fleet when it reached Miletus later in the summer (Arr. *Anab.* 1.18.4).[46] Following the crossing, we lose sight of the fleet until the army reaches Miletus.

Here, Alexander's surprising speed secured for him two of the three strategic objectives that had caused Philip such trouble at Perinthus, Selymbria, and Byzantium. By reaching Miletus with his fleet three days before the Persians arrived (Arr. *Anab.* 1.18.4), he was able to close the city's harbor and establish a zone of naval dominance around the city. Although inferior in number to the Persian fleet, he not only avoided a pitched naval battle, he was also able to deploy his army in such a way as to deny the Persians access to convenient anchorages and watering places. When Alexander began his assault of the city by land, his admiral Nicanor moved the fleet to the harbor and closed off the entrance by placing triremes side-by-side in the narrowest place with their bows turned outward (Arr. *Anab.* 1.19.3). This posture physically prevented the Persians from breaking into the harbor and the besieged from breaking out of it (Arr. *Anab.* 1.19.3–4).

We are not provided with any details, but it seems likely that the fleet was also used to attack the harbor defenses, at least toward the end of the siege, and was thus able to achieve the third objective learned from the failures of 340–39 (the effective application of force against the city's weakest defenses, often located at the harbor). We might reasonably conclude this from an episode recorded by Arrian (*Anab.* 1.19.4–5) toward the

---

45. Crossing: Arr. *Anab.* 1.11.6; Alexander's side trip: Diod. 17.17.1–3.

46. Morrison and Coates 1996, 3–4, argues that Arrian's total at Miletus applies only to the Greek allied fleet, but fails to explain why Arrian should have ignored the Macedonian squadron of 60. The natural conclusion from Arrian's narrative is that his source for these numbers (Callisthenes?) indicated a total fleet strength (whatever the origin of individual ships) of roughly 160 units. Diodorus's 60 ship squadron must therefore derive from a different source and cannot simply be added to Arrian's total. Furthermore, if Alexander only took his Macedonian squadron to the Troad, we would have to assume that he excluded his Greek allies from ceremonial acts that were intended for both Greek and Macedonian audiences. Finally, if Diodorus's statement (17.22.5) about the "few ships" he retained when he disbanded the fleet (see below) goes back to any reliable source, it implies a Macedonian squadron numbering far less than 60 units. Other problems arise from the kinds of vessels that were counted for the totals provided by our sources. Arrian defines his total as triremes, but we know there were other classes of warships in the fleet as well, such as triacontors (Arr. *Anab.* 2.7.2). Perhaps Justin's total of 182 (11.6.2) includes these smaller units.

end of the fight for control of the city. It seems that a group of mercenaries paddled in desperation on their upturned shields to a small, unnamed islet in the harbor while others boarded small skiffs and tried to evade "the triremes of the Macedonians" before getting captured by (other?) "threes" at the harbor mouth. Once Miletus was in his hands, Alexander himself (*autos*) sailed to the little island to deal with the mercenaries.[47] Its shores were steep, and so he ordered that ladders be carried at the prows of his triremes so they could land on its shore from their ships "as if attacking a city wall" (Arr. *Anab.* 1.19.5).[48] Although the mercenaries surrendered to avoid a fight, he and his men were clearly prepared to force a landing by employing a tactic of naval siege warfare. While the events at Miletus were not presented by our sources to highlight the fleet, its capabilities, or its importance to the campaign, these events demonstrate clearly that Alexander avoided the main mistakes that contributed to his father's earlier failures. Clearly adjustments had been made.

Alexander's next move struck both ancient and modern observers as surprising—even risky. Before proceeding southward to Halicarnassus, he disbanded his allied fleet, in spite of its apparent usefulness at Miletus.[49] Our sources record multiple reasons for this decision, but the fact remains that the Hellenic fleet was a clear mismatch for its Persian adversaries and Alexander was unwilling to risk defeat by allowing a pitched naval battle.[50] Rather than pay for a force he would have to restrain from fighting, and then dealing with morale problems that would certainly follow, he decided to send the fleet home except for his

---

47. It is unclear from the context whether Arrian uses the term "triremes of the Macedonians" to signify the entire Hellenic fleet, a specific Macedonian contingent of warships operating inside the harbor, or the triremes at the harbor mouth. The Greek is not clear. It is possible that we see here the Macedonian contingent in action, as Morrison and Coates 1996, 4, argues. The reflexive pronoun "himself" (αὐτός), describing Alexander's presence at the island, implies to me the presence of the Macedonian contingent. At this stage in the campaign, who else would attend the king when he joined the fleet in person?

48. Arr. *Anab.* 1.19.5: . . . καθάπερ πρὸς τεῖχος, ἐκ τῶν νεῶν τὴν ἀπόβασιν ποιησόμενος.

49. As many have noted, the decision might have caused problems but for the timely death of Memnon; Arr. *Anab.* 2.1.3; Plut. *Alex.* 18.5; Diod. 17.29.4, 30.7, 31.3; Curt. 3.1.21, 2.1; and Bosworth 1980, 143: "The Persian fleet *had* been effectively contained at Miletus and Alexander may have thought that the same tactics would work elsewhere. If so, he committed a colossal error, which the Persians exploited but not fully enough."

50. See Arr. *Anab.* 1.20.1; and Diod. 17.22.5. Alexander's decision not to risk a pitched battle with the Persian fleet is the subject of one of his famous disagreements with Parmenio; see Arr. *Anab.* 1.18.6–9. Modern scholars suspect that Alexander was uncertain of the fleet's loyalty; see Bosworth 1980, 143, for a summary of the different views.

core of Macedonian warships and 20 triremes from Athens who were assigned to transport his siege equipment.[51] We therefore hear nothing about the fleet at Halicarnassus although we see its indirect presence in the siege equipment that was used against the city. Where it anchored and how it avoided coming to blows with the Persians, we are not told.[52] The outcome of the siege here was less positive than the one at Miletus. Although Alexander eventually gained control of the city, he failed to capture the two citadels, Salamacis and Zephyrion, and the Persian fleet, based on Cos, remained operationally intact. A garrison, left behind by Alexander, proved insufficient to contain the Persian forces and the city "remained a bastion of Persian strength until early 332."[53]

After Halicarnassus, his men's lagging morale may have convinced Alexander to follow an operational strategy emphasizing forward movement and the avoidance of protracted sieges. This is not to say that he abandoned the strategy of attacking coastal cities, just that he carefully selected his targets to maximize the appearance of forward momentum.[54] The result was a string of successful approaches to towns in Lycia and Pamphylia that continued his progress and contributed to a healthier level of morale. And what of his fleet during these actions? After the brief statement of Diodorus mentioned above, the naval force remains invisible. Nowhere do we hear that he unpacked his siege equipment. We catch a glimpse of one triaconter just prior to the Battle of Issus, when Alexander sent some Companions up the coast to check on the whereabouts of Darius.[55] But, other than this, we hear nothing of the fleet as Alexander

---

51. Diod. 17.22.5. Although we are not specifically told that he kept his Macedonian squadron, it is logical to assume that he did so. The Macedonians had experience in siege warfare and their loyalty was beyond question.

52. Early inconclusive assaults, such as the attack on nearby Myndos, might have resulted from the late arrival of the siege equipment; Bosworth 1980, 144. The fleet must have anchored somewhere under the protection of the army as was done at Miletus.

53. Bosworth 1988, 48–49, describes the siege as much more difficult than Arrian presents, and feels that the men's morale was too low for Alexander to risk a second protracted siege of Salamacis and Zephyrion.

54. Arrian reports (*Anab.* 1.24.3–6, 26.1–5) that he took the following towns without a fight: Hyparna, Telmessus, Pinara, Xanthus, Patara, and about 30 smaller places (πολίσματα), Phaselis and other unnamed towns in Lower Lycia, Perga, and Side. At a few places where there was resistance (Syllion and Termessos: Arr. *Anab.* 1.26.5 and 1.27.5–28.2), Alexander chose to turn his attention to other more important nearby objectives (Aspendus and Sagalessus: Arr. *Anab.* 1.26.5–27.4 and 1.28.2–8). Upon occasion he was forced to fight (as at Sagalessus), but he always carefully picked his battles to maximize his victories.

55. Arr. *Anab.* 2.7.2.

defeated Darius at Issus, and then continued his march down the Levantine coast toward Egypt. Faced with his approach, the Phoenician ports of Arados, Sidon, and Byblos all surrendered without a blow. Tyre, which chose to deny him access to their city, was a different matter.

Alexander's Siege of Tyre (332)

Upon learning the decision of the Tyrians, Alexander abandoned his previous strategy of avoiding protracted sieges. He communicated this change in policy to his officers and men and Arrian may preserve the broad outlines of what he said (*Anab.* 2.17.3–4): "With the accession of Cyprus and the united fleets of Macedon and Phoenicia, our supremacy at sea would be guaranteed, and the expedition to Egypt would thus be a simple matter, and finally, with Egypt in our hands we shall have no further cause for uneasiness about Greece: we shall be able to march on Babylon with security at home, with enhanced prestige, and with Persia excluded not only from the sea, but from the whole continent up to the Euphrates."[56] Scholars have debated the authenticity of this speech, and some have questioned its grand justifications as irrelevant to the main issue—the siege of Tyre—facing Alexander and his men. But the inclusion of the Macedonian fleet as an element of strategy strikes me as believable, unexpected (given its low profile during Alexander's advance), and therefore possibly authentic, indicating that the speech, or its main strategic points, may descend from a genuine speech in the contemporary source on whom Arrian relied, probably Ptolemy.[57] Genuine or not, Alexander must have delivered some sort of explanation to his men because their avoidance of protracted sieges was about to change.

Once the decision was made and something of it communicated to his men, Alexander burrowed into the details of preparation. Although no one

---

56. Translation by de Sélincourt 1971, 132. Both Arrian and Curtius present a speech at this point in the campaign that justifies Alexander's decision to his men. Curtius's brief synopsis (4.2.17) lists various pretexts and religious justifications, while Arrian (2.17.3–4) writes a formal speech detailing a number of strategic objectives.

57. For the scholarly debate, see Bosworth 1980, 238–39. The following year (333), while Alexander marched from Gordion to Ancyra (Curt. 3.1.19–20), he ordered Hegelochus to gather a fleet to counter Persian advances won by Memnon and his nephew Pharnabazus in the Aegean (Arr. *Anab.* 2.1.1–5 with Bosworth 1980, 177–83). Although a large Persian offensive never materialized, guarding against this threat consumed the time and attention of the Macedonian fleet commanders as late as 331 when Alexander was in Egypt; Arr. *Anab.* 3.2.3–7; and Bosworth 1980, 266–69.

describes precisely how he proceeded, we can deduce the main outlines from the events that followed. Detailed discussions were held with his officers and engineers regarding where to initiate the attack, what kinds of machines to deploy, what forces to use, and where to get them. As Tyre was located on an island separated from the mainland by a narrow strait, he started by building a siege mole across the narrows. The twin factors of Tyrian naval dominance and threats of Carthaginian aid convinced him that he needed to gather a superior naval force as well. Precisely when he came to this decision is difficult to tell, but it must have been early since he lost no time in sending out messengers. Some went to Cyprus to ask the kings there for naval help, others went to Greece to lure away Phoenicians serving in Darius's fleet with promises of generous terms.[58] By spring, these diplomatic efforts had netted more than 200 warships, including a number of heavier galleys like "fours" and "fives."[59] In the meantime, crew chiefs were sent to the shipyards of Phoenicia to enroll shipwrights, carpenters, sawyers, and smiths and to requisition stocks of pitch, tow, leather, timber, copper, iron, and everything else that might prove useful.[60]

As part of his plan, Alexander built an earthen causeway for his siege machinery, or siege mole, from the mainland to the island. As this mole approached the city and his workmen along its front and sides came under increasing attack, the Macedonians erected leather screens on wooden scaffolds and deployed catapults in protective towers. In spite of these efforts, however, the attacks would not cease until Alexander achieved naval dominance and forced the defenders to divide their forces by attacking other sectors of the city walls.[61] I suspect he came to this conclusion long before a Tyrian fire ship destroyed his protective barriers or a spring storm eroded the foundations of his mole. In the meantime, his men continued to procure, cut, and stockpile timber, forge

58. Green 1991, 254, is surely wrong to suggest that Alexander waited until his mole had been destroyed before sending out ambassadors to raise a fleet. If messengers were dispatched during the spring, then this leaves too short a time for the gathering of the fleet and its transformation into a siege unit. For the dispatch in winter of small squadrons on special missions, see Thuc. 2.69, 3.88, 4.50; and Casson 1995, 270n3.

59. For the numbers of ships gathered, see Arr. *Anab.* 2.20.1–3; and Bosworth 1980, 242.

60. Philo (*Polior.* B 49–52) compiled a list of such useful supplies for his third century work on siege warfare; on Philo, see chapter 4.

61. A number of daring exploits of Tyrian resistance date to this period of the siege. For this phase of the struggle, see Bosworth 1980, 240–41.

metal fasteners, and construct the modular sections needed to transform the fleet into a siege unit.[62] Perhaps by April, the fleet had finally swelled to a size that exceeded the Tyrians' own force and, soon thereafter, Alexander brought it southward to Tyre, arrayed in battle order to insure an unopposed arrival.[63] Dismayed by the numbers that faced them, the Tyrians declined the challenge to fight, blocked up their harbors, and prepared to resist the coming naval siege.

By all accounts, the transformation of Alexander's fleet into a naval siege unit was carried out quickly. This speed highlights not only the skills of Alexander's engineers and their staff but also their high level of preparedness and the existence of a well-conceived plan to guide their actions. The results of their work were devastatingly effective. Although Tyre was thought to be virtually impregnable because of its location on an offshore island, the city fell to Alexander after a siege of only three to four months once his navy had been transformed.

A quick review of the tactics employed by this new force reveals its basic characteristics. The most important feature, by far, involved the placement of artillery and other kinds of siege machinery on the decks of his warships and transports. His engineers started with the horse transports and slower triremes (Arr. *Anab.* 2.21.1, 4) and then placed catapults (Curt. 4.3.13; Arr. *Anab.* 2.23.3), battering rams, and assault bridges (Arr. *Anab.* 2.21.4, 2.22.6–23.3; Curt. 4.3.13; Diod. 17.46.2) on other kinds of vessels. As the siege progressed, "threes" and "fours" were lashed together in pairs with their hulls spanned by a single, wide deck that carried both marines and machinery (Diod. 17.43.4, 46.1; Curt. 4.3.14–15). Along the front and sides of his advancing siege mole, where Tyrian defenders focused their disruptive attacks, we see warships, presumably fitted with artillery (Arr. *Anab.* 2.21.3–4), to defend the work crews and attack the city wall. Other specialists, working from vessels fitted with cranes (Arr. *Anab.* 2.21.5, 7), removed submerged obstacles strategically placed by the Tyrians to block access to their walls.[64] When Tyrian fighters in specially armored

---

62. Arr. *Anab.* 2.21.1, states that large work crews had been assembled from Cyprus and from various parts of Phoenicia; for the expedition to secure timber supplies, see Arr. *Anab.* 2.20.4–5; and Curt. 4.2.18 and 4.3.1. Modular designs were a feature ascribed to Diades; Vitr. 10.13.3; and above at n. 41.

63. For the likely time of year, see Bosworth 1980, 241–42.

64. There is a problem with the meaning of this passage: see Marsden 1969, 103; and Bosworth 1980, 248.

ships cut the mooring tackle of his work boats, Alexander deployed his own armored thirty-oared galleys in defense, and when this failed to stop Tyrian divers from cutting the lines, he replaced rope with chain (Arr. *Anab.* 2.21.6). The king focused other attacks on the harbor entrances where his larger vessels ("fours" and "fives") tried to break through floating barriers (*kleithra*) and sink galleys that had been deployed to prohibit entry (Arr. *Anab.* 2.24.1).[65]

Although the passage of time hinders our precise location of all these actions (his siege mole, the southern harbor, even the precise line of the city walls) on the modern landscape, the general outlines of Alexander's siege are clear—particularly its outcome. In the end, his vigorous attempts to attack the city from all directions bore fruit and his army and navy broke through the city's defenses at roughly the same time. The new kind of force crafted by the Macedonian king to accomplish this task deeply impressed everyone who participated. The lingering message was both simple and straight-forward: it was possible to shorten the siege of a coastal city by using the awesome new power of a naval siege unit against its harbor defenses. In less than two decades, this revelation would drive a naval arms race among Alexander's successors and spark a burst of forti-fied harbor construction throughout the eastern Mediterranean that would continue for more than a century.

Through his actions during this event, Alexander had provided a clear model for others to follow in building their own siege units. First, he started with a core of warships whose crews and commanders knew how to break down, set up, and transport siege equipment, as well as how to attack city walls from ladders mounted on the bows of their ships. These skills, probably developed in response to the failed sieges of 340–39, pre-pared his men to meet the demands of besieging Tyre. Second, he pos-sessed a corps of military engineers who had theorized how to adapt terrestrial siege engines for use aboard warships. Third, he was able to gather additional engineers who were skilled in building siege machinery from Phoenicia and Cyprus. Under the direction of Diades, these men, along with labor gathered from the nearby shipyards of Phoenicia, enabled him to convert a large number of ships into floating siege platforms of various designs in a short period of time. Fourth, he gained access to a number of Cyprian and Phoenician "fours" and "fives" whose crews would

---

65. Prow-to-prow ramming tactics and grappling hooks were used for ship-against-ship combat in these situations; Curt. 4.3.12; 4.4.7.

have understood the basic techniques of attacking harbor barriers and of fighting at harbor mouths.[66] And finally, he was willing and able to devote incredible amounts of money and manpower to the process of creating and then deploying this naval siege unit.

Anyone hoping to duplicate Alexander's force would have to be equally willing and able to spend lots of money, but money alone would not be enough. Success depended upon proper managerial oversight so that expenditures resulted in a labor force that was sufficient for the task at hand, that was supplied with the tools and raw materials it needed, and that was adequately protected, supervised, and held accountable for achieving its goals. Expert management of skilled personnel brought about the trans-formation of Alexander's fleet, and for this, Alexander deserves his full measure of credit. Those hoping to build, maintain, and wield a successful naval siege unit would have to be extraordinary managers, or at least be able to hire extraordinary ones to work for them.

Not surprisingly, following the surrender of Tyre and the shorter siege of Gaza that followed, the fleet did not figure prominently in Alexander's eastern campaigns except as a means of transport across bodies of water, or as a means of conveyance. As a result, the siege unit developed at Tyre appears only once during Alexander's reign. Following the king's return to Babylon from India in the spring of 323, we learn that he intended to gather a sizeable fleet that would operate out of Babylon and the Persian Gulf and facilitate his campaign against the Arabs. Starting with the core of Nearchus's fleet, he added a small number of warships (two "fives," three "fours," 12 "threes," and 30 triacontors) that had been cut into trans-portable sections and brought overland from Phoenicia to the Euphrates

---

66. Since we do not hear of "fours" or "fives" in the Macedonian fleet before the Phoenicians and Cyprians decide to join his fleet, I presume he adds these larger units to his fleet at this time. The Macedonians had more than one "five," as we can see from Curt. 4.3.11, and 4.4.7.9. Aside from their obvious employment as command ships (Arr. *Anab.* 2.22.2), the Macedonians learned their usefulness when the Phoenicians rammed and sank the three outer-most triremes blocking the northern harbor upon their arrival at the city (Arr. *Anab.* 2.20.9). Later, when the Tyrians mounted a daring breakout from their northern harbor, they chose three "fives," three "fours," and seven "threes" (Arr. *Anab.* 2.21.8–9) for the ac-tion. Caught off guard, Alexander eventually chased them back to the harbor from which they came. Notably, he used "fives" and "threes" for the task and with them rammed his enemies at the harbor mouth (Arr. *Anab.* 2.22.4–5). When the city finally fell, both harbors were forced: the Phoenicians broke through the barrier across the southern harbor and the Cyprians entered the northern harbor once the attention of the inhabitants turned elsewhere (Arr. *Anab.* 2.24.1–2). As with earlier actions at the harbor entrances, these forced entries were likely spearheaded by the heavier units of the fleet.

where they were reassembled (Arr. *Anab.* 7.19.3). He also planned to build new ships and sent out agents to arrange for supplies of timber, raw materials, and suitable workers. At the same time, he began to dredge a new harbor at Babylon, suitable for 1000 warships.[67] Although it is possible that Alexander gave orders for some experimental vessels larger than "fives," we hear of nothing larger than "fives" in the events leading up to or immediately following his death in June.[68] Once this occurred, these works were suspended along with a number of other plans considered too costly to complete (Diod. 18.4.1–6).

Antigonus Monophthalmus and Demetrius Poliorcetes

In the general mood of uncertainty that prevailed after Alexander's death, there was a noticeable lack of development and innovation in the areas of naval and siege warfare during a period that saw numerous attacks on coastal cities. In the period from 322 to 308, for example, the Diadochoi ("Successors"), or generals who divided Alexander's empire, fought vigorously with one another for control. Almost annually they sent out land and sea forces to attack their enemies and support their friends. More often than not, the military conflicts occurred around cities, and frequently these cities were located on the coast (Table 3.1). Despite this activity, the largest vessels still seem to be "fives," and the practice of attacking harbor defenses with large numbers of catapults mounted on warships appears to have been discontinued.

At Tyre, for example, when Antigonus faced a siege of the city in 314, we find no mention of the kind of warfare Alexander had waged in 332.[69] There was ample opportunity for its usage, however. Like Alexander, Antigonus lacked naval superiority and, as a result, he sent agents to gather ships and set in motion a large building program. He hired thousands of wood cutters, sawyers, and teams of draft animals to procure the needed

---

67. Strabo (16.1.11), citing Aristobulus as his authority, makes it sound as if the fleet had been completed. Arrian's account (*Anab.* 7.19.3–4), also based on Aristobulus, makes better sense and is the main source of my own comments.

68. Curt. 10.1.19 records an improbable order for 700 "sevens"; if there is any substance to Mnesigiton's claim (quoted by Pliny *NH* 7.207) that Alexander built ships up to "tens" in size, it should correspond to this period and might even reflect his unfulfilled plans.

69. In adopting the date 314–313 for the siege of Tyre, I am following the chronology outlined by Billows 1990, 109–16.

timber for construction at five different shipyards in Phoenicia, Cilicia, and Rhodes (Diod. 19.58.2–5). The similarities with Alexander, however, stop here. While Alexander used the opportunity to create a naval siege unit and storm the walls of the city from the decks of his ships, Antigonus simply enforced a blockade and waited 15 months for starvation to reduce the city.[70] We might ask what kept Antigonus from following a more aggressive battle plan for his siege of Tyre.

The answer cannot involve money since Antigonus had the largest reserves of all the successors, having recently collected some 35,000 talents from various royal treasuries in addition to annual revenues that totaled 11,000 talents (Diod 19.48.7–8; 56.4–5). A full treasury meant nothing, however, without the skilled personnel who were able to create and wield a siege unit such as the one Alexander created. We have seen how Alexander drew upon his father's corps of seasoned engineers to build his naval siege unit at Tyre. In 314, however, a specialized corps like this had to be reassembled and a workshop established, something difficult to accomplish on campaign. Faced with this reality, Antigonus may have decided it was more prudent to block the harbors and wait rather than employ untested machinery with men untrained in its use. However we explain his reasoning, the siege must have been frustrating and perhaps invited negative comparisons with Alexander's attack. If so, we do not see evidence for such a corps of engineers until six years later when Antigonus's son Demetrius emerges as his most trusted field commander.

Demetrius and the Siege of Mounychia (307)

In the spring of 307, Demetrius left Ephesus at the head of a large expeditionary force composed of 250 warships and an unknown number of supply ships. His war chest of 5000 talents gives a clear sense of the magnitude of the undertaking, which dwarfed all previous expeditions except for the force Antigonus had collected at Tyre in 313 (see Table 3.1). Antigonus dispatched his son to capture Athens' port city Piraeus, bring the city

---

70. Although Diodorus (19.61.5) clearly implies that he reckoned the 15 month duration of the siege from the period when Antigonus gained naval superiority, i.e., no earlier than the autumn of 314 (following Billows' dating), modern scholars date the beginning of the 15 month period from Antigonus's declaration before Tyre that he intended to besiege the city, perhaps in early summer 314 (19.58.1); see, for example, Merker 1958, 11; and Billows 1990, 116.

Table 3.1 Overseas Siege Operations From 322 to 308 BCE.

Fleets of large and small sizes are routinely dispatched with infantry forces to bring cities and regions into alliance through siege warfare.

Date (approx.)	Dynast	City/Region	Size of Force Sent: Naval	Infantry	Ancient source
322	Ptolemy	Cyrene	?	?	Diod. 18.21.7–9
319–18	Cassander	Piraeus	35 ships	4000	Diod. 18.68.1
319–18	Cassander	Aegina and Salamis	whole fleet (at least 35 ships)	?	Diod. 18.69.1–2
314–13	Antigonus	Tyre	120 ships by end of siege	? (3000 left to continue siege as Antigonus campaigned elsewhere)	Diod. 19.58.1–6, 59.2, and 62.8.
314	Seleucus	Erythrae	100	?	Diod. 19.60.3–4; cf. Diod. 19.58.5
314	Ptolemy	Cyprus	100 ships (+ 100 ships under Seleucus)	10,000 (+ 3000 previously sent)	Diod. 19.62.3–4; "strong force" = 100 ships and 10,000 infantry
313	Cassander	Lemnos	20 Athenian ships + fleet of Seleucus (= approx. 100 ships?)	?	Diod. 19.68.3–4; for the fleet of Seleucus (in 314), see 19.58.5

			Ships	Land forces	Reference
312	Antigonus	NW Black Sea Coast	?		Diod. 19.73.6
312	Antigonus	Peloponnesus	50 ships		Diod. 19.74.1
312	Antigonus	Miletus and Caria	?		Diod. 19.75.3–6
312	Cassander	Oreus (Euboea)	30 ships		Diod. 19.75.7–8
312	Antigonus sends relief force	Oreus	20 + 100; 100 recalled to Asia	1000	Diod. 19.75.7–8
312	Antigonus (after the capture of Chalcis, many places come over to Antigonus's side)	Chalcis, Oropus, Eretria, Carystus, Thebes, Phocis, Opountian Locris	150 ships + 10 Rhodian ships (Diod. 19.77.3)	5000 infantry and 500 cavalry + 2200 Boeotian infantry and 1300 cavalry	Diod. 19.77.2–4; 19.78.2–5
312	Ptolemy	Cyrene	?		Diod. 19.79.1–3
312	Ptolemy	Cyprus, Upper Syria, Cilicia	?		Diod. 19.79.4–7
Spr. 310	Ptolemy	Cilicia	?		Diod. 20.19.3–4
Spr. 309	Ptolemy	Lycia and Caria	? ("large force")	? ("large force")	Diod. 20.27.1–2; Plut. *Demetr.* 73
Spr. 308	Ptolemy	Andros, Corinth, Sicyon	?		Diod. 20.37.1–2

of Athens into an alliance, and then "free all the cities of Greece" (Diod. 20.45.1). This would require driving out the garrisons of Ptolemy and Cassander and replacing them with a confederation of Greek allies who relied on him for protection.[71] As Demetrius approached Athens, he ordered his fleet to remain near Cape Sounion while he sped ahead with a squadron of "threes" and effected a surprise entrance into the harbor (Polyaen. 4.7.6). There was apparently some resistance when his full fleet arrived and his men landed along the shore, but they quickly gained control of the walls and Piraeus was his, except for Cassander's garrison on the fortified hill of Mounychia. In order to dislodge this garrison, Demetrius set up his siege equipment and used his stone throwers and bolt projectors (catapults that shot stones and large arrows or "bolts") to shatter the parapets of the wall and hinder the defenders from killing his men as they ascended their ladders.[72] After a vigorous attack lasting two days, with his men fighting constantly in relays, he broke into the fortification and forced the defenders to surrender (Diod. 20.45.5–7). Soon thereafter, it seems likely that Demetrius sent a force to Megara, expelled Cassander's garrison by force, and restored autonomy there as well (Diod. 20.46.3).[73]

Although we are not given further details of the fighting and, thus, do not know the precise sizes of his ships or his full siege capabilities, it is clear that this force represented a major increase in size and strength over those sent out by sea before. For the next few years, moreover, we can detect a clear increase in power in the naval and siege forces that Demetrius takes into the field.[74] No doubt both father and son were encouraged by the considerable results of this first campaign. In military terms, the fighting was limited, the casualties were low, but the victory was decisive. The capture of Mounychia resulted in a wave of positive enthusiasm at Athens, Demetrius and his father were hailed as divine liberators, and the

---

71. He developed this policy as early as 314 while he was besieging Tyre; Billows 1990, 114.

72. His means of attack can be deduced from the equipment that he used: *lithoboloi* (stone throwers) and *katapeltes* (bolt projectors).

73. Plutarch (*Demetr.* 9) places the capture of Megara between the capture of Piraeus and the reduction of Mounychia. As this chronology would imply that Demetrius split his forces before Piraeus was firmly in his hands, it seems less likely than the sequence based on Diodorus that is presented in the text. Diodorus, to be sure, presents the information about Megara almost as an afterthought.

74. Plut. *Demetr.* 20.1–2; and Diod 20.45.6: "Demetrius was many times superior in the numbers of his soldiers and had a great advantage in his military equipment."

restored democracy joined the other Greek states allied with Antigonus.[75] Antigonus responded with a large gift of grain, the grant of control over the island of Imbros (an important harbor for grain fleets traveling to Athens), and timber for 100 warships, 30 of which were assigned to Demetrius for his next campaign (Diod. 20.46.4; 50.3). Acting on written orders from his father, Demetrius convened a meeting of his Greek allies to discuss a common defense policy against Cassander and then, in the spring of 306, set sail to continue the war against Ptolemy's generals on Cyprus, where he hoped to wrest control of the island from Ptolemy's grip.[76]

The Cyprus Campaign of Demetrius (306)

The Cyprus campaign of Demetrius in 306 provides an excellent case study for how best to attack or defend a coastal city with the aid of a fleet. As we can see from a siege manual written by Philo "the Byzantine," this campaign along with Ptolemy's response became "textbook" examples during the century that followed. Fortunately for us, Diodorus draws upon a source

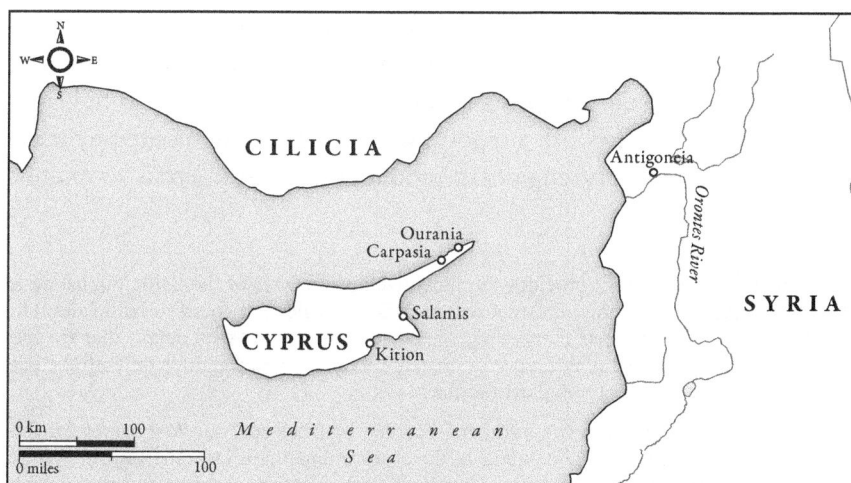

MAP 3.5 Cyprus and the Eastern Mediterranean.

---

75. The honors bestowed on Demetrius and Antigonus were considered excessive and somewhat shameful by Plutarch (*Demetr.* 10.3–13.2); but see Billows 1990, 149–50.

76. The Aegean islands, Cyprus, and the eastern Mediterranean littoral provided ripe areas for conflict between Antigonus and Ptolemy. For the maneuverings between the two during these years, see Will 1984, 53–57.

or sources (among them, Hieronymus of Cardia) who clearly understood both siege warfare and naval battles. As a result, he not only provides an excellent account of the whole campaign, he preserves our first clear description of a battle in which warships larger than "fives" took part.[77]

During the spring of 306, Demetrius sailed from Athens to Cilicia and gathered additional forces from his allies before crossing to Cyprus with 15,000 infantry, 400 cavalry, hundreds of transports, and roughly 163 warships (Diod. 20.46.6–47.1).[78] He proceeded to the coast of Carpasia on the northeast tip of the island where he landed his soldiers, beached his ships, and fortified his camp. At first he overwhelmed the nearby communities of Ourania and Carpasia, left his ships under guard, and advanced with his army toward Salamis. When he was 40 stades distant (approx 7.4 km.) from the city, he defeated a large force commanded by Ptolemy's brother Menelaus (Diod. 20.47.2–3) and drove it back into the city. As Demetrius set up his camp outside the city and both sides prepared for the siege that would follow, Menelaus sent messengers to Egypt reporting the recent defeat and requesting help (Diod. 20.47.7–8).

After surveying the city's defenses and the enemy's preparations for siege, Demetrius resolved to increase the scale of his attack and so he sent to Asia for "skilled workmen" as well as for stocks of iron, wood, and other supplies (Diod. 20.48.1). At that time, Antigonus was building his new capital in Syria (Diod. 20.47.5) and, presumably, he tapped into the labor source and supply network supporting this work.[79] Augmented by these resources, Demetrius's engineers produced a large *helepolis* or mobile

---

77. Seibert 1969, 190–206, provides the most detailed analysis of the battle published to date, including an evaluation of the sources and the strategies employed by both sides. His conclusion that Diodorus has merged a generic battle description with details that are specific to this battle misses the influence of the larger than normal warships on both the battle's outcome and the narratives that describe it.

78. There are problems with the numbers recorded by Diodorus, our best source for this episode; see Hauben 1976b, who builds on the observations made by Seibert 1969, 193–95. Hauben argues that the numbers have been confounded by textual errors and by the likely fact that Demetrius crossed to Cyprus with one total and then gained an additional number of ships from cities he subjugated before the battle. As a result, by the time of the battle with Ptolemy, Demetrius had either 180 or 190 warships (Hauben 1976b, 4). As for his transports, we know that Demetrius would have required hundreds of vessels from the fact that Ptolemy employed more than 200 transports to carry his 10,000 men to Cyprus (Diod. 20.49.2).

79. It is worth noting that Demetrius sent for "skilled workmen" (τεχνῖται) and not for "engineers" (μηχανικοί). Presumably, his engineers had already drawn up their plans and simply lacked the labor required to create the siege machinery Demetrius planned to build. The city, Antigoneia on Orontes, was later abandoned after the Battle of Ipsus when Seleucus founded Antioch (cf. Diod. 20.47.5, who wrongly calls the new town Seleucia).

siege tower that was 90 cubits high (about 41.6 m.), 45 cubits on a side (approx 20.8 m.), and mounted on four solid wheels 8 cubits in diameter (about 3.7 m.). It housed inside a force greater than 200 men who worked a mixed array of large, medium, and small stone throwers and bolt projectors arranged on nine separate levels. His engineers also produced two large covered rams for use against the city walls (Diod. 20.48.2–3).

Although we hear nothing specific about the fleet while Demetrius attacked the city's defenses by land, his use of catapults in the sea battle with Ptolemy (see below) suggests he may have used his fleet in some way to prosecute the siege at the harbor. At the very least, he must have used his fleet to enforce a blockade and thereby trap Menelaus's fleet of 60 ships inside the harbor of the city. For this reason, Ptolemy was forced to send messengers overland to Menelaus to inform him that he was at nearby Kition with a large force and wanted him to send his 60 ships *if he was able to do so* (Diod. 20.49.3).[80] Learning of Ptolemy's nearby position and his intention to arrive before the city with a relief force, Demetrius prepared for a sea battle. He left a part of his force in place around the city, manned all his ships, and embarked on them his strongest soldiers (*ton stratioton tous kratistous*), as well as stone throwers, 3-span bolt projectors (the bolt was roughly 70 cm. long), and a stock of projectiles. After mounting the bolt projectors at the bows of his ships, he anchored off the mouth of the harbor just beyond the defenders' catapult range. In so doing he was able to watch for Ptolemy's arrival and at the same time insure that Menelaus's 60 ships stayed in the harbor (Diod. 20.49.4–5).

Just before dawn, Demetrius assigned 10 "fives" under Antisthenes to continue the blockade of the narrow harbor mouth and ordered his cavalry to patrol the coast so they might assist those of his men who swam ashore from wrecked ships. At first light, when the enemy's ships could be seen on the horizon, he drew up his fleet (now numbering 170–180 units) in a line-abreast formation in front of the city, most likely parallel to the coast, and awaited Ptolemy's approach.[81] Intending to fight with his largest ships on the left wing, he drew up these ships in two lines. In the first, he placed

80. Cf. Seibert 1969, 196, who accepts Plutarch's version (*Demetr.* 16.1) that Ptolemy asked Menelaus to attack Demetrius's fleet from the rear at the height of the battle. Either way, Demetrius effectively used his fleet to enforce a blockade that kept Menelaus from sailing out.

81. For the numbers, see above, n. 78. Although Diodorus does not explain the relationship between the battle lines and the coast, Demetrius needed to block Ptolemy from setting up a camp near the city and from entering the narrow mouth of the harbor. The surest way to

seven Phoenician "sevens" and 30 Athenian "fours" and behind these, he placed 10 "sixes" and 10 "fives," presumably to increase the weight of the frontal attack he planned to unleash on this wing. He assigned his lightest ships to the middle of the battle line and the remainder of his fleet to the right wing, furthest toward the south.[82]

Upon seeing Demetrius arrayed for battle, Ptolemy ordered his transports to follow at a distance and, after making "an appropriate formation" for his 140 "fives" and "fours," he assumed command of the larger ships on his left wing (Diod. 20.49.2). Subsequent events show that his fleet assumed a line-abreast formation, parallel to the enemy's line. As the fleets slowly approached one another, the boatswains (*keleustai*) on both sides led their crews in prayers to the gods "as was the custom" and then, when the fleets were about three stades (555 m.) apart, Demetrius gave a prearranged signal to engage: the raising of a gilded shield.[83] As this signal was passed along the line in relays, Ptolemy gave a similar signal and the two fleets rowed toward one another. At a reasonable closing speed of roughly 5 kn. per side, the two sides would have collided in less than two minutes.[84]

During this period of roughly 1 minute and 48 seconds, trumpets blared the signals to engage, battle cries ("alalai alalai") erupted from both sides, and catapults discharged stones and arrows to kill from afar. As the ships drew closer, archers and javelineers launched thick volleys

---

do this was to adopt the battle formation described in the text. A battle line drawn up in front of the port and parallel to the shore also helps to explain Demetrius's disposition of cavalry along the shore and the ability of Ptolemy's left wing (i.e., the southern-most wing) to retreat southward toward Kition at the battle's end; see Seibert 1969, 198, with Abb. 1–4 (204–205) and map (206). On the other hand, Seibert believes (199) that high losses on Ptolemy's left might indicate they retreated with difficulty and thus support the notion of battle lines that were perpendicular to the shore. Because Ptolemy's losses might have resulted from any number of factors unrelated to the orientation of the battle lines, I prefer the scenario as I have described it.

82. The commanders were as follows: the nauarch (or commodore) Antisthenes commanded the 10 "fives" left at the harbor mouth; Medius, another nauarch, commanded the left wing; Themison of Samos and Marsyas, the author of a Macedonian history, commanded the center; Hegesippus of Halicarnassus and Pleistias of Cos, the *archikybernetes* or chief pilot of the entire fleet, commanded the right (Diod. 20.50.1, 3–4). For the rank of *archikybernetes* see Hauben 1987.

83. The stade or *stadion* varies slightly from place to place; I use here the Attic measurement of roughly 185 m.; see Wickander 2008, 766; and Hultsch 1882, Tab. IV, 699.

84. A vessel traveling at a rate of 10 kn. travels 308.6 m. in one minute. In 1.8 minutes (= 1 min. 48 sec.) it travels 555 meters or roughly the distance of three Attic stades.

into the sky, hitting their opponents with increasingly deadly effect. The helmsmen, meanwhile, chose their targets in the enemy line and decided whether to aim for the bow, the catheads, or the oars along the side; the boatswains urged on the rowers to increase the stroke; and the lines closed ever more quickly. At the last moment before impact, those on deck crouched down and desperately held on to avoid being knocked over by the force of prow meeting prow. Although no one ever recorded the action below decks, the boatswains probably timed the stroke so the oarsmen were pulling when the impact occurred, hoping that the pull would steady the crew and keep them in place during the collision and violent deceleration that followed.

Following the initial collisions, it was critical for the slower ships to maintain contact with their neighbors and not allow faster opponents to slip through their line. If either line was broken, as was likely when vessels sustained damage in the frontal collisions, or when the enemy swerved at the last moment to attack the oars along one side, these ships and other speedier vessels could try to slip past the enemy and deliver attacks from the rear. For this reason, adjacent ships supported one another by closing the gaps around ships either damaged or dead in the water and, at times like these, the skill of the oarcrew to reposition their vessels and the skill of the marines in warding off boarders played equal roles in the life or death of everyone aboard. Diodorus (20.51.3–4) attempts to capture these numerous possibilities of action in his description of what followed next:

(3) When the ships were driven together by force and violence, some swept off the oars of their opponents, and rendered them unable to flee or pursue and prevented those on board, though eager to resist, from joining in the fight. Others, colliding with their rams at the bows, backed astern for another charge, and the soldiers on each side inflicted many wounds since their opponents were so close. Some of the men, when their trierarchs had struck the enemy from the side and their rams became stuck, leapt onto the enemy ships to kill and be killed. (4) Some, grabbing onto the nearby hulls, lost their footing and fell overboard into the sea and were immediately killed by the spears of those standing above them. Others, gaining the upper hand, slew some of the enemy, and forcing others along the narrow deck, drove them overboard into the water. The fighting was utterly varied and full of surprises; often the weaker would prevail because of the height of their ships, and the stronger

would be afflicted by the inferiority of their position and the unexpected nature of this kind of fighting.

On the "sixes" and "sevens" which were presumably heavier and slower
than "fives" or "fours," the soldiers fended off boarders from lesser ships
that had become damaged and wedged close to their hulls. Demetrius,
"who fought most brilliantly of all" from the stern of his "seven," killed with
his javelins and spear a crowd of men who "rushed at him," presumably
from the bow or midship area (Diod. 20.52.1).

Eventually, Demetrius's heavier left wing overwhelmed Ptolemy's right
and drove it backward in flight. Free to turn his heavy ships toward the
enemy's center, Demetrius pressed forward into the enemy's line and
caused the ships there to flee backward as well. Further toward the south,
Ptolemy's left wing had gained the upper hand, destroying some ships
and capturing others with their crews. When Ptolemy turned back toward
the center, however, and saw his other ships in flight and Demetrius
bearing down on him with his heavier units, he sailed back to Kition with
only 20 ships, leaving behind the transports to fend for themselves. As a
result, Demetrius captured more than 100 of these transports along with
almost 8000 soldiers aboard them; he also captured 40 warships along
with their crews, and gained control of some 80 wrecks, which he towed
back to his camp full of seawater.[85] Only 20 of his own ships were put out
of action during the battle, but all were eventually refitted and placed back
into service (Diod. 20.52.6).

During the sea battle, a second conflict developed at the harbor mouth
where Demetrius had left Antisthenes with 10 "fives" to prevent the ships in
the harbor from joining Ptolemy. Although ordered by Menelaus to break
Antisthenes' blockade by force, these 60 ships were unable to effect a breakout until the main battle was almost over. In the end, they literally broke out
through brute force (*ton ek tes poleos biasamenon*) and caused Antisthenes to
withdraw to Demetrius's camp, but not before it was too late to join in the
fight (Diod. 20.52.5). No casualties are reported from this secondary conflict.

---

85. Plutarch (*Demetr.* 16.2–3) records different casualty totals, which Seibert 1969, 200–202
follows regarding the capture of the supply ships. Because Plutarch mentions no soldiers
among the camp followers and equipment that was taken, Seibert doubts the 8000 soldiers
mentioned by Diodorus (Seibert 1969, 202). I prefer to follow Diodorus who has otherwise
provided convincing details of this entire event. It is worth noting here that "fours" and
"fives" did not sink when "destroyed" (διεφθάρησαν) but, instead, remained afloat on the
surface "full of sea water" (πλήρεις οὔσας θαλάττης).

Unable to relieve the defenders, Ptolemy was forced to withdraw his forces and return to Egypt. As word of Ptolemy's defeat spread throughout the island, the results were immediate and tangible: all the cities and their garrisons surrendered to Demetrius, who reemployed the men, with the total force coming to roughly 16,000 infantry and approx. 600 cavalry (Diod. 20.53.1).[86] Demetrius quickly sent messengers to tell his father the good news. By dispatching them on one of his "sevens," he further emphasized the size, power, and effectiveness of his new weaponry. Antigonus was so elated when he heard the good news from his son that he declared royal status for both himself and for Demetrius (Diod. 20.53.2).

Henceforth, the price of naval dominance increased considerably and the main rivals of Demetrius chose not to challenge him with their fleets. Successful campaigns in coastal regions now required a large land army with developed siege capabilities supported by a large fleet. The best force required not only a developed unit of skilled engineers presiding over a staff of skilled workmen, but also skilled soldiers who were able to transport, erect, break down, and wield the heavy weaponry they created. It was also critical for the successful commander to maintain naval dominance over the region of the siege and for this, he required a navy that could protect large numbers of troop and supply ships, enforce blockades, and fight off attempts to relieve the defenders. Demetrius's effective use of "sixes" and "sevens" showed how additional weight and height provided an advantage when fighting "fours" and "fives" and, of course, led eventually to even larger vessels. The impetus for this development, however, occurred the following year when Demetrius used his fleet to besiege the island city of Rhodes.

The Siege of Rhodes (305)

Toward the end of the campaigning season of 306, Antigonus tried to invade Egypt with a large land and sea force. The fleet was largely intended to establish control of river crossings so that Antigonus could use his 80,000 infantry and 8000 cavalry to overpower Ptolemy's forces

---

86. Plutarch (*Demetr.* 16.7) records that Menelaus surrendered 12,000 infantry and 1200 cavalry and says that Demetrius reported to his father (17.5) a total of 16,800 prisoners as taken during the war; see Seibert 1969, 203 for a discussion of these numbers.

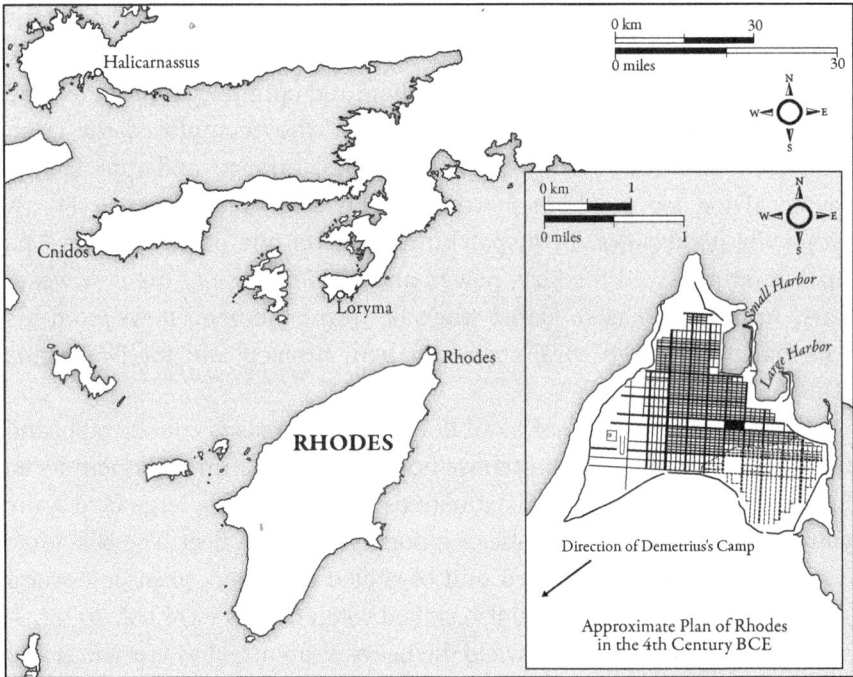

MAP 3.6 Rhodes and the opposite mainland with inset showing the harbors of Rhodes. Inset map adapted (with alterations) from Hoepfner and Schwandner 1994, Abb. 41 (inset on foldout plan between pp. 52 and 53).

along the river and march south to Memphis. A combination of bad luck, poor weather, and stout resistance on the part of Ptolemy's river garrisons prevented Demetrius, who commanded the fleet, from accomplishing this objective and so the expedition failed.[87] Antigonus intended to return to Egypt the following year when the Nile was lower and easier to cross (Diod. 20.76.5), but the loss of prestige that he felt from this failure made him focus his attention on the Rhodians first. During the previous year, this city had demurred when summoned by Demetrius to join the expedition to Cyprus (Diod. 20.46.6) and had also stood aloof from the failed campaign against Egypt during the autumn, citing treaty obligations as an excuse. Before making another frontal attack on Ptolemy, Antigonus apparently felt the need to make a demonstration of

87. On this episode, see Seibert 1969, 207–24; Hauben 1975–76; and Billows 1990, 162–64.

power at Rhodes and prevent this important city from falling further into Ptolemy's camp.[88]

The city was important to Antigonus and his rivals as a major mercantile center trading with Cyprus, Phoenicia, and Egypt. Back in 314, the city had agreed to build ships for Antigonus's siege of Tyre and, since then, had tried to maintain a balanced relationship with all the Diadochoi, and especially with Ptolemy, who was their major trading partner. When faced with another demand to join the war against Ptolemy, the Rhodians finally assented, but in the end could not agree to allow Demetrius full access to their harbors as he demanded (Diod. 20.82.3). As this would have led to a loss of control over their own internal affairs, they viewed the demand as a loss of independence.[89] And so, in spring 305, Demetrius assembled a large force on the Loryma peninsula opposite the city of Rhodes. He set out with 200 warships "of all sizes" and more than 170 "support" ships on which he embarked just under 40,000 soldiers along with an unknown number of cavalry and allied "pirates." In addition to these ships, there were almost 1000 private vessels that joined in the crossing, owned by merchants and pirates who hoped to profit from the campaign (Diod. 20.82.4–5).[90] Demetrius made the crossing in battle formation, with his fleet out front, three-span catapults mounted at the bows, followed by his troop ships and horse transports. As he crossed, his forces filled the sea from mainland to island, providing an awesome spectacle to those in the city who watched his approach (Diod. 20.83.1–2).

Located on the northern tip of the island, the city of Rhodes possessed three bays along its eastern shore that served as natural harbors, two of which figure in accounts of the siege. Although their precise layout is unclear at the time of Demetrius's attack, Diodorus paints a reasonably clear picture of their general configurations. The northernmost bay, which he calls the "small harbor," was closed by some sort of floating barrier

88. For an excellent discussion of the problems, see Hauben 1977, 328–39, who argues that Diodorus draws his information from a Rhodian source named Zenon and that his characterization of Rhodian foreign policy is largely correct; and Billows 1990, 165–66 with n. 5, who believes more caution is warranted. Diodorus (20.82.1–2) records that Antigonus provoked the Rhodians to attack a squadron of warships he had sent, probably in early 305, to intercept Rhodian merchants sailing to Egypt and confiscate their cargoes.

89. See Hauben 1977, 328–29, and his synopsis of events leading up to war, 330; this view is reflected in Berthold 1984, 66, who presents a good summary of the siege, 66–80.

90. On the nature of these merchants and pirates, see de Souza 1999, 44–45.

(*kleithra*) and protected along its eastern side by a breakwater or mole. Immediately to the southeast was the "great harbor," also protected from the seas by a mole whose end was located about 500 feet from the city wall where a gate led into the city. There was apparently no harbor barrier here and the shoreline next to the wall was somewhat rugged. The city wall ran along the shore inside both harbors and was lower here and not as strongly constructed as it was elsewhere in the circuit.[91]

Landing somewhere southwest of the city along the Gulf of Ialysus, Demetrius established a camp, protecting it with a triple stockade made from local trees and from farm enclosures. While he constructed his camp and built a mole to protect his fleet, he gave free rein to those who wished to plunder the island by land and sea (Diod. 20.83.3–4). At first, the Rhodians tried to negotiate with him, but after their messengers were ignored, they dispatched envoys to the other Diadochoi—Ptolemy, Lysimachus, and Cassander—begging them for aid (Diod. 20.84.1). Inside the city, they prepared their forces, enrolled in the army all foreigners who wished to share the danger, and expelled those who did not. They enacted a number of measures aimed at raising civic pride and bolstering morale, repaired their catapults, stockpiled projectiles, rebuilt damaged sections of the defensive circuit, and stacked piles of stones next to the walls (Diod. 20.84.2–5). They also sent out three of their fastest ships (*ton arista pleouson neon treis*) against those who were plundering the island and had some success, burning ships and capturing prisoners whom they brought back to the city to ransom (Diod. 20.84.6).

As one might expect from Demetrius's past actions, he prepared for this siege on a grand scale, far exceeding what he had done before. Judging correctly that capture of the harbors was critical for his success, Demetrius focused his attention there and asked his engineers to prepare machines that could be mounted aboard his warships and freighters. He produced two large "turtles" (*chelonai*) or protective coverings for his artillery; in one he placed a battery of stone throwers (*petroboloi*), and in the other a battery of bolt projectors (*oxybeleis*). Each turtle was so large that he had to support it on a pair of yoked freighters. He also joined together

---

91. See Diod 20.85.3 (low harbor wall); 85.4 ("small harbor"; harbor barrier); 86.1 (distance of mole in "great harbor" from circuit); 87.1 (harbor wall along the "great harbor"; ruggedness of shore); 88.7 (gate near base of mole). On the nature of Rhodes' harbors during the Hellenistic period, see Lehmann-Hartleben 1923, 128.

freighters to support two floating siege towers, which were designed to exceed the height of the harbor towers (Diod. 20.85.1). In order to protect these ponderous constructions from attack, he built a long floating barrier made of squared logs held together by iron plates and spikes (large nails).[92] Deployed in the water around the floating machines, the barriers prevented enemy vessels from reaching the hulls on which the machines rested. He also adapted small open galleys called *lemboi* for attack purposes by adding protective coverings for three-span bolt projectors. Manned with catapult crews and Cretan archers, these *lemboi* shot at the men who worked to increase the height of the city wall running along the shores of the harbor (Diod. 20.85.3).

Perceiving by his preparations that Demetrius was focusing his attacks on the harbors, the Rhodians placed two catapult batteries on the small harbor's mole and three more on freighters near its *kleithra* or harbor boom. These stout defenses may have convinced Demetrius to focus his attacks on the great harbor, which had a low stretch of wall and no *kleithra*. In order to bolster their defenses here, the Rhodians placed catapults on freighters anchored in the harbor and worked feverishly to strengthen and heighten the defensive walls along the shore and across the base of the mole, where they also placed a number of catapults.[93]

When everything was ready, Demetrius learned to his dismay that his massive assault machines were too large and top-heavy for the local sea conditions. As a result, he was forced to move them up the coast during the night when the diurnal westerlies gave way to calm weather (Diod. 20.86.1).[94] One night while his crews towed the machines from his camp, he seized and fortified the end of the harbor mole, established a catapult position to cover the harbor entrance, and then brought his

92. Diodorus (20.85.2) describes this barrier as "held together by nails" (καθηλωμένον) and also as a χάραξ, or defensive palisade, overlaid with iron (20.88.5: τὸν σεσιδηρωμένον χάρακα). We should probably envision a long boom made of squared logs held together with iron nails and reinforcement plates at the joins between the logs.

93. These actions can be deduced from Diod. 20.85.4; 86.2; 87.1; 88.2. Because we never hear that Demetrius forced the barrier of the small harbor, we can safely assume that his attacks occurred inside the great harbor. This is where the Rhodians placed catapults on individual freighters (Diod. 20.86.4) and where their ships (presumably these catapult ships) were attacked with fire arrows (Diod. 20.88.2).

94. These wind conditions prevail today during the spring at the city of Rhodes; Watts 1975, 544: "Here spring mornings see either calms off the Turkish southern coastline or a gentle offshore feed. . . . Yet by afternoon in spring there is a wind from W or NW that is most

floating assault machines into the harbor at dawn. Their entry was accompanied by shouts and trumpet blasts and then followed with catapult attacks on the walls and work crews around the harbor, particularly at the mole's base where the wall was weak and low (Diod. 20.86.2). Toward nightfall, Demetrius towed his assault machines back toward the harbor mouth, and when he did so, the Rhodians launched an attack with small fire ships but were kept from reaching the freighters by the floating barrier and by catapult fire (Diod. 20.86.3–4).

For eight days, Demetrius attacked the great harbor with his assault machines; he broke the constructions the enemy had placed on the mole and weakened the walls with his stone throwers, but was unable to break into the city. At one point, Demetrius sent a wave of men from his ships to land on the shore and climb the wall with ladders. These, too, were beaten back and the Rhodians burned the enemy ships that had run aground (Diod. 20.87.1–3).[95] After seven days of repairs, Demetrius resumed his attacks on the great harbor's walls with his floating artillery batteries. This renewed effort, plus the fire arrows he shot at the freighters in the harbor, caused a great deal of alarm. Fearing the worst if his assaults continued unchecked, the Rhodians manned three of their strongest (*kratistous*) ships with their best men to attack the freighters supporting Demetrius's assault machines.

> Diod. 20.88.5–6: Although many projectiles were hurled at them, they first forced their way to the iron-bound barrier and broke it apart. Then, making repeated ram strikes against the boats [on which the machines were mounted] and filling them with seawater, they knocked down two of the machines. When the third machine was towed back by Demetrius's ships, the Rhodians, emboldened by their success, pressed on into battle more boldly than was prudent. (6) And thus, after many large ships surrounded them and broke their hulls in many places with their rams, the nauarch [commodore] Execestus, the trierarch, and some others were wounded

---

frequently moderate, but can also be fresh to strong and even gale. This wind has often eased by the evenings of spring, but the fresh to strong W wind is as frequent at this time as it was earlier in the day. Even so, a quarter of the spring evenings are calm and another quarter have only light winds from the W."

95. The *akrostolia* taken by the Rhodians from these ships (Diod. 20.87.2, 4) were prow or stern ornaments and not rams, or "beaks," as translated by Geer 1954, 371, 373.

and captured. The rest of the crew jumped overboard and swam away to their comrades and one of the ships fell into the hands of Demetrius; the other ships escaped from the battle.

Undaunted, Demetrius constructed another machine "three times the size of the former in height and breadth," but when he brought it up to the harbor, it was overturned by a south gale (Diod. 20.88.7).[96] At this point, a force of Rhodians issued forth from the harbor gate and attacked the mole that Demetrius had occupied since the first day of the siege. Since the gale prevented Demetrius from sending reinforcements, his 400 men eventually surrendered and gave up the position (Diod. 20.88.8). Following these setbacks, a relief force of 750 men sailed into the city, underscoring Demetrius's inability to shut off the city from the sea (Diod. 20.88.9).

Unsuccessful in his harbor attacks, Demetrius decided to focus his subsequent energy on the landward side of the city (Diod. 20.91.1). And although we hear of occasional fighting at the harbor, the actions were aimed at diverting resources from city's landward defenses (Diod. 20.95.3; 98.7–8). Because Demetrius was never able to close either harbor, ships carrying food, supplies, and additional forces repeatedly brought aid to the besieged city.[97] Furthermore, on more than one occasion, Rhodian squadrons sailed out of the harbors to intercept Demetrius's supplies and redirect them to the city (Diod. 20.93.2–5; 97.5–6). Thus, despite his massive land and sea force, his team of engineers, the weapons they built, and the labor force at their disposal, Demetrius was unable to take the city of Rhodes.[98] After a year of inconclusive fighting, when developments in Greece demanded his son's attention, Antigonus wrote a letter directing Demetrius to come to terms with the Rhodians (Diod. 20.99.1) and move his forces to Greece.

---

96. Southeast gales are most frequent at Rhodes during the spring; Watts 1975, 544: "The other strong to gale direction in spring is SE and that again is diurnal growing to maximum frequency in the afternoons. . . ."

97. Diodorus (20.96.1–3; 98.1) seems to imply that this occurred on at least four separate occasions.

98. Although we know only three of his engineers by name (see Billows 1990, App. 3, nos. 37, 47, 124), his staff was surely large: on one raiding mission, the Rhodians captured a convoy of supply ships, on which were 11 craftsmen (τεχνῖται) "who excelled others of note in their ability to make missiles and catapults" (Diod. 20.93.5). Among his most well known constructions was a *helepolis*, a massive siege tower that was larger than anything built before (Diod. 20.91.2–8); 10 long *chelonai* ("turtles" or "penthouses"), eight to protect the men digging mines under the wall and two more to cover his two battering rams. Each of

The After-Effects of Rhodes

One wonders what Demetrius thought of his fleet's performance at Rhodes. For all its success at Salamis, the fleet seemed far less effective a year later. It failed to establish a zone of naval dominance around the city and allowed attacks on supply convoys both near the island and further afield. Unable to enforce a blockade of the city's two harbors, repeated shipments of supplies and reinforcements arrived to strengthen the people's resolve to hold out. The "sixes" and "sevens" that had proved so helpful at Salamis played no visible role at Rhodes, and were passed over by Demetrius as carriers for his primary assault machines. He built these weapons so large that he was forced to place them on yoked freighters, and when these were overthrown by the enemy and the elements, his solution was to build an even larger construction. The result was predictable: the machine collapsed.

On the other hand, it would be wrong to conclude that the failure to take Rhodes represented a lasting blow to Antigonid prestige.[99] At Rhodes, to be sure, the citizens erected statues of Cassander and Lysimachus and honored Ptolemy as a god (Diod. 20.100.2–4), but elsewhere the impact was hard to observe. This was because Demetrius's "failure" was also a massive demonstration of power that awed those very men whom the Rhodians honored. The Rhodians, moreover, were a unique opponent, possessing resources that few other cities commanded—resources that had enabled them to outlast the kind of siege only Demetrius could wage. In particular, the island state was extremely wealthy and possessed a large stock of catapults of all sizes with trained crews to man and repair them. It also had an effective naval force with commanders and oarcrews who displayed a high level of seamanship. Equally important was the city's strong civic pride, which enabled everyone under siege to hold out bravely

---

these rams was 120 cubits long (55.5 m.), sheathed with iron and able to deliver a blow "equal to the ram strike of a ship" (Diod 20.95.1). When Demetrius moved these machines up to the city wall, he used the crews of his ships to clear a space 4 stades wide (approximately 740 m.); the labor force amounted to almost 30,000 men (Diod. 20.91.8).

99. See, for example, Hauben 1977, 338: "they lost considerable prestige . . . especially among the Greek poleis . . ."; Billows 1990, 169: "the failure to win a clear victory represented a sharp blow to Antigonid prestige," and idem, 186, where he lists "the debacle at Rhodes" among the times when Antigonus, to his detriment, placed excessive trust in the abilities of his son; and finally Berthold 1984, 79, who calls the siege "one of the greatest failures of Antigonid foreign policy."

when conditions looked worst. Because most cities were less endowed
with such advantages and knew they could not withstand a similar attack,
the demonstration of power at Rhodes had a positive impact that far
exceeded any temporary loss of prestige.

By early summer 304, Demetrius left Rhodes and sailed through the
Cyclades with "his whole force" (Diod. 20.100.5); Plutarch (*Demetr.* 23.1)
says he responded to a plea from Athens, where Cassander had the city
under siege, and took with him 330 ships, presumably including the transports, and a large force of hoplites. From the moment he landed at Aulus
in Boeotia, Demetrius met with a string of successes that he owed in part
to his obstinate siege of Rhodes. He freed the nearby city of Chalcis from
its Boeotian garrison and forced the Boeotians to renounce their friendship with Cassander and ally themselves with himself and his father
(Diod. 20.100.6). He made an alliance with the Aetolians (long-time enemies of Cassander), raised the siege of Athens, and removed Cassander's
forces from central Greece up to Thermopylae. Driving Cassander back to
Macedonia in headlong flight, he captured the city of Herakleia (just past
Thermopylae), where 6000 Macedonian soldiers came over to him.
Turning south, he took Cenchreae, the eastern port of Corinth, and
expelled two of Cassander's garrisons from hill forts in Attica, handing
both places back to the Athenians (Plut. *Demetr.* 23.1–3). While we lack the
specifics of the fighting, his recent reputation, his siege machinery, and
his nearby fleet surely played a role in these rapid gains.

Such a conclusion is warranted from the details of the following year's
campaign. At the beginning of spring 303, Demetrius moved first to Cenchreae, east of Corinth, to create a diversion. Suspecting that Corinth was
his next target, the Sicyonians were unprepared when he attacked their
harbor and city simultaneously. Unknown to them, he had dispatched a
squadron of ships into the Corinthian Gulf with orders to coordinate their
attack on the harbor with his own attacks on the city (Polyaen. 4.7.3). As
the harbor seems to have been poorly fortified (Diod. 20.102.2), the ships
were no doubt assigned to secure the area and then wait for a signal to
offload the siege equipment.[100] Because the attack occurred unexpectedly

---

100. Surprisingly, the manuscripts of Diod. 20.102.2 describe the harbor region as ὀχύρου
(strong or secure) to explain why Demetrius later destroyed the harbor community when he
resettled the city in a more defensible location. Sensing a corruption of the text, L. Dindorf
(Diodorus 1831 and Diodorus 1844) suggested that the original reading was <ἀν>οχύρου
("weak or indefensible") and this view has been followed by subsequent editors.

at night, and from multiple directions (Polyaen. 4.7.3), Demetrius was able to steal inside the walls and drive the garrison up to the acropolis.[101] When these men saw that he intended to use his siege equipment, they panicked and surrendered on terms (Diod. 20.102.2). Following this success, and after resettling the city in a more defensible location, Demetrius turned next to Corinth where events followed a similar course. He attacked during the night from multiple directions, entered the city through a postern gate, gained control of Corinth's western harbor at Lechaion, and drove the garrison to higher ground (Diod. 20.103.1–2). Here, he unpacked his siege equipment and dislodged "by force" a portion of the garrison that had fled to a place called Sisyphion somewhere on the slopes of Acrocorinth. Turning to the rest of the garrison who had occupied the top of the precipitous hill, he "struck the men with terror and forced them to hand over the heights" (Diod. 20.103.2–3).[102] After settling affairs at Corinth, where he was asked (no doubt by his supporters) to leave a garrison until the war with Cassander was over, Demetrius continued his campaign into the Argolid, Achaea, and Arcadia, dislodging the forces of his enemies and bringing the cities into alliance.

By the end of autumn 303, he had brought the entire northern and central Peloponnesus under his control and proved beyond a shadow of doubt the value of a strong siege force that could be deployed by sea if necessary.[103] The following spring, he orchestrated a meeting of Greek allies who voted into existence a new "League of Corinth" designed to work in alliance with himself and his father on the model of the league established by Philip II, 35 years before. The rival Diadochoi viewed these developments with alarm and agreed to cooperate to break the power of Antigonus and his son. At the beginning of spring 301, they accomplished this fact at Ipsus, near a city called Synnada in central Asia Minor. By the end of the battle that was fought there, Antigonus lay dead while Demetrius fled westward to join his fleet at Ephesus to try to regroup and recover (Plut. *Demetr.* 30.1–2).[104]

---

101. Diod. 20.102.2: παρεισέπεσεν ἐντὸς τοῦ τείχους, "he got inside the walls by the side," i.e., he stole into the city.

102. For a clear reconstruction of these events, see Billows 1990, 171.

103. See Billows 1990, 171–72, for an excellent description of these events.

104. For a clear and detailed account of the battle and the events leading up to it, see Billows 1990, 175–85; Diodorus (21.1.4b) records, less plausibly, that he fled to Cyprus with his family following the battle.

Demetrius following Ipsus (301–283)

Always resilient, Demetrius returned to Greece to salvage what he could while his rivals carved up his Asiatic empire "like a big carcass" (Plut. *Demetr.* 30.1). Athens requested that he not enter the city, but agreed to send him the ships he had in their harbors which included one "thirteen." Apparently his largest ships had increased in size during the busy years since the battle off Salamis, but unfortunately we know nothing of the details aside from the fact that he also possessed an "eleven," known for the quality of the wood used in its construction (Theophr. *Hist. pl.* 5.8.1). We do know that thanks to his fleet, Demetrius managed to keep his hold on Corinth, the Cyclades, Cyprus, the chief cities of western Asia Minor, Sidon, and Tyre. We also know that he took this "thirteen" along with his daughter Stratonice and his "whole fleet" to Syria in 299 or 298 after Seleucus, the Diadochos who ruled Syria, requested her for a wife. Demetrius hosted a banquet for the king on the deck of this "thirteen" (Plut. *Demetr.* 32.2–3), and then sailed off to Cilicia where he recovered the cities taken by Cassander's brother Pleistarchus after Ipsus. While he was besieging Soloi, Lysimachus arrived with a force to help his ally, but was so awed by the size and nature of Demetrius's force that he prudently withdrew.[105] Presumably Demetrius's "thirteen" participated in this siege, but we are left to guess how the vessel was used.

Demetrius's next major adventure involved Athens, where unsettled conditions in 297 gave him an opening to interfere.[106] An Athenian general named Lachares had assumed tyrannical powers over the city and civil war had broken out as a result. Summoned by the anti-Lachares faction who had occupied the port city, Demetrius crossed to Attica, but lost a number of ships and men in a storm off the coast. Undaunted, he summoned reinforcements from Cyprus and then marched into the Peloponnesus where he received the submission of a number of cities that had

---

105. Plutarch (*Demtr.* 20.8–9; 33.4) records that Lysimachus sent a message to Demetrius asking him to show him his *mechanai* and his fleet, and that after viewing his full array of weaponry, he withdrew in awe. On this campaign, see Lund 1992, 89: "The Soli incident may represent just one episode in a campaign fought by Ptolemy and Lysimachus, of which the other details are lost. . . ."

106. For the date, see Habicht 1997, 85.

revolted from him.[107] After his forces arrived from Cyprus, he returned to Athens, now with a fleet of 300 ships, and cut off the food supply.

While Demetrius was thus engaged, Seleucus moved against Cilicia, Lysimachus threw himself against Demetrius's forces in western Asia Minor, and Ptolemy attacked Cyprus, now denuded of forces. Ptolemy also sent a fleet of 150 ships into the Saronic Gulf, but in the face of Demetrius's superior force, they withdrew. Demetrius eventually gained control of Athens in the spring of 295, established a fortified garrison on the Mouseion Hill, which he included inside the city circuit, and assumed control of Lemnos and Imbros, so important to Athens' grain trade.[108] At this time, he learned that Lysimachus had "seized the cities in Asia that belonged to him" and that Ptolemy had done the same in Cyprus save for Salamis, where his mother and children were currently under siege (Plut. *Demetr.* 35.5). Demetrius, ever busy, campaigned briefly in the Peloponnesus against Sparta, but withdrew his forces back northward when he received a request from one of Cassander's sons, Alexander, to help him in a dispute with his brother and co-regent Antipater. Arriving too late to help him (Pyrrhus had already done so), Demetrius nevertheless had the young king murdered at a banquet, seized the throne, and convinced Alexander's army to ratify the act and escort him back to Macedonia, which they did (Plut. *Demetr.* 36–37).[109]

During the following seven years, while Demetrius reigned as king of Macedonia, he held sway over most of mainland Greece save for Sparta and the regions of Aetolia and Epirus. His authority did not go unchallenged, however, and he was repeatedly forced to wage campaigns against the Boeotians, aided by their allies from Aetolia and Epirus. In spite of his overall success, he never gave up a desire to recover his Asiatic possessions and, following a failed campaign into Aetolia, a near fatal sickness, and an attack by Pyrrhus on Macedonia (which he repelled and then concluded with a truce), he began preparations, probably in 288, for a major campaign into Asia Minor. According to Plutarch's biography, he laid his

107. He also besieged Messene and almost lost his life when struck in the face with a catapult bolt (Plut. *Demetr.* 33.3–5).

108. See Habicht 1997, 85–86.

109. Justin (16.1.1–19) tells a similar story, except that he does not mention Pyrrhus and says that Lysimachus convinced his son-in-law Antipater to make up with his brother and thus avoid any dealing with Demetrius.

plans on a grandiose scale with numbers that are unbelievable but, nevertheless, provide an idea of the reports that reached the ears of his rivals. He enrolled 98,000 infantry, almost 12,000 cavalry, and laid down the keels for 500 warships, using the naval yards in Piraeus, Corinth, Chalcis, and Pella. His ships were not only numerous, they were large, including a "fifteen" and "sixteen," whose "speed and design were more admirable than their size" (Plut. *Demetr.* 43.7).[110] Confronted by this threat, Ptolemy, Lysimachus, Seleucus, and Pyrrhus agreed to make a preemptive attack on Macedonia in the spring of 287. Demetrius was caught totally unprepared.

Faced with armies from the east led by Lysimachus and from the west by Pyrrhus, Demetrius lost control of his troops, who eventually deserted him. Then, left with no option but flight, he slipped from the kingdom and tried to rally his generals and supporters in Greece as best he could. Encouraged by news from Macedonia, Athens decided to rebel during the spring of 287, stormed the Mouseion hill and expelled the Macedonian garrison. Demetrius arrived from Corinth and surrounded the city with his army, but not before a force sent by Ptolemy from Andros helped the Athenians to gather in their harvest.[111] As Demetrius began a siege of the city, the Athenians sent to Pyrrhus for help, but by the time he arrived with an army, Demetrius had already agreed to discuss terms. It seems that Ptolemy had sent his own representative, one Sostratus of Cnidos, and Demetrius agreed to break off the siege so long as he retained control of Piraeus and the forts of Attica. Apparently he made a separate agreement with Pyrrhus regarding the situation (Plut. *Pyr.* 12.6).[112]

Soon after these terms were accepted (according to Habicht "hostilities ended . . . not later than July 287"), he assigned the care of his Greek

---

110. Plut *Demetr.* 43.7: ἀλλὰ τὸ τάχος καὶ τὸ ἔργον ἀξιοθεατότερον τοῦ μεγέθους παρεῖχον. Merker 1958, 34, accepts the numbers and argues that Demetrius's plan was "to recover the absolute mastery of the sea which he had to some extent lost with the seizure of his eastern possessions by Ptolemy and Lysimachus."

111. For the base on Andros see Shear 1978, p. 2, lines 19–20, with pp. 17–19; the relevant text can be found in *SEG* 28, 60 = Austin 2006, no. 55, lines 19–20; for events at Athens, see Habicht 1997, 96–97.

112. This is the view of Habicht 1979, 62–67. Shear 1978, 74–78 includes Lysimachus as a party to this agreement, something doubted by Habicht 1979, 64; cf. Lund 1992, 102: "The argument that Demetrius aimed, in making peace with Ptolemy and Pyrrhus, to reduce the number of his enemies, enabling him to focus on Lysimachus's possessions in Asia is compelling."

possessions to his son Antigonus, gathered "as many ships as he had, embarked on them 11,000 soldiers along with his cavalry, and sailed off to Asia in order to detach Lydia and Caria from Lysimachus" (Plut. *Demetr.* 46.4).[113] Plutarch's wording leaves the impression of haste and implies that his departure was rushed. Although no figures survive for the size of his fleet, we might guess from past operations that it included a large number of transports and enough warships to convince Ptolemy not to interfere from his base on Andros. Nevertheless, it fell far short of the force envisioned in 288. In fact, when he arrived at Miletus, his fleet was insufficiently large to scare the city into immediate submission (see below). We might therefore suspect that Demetrius hastened his departure from Athens in order to pass by Andros before Ptolemy was able to strengthen his forces.[114] We might also wonder if his new "fifteen" and "sixteen" accompanied him on the voyage, because no stories involving these ships survive as they did when he took his "thirteen" eastward in 299 or 298.

Once he arrived in Asia Minor, his actions reveal the moves of a desperate man and underscore the inadequacies of his forces. *Near* Miletus (i.e., he was not received by the city upon his arrival), he met with Eurydice, the sister of his deceased wife Phila, and married her daughter Ptolemais in a move to "mobilize more local sympathy and support."[115] If ever there was a time to show off his grand armada, this was it, but we read of no feasts aboard the wide decks of his flagship. Following this hurried act of public relations, he turned to the cities of Ionia in a campaign whose details are not recorded. Plutarch (*Demetr.* 46.6) merely states that "many came over willingly, while others had to be forced." There are good reasons to doubt the widespread, enthusiastic adherence of Ionian cities to his cause. First of all, conditions in Ionia had been relatively peaceful prior to Demetrius's arrival, and contemporary inscriptions reveal that the area had "experienced a form of pragmatic and basically city-friendly royal imperial

---

113. For the date, see Habicht 1997, 97.

114. We learn from an Athenian decree (*IG* II² 650, lines 8–10) that the commander sent by Ptolemy to aid the city in May 287 commanded a squadron of small open galleys (*aphraktoi*). If this was representative of the force at Andros, it was presumably still too weak to pose a serous threat to Demetrius's invasion fleet.

115. Errington 2008, 57; cf. Plut. *Demetr.* 46.5: δέχεται δ' αὐτὸν Εὐρυδίκη περὶ Μίλητον ἀδελφὴ Φίλας, "Eurydice the sister of Phila received him in the environs of Miletus."

administration" for the past 15 years.[116] If Demetrius was unable to count on widespread discontent among the cities of Ionia, his success depended squarely on their perceived strength of his naval siege unit. As events were soon to show, however, Demetrius himself questioned the capabilities of this force. Whatever he did, and however much success he achieved, he must have spent the autumn and winter of 287/86 engaged in these events.

Sometime during the spring of 286, following the capture of Sardis and the desertion of "several of Lysimachus's officers," who brought with them both money and men, Lysimachus sent his son Agathocles with an army to confront Demetrius (Plut. *Demetr.* 46.6–7). Rather than face Agathocles head-on, Demetrius elected to leave his fleet behind and march inland. In other words, Demetrius decided not to hunker down among the cities of Ionia or Caria to engage Agathocles in counter-siege warfare. And this reinforces the impression left by Plutarch that he was forced to leave Greece before his siege unit was adequately prepared, perhaps in a rush following the settlement at Athens. This also reinforces our suspicions about Demetrius's popularity among the Ionian cities. Whatever we conclude, however, the outcome was disastrous, for he was pursued and harassed by Agathocles' force, cut off from provisions and forage, and lost 8000 men in the process. Blocked from descending into Syria by a second army commanded by Seleucus, Demetrius vainly hoped to reach his fleet at Caunus, tried to negotiate, but was eventually convinced by his friends to surrender himself to Seleucus (Plut. *Demetr.* 46.7–49.9). During the winter months of 286/85, his remaining men deserted to Seleucus, who thereupon took Demetrius into custody and kept him under house arrest until he died in the first few months of 282.[117]

Conclusions

Of all the dynasts who succeeded Alexander, Demetrius advanced the big ship phenomenon more than anyone else, and yet our sources (principally Diodorus and Plutarch) provide us with few details of this process and

---

116. See Errington 2008, 56–58 for the evidence. Plutarch's belief that Demetrius hoped to reach his fleet at Caunus (Plut. *Demetr.* 49.5; see below, text) also implies a tenuous hold on Ionia. Had he acquired the cities of Ionia, why did he expect his fleet to be wintering at Caunus in Caria? Tarn 1913, 99, paints a different picture: "He had been popular in Asia; Lysimachus was not. Some of the cities opened their gates; some he stormed; men gathered to the great adventurer's standard."

117. See Wheatley 1997, 19–27, esp. 27.

leave us guessing at his reasons for doing so. Broadly speaking, we know that he had "sixes" and "sevens" by 306, an "eleven" (presumably) and a "thirteen" by 301, plus a "fifteen" and "sixteen" by the time of his final expedition to Asia Minor. As for their use, we know that his "sixes" and "sevens" provided a height and weight advantage over Ptolemy's "fours" and "fives" at Salamis. We also know that his "thirteen" had wide enough decks to host a wedding feast, that she was present in the fleet for his recovery of Cilicia in 299 or 298, that this involved at least one siege at Soloi, and that Lysimachus was so awed by his firepower that he withdrew. We know that his "fifteen" and "sixteen" were admired for their design and speed and that they figured in Demetrius's plans to recover his Asiatic possessions. We also have no solid indication that they ever saw action.[118] This record, though meager, can be augmented by what we know of the development of warships prior to Demetrius.

As early as the Peloponnesian War, warships with strengthened bows were used to defeat "fast triremes" in confined areas like straits or harbors. Soon thereafter, the same city that employed their "threes" in this way against the Athenians introduced the first "fives," the same class that Alexander employed to break into the harbor at Tyre. Considering their increased weight and size, it makes sense that we find galleys larger than "threes" in combat around harbor mouths where their superiority in frontal ramming was a desirable characteristic. At this same time, we also observe the development of catapult artillery, which was used by most generals for offensive and defensive siege warfare. Initially developed for unrelated reasons, these two weapons systems—larger warships and catapults—were effectively united by Alexander when he besieged Tyre. This, more than anything else, explains the love affair between Demetrius and these larger vessels.

Of all the successors, Demetrius gained the reputation for being skillful at waging siege warfare, even taking a personal role in the designs of his research and development teams (Plut. *Demetr.* 43.4). Throughout his career, he engaged in numerous sieges of coastal cities for which he and his engineers developed large and elaborate wooden constructions. At

---

118. The fact that Philostephanus (Pliny *NH* 7.208) records Demetrius's largest ship as a "fifteen" suggests a degree of confusion in antiquity over his largest vessel. Living in Alexandria at the time of Ptolemy IV Philopator (222–206), Philostephanus should have had access to such information if it existed. This confusion might be explained if these ships played a minor role in 288 or perhaps no role at all.

Salamis, we find our first reference to the use of bolt projectors in a sea battle, and learn that the new "sixes" and "sevens" imparted a height and weight advantage to the victor. Slower and less maneuverable than Ptolemy's "fours" and "fives," these new vessels must have excelled in the frontal charge described by Diodorus at the battle's start. As for the battle characteristics of Demetrius's largest warships (his "eleven," "thirteen," "fifteen," and "sixteen") we are on less secure ground. The proposed oar-systems that define these classes demand an increase in weight and breadth as more men were placed side-by-side on each oar. We might also suspect from the ram sockets at Nikopolis that these larger vessels possessed bows and rams that were heavier and more deadly in frontal collisions with each increase in size.

The reason behind Demetrius's desire to build progressively larger warships might well be found in the problems he faced when attacking the harbors of Rhodes. First, there was the failure of his floating assault machines that were mounted on pairs of freighters. We can see from these constructions and from the lofty *helepolis* he built for his subsequent land attack that he felt elevation was important for his catapult attacks on city walls. This explains his curious decision to build an even taller construction when his first generation of machines was overthrown by the enemy. When his ships were simply unable to support his new construction and the whole thing collapsed, he turned his attention to the land defenses, where it was easier to achieve a higher elevation for his catapults. His second major difficulty involved the catapult batteries and barrier across the small harbor that he chose not to attack. The solution to this failure probably led him to propose larger and larger ship classes. While we might question the "thirteen's" ability to support his tallest siege towers, it is easy to imagine how a heavy galley, fitted with a massive ram and catapults, might effectively attack a harbor barrier and catapult batteries located on anchored freighters.

As I stated in the Introduction, most scholars interested in the development of classes larger than "threes" assume that they were constructed primarily for naval warfare between fleets on the high seas. In this chapter, I have argued that a desire to capture coastal cities and to maintain control of their harbors makes better historical sense for explaining the invention and subsequent development of these larger vessels. Such an explanation takes into account more than a century of naval development as well as the primary role played by Demetrius in accelerating this phenomenon during his lifetime. It also explains the curious fact that Demetrius increased the sizes of his warships during a period when he enjoyed naval superiority over his rivals and when we find no major sea battles apart from the one off Salamis, itself part of a siege action. Because our historical record is so poor, however, we lack clear narratives that describe these big ships in action, leaving us to guess how they were used. Fortunately, we possess a remarkable text that provides us with some of the answers we seek. Written by Philo the Byzantine in the half-century following the death of Demetrius, it provides the next evidence we must consider.

4

Philo the Byzantine and the Requirements of Naval Siege Warfare

Introduction

Sometime between the 240s and the 220s BCE, an engineer named Philon submitted a detailed report to his patron, a general named Ariston, explaining exactly how to attack and defend a Hellenistic city.[1] Surprisingly, his advice includes lengthy sections on how to use one's navy to facilitate the process. Philo (as we call him in English) submitted other such reports to Ariston, which comprised a corpus he titled "The Compendium of Mechanics" (*He Mechanike Syntaxis*).[2] Three of these reports still survive: a discussion of artillery construction (*Belopoiika*), another on pneumatic devices (*Pneumatika*), and a third on siege warfare, the work that concerns us now.[3] In addition to these subjects, the full "Compendium" included an introduction (*Eisagoge*) plus books on harbor construction (*Limenopoiika*), levers (*Mochlika*), automatic devices (*Automata*), and perhaps another on sending secret messages.[4]

---

1. Because other parts of Philo's work include detailed discussions of weapons and defense systems as well as methods of leadership, Ariston must be a military official in some position of authority. See D 28 where Philo urges his patron to take no undue risks during the course of the siege "for, in regard to all your plans, you could not accomplish anything as great with your own body as you would damage by suffering harm." Garlan 1974, 285, feels he might be a military engineer as well as a general.

2. Philo *Bel.* 14 [56.10–13]; the numbers inside the square brackets refer to the page and line numbers of Thévenot et al. 1693. Although this is roughly the numbering system used by Marsden 1971 (see next note), his line numbers do not exactly correspond to those of Thévenot's text because his column width is wider; see Marsden 1971, 15.

3. For accessible texts and translations of these works in English see, for the *Belopoiika*, Marsden 1971, 105–84; and DeVoto 1996, 4–94; and for the *Pneumatika*, which survives through Arabic and Latin translations, see Prager 1974.

4. See Garlan 1974, 281–82.

Philo's discussion of siege warfare is traditionally considered the fifth book of his "Compendium" and is titled *Poliorketika* from its content. The text falls into four subdivisions or chapters, which correspond to the following topics: (A) advice on the construction of fortifications, (B) preparations for a siege, (C) defense against a besieger, and (D) the art of besieging.[5] The last two of these sections, namely C and D, present revealing evidence concerning naval siege warfare and the full range of uses to which Hellenistic warships were put during siege and countersiege operations. In other words, Philo paints a full picture of the many ways in which naval power could be utilized to defend as well as to attack coastal cities. The resulting text is systematic, scientific, devoid of any political agenda, and provides excellent evidence for the use of a fleet during the big ship era.

As for Philo himself, we might infer from his epithet "the Byzantine" (*Byzantios*) that he had some connection with this city, which was perhaps his birthplace, the location where he first learned his craft, or attained his reputation.[6] Beyond that, we must rely on what he tells us about himself in his surviving works. From his report on catapult construction (*Bel.* 5 [51.15–23]), we learn that he spent some time among the military engineers at Alexandria and Rhodes, but in what capacity, he does not say.[7] Although Ariston is too common a name to reveal the identity of his patron or the conditions that called for his advice, we might glean some useful clues from regional hints that appear in the *Poliorketika*. For example, Philo advises those under siege to gather dates growing inside the city walls for food (B 48), and to hang planks of date palm wood off their walls to cushion the blows of stones from catapults (C 3; D 10, 17; cf. B 52). According to A. W. Lawrence, "Dates scarcely ever ripen outside a sharply-defined climatic belt," which he says "does not extend as far north as Asia Minor, but includes part of Syria, Phoenicia, and Palestine."[8] If this was the

---

5. The book's actual position in Philo's "Compendium" is unclear. Some editors prefer to place it following the fourth book on catapult construction (where it appears in some manuscripts of Renaissance date) and count it as the fifth book of the "Compendium." Others count the surviving text as two separate books, with sections A and B comprising the "Preparations" for a siege (Παρασκευαστικά) and C and D the book on "Siege Warfare" (Πολιορκητικά). Still others prefer to take each of the chapters as separate books. For all the possibilities with the relevant literature, see Garlan 1974, 281–83, whose text (279–404), accompanied by a critical apparatus, French translation, and commentary, now serves as the best modern edition. I have adopted Garlan's practice of counting the whole text as a single book divided into four subdivisions signified by capital letters.

6. For his epithet, see Garlan 1974, 284.

7. See Marsden 1971, 109 with n. 8.

8. Lawrence 1979, 70.

region of Philo's concern, it helps to explain his advice to those expecting a siege to stockpile naphtha from Babylon along with two poisons for their pointed projectiles: one from Arabia, and another from a shellfish found in a marsh close to Ake (modern Akko in Israel; B 53).[9]

General time indicators are provided by Philo's discussion of Ctesibius's design for a catapult powered by bronze springs. Ctesibius, a famous engineer who worked for Ptolemy II, was apparently dead when Philo visited Alexandria, because he did not learn the details of his design from the master himself, but from conversations with Ctesibius's coworkers (*Bel.* 49 [72.36–39]).[10] This suggests to some a date as early as the 240s for Philo's reports to Ariston, while others prefer a date in the 220s. Based on these regional and chronological indicators, A. W. Lawrence makes a compelling argument that Philo's *Poliorketika* was written toward the end of his career and concerns those cities affected by the campaigns of Ptolemy III into Phoenicia and Syria between 246 and 240.[11] Even if we date the work slightly later than this, his work on siege and countersiege warfare reflects techniques derived from forces built up during the reign of Ptolemy II, a king who amassed the largest fleet and built more big ships than anyone else in the ancient world (see chapter 6).[12] It is quite likely, therefore, that Philo's text reveals in detail the tactical and strategic objectives behind such a fleet's creation. As we now turn to consider what Philo has to say, the reader should note that I have reordered the topics contained in his original discussion for the sake of clarity. Those who wish to see the original order

---

9. The word Ἄκης (Akko) represents an emendation of the meaningless ἀκτὶς (mainland or promontory) which appears in the manuscripts.

10. For the problems involved in dating Ctesibius, see Marsden 1971, 6–8. Two contradictory passages in Athenaeus's *Deipnosophistae* suggest dates during the reigns of Ptolemy II ("not long after 270") and Ptolemy VII Euergetes II (145–16). Even if there were two engineers of the same name, Marsden (6–7) argues convincingly for the earlier date for the Ctesibius mentioned by Philo, based on the nature of his catapult designs. Prager 1974, 13, argues from *Bel.* 61 [77.46–50] ("Ctesibius demonstrated this for us by showing the nature of air—that its motion is strong and sharp . . .") that Philo was among Ctesibius's pupils and was thus a younger contemporary. The reference to "us," however, need imply nothing more than the general scientific community.

11. Lawrence 1979, 69–71; and Garlan 1974, 283–84, who expresses the generally held opinion that Philo's work should be dated ca. 225 BCE; references to earlier views can be found in Garlan's notes.

12. See C 54 which advises the placement of unused warship rams on a harbor barrier. Philo's assumption that his patron might have access to unused stocks of warship rams strongly suggests that he worked for a major naval power. Considering the other indicators in his text, this can only be Ptolemy II or III.

and thereby understand the full intent of Philo's advice to his patron may consult the translation of Philo's naval sections presented in Appendix E.

How to Carry Out a Naval Siege: The Naval Siege Unit

Before we can contemplate a full-scale attack on a coastal city, we must understand the nature of the naval force that will carry out the attacks. The naval siege unit, as I like to call this force, is a mix of varied types and sizes of vessels, specifically designed to perform different, but complementary tasks. In a sense, the force described by Philo is analogous to the land army in the diversity of its constituent components. Although he tends to use overlapping terms for the vessels he describes, certain characteristics of the siege unit can be extracted from his text.

Among the attacking force, he mentions "naval vessels" (*nees*: C 58; D 110), a "warship" (*polemia naus*: D 103), "cataphract ships" (*kataphraktoi nees*: D 22), "long ships" (*skaphai makrai*: D 5), "ships" (*skaphe*: D 105), "large ships," presumably fitted with rams (*poieteon d' estin . . . embolas . . . ton megalon skaphon*: D 29), "boats" (*ploia*: D 53, 101, 105), "undecked boats" (*aphrakta <ploia>*: D 103), "support boats" (*hyperetika <ploia>*: D103), small warships called *lemboi* (D 21, 38), and bulk transports called *holkades* (C 55; D 21, 23, 101). The position of honor was reserved for the heavy galleys called "cataphracts," whose upper deck served both as a fighting platform and a protective covering over the oarcrew.[13] These vessels, also called "large" or "big ships" by Philo (D 29), were armed with bronze rams at their bows and carried deck soldiers on their *katastroma*, or upper deck. They were used for a multitude of tasks and served as the unit's most powerful offensive naval weapon. For example, Philo specifically mentions their use to break through the harbor barrier (D 22). The unit's cataphracts were augmented by smaller, open galleys—the aphracts—whose oarcrews were unprotected by a covering deck. In the battle line, these smaller galleys were placed alongside larger warships to deter enemy attacks on their sides or oars. Among these smaller ships

---

13. During the Hellenistic period, the term usually applies to vessels the size of "fours" and larger, although some "threes" were protected with extra planking and classified as cataphracts; see App. *Mith.* 17 and 92; Memnon of Herakleia, *FGrH* 434, F1, 21 (=Dritter Teil, Text, XXIV. Herakleia am Pontos, p. 351); and Caes. *BC* 2.23.

were the *lemboi,* a type originating as an Adriatic pirate galley that was adopted during the third century as a cheaper alternative to the "three." These *lemboi* could exhibit considerable variations in design but were noted for their speed and maneuverability.[14] In spite of their lightness, Philo makes it clear that *lemboi* could be adapted to carry a small stone projector by the addition of a specially constructed base with a curved roof made of stout planks (D 38). Last, but not least, the siege unit also employed cargo vessels, called *holkades* (literally "towed vessels"), which were valued for their stability and carrying capabilities. Although Philo does not mention their obvious use as cargo carriers and troop transports, he notes them as suitable platforms for artillery and siege machinery (D 21, 23), and as buoyant stations along the harbor barriers called *zeugmata* (D 101; on the *zeugma,* see below).

Siege warfare made stern demands on both the besieger and besieged as it involved every conceivable kind of fighting. As a result, the best naval siege units possessed not only a wide array of vessels but also the appropriate expert personnel. This included military engineers and expert craftsmen (B 49), crack artillery crews and specialists who fought from the siege "machinery," and last, but not least, the deck soldiers who fought on the cataphract warships. On two separate occasions (D 22, 103), Philo remarks that you should be careful to employ only deck soldiers who were experienced in "fighting at sea"—ones with enough discipline "to use the ram" and resist the urge to board the enemy. In sum, the naval siege unit described by Philo was a complex force that compares favorably to contemporary land armies in the diversity of its constituent elements and the specialized expertise exhibited by its personnel.

The Procedure of Attack
Use of Stealth and Deceit

The best way to take a city is through stealth or deceit, when the enemy is least prepared for an attack (D 2–3).[15] In this way, both the attacker and defender sustain the fewest casualties. If the city cannot be fooled

---

14. See Casson 1995, 125–27.

15. This explains the popularity of preserved lists of successful tricks, called *strategemata,* by Polyaenus and Frontinus. Glorified in Greek myth and epic (e.g. the Trojan Horse), examples of ruses, tricks and deceit lie behind many important events in Greek history (such as

into surrender, however, and a frontal attack is necessary, then it must be carried out vigorously, continuously, and in as many places around the city's defensive circuit as possible (D 24–26). The most effective action involves a simultaneous attack by land and sea, which both inspires fear and divides the forces of those inside the walls (D 24), an observation that is supported fully by preserved stratagems in Frontinus and Polyaenus.[16]

Effective Blockade

A major objective for anyone who hopes to gain control of a hostile coastal city is to cut off the defenders as quickly and as fully as possible from all hope of outside help. To insure this, the attacker must first build a stockade around the city and blockade the harbor entrances with his warships so that nothing can sail in or out (D 5).[17] Philo describes the process as "anchoring against the harbor" (*epi tou limenos ephormein*), which sounds like a simple task, but it was often difficult to carry out in practice. For example, energetic defenders might attack hostile ships by sending out divers to drill through hulls or to cut anchor lines (C 60), so the attacker had to be prepared with the appropriate counter-measures. Philo suggests that guards armed with long tridents be stationed on rafts around the attacker's ships to intercept incoming divers (D 54). He also recommends the use of anchor chain instead of rope to prevent the enemy from tampering with the moorings (D 53).[18] Although the attacker must be extra diligent at the harbor entrance, he should not relax his attention elsewhere, or the enemy might slip into the city by entering from the landward side, particularly at night (D 102).

---

how Pisistratus first gained control of Athens: Hdt. 1.59.3). Frontinus and Polyaenus give numerous examples where victory was obtained through tricks or by cunning; for a few examples related to naval sieges, see Fron. *Str.* 3.2.2, 10, 11, 3.7; 4.7.23; and Polyaen. 4.7.8, 12.3; 5.19.1, 23.1; 5.35; 5.41.

16. See, for example: Polyaen. 4.7.3; and Fron. *Str.* 3.9.5, 6, 8, 10.

17. Failure to maintain an effective blockade by land and sea could doom even the most energetic attacks on the city's defenses. In the most famous siege of antiquity, Demetrius Poliorcetes failed to capture Rhodes (305–304 BCE), in part, because he was unable to intercept Ptolemy's occasional shipments of reinforcements and supplies.

18. In shallow water, he suggests the use of protective devices called "funnels" (χῶναι) that must have somehow protected the mooring lines from being cut. Exactly how they worked is unclear. Garlan 1974, 321, translates the noun as "gaines" or "sheaths" in English.

Frontal Attack

The actual frontal attack on the harbor defenses was carried out by the naval siege unit composed, as stated before, of both large and small warships, as well as cargo vessels. Although Philo does not describe in detail the weaponry of this unit, because it would be well known to his patron, he assumes that the attacker will possess ample quantities of wood for constructing siege machinery (*mechanemata*) and protective coverings.[19] These constructions could be placed on *lemboi* and cargo vessels (D 21) and might include assault towers, landing gangways, and artillery bases (cf. C 59; D 25 and D 38). Philo also assumes the attacker will have ample supplies of artillery and missiles, which should include both stone (D 38, 105) and arrow projectors of varying sizes (B 49; D 105).[20]

Breaking the Harbor Barrier

The act of breaking into the harbor with a naval siege unit involved breaching a physical barrier that was strung across the harbor mouth. Various kinds of barriers were constructed during this period. The simplest, called a *phragma* or *kleithron*, might be little more than a large chain supported by buoys (D 52; see Fig. E.1).[21] Others required periodic drying out and caulking in order to keep them serviceable (Aen. Tact. 11.3). Because the barrier, however it was constructed, formed the harbor's first line of defense, the besieger could expect his attack here to be met by a vigorous resistance (C 54–58). In such a fight, where marines formed the main target of every enemy marksman and catapult (D 105), Philo advises the attacker to use his most experienced men, particularly those most accustomed to fighting at sea (D 22).[22] This fight could be fierce, depending on the preparations

---

19. Although cognate with the English noun "machines," the Greek word μηχανήματα is best translated by some periphrasis like "timber constructions" to avoid confusion with the industrial age connotations of the English word.

20. There is a limit to the size of stone projector that can be placed on a small warship like a *lembos*. See chapter 5 for the details.

21. For more details on these kinds of barriers, including a list of harbors with attested *kleithra*, see Garlan 1974, 388. A similar barrier closed off the entrance to the Golden Horn in 1453; the massive chain can be seen on display in the Istanbul Military Museum.

22. Those accustomed to fighting at sea would be steadier under fire and more likely to remember and follow orders in the heat of the battle (D 103). At Salamis in 306, those unaccustomed to fighting at sea complained that "often the weaker would prevail because of the

of the defenders, which might be considerable if they had also followed Philo's advice (cf. C 58).

The best kind of barrier was a "yoked" affair called a *zeugma*, comprised of warships and small boats joined together into a more or less rigid unit by timbers. For extra protection, Philo urges the construction of ram-like projections from the bows of the constituent ships if the defender possessed extra warship rams (C 54). This pontoon barrier would be further protected by rowboats stocked full of incendiary materials (C 55), by heavy weights (Philo calls them "lead amphoras") suspended from overhanging beams which could be made to plummet down on the attackers' warships, and by two 20 mina (8.7 kg.) stone projectors (C 56) on each side of the harbor entrance. If the harbor mouth was so wide that the center passage lay outside the range of the defender's harbor batteries, he should build a central tower in the middle of the entrance and place in it an artillery piece that discharged 30 mina (13.1 kg.) projectiles (C 57).

Depending upon the attacker's resources and the construction of the barrier, Philo presents two methods that might be used to break through it. If the barrier was a simple *kleithron*, the attacker might first try brute force by smashing through it with his larger warships (D 23). Surely we see in this piece of advice one reason behind the construction of the largest polyremes whose extra weight, mass, and large rams would be effective in dislodging or breaking such barriers. If direct attacks on the barrier were unsuccessful, the attacker might try to dismantle it by dragging the connecting chains up on deck to break apart their fastenings.[23] For this chore, he could use his cargo vessels, along with their anchors and winches, as floating demolition platforms (D 23). Against a well defended *zeugma*, or pontoon barrier, the attacker would need his largest ships and his most experienced men, particularly those who "are able to fight at sea" (D 22).

Above all, the attacker must maintain pressure on other sectors of the city while he is trying to get into the harbor (D 24–27). Aside from using his

---

height of their ships, and the stronger would be afflicted by the inferiority of their position and the unexpected nature of this kind of fighting" (Diod. 20.51.4). Philo's observations were much more precise in that those accustomed to fighting at sea were able to anticipate conditions that others would call "unexpected."

23. This brings to mind the unsuccessful attempts of the Athenians to undo the fastenings of the barrier that blocked their escape from the Great Harbor at Syracuse in 413; see Thuc. 7.59.3, 69.4, and 70.2. Diodorus (13.14.2) says that the Syracusans built the barrier in three days out of various vessels placed side-by-side, joined by iron chains and planking.

land forces, he might carry out ramming attacks on seaside sections of the circuit wall with "the vessel least serviceable for war among the big ships" (D 29; C 59) in hopes that the wall might collapse (D 29).[24] He might also attempt to land men on the wall by using gangways slung out from his ships (C 59). As a defense against these actions, Philo urges the defenders to deposit piles of rubble in the sea next to vulnerable sections of their circuit to keep the enemy vessels from approaching the wall too closely (C 59).[25]

The Defense Against a Relieving Force with Naval Capabilities

If an ally of the besieged sends a relieving force, Philo advises the besieger to close up the harbor with debris (D 101). Although Philo does not state the obvious, the besieger will leave a restricted entrance to allow his own ships to move in and out. The goal was to reduce access into the harbor to an easily defended space. In this way, no relief vessels can slip into the harbor. If it is impossible to close the harbor entrance by this means, then the besieger must build his own pontoon barrier across the harbor mouth (D 101).[26] Since this barrier will form the center of one's line if the reliever decides to fight a naval battle (D 103), the besieger must start with stable vessels like cargo carriers that can serve as artillery platforms (D 101), placing them side-by-side and then joining them together with timber beams.[27]

Any foe worth discussion will have brought a relieving force large enough to defeat the besieger, and if this force is considerably larger than the besieger's force, common sense dictates that the besieger must break off the siege and withdraw. Rather than discuss the obvious, Philo focuses on a scenario where the besieger's force is slightly inferior to that of the

---

24. The chance for damage to the warship was apparently high enough for Philo to advise the use of the least serviceable vessel for this task. Nevertheless, the mere possibility that a large cataphract warship might actually cause a fortification wall to collapse reveals the immense power of their ramming blows. See note on C 29 in Appendix E.

25. Alexander cleared such piles of underwater debris during his attack on Tyre in 332; see Arr. *Anab.* 2.21.4–7.

26. The barrier built by the besieger is also called a *zeugma* or "yoked construction." Examples of harbor-closing strategies can be found in Thucydides' account of hostilities at Pylos in 425 (4.8.5–7; unrealized) and at Syracuse in 413 (7.59.3; 7.70.2; realized). For the *zeugma* built in 413 at Syracuse, see also Diod. 13.14.1–2, who says it was completed in three days. See also below at "The Defense Against a Naval Siege Unit."

27. Philo says you should use "what wood you have around," knowing well that a besieger will have large stocks of wood at his disposal.

reliever and is thus forced to fight in front of the harbor. In such a case, he advises the besieger to place his most experienced marines on his cata-phracts and instruct them not to board the enemy but to rely on ramming attacks (D 103). The besieger should array his line in a crescent-shaped formation with his attack ships (i.e., his fastest and most maneuverable warships) drawn forward on the wings (D 103). At the center of the line, which is formed by the besieger's barrier at the harbor mouth, Philo ad-vises the placement of artillery batteries, aphract galleys, and support ships. No big ships are mentioned, but presumably they would be sta-tioned between the barrier and the attack ships. Since the besieger's posi-tion is essentially anchored to the barrier he has constructed, he must assume a defensive posture and wait for the reliever to engage (D 104).

When the battle is finally joined, Philo advises the adoption of three main strategies (D 105). First, the besieger should target the enemy's deck soldiers by striking them with long-range projectiles, primarily stones and arrows shot from catapults, although he also mentions devices called *dory-boloi* or "spear projectors" (D 105; cf. C 58). Second, he should burn the enemy hulls by using incendiary missiles, burning caltrops, torches, and pitch (Fig. E.3).[28] And finally, he advises the besieger to crush and shatter his opponent's hulls, by striking them with heavy projectiles "from the land, from the timber constructions and from the other boats" (D 105).[29]

If the reliever does not attack the pontoon barrier and the besieger wishes to engage the enemy anyway, he must first reform his battle line by collecting together his forces from both wings in front of the barrier (D 106). Once this has been done, the besieger can then advance toward the enemy to fight a regular sea battle. The attack might be carried out in various complementary ways. On the wings, the besieger might utilize his attack ships to out-maneuver the enemy so that he can take them in their sides. Elsewhere along the line he might challenge the enemy in prow-to-prow contests with his larger vessels. And near the barrier, where he has stocks of

---

28. At C 55, Philo advises the defenders to station rowboats stocked with these incendiary weapons along the interstices of the pontoon barrier. Vegetius (*Mil.* 3.24) tells us that "a caltrop is a defensive weapon made from four spikes, and whatever way you throw it, it stands on three spikes, and causes injury by the fourth which stands erect." Here, they are wrapped in twine, coated with some flammable substance, like pitch, and set afire. They are then thrown, ablaze, at the wooden hull of an enemy ship into which their points stick.

29. See the comments above in the section "Breaking the Harbor Barrier" which are also relevant here.

missiles and long-range artillery, he might attack the enemy with incendiary weapons (D 107). On no occasion does Philo recommend the use of boarding parties. In general, the men are to fight with discipline, and are specifically ordered not to climb out along the side of the vessel or to board the enemy.[30] They are told, instead, to place their trust in the effectiveness of their warship's ramming strikes (D 103).

The Pursuit of a Defeated or Fleeing Enemy

Although Philo has not set out to write a general tactical manual on naval warfare, he does provide a few insightful statements concerning the pursuit of a fleeing enemy. Such a pursuit was potentially dangerous and therefore should only be made "in formation with the entire fleet" (D 108). This general admonition applies as well to attacks made on a disorganized fleet. If the attacker should overtake his enemy and force him to turn about for a confrontation, the attacker can best defeat his enemy by attacking from a unified formation. In this way, the attacker can revert to the three tactical objectives Philo outlined previously: 1) attack the marines, and 2) burn and 3) crush the enemy hulls.

If the enemy chooses to avoid the confrontation and continue their flight, the attacker must focus his attacks on the enemy's steering and propulsive oars. By acting in this way, the attacker will either force his enemy to turn and fight, drive them toward the shore, or disable the vessels at sea. In this last case, the attacker might then kill their deck soldiers at his leisure with long-range projectiles, and then either swamp the helpless vessels by ramming, burn them (D 107, 108), or capture them and tow them back to his camp (D 109). There is no explicit talk of boarding as a fighting tactic, although eventually one would have to board those vessels whose oars had been destroyed and deck soldiers eliminated in order to capture them.

---

30. If the verb ἀκρωτηριάζειν were translated "to cut off akroteria," Philo might be saying that the men are specifically ordered not to cut off any trophies (i.e., the enemy akroteria) nor to board any enemy ship. Garlan 1974, 326 (at D 103), has Philo ordering the men not to disarm or board any enemy ship and explains in his note to the passage (n. 103b on p. 403) that during the *diekplous*, the goal was to pull away the oars from the enemy vessel. However we choose to translate this passage, the admonition against boarding remains the central theme and our translation of ἀκρωτηριάζειν should amplify or supplement this statement. For this reason, I prefer what I have presented in the text.

The Defense Against a Naval Siege Unit

There are two major ways to defend against amphibious attacks according to Philo's text. The first is to hinder the enemy from gaining a foothold on one's shore by denying him the landing places for his troops and by dispersing a variety of anti-personnel devices (C 51). This strategy was intended to tip the odds in the favor of the defenders who might be intimidated in the face of the attack.[31] Philo advises the defenders to close off their more accessible places with stockades, conceal doors studded with nails, and disperse iron and boxwood caltrops at the landing places (Fig. E.3). He also advises placing stakes, joined together in opposite directions with iron bands, set just beneath the surface of the water (C 53; see Fig. E.2).

Because gaining control of the harbor would be a primary goal of the attacker, the second (and perhaps main) area of concern was at the harbor, whose entrance should be blocked by a physical barrier (C 52). Philo advises using a boom (*kleithron*) or chain supported by floats (C 52, 55; Fig. E.1) or, lacking this, a pontoon barrier (*zeugma*) made of cargo vessels and warships joined together with wooden beams (C 54–55).[32] In both cases the objective is to keep the enemy from getting too close to one's defenses. To this end, the defenders should place underwater obstructions off seaside stretches of their walls (C 59), deploy artillery in strategic places (C 56–57), and stockpile incendiary weapons in rowboats at various places along the harbor barrier (C55). Maintaining control of the harbor entrance was the main concern for the defenders and the key to a successful resistance. Philo accordingly advises the placement of a 20 mina (8.7 kg.) stone projector on each side of the entrance. If the entrance is too wide for the weapons to provide overlapping fire, a tower large enough for a 30 mina (13.1 kg.) weapon should also be placed in the middle.[33]

---

31. For an example of this factor, see the speech of Demosthenes to his men at Pylos (425), as recorded by Thucydides (4.10.5), himself a commander of warships: "I call upon you as Athenians who know from experience all about landing from ships on foreign shores and how impossible it is to force a landing if the defenders stand firm and do not give way through fear of the surf or the frightening appearance of the ships as they sail in. . . ." Trans. Warner 1972, 270.

32. This barrier or *zeugma* (n. 26) might be strengthened further by the addition of timber constructions tipped with a warship ram that were built in front of each ship making up the barrier (C 54).

33. Advice like this would have been included in his lost work on harbor construction.

The main target for these heavy pieces was the enemy's siege machinery (C 58, 67–70), which were also attacked with incendiary missiles and large bolt projectors. Philo is quite clear about the limitations of these weapons when used against ships. They might help to destroy *some* of the enemy vessels at the barrier, but only under certain specific conditions (C 56): the boats must be small (*ton mikron tines*); they must be unable to move freely (*peri tous embolous peripageisai*); and they must be hit, presumably more than once, by lead amphoras and by 20 mina stone shot (*tuptomenai tois te molibois amphoreusi kai tois petrobolois*).

It is important to briefly note something about Philo's discussion of catapults. Nowhere do we find evidence for the modern view that catapults were used to harm a warship's oarcrew by penetrating the vessel's protective deck.[34] That such a possibility does not even occur to Philo demonstrates this theory as groundless and warns us against arguments based on the assumption that if something was possible (within the limits of ancient technology), then it must have been done.

Conclusion

In general, Philo's remarks nicely supplement what we have learned from a series of naval sieges ranging from Syracuse (415–13) to Rhodes (305) and described by historical authors like Thucydides, Diodorus, and others. Philo specifically details the range of different vessels from rowboats to freighters that were pressed into service for various purposes. He recommends the use of one's largest warships for attacking the harbor barrier, for crushing enemy ships, and even for ramming the foundations of city walls built where ships could approach them. The best deck fighters were skilled, practiced in fighting at sea and disciplined enough to rely on their ships' ramming abilities and thus resist boarding the enemy. Catapults were omnipresent (see C 25) with stone and bolt projectors being placed on the city wall in towers and on vessels of varying sizes from *lemboi* to cataphracts to freighters.

Surprisingly, the use of catapults, which many historians credit with driving the big ship phenomenon, receives less attention from Philo than we might like. In his discussions of attack and defense at the harbor, he

---

34. See Foley and Soedel 1981, 160–162, and chapter 5. The view has been endorsed most recently by Morrison and Coates 1996, 310, and 369–70.

provides few details of catapult sizes, mentioning specifics only when describing the defenses at the city's main harbor (C 56–57, 67).[35] Elsewhere he assumes the reader will know what sizes to use and where to place them when attacking the city wall (C 21, 25), when trying to "harm the marines" of a relief force (D 105), when attacking the harbor barrier (D 21–23), or when placing them on *lemboi* fitted with protective coverings (D21, 38). Since the use of catapults on polyremes is frequently cited as a driving force behind the development of big ship navies, and since they are clearly important elements of Philo's naval siege unit, we will examine this subject in more detail in the following chapter.

---

35. Philo specifically mentions catapult sizes in six different sections of his work on siege-craft (C 6, C 26, C 56–57, C 67, D 17, D 31). These sections, and what they imply for the sizes placed aboard warships, are discussed in chapter 5.

5

Big Ships, Boarding, and Catapults

It had taken perhaps half a century to go from a "four" to a "six," and well over a quarter of a century from a "six" to a "seven." With the introduction of the "seven," the pace of development quickened dramatically. In but 25 years or so, the gamut was run from a "seven" to a "sixteen," thanks to the drive, inventiveness and daring of Demetrius the Besieger of Cities.

—CASSON 1995, *137.*

Introduction

The drive to build large warships following Alexander's death produced a unique period of naval history whose significance has been only partly understood. We have already seen how the roots of the phenomenon go back to the turn of the fourth century with the introduction of "fours" and "fives" at Carthage and Syracuse. By mid-century a desire for ships larger than "threes" had spread to Phoenicia and Cyprus and produced "sixes" during the reign of Dionysius II of Syracuse (367–44 BCE) (Aelian *Var. Hist.* 6.12; Pliny *NH* 7.207). The fact that the Athenians resisted the trend until the 330s (when they built their first "fours" and, a few years later, their first "fives"), shows that "bigger" was not immediately recognized as "better" by everyone.[1] The same can be said for Alexander who left Europe for Asia in 334 with nothing larger than "threes" in his fleet. This changed during his siege of Tyre when we find him using the "fours" and "fives" of his Phoenician and Cypriot allies. Toward the end of his reign, shortly before 322, we learn he planned to build a new fleet station in Babylon and

---

1. For the dates when "fours" and "fives" first appear in the Athenian fleet, see Appendices A and B at "Historical Development."

construct ships larger than "fives," but these ideas were abandoned upon his death.[2]

When Antigonus and his son Demetrius set about acquiring naval dominance over their rivals, we notice a concerted effort on their part to build increasingly large warships. Demetrius used "sixes" and "sevens" to defeat Ptolemy off Cyprian Salamis in 306. Then, following his capture of Cyprus, he built an "eleven" from impressively long Cypriot timber (Theophr. *Hist. pl.* 5.8.1; Pliny *NH* 16.203) and a "thirteen," which he stationed at Piraeus before the Battle of Ipsus in 301 (Plut. *Demetr.* 31). By the time of his last campaign into Asia Minor, in 288, he had added a "fifteen" and "sixteen" to his collection (Plut. *Demetr.* 43.3–7; see chapter 3, pp. 123–24).

We might well ask what drove this rapid development of larger and larger warships. The theory that is currently favored explains the big ship phenomenon as an outgrowth of new tactics of galley warfare that were developed during the Hellenistic Age. As Lionel Casson explained it, "one feature above all others governs this stage of development: boarding now became an important naval tactic, and galleys more and more ceased to become man-propelled missiles to become carrying platforms for fighting men and—a new naval weapon—catapults."[3] In other words, sea battles between fleets with big ships began with volleys of catapult fire that were followed by close-in grappling and boarding, with the final victory going to the side possessing the best marines, that is, the ones with superior deck-fighting skills.[4]

Unfortunately, the few examples we have of big ships in action do not accord well with this theory. Consider, for example, the "ten" that fought in the battle off Chios between Philip V and Attalus of Pergamon in 201 BCE (Polyb. 16.3.3–6). This ship, which carried Philip's flag, attacked a *triemiolia* (a warship smaller than a "three") by ramming her amidships. The "ten's" prow got stuck beneath the enemy's lowest (thranite) bench of oars and the helmsman was unable to disengage. Thus immobilized, the "ten" was attacked by two "fives," one on each side, who eventually destroyed her and killed everyone aboard including Philip's admiral Democrates. In this sole example, we see the "ten's"

---

2. See chapter 3, p. 100.

3. Casson 1995, 103; for similar views, see also Meiggs (1982) 1998, 137; Morrison, Coates, and Rankov 2000, 48–49; and Basch 1987, 345.

4. See, for example, de Souza 2007, 359–360.

commander consciously choosing to ram his opponent rather than grapple and board her. Was this example an oddity, and thus recorded, or does it suggest that "tens" and other big ships were built for the force of their ramming blows?

In previous chapters I have tried to explain the popularity of big ships in terms of naval siege warfare, arguing that warships were built with heavy bows and strong rams to excel in frontal ramming, thereby facilitating the attack and defense of coastal cities. Let me, for a moment, play devil's advocate and frame the issue in terms of naval combat. Is it possible that big galleys were developed for combat in pitched naval battles? We have seen how catapults helped to define the naval siege unit as early as Alexander's siege of Tyre (332 BCE). We have also learned from Philo precisely how catapults and deck soldiers contributed to the power of the naval siege unit's attacks. Considering that sea battles drove the development of warships throughout the Archaic and Classical periods, is it not likely that catapults—both their invention and subsequent use with boarding parties of marines—drove the development of warships bigger than "threes," as Casson and others have suggested? I believe that the answer is "no," and the reasons why are instructive enough for a detailed examination of this theory in the chapter that follows.

Catapults

First, we must define the terminology that enables our discussion. From the perspective of the projectiles that are thrown, there are two basic types of catapult: one that projects arrows—the *katapeltes oxybeles* or "sharp shooter" and another that projects stones—the *katapeltes petrobolos* or *katapeltes lithobolos*.[5] The specific details of these weapons, their invention and subsequent evolution can be derived from a number of constructional handbooks and scientific treatises written at various times between the mid-third century BCE and the early second century CE. The evidence is thoroughly described in a well-known study by E. W. Marsden titled *Greek and Roman Artillery*.[6] Most of what I will say about catapults is based, at least in part, on this learned work.

---

5. The noun καταπέλτης (-αι), also spelled καταπάλτης (-αι), is sometimes present, sometimes not. I use the English term "stone projector" for both πετροβόλος and λιθοβόλος, and "bolt projector" for ὀξυβελής.

6. The work consists of two volumes: Marsden 1969 and Marsden 1971.

Catapults were invented during the first years of the fourth century and soon thereafter underwent a series of significant changes that primarily affected the mechanism propelling the projectile. At first, catapult designers employed larger than normal bows for this power, but eventually found—probably during the reign of Philip II (359–336)—that they could achieve more power with a torsion design for the propulsion system. By the time of the first siege of Tyre (332), we can delineate certain basic features in these torsion weapons that remained largely constant throughout the rest of the Hellenistic period. For example, the propulsive force was generated by a special "spring cord" made of sinew fibers wound tightly in two thick bundles or springs (*tonoi*) on either side of the spring frame (Fig. 5.1). Since the springs imparted the propulsive force to the arms and bow string of the weapon, an increase in size or weight to the projectile demanded a proportional increase to the diameter of each spring bundle. As a result, the wooden frame holding these bundles had to increase in size and weight as well, as did all the other parts of the weapon. Through a process of trial and error, the builders learned that each machine had a maximum performance level that was only achieved when it was made of perfectly balanced parts and shot a projectile of appropriate size and weight.

By the third century, the builders had worked out two design formulas, one for machines that shot stones and another for ones that shot arrows. Based on the length of the bolt or the weight of the stone, these formulas specified the diameter of the spring as well as the dimensions of each of the machine's constituent pieces. Because each machine shot a projectile that was matched to its size, we can calculate the dimensions and weights of weapons whose projectile characteristics are given by our sources (for example, a three-span *oxybeles*, or a ten-mina *lithobolos*). We can do the same for machines that shot projectiles found in the contexts of historical sieges.

Not surprisingly, bolt projectors and their ammunition were much smaller and lighter than were stone projectors and were thus easier to mount and use aboard a warship. Demetrius Poliorcetes preferred the three-span machine, which shot a bolt roughly 70 cm. in length, and weighed approximately 112 lbs (50.8 kg).[7] According to Diodorus (20.85.3), this weapon had the greatest range and, for this reason, Demetrius mounted

---

7. Marsden 1969, 171; in referring to "hundredweight," Marsden presumably refers to the British Imperial value of 50.8 kg. or 112 pounds.

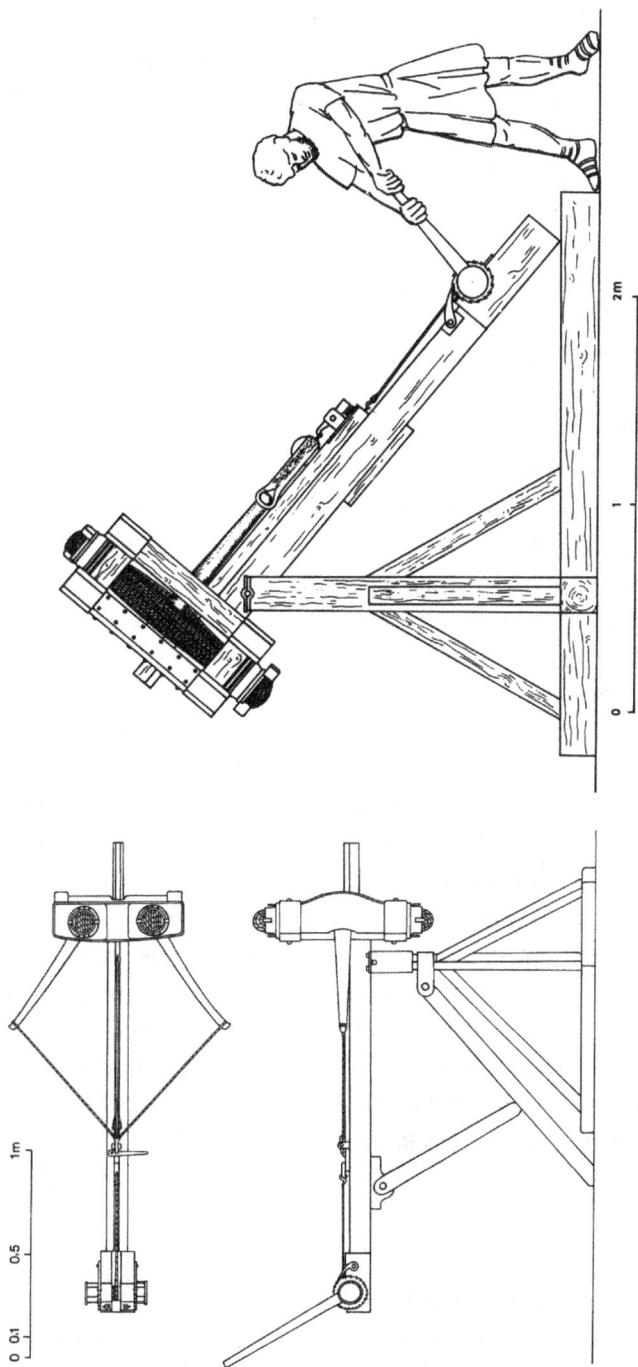

FIGURE 5.1 (Left): Torsion two-cubit *oxybeles* (as designed by Vitruvius), side and top views. (Right): Torsion 10 mina *lithobolos* from Hatra. Both left and right images presented at the same scale. Reconstructions by D. Baatz.

them on the bows of his warships to meet Ptolemy off Cyprian Salamis in 306. They are attested in at least three different naval battles: in the battle just referred to at Salamis, at Naulochus in 36, and at Actium in 31. Alexander placed such weapons in deck towers for his assault on Tyre in 332, and in 305 Demetrius put them aboard small craft for attacking workmen who were building fortifications in the harbor at Rhodes. At Naulochus, Agrippa used a heavier catapult to shoot a grappling hook fitted to the end of a five cubit (2.3 m.) wooden shaft, called a *harpax* or "grip," attached to a long rope. The device was shot onto an enemy warship and its trailing line hauled back aboard, hopefully dragging the struck ship alongside for boarding.[8]

Although stone projectors are specifically attested in only two naval battles during the Hellenistic period—at Cyprian Salamis in 306 and at Actium in 31—Marsden believed that they were regularly employed for naval combat "particularly when the opposing admirals decided mainly to adopt the tactic of laying their ships alongside enemy vessels and boarding them."[9] While Philo might not agree fully with such advice, we have seen how naval forces were frequently sent on missions to attack or defend coastal cities and, thus, it is likely that catapults were generally available for naval battles if the commanders chose to use them. Placing them aboard warships required some care, however, as revealed by the dimensions in Table 5.1. Torsion weapons were also susceptible to damage by water and required restringing in the field when this occurred, which was often impossible (Philo *Bel.* 17 [57.50–58.5] and 48 [72.13–25]). According to Philo (*Bel.* 17 [58.4–5]): "This happens not infrequently in land-campaigns, and is common in naval warfare." For these reasons, the Romans encased the springs of their bolt projectors in metal cylinders, while naval commanders kept their artillery safely stored away from their deck mounts until right before battle.[10] As a result, images showing catapults on warships are extremely rare. The first century BCE Praeneste relief probably depicts two bases for bolt projectors in a deck tower on the ship's bow (Fig. 5.2), but the catapults are not present. I know of only one clear depiction of catapults on a warship, and they appear on a Roman tombstone of first or second century

---

8. See Appendix F for specific references to the episodes described above.

9. Marsden 1969, 172, was following the long-established view of Tarn (1930) 1960, 145, that commanders of big ship fleets had to choose between ramming or boarding as their dominant tactic in battle.

10. Marsden 1969, 168 with n. 4.

Table 5.1 **Estimated Dimensions and Weights of Catapults.**

Catapult Size	Weight or Length of Projectile	Catapult Dimensions in m.			Catapult Weight (approx.) in kg.
		Length	Width	Height	
3-span *oxybeles*[1]	0.69 m. bolt	2.74	1.08	1.47	50.8 kg.
5-span (?) *oxybeles*[2]	1.23 m. bolt	3.7	1.9	–	–
5 mina *petrobolos*[3]	2.2 kg. stone	3.7	1.94	2.7	1820 kg. (?)
10 mina *petrobolos*[4]	4.4 kg. stone	6.4	3.2	–	–
20 mina *petrobolos*[5]	8.7 kg. stone	8.0	4.0	–	–
30 mina *petrobolos*[6]	13.1 kg. stone	9.2	4.6	–	–
1 talent *petrobolos* Garlan estimate[7]	26.2 kg. stone	7.75	5	6.35	–
1 talent *petrobolos* Nossov estimate[8]	26.2 kg. stone	11.5	5.8	–	–
1 talent *petrobolos* BBC Model[9]	26.2 kg. stone	7.5	8.5	–	12 tons

1. Marsden 1969, 171; Nossov 2005, 139.
2. The length of a bolt from a 5-span weapon should be 1.16 m. in length. Nossov 2005, 139 calculates the size of a slightly larger weapon based on the diameter of metal washers from a spring mechanism found in Epirus. I include it here for comparative purposes.
3. These calculations are based on Marsden 1969, 25, 34, 46–47 and Fig. 1.22, who gives the weight of a "small" petrobolos (5 mina?) as two tons, 171.
4. Nossov 2005, 139.
5. Nossov 2005, 140.
6. Nossov 2005, 140.
7. Garlan 1984, 358.
8. Nossov 2005, 140.
9. A 1 talent model was built in 2002 for a BBC production, titled "Building the Impossible— The Roman War Machine," by Carpenter Oak and Woodland (UK). The machine only shot twice; on the second occasion, the spring carrier cracked, showing that it was not made heavy enough. For details, see the following URL (http://www.carpenteroakandwoodland. com/portfolio/on-television/building-the-impossible—the-roman-war-machine).

CE date found near Mainz (Fig. 5.3).[11] In spite of the difficulties involved with their use at sea (or on other bodies of water), many ancient commanders must have taken the necessary precautions in order to increase their firepower.

---

11. See Bockius 2001 who interprets the weapons as two bolt projectors. Their scale seems rather large for bolt projectors and makes me wonder if the artist intended to depict small (one to two mina) stone projectors instead. Regardless of their type, the weapons are clearly catapults.

FIGURE 5.2 Depiction of a warship with deck tower and catapult bases (?) on a relief from Praeneste. Second half of first century BCE.

FIGURE 5.3 Roman tombstone from Mainz (district of Weisenau). Photo of a copy in the Museum für Antike Schiffahrt, Römisch-Germanisches Zentralmuseum, Mainz. First or second century CE.

Catapult Balls from the Battle of Actium?

A discovery made off western Greece in 1994 may allow us to gauge the size and weight of stone projectors used in the Battle of Actium (31 BCE). During the summers of 1993 and 1994, I codirected a team of Greek and American researchers searching for battle debris still lying on the sea floor at the entrance to the Ambracian Gulf near modern Preveza.[12] At a spot roughly 3.5 km. west of the Preveza Peninsula (Map 5.1), the team located a number of small ovoid stones reminiscent of catapult shot (Map 5.2). Unfortunately, when we returned to retrieve these stones in 1997, large areas of the sea floor had become obscured by sediments produced by a nearby construction project.[13] As a result, the divers sent to retrieve the stones were unable to locate them and we are thus forced to rely on the low-resolution images recorded in 1994.

Because the stones in the images looked like river cobbles, worn smooth by the action of running water, the scientists on our team declared them intrusive, that is, brought in through human agency.[14] Thinking that fishermen may have brought them from shore, we asked our captain, a local fisherman, to show photographs to his friends and colleagues. No one, man or woman, recognized the stones as having any use in modern fishing.[15] We next thought these stones might have come from sixteenth century cannons used in the skirmishes preceding a naval battle fought near Preveza in 1538 CE. But then we learned that stones shot

12. For a brief description of the Actium Project: French 1993–94, 40; Tomlinson 1994–95, 32; and Blackman 1997–98, 66–68. For the rams lost during the battle: Murray and Petsas 1989, 137–41; and Murray 2002a, 346–47.

13. In 1995, the Greek government commenced work on an underwater tunnel for cars and small trucks from the Preveza Peninsula to Cape Actium. Preformed sections of the tunnel were constructed on land and lowered into a trench excavated into the sea floor across the region of the Actium Straits. All the excavated sediment was placed on barges and then dumped into the sea outside the entrance to the Ambracian Gulf, whereupon currents spread the sediment northward over the battle zone. The tunnel opened in 2002.

14. Personal communications with Prof. Norman Blake, a marine biologist from the University of South Florida at St. Petersburg, Florida (August 1994) and with Dr. Vasilis Lykousis, a marine geologist and oceanographer from the National Center for Marine Research, Athens, Greece (March 26, 1996).

15. Personal communication with Mr. Spiros Boukouras and his wife (April 10, 1996). Mr. Boukouras has been actively fishing these waters for more than 50 years.

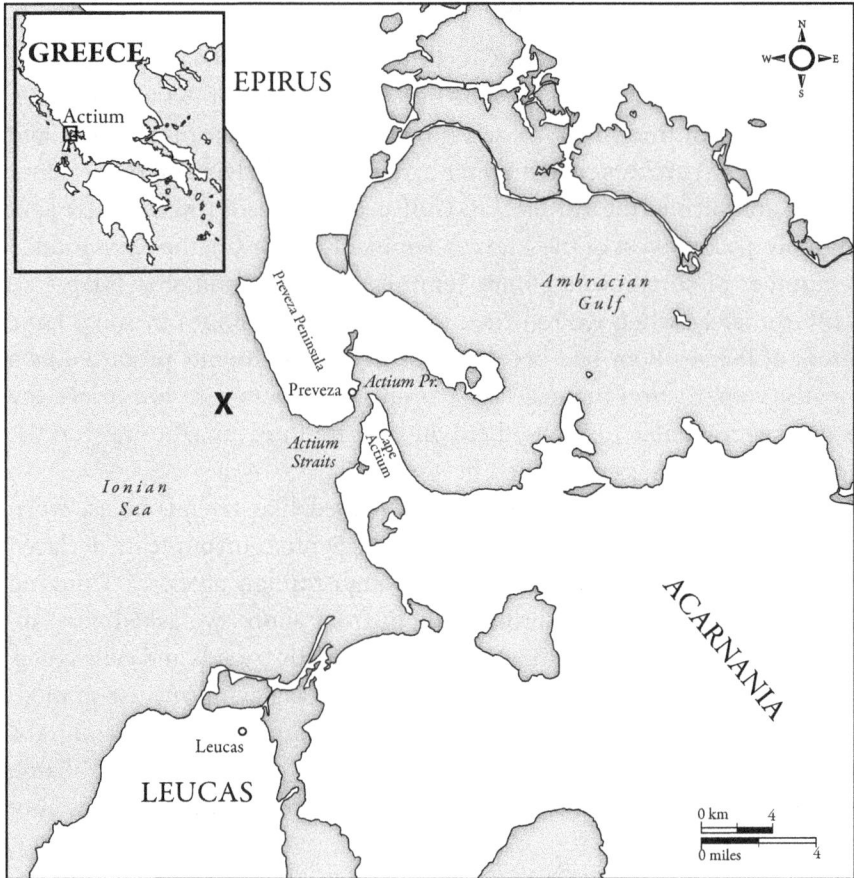

MAP 5.1 Location of Target 136.1.

from cannons must be spherical so these ovoid stones cannot derive from this battle.[16]

What about the Battle of Actium? The stones, measuring roughly 12 cm. in maximum diameter, are appropriate in size and shape for catapult shot and could provide tangible evidence for the use of small *petroboloi*

---

16. For the actions that occurred prior to the battle, the battle itself, and the locations of various military movements, see Guilmartin 1974, 42–56, and especially his Map 2, 49. Because stone shot had to be carefully cut into spheres to block the gasses propelling them through the cannon's barrel, they were more expensive to make than were iron shot and this eventually led to their abandonment; see Guilmartin 1974, 170 and 272.

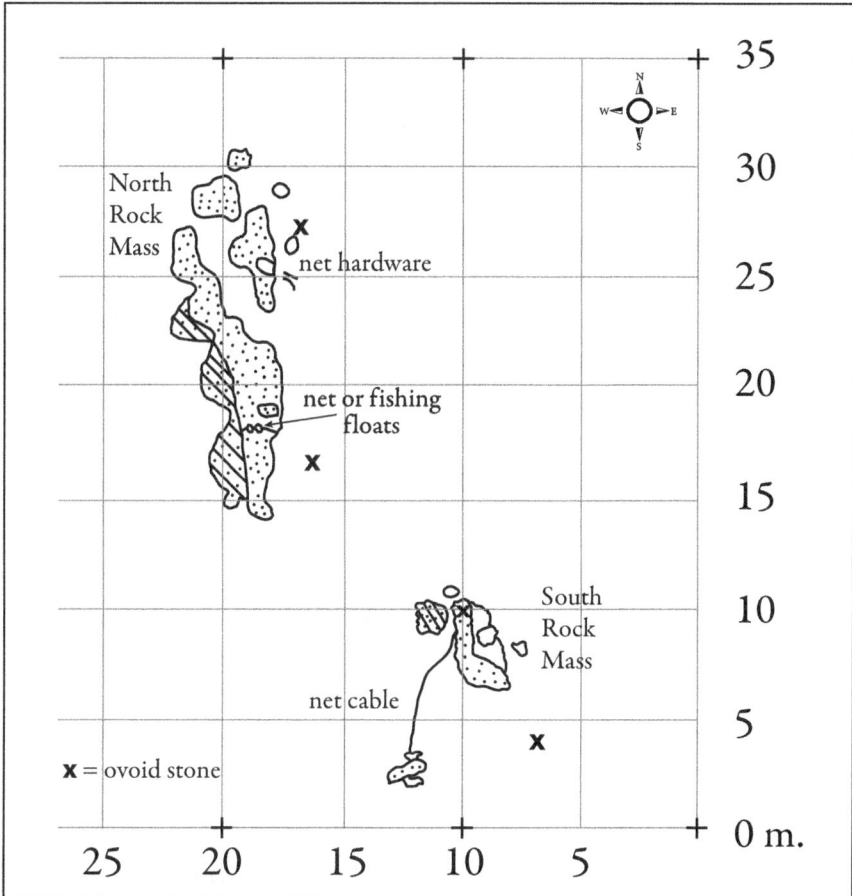

MAP 5.2 Target 136.1. Map adapted from Blackman 1997–98, 67, Fig. 101.

during the course of the battle. The stones' current location 3 km. offshore corresponds well with the position of Antony's right wing as described by Dio and Plutarch when the two battle lines finally engaged (Map 5.1). Indeed, Dio (50.32.4–5) implies that both sides employed *petroboloi* when he describes dense showers of arrows and stones and the use, by both sides, of "machines" to hurl pots full of charcoal and pitch (50.34.2). We might explain the "clean" appearance of the stones by the recent action of fishermen in the area. Our sonar revealed long parallel grooves in the bottom sediments adjacent to the mouth of the gulf that are clearly the result of drag nets pulled by trawlers. It is therefore possible that modern drag nets swept these stones from the sediment and left them exposed near the rocks on which they became entangled.[17]

Despite the inconclusive nature of the evidence, we can still explore the possibility that these stones represent small caliber projectiles and originate from the Battle of Actium. What we know about stone projectors of small caliber would seem to support such a hypothesis. For example, Philo (*Polior.* D 105) urged the use of both bolt and stone projectors as antipersonnel weapons in sea battles as well as in naval siege warfare. His advice to target the marines makes this quite clear. While he did not indicate the sizes involved for such attacks, there are ways to figure this out. We know, for example, that Demetrius mounted *both* three-span bolt projectors and *petroboloi* on the ships that fought Ptolemy off Salamis in 306 (Diod. 20.48.4). Since the three-span weapons were mounted at the bows, he must have placed the stone throwing artillery back from the bow, along the ship's center line. Their maximum size would have been determined by the classes of warships he used, the widths of their decks, and the carrying capacity of their hulls. While we lack these technical details, we are told by Diodorus that he possessed some 53 "heavier transports," which he describes elsewhere as "fives," "sixes," and "sevens." Surely these are the vessels on which his *petroboloi* were mounted.[18]

---

17. There is much net hardware lying next to and around the rocks where these ovoid stones were located. Mr. Boukouras (personal communication, April 10, 1996) claims that trawlers no longer operate in this area because they lost too many nets on multiple underwater obstructions. Considering the locations of the rocks we charted by sonar in 1993 and 1994 and the north-to-south orientation of their dragging operations, as evidenced by the sonar record, I believe it unlikely that trawlers dragged the stones very far before their nets became entangled. I therefore feel that the stones' current locations may still be significant. I have argued elsewhere (Murray 2002a, 348–52) that Antony would have placed his heaviest ships on the north end of his battle line and moved them northward in order to gain a favorable angle to the freshening sea breeze. In this way he stood the best chance of avoiding Leucas Island when his ships raised their sails and turned toward the southwest. Dr. Lykousis (personal communication, March 26, 1996) believes the natural rate of sedimentation in this area is very low—on the order of a centimeter or so per 1000 years. Both he and Dr. Blake (see n. 14) also believe it possible to account for the clean nature of the stones by shifting sediments moved by known bottom currents in the region (in October 1997, our divers reported a current on the bottom of roughly half a knot).

18. Diodorus's text is not internally consistent regarding the composition of this fleet. Despite these problems, we can see from Diod. 20.47.1 and 50.1–3 that the 53 heavier transports mentioned in the first passage must include the "fives," "sixes," and "sevens" mentioned in the second one; in like manner, the 110 swift "threes" of the first passage must include the 30 Athenian "fours" in the second one. See, further, chapter 3, n. 78.

Small Caliber Catapult Balls

Because of the ubiquitous presence of catapults, their projectiles are found in all sizes at countless sites throughout the Mediterranean basin. These stones, some marked with numerals indicating their weights in minae, allow us to judge the weight and shape of the stones in the battle zone off Actium.[19] For example, rather complete collections of catapult balls have been found both at Pergamon and at Rhodes where city arsenals preserved a large number of balls of all sizes (Fig. 5.4, C).[20] From these examples, we can see that stones from the smallest sizes were generally ovoid or irregular in shape like the Actium examples. Larger balls were made spherical to insure a similar trajectory to each shot, an important consideration when heavier projectiles were fired repeatedly from fixed positions against stationary targets like the parapets on city walls. Since the smallest sizes were shot at close range into masses of men, a similar trajectory for each shot was unimportant. This was especially true when artillery weapons were mounted on the decks of moving warships.

Other sites like Tell Dor (Hellenistic *Dora*) and Piraeus provide evidence for the local origin of some catapult balls thrown during historically attested sieges. As might be expected, attackers relied on a mix of imported (i.e., brought with them) and local stone for their catapult ammunition. At Dor, a petrographic analysis of 25 balls revealed three types of stone: basalt (an import), limestone (from the Mt. Carmel region, just to the east of Dor), and kurkar.[21] The kurkar, a calcareous sandstone formed along the coast, is of two types—one that is local, and another that occurs to the north of Haifa at a distance of roughly 70 km. The balls, therefore, reveal that the attacker came to Dor prepared with some ammunition, but augmented this supply with balls made from limestone and kurkar procured locally. At Piraeus, the local source of stone can be seen from inscribed letters remaining on the balls' surfaces. These make it clear that the attacker fashioned some of his projectiles from grave markers taken from tombs just outside the walls being attacked.[22]

---

19. See Marsden 1969, xix, for the various weight and length measurements and their equivalencies.

20. For Rhodes, see Laurenzi 1938–46; for Pergamon, see Von Szalay and Boehringer 1937.

21. Shatzman 1995, 63–64.

22. Small funerary columns with the appropriate diameters were cut into cylinders with heights that equaled their diameters. These cylinders were then rounded into spheres, thus preserving some of the inscribed letters on the column's surface; see Kyriacopoulos 1992, 219, Figs. 2–3.

This brings us back to the Actium stones, which resemble river cobbles. During the summer of 1997, I saw a small mountain of such stones that had been brought to Cape Actium for use in building the underwater tunnel across the Actium Straits (see n. 13). I was told by friends in Preveza that these stones were taken from the Evenus River in nearby Aetolia. Although I was unable to verify the precise origin of these stones, I have personally seen such cobbles in the bed of the Achelous River near Stratos and in dry stream beds called *remata* throughout the region. In other words, the forces of both Octavian and Antony could have procured their ammunition ready-made from the beds of nearby streams and rivers. Catapult balls clearly made from stones smoothed by water have been found by E. Serbeti in destruction levels at nearby Oiniadai, and she concludes that they came ready-made from the adjacent Achelous River (Fig. 5.4, D).[23] In light of this evidence plus the stones from Piraeus and from Dor, it seems quite possible, even likely, that both sides collected cobbles from nearby river beds to use as ammunition for their deck-mounted *petroboloi*.

Small Caliber Stone Projectors

Table 5.2 presents a few examples of catapult balls of a size and shape that are similar to the stones noted on the sea floor in the Actian battle zone. If we may judge from these examples, a weight between 5 and 7 minae would seem to be reasonable. Estimates for the dimension of the weapon that shot such a stone can be found in Table 5.1. According to one estimate, the 5 mina machine would have measured roughly 3.7 m. (length) by almost 2.0 m. (width) by 2.7 m. (height) and would have required a clear space of 5.05 m. by 2.50 m. to work effectively. More importantly, the weapon would have weighed around two tons (1820 kg).[24] In comparison, a heavy catapult was much larger in size, required much more space to work properly, and would have weighed far too much to be placed on a warship or freighter. For example, a 1 talent machine (i.e., a weapon that shot a ball weighing 1 talent = 60 minae or 26.2 kg.) would have measured

23. Serbeti 2001, 105; and Table 5.2 below.

24. Marsden 1969, 171, does not provide a direct weight calculation, but gives the weight of a "small" *petrobolos* (presumably he had this example in mind) as roughly two tons. For the origins of these calculations, see my Table 5.1.

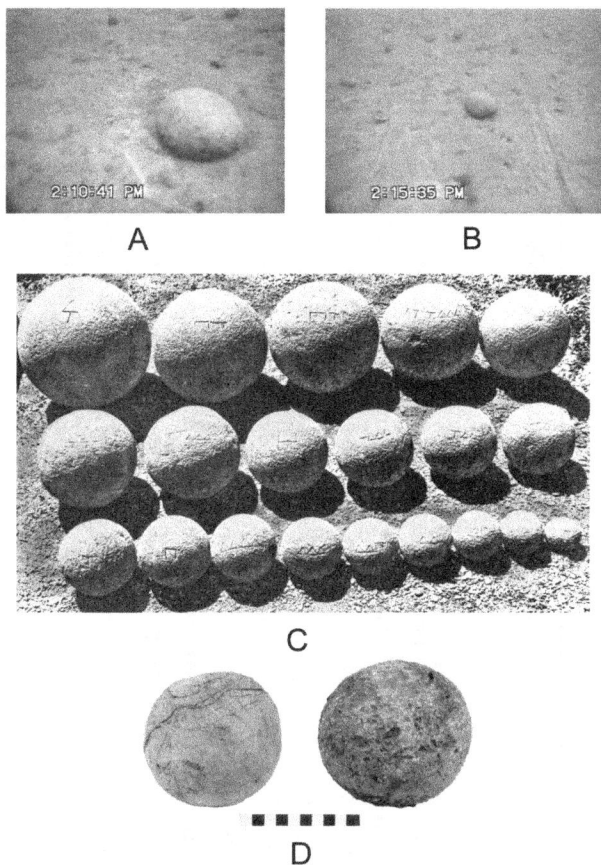

FIGURE 5.4 (A-B): Actian catapult ball (?); B shows impressions from lower skids of ROV. (C): Catapult balls from the arsenal at Rhodes. (D): Catapult balls Λ 20 and Λ 14 from Oiniadai.

roughly 7.75 m. (length) by 5.0 m. (width) by approximately 6.35 m (height) and weighed more than 12 tons.[25] This surely explains why Philo advised the placement of moderate sized weapons, like those shooting balls weighing 20 or 30 minae, in towers at harbor entrances (Philo *Polior.* C 56–57).

In comparison, the three-span *oxybeles* was much smaller and lighter than its stone-throwing relatives. Marsden built a three-quarter scale model of this weapon and reckoned that the full-scale version with iron

---

25. See Table. 5.1.

Table 5.2 Examples of Small Catapult Balls.

(D = diameter; max. = maximum; wt. = weight)

Site (findspot; date, if known)	Description of stones	Wt. in minae[1]
Dura Europa (found in mines of the siege ramp zone, south of tower 19; dated to siege of 256 CE).	The stones are approx. 6–8 cm. in diameter; the weights are not recorded in the published literature.[2]	1? 2?
Piraeus (found at 39 Gounaris Street in Piraeus; Hellenistic period; perhaps 86 BCE).	6 marble stones, some clearly cut from funerary columns, were found together in this location; Inv # 5762/6 is closest in shape and size to the Actian examples: max. D = 12.0 cm.; min. D = 10.0 cm.; wt. = 2.1 kg.[3]	4.8
Rhodes (found in Hellenistic arsenal).	The smallest has the following characteristics: ovoid; marked with the Greek letter "Pi" (indicating a weight of 5 minae); max. D = 12.0 cm.; wt. = 2.180 kg.[4]	5
Pergamon (found in Hellenistic arsenal).	The smallest example had the following characteristics: broken; D = less than 15 cm.; wt. = 2.8 kg. Perhaps originally 10 minae in weight (or less).[5]	6.41 (broken; originally 10?)
Numantia (found in various forts of Scipio's siege encampment; 133 BCE).	Among the stones, there were the following sizes: three 10 mina balls; one 5–6 mina (it is broken), two 3 mina; one 1 mina; and (perhaps) one 1/2 mina.[6]	10 5–6 3 1, 0.5?
Numantia (found inside the city).	The following sizes were reported among those found: one 3 mina (D = 10 cm.); three 2 mina (D = 7.5–8.7 cm.); five 1 mina (D = 6.0–7.0 cm.).[7]	3 2 1

Masada (found in locus 1039 in a room of the casemate wall on the NW periphery of the circuit. The deposit is dated to period of the final siege, 72–73 CE).[8]	"Hundreds of ballista stones, the size of oranges, were found on the floor of the room, partly in heaps, partly dispersed . . ."; one ball (locus 406) is similar to the Actian examples (wt. = 2.9 kg.; D = 12.2 cm. × 11.7 cm.).[9]	6.64
Oiniadai (found in the Agora; Hellenistic in date).	10 catapult balls were found ranging in weight from 2.5 to 6 kg.; the smallest of these examples (Λ20/89; max. D = 12 cm.; wt. = 2.5 kg.) compares favorably with the Actian stones.[10]	5.73 to 13.74
Tell Dor (found on the Tell; probably deriving from sieges of Antiochus III in 219 BCE, or Antiochus VII in 138/7 BCE, who attacked by land and sea.[11]	207 catapult balls (exclusive of fragmentary ones); stones are of varying sizes that divide into 14 groups. The smallest sizes (expressed in minae) are 3 (6 examples), 5 (18 examples), and 8 (11 examples). Some of the stones bear letters that clearly indicate their weight.[12]	3 5 8
Tell Dor (found in Tantura Lagoon, just to the south of the Tell; for date, same as above).	The weights of the 10 stones found in Tantura lagoon range from 1.5 to 16.8 kg.; three are close in size to the Actian examples: 75–677 (kurkar limestone; wt. = 1.5 kg., D = 11.0 × 10.0 cm.); 95–670 (basalt; wt. = 2.8 kg., D = 11.75 × 10.5 cm.); 95–669 (limestone; wt. = 3.5 kg., D = 11.5 × 14 cm.).[13]	3.44 to 38.48 3.44 6.4 8.01

(continued)

Table 5.2 Examples of Small Catapult Balls.

(D = diameter; max. = maximum; wt. = weight)

Carthage (approx. 2500 stones have been found in and around the war harbor and the arsenal in the destruction level of 146 BCE; in all, some 5600 stones have been found at Carthage in various locations).[14]	Approx. 700 stones from the Bardo museum range in weight from 2.5 kg. to 40.5 kg. The smallest examples for which measurements are given included 16 stones (2.75–3.5 kg.) with diameters ranging from 13.05 to 14 cm.[15]	6.3 to 8
Lambaesis (300 stones found in the camp of the Roman III Legion; 3rd century CE or later).[16]	136 stones remained in 1910 for study; they ranged in size from 7.3 cm. (0.45 kg.) to 15.3 cm. (4.5 kg.) in diameter. The following sizes are included: D=12.7 cm. (wt.= 2.0 kg.): 12 examples D=13.4 cm. (wt.=2.75 kg.): 8 examples D=13.7 cm. (wt.=3.154 kg.): 13 examples	4.6 6.3 7.3

1. According to Marsden 1969, xix, Greek artillerymen "probably used as their standard the Attic-Euboic mina which was equivalent to 436.6 grammes or to 0.96 lb. (British)...." This is the exactly the value indicated on the Rhodian example appearing in the table that is marked with the numeral for 5. Since peoples in different geographical locations probably employed different standards for the mina, these values are only approximations for the purpose of comparison.

2. Garlan 1974, 397–98, note at 3i:c, and du Buisson 1944: 44.

3. Kyriacopoulos 1992, Fig.8, p. 224, A 26. These balls are currently in the Piraeus Archaeological Museum, where I saw them in March, 1996, thanks to the courtesy of G. Steinhauer.

4. The ball is currently in the Rhodes Archaeological Museum; see Laurenzi 1938–46, 33, #1 in the table; the ball is also shown as the smallest example in Tav. XXVIII.

5. Von Szalay 1937, 52; the stone appears as #9 in the table, 50.

6. Schulten 1927, Tafel 53 with p, 264; see also Schulten 1933, 125–26. Schulten remarks (1933, 125) that the 1–2 mina stones would have been shot, like the arrows, in a more horizontal trajectory against "small targets" as compared to the larger calibers, which would have been shot more in an arc and used against "large targets" like masses of men or fortification walls.

7. See Schulten 1927, 265.

8. The western (exterior) wall of the room had completely disintegrated, and other objects had clearly fallen into the room from a tower which adjoined it to the south. Whether the balls came from this tower, or were thrown into the city is unclear; Holley 1994, 360–62 and 365.

9. For the quote, see Yadin 1965, 80 with plate 15B; the ballista balls are analyzed by Holley 1994, 353–65, who presents a listing of stones and their findspots, 365. Balls range in size from 0.6 kg. (D = 6.7 cm.×6.3 cm.) to 22 kg. (D = 25 cm.); Holley 1994, Appendix B, p. 364.

10. The catapult stones ranged in size from 11 to 17.5 cm. in maximum diameter (2.5–6 kg.). A20/89 was found in the destruction level of a structure situated between the Bouleuterion and a series of store rooms or shops in the Agora; the function of the structure was not identified. See Serbeti 2001, 105–106 and 152–56 with pl. 18.

11. For the first siege, see Polyb. 5.62–69; for the second, see 1 Macc. 15.10–14, 25, 37; Jos. *AJ* 13.223–24; Charax in *Steph. Byz. s.v. Dōros = FGrH* 103F 29; and App. *Syr.* 68.

12. Cf. Stern 1994, 208–11; Shatzman 1995.

13. The stones were originally found by Kurt Raveh and Shelley Wachsmann. I wish to thank Dr. Israel Shatzman for alerting me to the number of stones found in the lagoon and Ms. Bracha Zilberstein, the conservator at the Kibbutz Nahsholim Museum, where the balls were displayed when I saw them in June 1997. The weights and types of stone were recorded in the records of the museum.

14. Rathgen 1909–11, 235–41.

15. Rathgen, 1909–11, 238–39 with table on p. 240.

16. Rathgen, 1909–11, 241–44. esp. p. 242.

plating would have weighed roughly 50 kg. with the following dimensions: 2.74 m. (length) by 1.08 m. (width) by 1.47 m. (height).[26] From these calculations, he estimated that a Roman qinquereme or "five" might have carried "ten three-span arrow-firers (10 cwt.), two comparatively small stone-throwers weighing 2 tons apiece (4 tons), expert artillerymen and ammunition (1½ tons), and still be able to carry forty marines (3 tons)."[27] Bigger warships could have carried even more.

Catapults, Big Ships, and Boarding

Most naval historians think that the development of catapults and big ships was closely related and that the adoption of naval catapults drove the development of larger and larger warships. For example, W. L. Rodgers wrote that Dionysius had "little use in building large ships" unless his "new artillery was installed on their upper decks."[28] The theory has been accepted for years, despite the fact that Dionysius used relatively small artillery, which he positioned on his siege mole, not his ships, when besieging the offshore island of Motya in 397 (Diod. 14.51.1).[29] Regardless of these nagging details, most liked the theory because the wide decks of bigger and bigger warships made perfect sense as platforms for bigger and bigger catapults. The theory also fit with scholars' notions about the scarcity of skilled oarcrews during the fourth and third centuries BCE when multiple-man sweeps required only one skilled man per oar.[30] Bigger ships, larger catapults, and a lack of skilled oarsmen forced naval commanders to rely increasingly on boarding over ramming when warships grew significantly larger than "threes."[31]

According to Vernard Foley and Werner Soedel, catapults actually countered the effectiveness of ram strikes by shooting heavy bolts through

---

26. The dimensions have been calculated from the design formula diagram presented by Marsden 1969, 25, 171, and Fig. 1.21 (facing 42).

27. Marsden 1969, 171; for the term "cwt.," i.e., hundredweight, see n. 7.

28. Rodgers (1937) 1964, 197.

29. For the "belly bow" or *gastraphetes* from the time of Dionysius and its use at Motya: Marsden 1969, 5–12, and 54–56; for the continuing belief that they were stationed aboard Dionysius's ships: Meijer 1986, 121.

30. The idea that multiple-man sweeps eased the labor problem of securing trained oar crews is most fully explained by Casson 1991, 112 and 130.

31. See, for example, Marsden 1969, 173; Meijer 1986, 133–34; Basch 1987, 345; and Morrison, Coates, and Rankov 2000, 48–49, who all come to similar conclusions.

the enemies' decks to disrupt the oarcrews.[32] With tactics like these, "catapults were able to neutralize at least part of the threat presented by rams and bring boarding tactics back into favor."[33] The theory sounded reasonable and gained immediate acceptance by most scholars.[34] As a result, when J. F. Coates theorized how midsized polyremes would have been designed, he cites these deck-penetrating bolts as a design consideration. In general, he observed: "Surviving accounts suggest that polyremes larger than sevens were built in relatively small numbers, and were probably attempts to create a ship invulnerable to ramming, difficult to capture by boarding, and at the same time carrying a powerful armament of catapults and troops so able to grapple and overwhelm any lesser type by boarding."[35] He concluded that such ships would have had no "tactical need" for attaining speeds higher than 4–5 kt. Those bold enough to offer an opinion suggested that combat between the biggest warships involved fights between "floating fortresses" where super-galleys, like Ptolemy's "forty," would "plow into clusters of smaller craft with its catapults volleying stones and darts, its archers firing arrows, and boarding parties readying at given points to hurl grapnels and eventually leap."[36]

Summary

Considering the conflicting views expressed above, a summary now seems desirable. The first warships larger than "threes" were developed for their frontal ramming capabilities. In order to achieve greater weight and heavier ramming blows, the designers of these ships sacrificed a degree of speed and maneuverability when their new designs were compared to "threes."[37] Literary allusions to the performance characteristics of

---

32. See Foley and Soedel 1981, 160–62, esp. 161.

33. Foley and Soedel 1981, 162.

34. Meijer 1986, 133–34, argues that the presence of Demetrius's "sixes" and "sevens" at Salamis in 306 reveals his reliance on boarding tactics. Diodorus (20.51–52), our best source for the battle, makes no such observation, however. Indeed, he lists Ptolemy's losses as 80 ships "destroyed" and 40 ships "captured" (Diod. 20.52.6), implying that ram strikes disabled more than twice as many ships as were captured by boarding.

35. Coates in Morrison and Coates 1996, 309; Coates cites the views of Foley and Soedel, 310.

36. "Floating fortresses": Garlan 1984, 361; "plow into clusters . . .": Casson 1995, 110.

37. By "maneuverability," I mean the speed with which the vessel responds to the helm, how many boat lengths it takes to execute a 360° turn, how quickly the vessel accelerates,

"threes," "fours," and "fives," reveal that the best "threes" were generally faster and more maneuverable than were the best "fours" and "fives." What the larger vessels gave up in speed and maneuverability to their smaller relatives the designers tried to offset with an increased space for deck troops, who were charged with targeting enemy marines and protecting their vessels from boarding attempts. Such attempts generally followed ram strikes when two ships became entangled, or when the attacker's ram stuck fast and did not allow it to back away from the struck ship (for examples: Polyb. 16.3.8–11, the battle off Chios in 201; and Livy 37.30, the battle off Myonnesus in 190).

Alexander demonstrated the effectiveness of naval catapults when he reduced Tyre in 332. Following his death, generals like Demetrius utilized both three-span bolt projectors and small *petroboloi* in naval battles as well as naval sieges. The three-span weapons weighed roughly 50 kg. and were small and light enough to be mounted on most warships at the bow. Diodorus (17.45.2) informs us that Alexander placed such weapons in deck towers at Tyre, presumably on his larger "fours" or "fives." Warships as small as *lemboi* could be fitted with special platforms to carry small *petroboloi*, but in general, their great weight and large size demanded their placement on vessels larger than "threes" and "fours." Marsden calculated that a "five" might have carried ten three-spans and a pair of small *petroboloi* by reducing the marine contingent by roughly 40 men. There is no clear evidence to suggest that catapults drove the development of warship design, no ancient author who implies their use to negate the role of ramming attacks, and finally, no evidence to suggest that catapult crews ever purposefully shot bolts through the decks of warships to disrupt the oar-crews. Philo, who describes in detail how naval catapults were used for attack and defense, would surely have described such tactics had they existed in practice.

An Alternate Theory

While there is no direct evidence for the precise size limitations placed on naval artillery, it seems logical to assume that the same warship might

---

comes to a stop, backs water, etc. Sea handling qualities were a different matter. There is some evidence that heavier "fives" were able to weather choppy seas and stormy weather better than "threes" and "fours." See Appendix B.

Table 5.3 Attested Sizes of Catapults in Philo's Text.

Size in minae	Particulars of Use	Intended Purpose	Philo *Polior.*
2	In mines dug under the city wall, 2 mina *petroboloi* are used.	antipersonnel	D 31
10	For the defense of a city, the community should provide at public expense one 10 mina *lithobolos* and two 3-span catapults for each parallel street.	antipersonnel	C 26
10	Two 10 mina *lithoboloi* should be stationed against enemy *petroboloi* aimed at the city wall in order to attack them.	antiweapon and antipersonnel	C 6
10	When attacking a city wall with your mobile towers, place two 10 mina machines and one 5-span *oxybeles* opposite each of their *lithoboloi*.	antiweapon and antipersonnel	D 17
20–30	At the mouths of harbors, station 20 and 30 mina *petroboloi* for the purposes of attacking ships attempting to force an entry.	antiweapon and antipersonnel	C 56–57, 67

Table 5.4 Known Warship Casualty Figures Sustained by Defeated Forces in Naval Battles from 306 to 31 BCE.

BATTLE	DATE	CASUALITIES (Warships)
Salamis (Cyprus)	306	Losses = 85.7% of total fleet; 77% by ramming; 33% by boarding. Ptolemy lost 120 warships out of a total force of 140 (40 with crews by capture, 80 by ramming). Those destroyed by ramming were eventually towed, full of sea water, to Demetrius's camp before the city of Salamis.[1]
Mylae (Sicily)	260	Losses = 33.8% of total fleet; 30% by ramming; 70% by boarding. The Carthaginians lost 44 warships out of a total of 130 (31 by capture, 13 by ramming).[2]
Ecnomus (Sicily)	256	Losses = 26.9% of total fleet; 32% by ramming; 68% by boarding. The Carthaginians lost more than 94 warships out of a total force of 350 (64 by capture, and more than 30 by ramming).[3]
Chios	201	Losses = 50.7% of total fleet; 90% by ramming; 10% by boarding. Philip V lost 103 warships out of a total force of 203 (10 by capture, 93 by ramming).[4]
Myonnesus (Ionia)	190	Losses = 47.2% of total fleet; 69% by ramming; 31% by boarding. Antiochus III lost 42 warships out of a total force of 89 (29 by ramming and by fire, 13 by capture).[5]
Mylae (Sicily)	36	Losses = 19.4% of total fleet. Sextus Pompey lost 30 out of a total force of 155.[6]
Naulochus (Sicily)	36	Losses = 94.3% of total fleet; 10% by ramming; ? % by boarding. Sextus Pompey lost 283 warships out of a total force of approx. 300 (28 by ramming and 255 by capture and by fire).[7]
Actium	31	Losses = 60.9% of total fleet; ? % by ramming; ? % by boarding. Antony lost approx. 140 warships out of a total force of 230 (approx. 80 by ramming and/or capture, and approx. 60 by fire).[8]

1. Diod. 20.49.2 (fleet size); 20.52.6 (casualty totals).
2. Polyb. 1.23;3 (fleet size); *CIL* VI 31611 = *ILS* 65 (casualty totals; cf. Polyb. 1.23,10 who records the total of lost ships as 50).
3. Polyb. 1.25-9 (fleet size); 1.28.12, 14 (casualty totals).
4. Philip's force consisted of 53 cataphracts, an unknown number of open galleys like *triemioliai*, and 150 small open galleys called *lemboi* and *pristeis* (Polyb. 16.2.9). Of the 50 warships disabled by the Rhodians, 40 were *lemboi* (Polyb. 16.7.2). We must add to the totals given by Polybius at the end of his account (16.7,1–3) one "eight" that was destroyed (16.3,2), and another that was captured (16.3,8-11) during the battle.
5. Livy 37.30.1–2 (fleet size); 37.30.7–8 (casualty totals).
6. App. *BC* 5.105 (fleet size); 5.108 (casualty total).
7. App. *BC* 5.118 (fleet size); 5.121 (casualty totals).
8. Various numbers are preserved by Florus (2.21.5), Orosius (6.19.9, 11) and Plutarch (*Ant.* 61.1); see Murray 1989, 133–34, and Murray 2002a, 346 with n.

28

carry larger caliber weapons for siege warfare than for combat at sea. Table 5.3 presents the few indicators Philo provides in the text of his *Poliorketika* regarding the use of various sized weapons. From this evidence, it seems that machines of calibers up to ten mina in size were employed against human targets, while machines of ten mina and larger targeted structures built of wood and stone. Since the ten-mina caliber targeted *both* men and machines, we might consider this to have been the maximum caliber used aboard warships because of their effectiveness against men, catapults, deck towers, and siege machinery.

If the enemy possessed far superior seamanship skills, as did the Carthaginians at the outbreak of the First Punic War, it seems that Roman commanders considered boarding without ramming to be a useful tactic. Surely W. W. Tarn goes too far, however, when he states that commanders had to choose whether to ram or board as their dominant tactic.[38] Such a view is much too simplistic. The same can be said for his generalized view that Romans and Macedonians picked boarding over ramming as their primary tactic. More than 50 years ago, H. T. Wallinga demonstrated that Tarn's conclusions were based on "an over-simplified view of the tactics of an ancient sea-battle, and on the mistaken idea that in such a battle boarding was so easy, that any new-made naval power could gain victories merely by adopting it."[39] Boarding an enemy was not only difficult, it offered unexpected variables that many commanders tried to avoid if they could. As Diodorus (20.51.5) noted in reference to the battle off Cyprian Salamis in 306, "in naval battles there are many different reasons by which those who should rightly gain victory are unexpectedly defeated."

While it is true that many accounts stress the Roman preference for boarding, we should recognize the skewed nature of our sources. Accounts of individual engagements (see Table 5.4) make it quite clear that marines, and particularly the officers, provided the details that make up our battle accounts. For this reason, naval battles are frequently defined by the exploits of various individuals who participated in deck fighting. At Chios, for example, we learn the exploits of Attalus, Deinocrates, Dionysodorus, Autolycus, Theophiliscus, and Philostratus—all involved in deck fighting. And yet, when we read that the marines on a particular vessel were killed, we rarely learn the fate of the oarcrews. Neither these men

---

38. Tarn 1930, 245.

39. Wallinga 1956, 28–29.

nor their relatives came from a class who mattered to the historians re-
cording these events and so, their accomplishments and their fates were
routinely ignored. The effect of this methodological approach by those
who chronicled these events leaves us with the impression that many conflicts were resolved by the marines in deck fighting. For some battles, the
raw casualty totals tell a different story, as Livy's account of the battle off
Myonnesus makes clear. After reporting 29 ships destroyed by ramming
and 13 by capture, the historian concluded (Livy 37.30.6), "as usual, the
valor of the marines had the greatest effect in the battle." Based on raw
numbers, this simply cannot be true.

Wallinga also found fault with Tarn's notion that fleet commanders
purposefully chose whether to make boarding or ramming their dominant tactic and demonstrated how many Hellenistic naval battles followed
a complex trajectory that might involve both ramming and boarding.[40] As
Wallinga saw it, most battles exhibited different phases during which the
combat varied depending on the strength and endurance of the oarcrews.

> . . . [D]uring the first phase the mode of fighting was dictated by the
> side which had the faster ships and the attacks on the ships them-
> selves prevailed; the second phase brought to the fore the marines,
> who continued the attack with missiles, which had started already
> in the first phase but gave better chances now that the ships had
> lost some of their initial speed . . . ; in the third phase the speed of
> the ships had diminished so much that it became possible to
> grapple and board, boarding having been possible during the sec-
> ond phase only in the exceptional case that a ram stuck.[41]

Wallinga's three-phase scheme better accounts for the complexity of naval
combat, especially when fleets contained ships of varying sizes and performance characteristics. Even so, no rigid scheme can possibly cover the
infinite variations of battle as the sea fights off Naulochus and Actium
show. In both cases hostilities concluded with the victors burning the fleet
of the vanquished, implying that some commanders destroyed their enemies from a distance with volleys of missiles and incendiary projectiles,
rather than close-in boarding. In such cases, boarding, when and where it

---

40. Wallinga 1956, 29–50.

41. Wallinga 1956, 49–50.

occurred, may have consisted of little more than crossing to defenseless, empty, or burned out hulls to place them under tow for salvage.

Conclusion

Despite popular theories to the contrary, it seems that a desire for dominance in naval siege warfare, and especially for dominance in frontal ramming, provided the fuel that touched off the naval arms race during the reign of Demetrius Poliorcetes. This said, no one can doubt the critical importance of catapults. They were essential to the success of naval siege warfare and served as effective antipersonnel weapons in naval battles. Their importance in driving the development of larger classes is undeniable. These catapults, however, were not employed because the ships that carried them were incapable of ramming. We have seen from Philip's "ten" at Chios that its commander expected to attack his opponents with ramming strikes. But as the battle wore on, when the oarcrews tired and the ships became packed close together, success and safety often depended upon the excellence of one's marines in repelling boarding parties from damaged ships. As long as was prudent, however, the marines on undamaged ships heeded Philo's advice: they relied on their ships' rams and resisted boarding the enemy. What then do we make of the galleys that were even larger than Demetrius's "sixteen"—galleys that have been convincingly described as giant two-hulled catamarans by Casson? How else could such galleys function if not to "plow into clusters of smaller craft" with catapults volleying stones and darts, archers firing arrows, and boarding parties readying to hurl grapnels and leap?[42] These are good questions that demand serious answers and thus form the subject of the next chapter.

---

42. Casson 1995, 110.

6

The Culmination of the Big Ship Phenomenon

MOST AGREE THAT Demetrius Poliorcetes, more than any of Alexander's successors, drove the development of the big ship phenomenon. Following his defeat of Ptolemy off Cyprus in 306, no one dared to challenge him at sea. Thereafter, his success in waging sieges on coastal cities spurred his rivals to experiment with a small number of extraordinary warships that some modern scholars have dubbed "super-galleys." Although these vessels reached an impressive level of size and decoration in Ptolemy IV's "forty," they were not the ultimate expression of the big ship phenomenon as most believe. This is because big ships were a fleet phenomenon, and were never intended to function as individuals. The true culmination of the big ship phenomenon occurred during the reign of Ptolemy II Philadelphus (282–246) and his successor Ptolemy III Euergetes (246–222), when they amassed the largest fleet of big ships ever built. This chapter will attempt to answer the obvious question "Why?" We must start, however, with the first of these new super galleys—an "eight" of extraordinary size and beauty called *Leontophoros* or "Lion Bearer."

Leontophoros

Antigonus, the son of Demetrius, having learned what had happened [i.e., the death of Seleucus and Ptolemy Ceraunus's seizure of his kingdom], undertook to cross over to Macedonia with a land and naval force, hurrying to anticipate Ptolemy. And Ptolemy, having the ships of Lysimachus, departed and arrayed himself in opposition. Among his fleet there were others, but also the ones sent from Herakleia: "sixes" and "fives" and open galleys (*aphraktoi*), and one "eight" called *Leontophoros* which was considered a marvel on account of its size and beauty. For in it, 100 men rowed each file, so that there were 800 in each part and 1600 from both sides. Those fighting from the upper decks numbered 1200, and there were two helmsmen. When the battle occurred, Ptolemy prevailed, routing the naval force of Antigonus, with the ships from Herakleia fighting most bravely of all. And of those from Herakleia, the *Leontophoros* "eight" carried the select contingent. Having fared so poorly, Antigonus withdrew to Boeotia. And Ptolemy advanced into Macedonia and held the throne securely.

—MEMNON IN PHOT. *BIBL.* 224.226B 14–33[1]

We learn of this warship from a synopsis made by Photius, a ninth century Patriarch of Constantinople, of a book containing the local history of Herakleia, a city on the south shore of the Black Sea. A Herakleiote named Memnon wrote the history during the first or second century CE and imbued his text with the pride he felt for his city's past achievements.[2] According to this text, a son of Ptolemy I surnamed Ceraunus declared himself king and used the vessel, normally stationed at Herakleia on the south shore of the Black Sea, to gain control of Macedonia in the autumn of 281.[3] No details of the fighting are given, but according to Memnon, the vessel's size and beauty were remarkable and she carried "the select contingent" (*to exaireton*) of Herakleian fighters in a victorious battle fought with Antigonus Gonatas, son and successor of Demetrius Poliorcetes. Memnon's description of the ship is odd and displays the unhappy effects of abbreviation. As a result, the text has resulted in two different interpretations. The ship, according to the text of Photius, was powered by 100 men per file (*stoichos*), "so that there were 800 in each part and 1600 counting from both sides."[4] Additionally, we read there were 1200 deck soldiers, and two helmsmen.

In an article written more than 40 years ago, Lionel Casson suggested that Memnon was describing a catamaran with two separate hulls spanned by a wide fighting deck, nicely explaining the reference to a two-part hull, the two helmsmen, and the large number of oarsmen and deck fighters.[5]

---

1. Phot. *Bibl.* 224.226b 14–33 = *FGrH* 434, F1 8.4–6 = *TLG*, Memnon Frag. 13.1–20.

2. Photius presented a synopsis of books 9–16 of Memnon's work in his *Bibliotheca* or *Myriobiblion*. See *FGrH*, Dritter Teil, Kommentar, 24. Herakleia am Pontos, pp. 267–68; and Dueck 2006, 44.

3. For the date and circumstances of this event, see Walbank 1988, 242–45.

4. Phot. *Bibl.* 226b 22–24 = *FGrH* 434, F1 8.5 = *TLG*, Memnon Frag. 13.9–12: . . . ἐν ταύτῃ γὰρ ρ [= 100] μὲν ἄνδρες ἕκαστον στοῖχον ἤρεττον, ὡς ω [= 800] ἐκ θατέρου μέρους γενέσθαι, ἐξ ἑκατέρων δὲ χιλίους καὶ χ [= 600]·

5. Casson 1969, 191; and more recently Casson 1995, 112. Throughout this chapter I will use the term "double-hull" or "multi-hull" instead of catamaran, which carries a connotation of two separate hulls, spaced apart from one another. Because I remain uncertain whether the ancient multi-hull warships had two separate hulls, spanned by a deck (like a modern catamaran sailboat), or two hulls positioned side-by-side without a space in between, I utilize these terms to retain this ambiguity.

A problem remains, however, because the Greek text clearly says that 100 men rowed in each *stoichos*, a term known from military writers to mean a file or column of men, and presumably, in this case, a fore-to-aft line of rowers. Adhering to this sense of *stoichos*, J. S. Morrison suggested in 1980 that the rowers must have sat in long files down the sides of the vessel, with eight files per lateral half of a single hull. He argued that the ship must have been extremely long and narrow to accommodate the oarsmen, perhaps 110 meters in overall length and almost 10 meters wide. Such a long vessel would have been difficult to turn, and this explains, to Morrison's way of thinking, the need for two helmsmen to maneuver the large steering oars.[6]

The problem with this view involves the vessel's length, which would be "substantially longer . . . than the longest wooden line-of-battle ship ever built in the 19th century!"[7] When ships become too long, their hulls cannot withstand the differential pressures caused by surface waves along their lengths. Based on what we know from other periods of history, a seagoing ship built entirely of wood might safely be 70–75 meters in length, but when the hull got longer than this, naval architects employed metal bracing, like iron or steel girders inside the hull.[8] When faced with Morrison's suggested design, J. F. Coates observed: "It would . . . be surprising if [ships like *Leontophoros*] did not in fact suffer from severe structural weaknesses of one kind or another. . . ."[9]

The problem facing us can be summed up as follows. Do we have in this vessel the first of the large double-hull warships, known to have existed in the later fleet of Ptolemy II—vessels that Casson describes as giant battle ships, forcing their way into clusters of smaller ships, to bombard, grapple, and smother their enemies with boarding parties? Or, do we have a dangerously long, single-hull galley designed to ram and board its opponents, as Morrison argues? While naval historians might disagree over which of the theories they prefer, most would agree that *Leontophoros* was built to defeat Demetrius's largest ship—perhaps a "thirteen" or even a "sixteen"—in a pitched sea battle.[10] But is this reasonable? We have learned

---

6. Morrison 1980, 46, and Morrison and Coates 1996, 272–73.

7. J. F. Coates in Morrison and Coates 1996, 311.

8. Sleeswyk and Meijer 1994, 115.

9. J. F. Coates in Morrison and Coates 1996, 311.

10. See, for example, Casson 1995, 138–39; Meijer 1986, 136–39; and Anderson 1976, 28.

that most big ships were designed with frontal ramming and harbor fighting in mind and, if this is true, then Lysimachus probably built his "eight" to facilitate an attack on harbor defenses, not to face other ships in pitched naval battles. The same conclusion emerges from the historical context that produced this extraordinary "eight."

Scholars have long felt that Lysimachus was motivated to build his *Leontophoros* "eight" following a confrontation with Demetrius on the Cilician coast of Asia Minor. The details are preserved by Plutarch (*Demetr.* 20.7–8):

> His enemies would stand on the shore and admire his "fifteens" and "sixteens" sailing past them, and his *helepoleis* [mobile siege towers] were a spectacle to those he was besieging as the following demonstrates. For Lysimachus, although he was the bitterest enemy Demetrius had among the kings, and had drawn up his forces against him when Demetrius was besieging Soloi in Cilicia, sent and asked Demetrius to show him his engines of war, and his ships in full parade; and when Demetrius had shown them, Lysimachus went away in amazement.

Curiously, the story has led to a misconception that Lysimachus asked permission to inspect Demetrius's fleet, and that Demetrius reluctantly agreed. After inspecting his largest ship, so the story goes, Lysimachus departed in amazement and thereafter built his *Leontophoros* as an answer to what he had seen.[11] Actually, Plutarch says nothing of the sort. This event involved no chivalrous (if reluctant) offer of a guided tour, but rather an in-your-face demonstration of superior naval power. The episode in question probably occurred in 298, just after Demetrius had married his daughter to Seleucus and held a banquet on the deck of his "thirteen"; I have argued in chapter 3 that Demetrius presumably had this "thirteen" with him for the siege of Soloi.

From Plutarch's account, we can see that Lysimachus had approached Soloi with a relief force in hopes of raising the siege. He apparently sent a message to Demetrius, demanding that he depart and, in response, Demetrius held some sort of naval review in front of Lysimachus to demonstrate

---

11. The idea seems to have originated with Tarn 1910, 211; and can be seen more recently in Casson 1995, 138; and Meijer 1986, 136–37.

his superiority. In the face of such naval power, Lysimachus prudently withdrew.[12] I suggest that soon thereafter, Lysimachus addressed his impotence by strengthening his naval siege unit in order to dislodge Demetrius's harbor garrisons. His largest vessel, therefore, was built to breach harbor barriers and not to duel with Demetrius's "thirteen." Indeed, what little we know about these years suggests that Lysimachus considered the recovery of Greek cities in Ionia to be a high priority objective.[13] A few years later (in summer 294), while Demetrius was engaged in Greece, we learn from Plutarch (*Demetr.* 35.5) that Lysimachus had recaptured the cities he coveted.[14] Although no details survive beyond this brief remark of Plutarch, I suspect *Leontophoros* contributed to Lysimachus's success and, thereafter, served as a deterrent to those who might defect from his side. We are not told where the vessel was built, but if it was Herakleia, where she appears in 281, then Lysimachus could have initiated the construction at any time after his marriage to the city's queen Amastris in 302 BCE.[15]

The occasion most scholars accept as the reason for the construction of *Leontophoros* was Demetrius's planned invasion of Asia Minor in the early 280s.[16] This theory only makes sense, however, if Lysimachus set aside his wounded pride for a decade and somehow managed to retake Demetrius's coastal cities in Ionia with the forces he had. We would then have to explain the odd fact that the warship his architects produced had characteristics that were better suited for a floating siege platform than a ramming warship. If we accept Morrison's design, which seems required for a ramming warship, then its hull is too long and too weak to sustain

---

12. For the context of this episode, see Lund 1992, 88–89.

13. Lund 1992, 88, suggests that Lysimachus allied with Ptolemy in the early 290s because he recognized his inability to deal with Demetrius's fleet and hoped this alliance would result in naval support for the recovery of Greek cities under Demetrius's control. The existence of Ptolemaic troops at Aspendus ca. 297 has been seen in this context; see Burstein 1980, 78.

14. According to this same passage in Plutarch, Ptolemy regained control of Cyprus and Seleucus regained control of his cities in Cilicia at this same time. For these events and their chronology, see Lund 1992, 91–95.

15. For this period of Herakleia's history and the relationship between Amastris and Lysimachus, see Burstein 1976, 81–84.

16. See Tarn 1910, 211, who argues that the ship was built in Herakleia in response to rumors about Demetrius's preparations for his Asiatic campaign. Burstein 1976, 84, accepts this view presumably because, like most scholars, he believes that *Leontophoros* was built to resist Demetrius's "fifteen" and "sixteen" in battle.

repeated collisions. If, on the other hand, we accept Casson's design, the vessel's deck, which was sufficient for 1200 soldiers, works well as a platform for siege operations. I therefore suggest that either Photius or Memnon misunderstood the original source, incorrectly used the term *stoichos*, and unwittingly transmitted an impossible description of the ship's oarsystem. For this reason, I prefer Casson's reading over Morrison's and interpret *Leontophoros* as a large self-propelled two-hulled galley.

If this interpretation is correct, it suggests that Lysimachus built the first self-propelled naval siege platform, replacing the yoked freighters that Demetrius employed at Rhodes in 305. Such a vessel would not require towships to approach a city's harbor defenses, and with the two hulls fixed firmly side-by-side, would be resistant to collapse caused by wave action. However we choose to envision this ship, the record of siege warfare during the period of its construction makes it unlikely that *Leontophoros* was a revolutionary form of battleship that forced its way into clusters of smaller ships, first bombarding, then grappling and smothering their enemies with marines.[17] *Leontophoros* makes much more sense as a maneuverable and no doubt heavily fortified siege platform.

If Lysimachus built *Leontophoros* during the first half of the 290s, then Demetrius designed his "fifteen" and "sixteen" in response to Lysimachus's vessel, and not the other way around. These warships, the largest single-hulled galleys ever built, were presumably more maneuverable than a double-hull "eight" and thus effective as massive ramming weapons that could break through defensive barriers whether they were found at harbor entrances or placed around siege platforms like *Leontophoros*. As we have seen from both Diodorus and Philo, these barriers included floating booms held together with iron plates and spikes, and elaborate pontoon barriers called *zeugmata* or *schediai*.[18] Doubtless, Demetrius designed his newest big ships with the coastal cities of Ionia in mind, but the expected battles were quite different from those envisioned by most modern scholars. If my view of these vessels is basically correct, they were not intended for sea battles at all, but served the purposes of siege and countersiege warfare once naval dominance had been secured with other, more maneuverable warships.

---

17. See Casson 1995, 110.

18. Diod. 20.85.2 (booms fixed with iron); Philo *Polior.* C 54–55 (*zeugma*); Philo *Polior.* D 101, 103 (*schedia*).

When Ptolemy Ceraunus brought Lysimachus's extraordinary "eight" to Macedonia in 281, he did so to help him gain coastal cities by intimidation and by force, if necessary. The plan worked and, after Antigonus failed to block his rival at sea, the Macedonians quickly accepted Ceraunus as their king. Concerning the vessel's performance in battle, Memnon's words seem vague and carefully chosen: ". . . the ships from Herakleia fought more bravely than the others. And of those from Herakleia, the *Leontophoros* carried the select contingent."[19] Indeed, the men on board had to protect this slow moving siege platform by firing catapults and *lithoboloi*, shooting arrows, and by throwing javelins and sling bullets. Considering the vulnerability of such a slow moving vessel as well as its requirement of a highly trained crew to manage the ship and run the siege machinery once the vessel was on station, it comes as no surprise that these men were deemed "select" (*exaireton*). They performed their duty, the ship was not harmed, and Memnon gives them their due in his patriotic account, even though he neglects, or is unable, to report the details of their fighting.

Can we make anything of the name *Leontophoros*—"Lion Carrier"—or the vessel's designation as an "eight"? Years ago, W. W. Tarn suggested that "Lion Carrier" referred in some way to Lysimachus who may have chosen the lion for his personal symbol.[20] While this sounds reasonable enough, we might also note the term *mechanophoroi nees* used by Arrian (*Anab.* 2.22.6, 23.2) in a technical sense to describe Alexander's "machine-carrying warships" at Tyre in 332.[21] The name might therefore refer to a large assault tower, or other piece of machinery, identified with the king.[22] Her designation as an "eight" needs to be paired with the rest of the description: she was "a marvel for her size and beauty" (*megethous heneka kai kallous hekousa eis thauma*). Because *Leontophoros* was somehow different than warships built before her, we can detect in her description the confusion over how to signify her classification. If she was a warship with two

---

19. Phot. *Bib.* 224.226b.27–30 (= *TLG*, Memnon Frg. 13.15–18). Tarn 1910, 210, makes the unsupported statement that *Leontophoros* "was largely responsible for the very important defeat at sea which Gonatas suffered at the hands of Ptolemy Ceraunus . . ." and others have followed him: e.g., Morrison and Coates 1996, 36.

20. Tarn 1913, 131, says the lion referred to Lysimachus's *parasemon* or identifying symbol.

21. The only other appearance of the adjective *mechanophoros* occurs in Plut. *Ant.* 38.5 to describe wagons that carried siege machinery.

22. A lion is mentioned more than once in conjunction with Lysimachus. For example, he killed one when hunting in Syria that sliced his shoulder to the bone (Curt. 8.1.15); later (in

separate hulls, then she might be called a "double-eight" or even a "sixteen." Subsequent multi-hulled warships built by Ptolemy II reveal that the latter method of naming was eventually adopted, but for Lysimachus's prototype vessel, the term *okteres* was apparently retained, with the additional comment that her size was exceptional.

"Twenty," "Thirty," and "Forty"

We can now consider the three classes of double-hull warships that appear in Ptolemaic fleets: a "twenty" and two "thirties" built during the reign of Ptolemy II Philadelphus, and a gargantuan "forty" built during the reign of Ptolemy IV Philopator. A consensus of opinion regarding these vessels and the oarsystems that propelled them has never been achieved because the sources available to us allow for various interpretations, at least about the "forty." Our information comes mainly from a work, "About Alexandria," written by Callixenus of Rhodes as quoted by Athenaeus of Naukratis in his *Deipnosophistai* ("The Learned Banqueters").[23] Callixenus's description of both the ship and the method by which she was launched is important enough to quote in full. Athenaeus introduces the quote as follows:

> Since we have discussed ship construction, we must now say something (for it is worth hearing) about the ships built by King Philopator. Callixenus himself wrote as follows about these in the first book of his work "About Alexandria":
> "The 'forty' was built by Philopator [221–204 BCE]. It was 280 cubits long, 38 from gangway to gangway, and 48 cubits up to the prow ornament [*akrostolion*]. From the stern ornaments [*aphlasta*] to the part where the ship entered the water was 53 cubits. There were four steering oars that were 30 cubits long, and thranite oars—the longest aboard—that were 38 cubits; these, by virtue of their having lead in the handles and being heavily weighted inboard, were very

---

328 or so), when hunting with Alexander, he was rebuked by the king for preparing to kill the lion in advance of himself (Curt. 8.1.14). Curtius wonders (8.1.17) whether or not this was the reason behind the widespread but unsubstantiated story that Alexander deliberately exposed Lysimachus to a lion (Sen. *Ira* 3.17.2 = *Dial.* 5.17.2; *Cl.* 1.25.1; Pliny *NH* 8.54; Paus. 1.9.5; Just. 15.3.7–8; Lucian *Dial. mort.* 14.4 (397); Plut. *Demetr.* 27.3).

23. For Callixenus and his work "About Alexandria," see Rice 1983, 134–79.

easy to use because of their balance. The ship was double-prowed and double-sterned, and had seven rams. Of these, one was the chief ram out front, and the rest angled back to the catheads [*epotides*], which also had rams on them. It took 12 undergirds [*hypozomata*], each 600 cubits (in length). The ship was extremely well-proportioned and was a marvel in its other decoration, as it had animals, no less than 12 cubits in size at the bow and stern, and every surface was covered with painted decoration, and the hull from the oars down to the keel had ivy leaves and *thyrsoi* all over its surface. The ship's tackle was entirely ship-shape and ample. During a trial run, the ship held over 4000 oarsmen and 400 other officers, ratings and deckhands, and 2850 marines on the deck; and off under the thwarts there was another crowd of men and a large supply of provisions.

"The ship was launched originally from a sort of cradle, which they say was constructed with the timber of 50 'fives.' It was drawn down by a mass of men with shouting and trumpets. After that, the launching was devised by a man from Phoenicia. He prepared a ditch, as long as the ship, which he dug adjacent to the harbor. He built the foundations of this ditch with hard stone to a depth of 5 cubits, and thrust logs across them crosswise, running the whole width of the trench, leaving a space 4 cubits deep (on top of the logs). And making an inlet from the sea, he filled with sea water the whole excavated space into which he easily led the ship with the help of whatever men happened to be at hand. . . . Then, closing the original entrance (of the channel from the sea), they drained away the water with pumps. When this had been done, the ship settled safely onto the previously mentioned logs."

Athen. *Deip.* 5.203e–204b (= *TLG*, 5.37.5–48 = Callixenus *FGrH* 627 F1 = *TLG*, Callixenus Frag. 1.1–60).[24]

Casson was surely right to see in this description a large double-hull vessel, rowed at three levels, spanned by a fighting deck. This explained the presence of two prows, two sterns, and four steering oars. It also

---

24. Plut. *Demetr.* 43.5 also mentions this vessel and gives similar specifications (length = 280 cubits; height to top of prow ornament = 48 cubits; 400 sailors; 4,000 oarsmen; room on her gangways and fighting deck for nearly 3000 marines).

Table 6.1 Characteristics of the "Forty."

	Cubits	Meters[1] (1 Attic cubit = 0.462 m.)	Feet
Length	280	129.5	420
Beam	38	17.6	57
Ht. from waterline to tip of sterns (pl.)	53	24.5	79.5
Ht. from waterline to prow ornament (sing.)	48	22.2	72
Draft (when empty)	< 4	< 1.85	< 6
Steering oars (4)	30	13.9	45
Thranite oars	38	17.6	57
Personnel: Oarsmen		4000	
Hyperesia = Officers, Ratings, Deckhands		400	
Marines		2850	
Total Crew		7250	

1. Morrison 1996, 275, notes that there are two possible values for the Egyptian cubit used at this time; cf. his text for the values calculated on a cubit of 0.5325 m.

explained the existence of thranite oars, which suggested the presence of zygian and thalamian oars as well, thus indicating oarsmen at three levels.[25] By placing oarsmen on both sides of each hull, Casson felt that the 4000 men could be accommodated in such a design. According to his view, the "forty," was essentially a double "twenty."

Because of the 38 cubit beam "from gangway to gangway" (*apo parodou epi parodon*) recorded by Callixenus, Morrison found a problem with Casson's interpretation of the "forty's" rowing system. He felt that such a dimension did not allow enough space for men to work their oars from *both* sides of each hull. As a result, Casson's system required the oarsmen on the inner sides of each hull to interleave their oars with ones from the adjacent hull, producing a difficult situation at best, an impossible one at

25. Casson 1969, 188–191; and Casson 1995, 108–112. He suggested placing eight men on each thranite oar, seven on each zygian, and five on the thalamian oar: Casson 1969, 189; and Casson 1995, 111.

worst.[26] For this reason, Morrison suggested that the two hulls were stationed firmly side-by-side and that all 4000 oarsmen had to be accommodated on the outer sides of each hull. He proposed a push-pull system with rowers seated on *both* sides of each oar, attested from a seventeenth century model, but not from actual historical practice.[27]

Given our current evidence, the answer to the placement of hulls in Philopator's "forty" is unknowable and probably lies in what Callixenus (or his source) meant by the expression "from gangway to gangway." If each half-hull possessed two gangways (*parodoi*), then Callixenus might have recorded the beam for one of the hulls and not for the overall width of the *katastroma*, or fighting deck.[28] This would allow us to move the hulls further apart and create more space for Casson's interior oars to work without interfering with one another. While technically this would solve the problem of space for the inner files of oars, it does not address the issue of hull integrity. Two hulls placed far apart would require massive connecting timbers, and these pose their own structural problems.[29] Because we must rely on a quote from an author whose sources are unknown, I am inclined to reserve judgment and turn to other details that are less controversial.[30]

Casson and Morrison agreed about one thing: the other extraordinary vessels, whose designs led to the "forty," were built primarily to defeat ships of smaller size in pitched sea battles. In fact, this supposition underlies most arguments put forth by scholars regarding these so-called

---

26. Basch 1987, 352–53, points out the main problems with the design as represented in Casson's sketch plan and shows in a diagram (Fig. 741, at 353) the impossibility of the oar arrangement. To meet such objections, Casson 1995, 112, offered as another possibility a design with the two hulls placed close together, side-by-side. The interior benches would have been manned by rowers who "had no oars but were stationed there to serve as a spare crew" ready to take over when the original oarsmen got tired. Sleeswyk and Meijer 1994 adopt such a design as shown in their cross-sectional drawing, 117.

27. See Morrison 1972, 232, under his comments on Casson, 108 ff.; and also Rice 1983, 143n20.

28. This is the solution adopted by Meijer 1986, 140; Morrison in Morrison and Coates 1996, 276, disagrees because he feels that the order in which the dimensions are given implies a breadth for the whole ship. In Meijer's defense, the dimensions might equally apply to one hull. Callixenus first mentions the length of the hull, the breadth from gangway to gangway, and the height to the singular bow ornament, i.e., of one hull. He then mentions the height of the stern ornaments of both hulls, and the fact that there were two prows, two sterns, four rudders, etc.

29. Cf. the comments of Basch 1987, 353, regarding this problem with the design proposed by Foley and Soedel 1981, 126–27. Such considerations are reflected in the hull design proposed by Sleeswyk and Meijer 1994, 117 Fig. 1.

30. For the problems involved in evaluating Callixenus's sources, see Rice 1983, 135–38.

super-galleys.[31] If only we had a better record of naval battles, so the reasoning goes, we would have to rethink everything. Perhaps Tarn says it most plainly:

> It is unfortunate that most of the story has perished. We possess no description of a Hellenistic naval battle between Salamis in 306 and Chios in 201; that is to say, we know nothing at all about the battles between Egypt and Macedonia, in which much larger ships took part than in any that fought in the battles of which we possess accounts. If an even tolerable account had survived of, let us say, the battle of Cos, about 258, in which Macedonia deprived Egypt of the command of the sea, everything that has been written about ancient naval warfare would have to be rewritten from a somewhat different angle. . . .[32]

I have tried to avoid Tarn's assumption in favor of another approach—one that places the goals of naval siege warfare as the driving force behind the development of increasingly large warships. I therefore assume that even larger warships, like *Leontophoros*, the "twenty," and "thirty" were built for similar purposes and interpret these vessels as naval assault platforms. They also make sense as attempts to solve the problems encountered by Demetrius's yoked freighters during the siege of Rhodes in 305. Specifically, these problems involved 1) a lack of propulsion, and 2) susceptibility to wave action. These double-hull vessels could have moved into and out of position under enemy fire without risking the lives of towboat crews and would have presented steadier platforms when confronted by waves that caused yoked hulls to rock in different directions.

Resistance to wave action is an important consideration for anyone intending to mount lofty "timber constructions" on floating platforms like warships. The classic example was provided by Demetrius's largest naval assault tower at Rhodes (Diod. 20.88.7), which collapsed during a bout of stormy weather, brought down presumably by the differential rocking of the two freighters which carried it. This precise situation was discussed by Athenaeus Mechanicus (Athen. Mech. 32) who proposed a device called

---

31. See, for example, Tarn (1930) 1960, 132–34; Casson 1995, 110; Landels 1978, 153; Foley and Soedel 1981, 160; Meijer 1986, 139–41; Basch 1987, 338 and 345; Morrison and Coates 1996, 275–77.

32. Tarn (1930) 1960, 123.

"the little ape" (*pithakion*) that he claimed would offset the tendency of yoked hulls to rock in opposite directions.[33] While scholars have debated the effectiveness of his proposal, I have always felt that the *pithakion* represented a poor man's solution for a problem best addressed by a double-hull warship. Lysimachus, then, was the first to solve the problem of differential hull movement by joining two adjacent hulls into a single rigid unit, but this was so expensive that only a few rulers ever turned to his solution.

However one decides to visualize the oar arrangements of the "forty," no one disputes that it carried 2850 marines on its maiden voyage. Such a deck, even if the men were packed closely side-by-side, would serve well as a base for various kinds of siege machinery. If the "forty" was basically a large floating platform, what purpose did the rams serve? The answer may be seen in the odd V-shaped construction that carried them, all seven in number. How, precisely, this construction was fashioned we are not told, aside from the fact that a primary ram was out front, presumably at the tip of the "V," and the others angled back to the catheads (*epotides*) where the sixth and seventh rams were mounted. This multi-ram construction linked both prows and brings to mind the ram projections that Philo advised defenders to place on the *zeugmata* or pontoon barriers they built across harbor entrances (Philo *Polior.* C 54). If this is a correct parallel, the "forty's" rams were not designed for offensive ramming attacks, but served a defensive purpose deterring enemy vessels from attacking the space between the two hulls.[34]

For us, the value of Callixenus's description lies not so much in what we learn about Philopator's "forty," interesting as it is, but rather for what it implies about the designs of Philadelphus's "twenty" and two "thirties." I say this because Plutarch pronounced the "forty" a showpiece rather than a working warship. According to him (*Demetr.* 43.5–6), the vessel "differed little from a stationary building on land, and since she was designed for exhibition rather than for use, she could only be moved with great difficulty and danger."[35] This was not the case for Philadelphus's

---

33. For various attempts to explain this device, see Whitehead and Blyth 2004, 145–47 (who feel that it had little likelihood of success); and Lendle 1983, 158–60.

34. Such a space would exist (at least at the prow) no matter if the hulls were fixed closely side-by-side or set far enough apart to allow the inner oars to work.

35. Rice 1983, 140, questions the independent judgment of Plutarch as perhaps being "based upon his own understanding of ships built half a millennium before his own time."

"twenty" and "thirty." As Casson observed, Plutarch knew Ptolemy IV as a builder of exhibition pieces, not as an innovator. And so, there is no reason to credit him with the invention of the double-hull warship. "It is far easier to assume that examples were right under his eyes—in Ptolemy II's 'twenty' and two 'thirties.'"[36] Most scholars agree that Demetrius's "sixteen" represents the largest practical size for a single-hull warship with multiple-man oars. If this is so, then the "twenty" and two "thirties" built by Ptolemy II must have been double-hull warships like the "forty," with two prows and two sterns each.[37] That these two classes were built along similar lines is also implied by the fact that the "twenty" and "thirty" were designed by the same architect, a man named Pyrgoteles. Considering the well established progression from "small" to "large" in warship designs, the smaller "twenty" was probably built first and then enlarged to produce the "thirty."[38] Both these vessels worked so well that Philadelphus honored their designer with a statue at the sanctuary of Paphian Aphrodite on Cyprus. A base was found at the sanctuary in 1888 bearing the inscription, "King Ptolemy [dedicated the statue of] Pyrgoteles, son of Zoes, the one who designed the 'thirty' and 'twenty.'"[39] Then, following the dedication of this statue, Ptolemy apparently decided he needed a second "thirty," so the first vessel clearly met or exceeded his expectations (Athen. *Deip.* 5.203d = *TLG*, 5.36.15). Before addressing the obvious question about Ptolemy's need for such a collection of super-galleys, we

---

In fact, Rice suggests, 141, that the vessel "may have been intended to announce that Egypt was far from finished as a naval power." Regardless of Philopator's intentions for building the vessel, Plutarch's judgment should not be dismissed lightly. Since he repeats exactly some of the dimensions and crew numbers recorded by Callixenus (n. 24), the possibility exists that he also consulted the work "About Alexandria." And while Callixenus describes the "forty" as "extremely well-proportioned" (εὔρυθμος δ' ἦν καθ' ὑπερβολήν), this says nothing about the problems involved with navigating the vessel. For an engineer's opinion, see Sleeswyk and Meijer 1994.

36. Casson 1995, 112.

37. Casson 1995, 100 n. 20, points out the limit of placing eight men on a single oar known from better documented periods of history, and since a "thirty" would require ten- or eleven-man oars at the upper level, the "thirty," like the "forty," could not be a single-hull vessel named on the traditional pattern found in warships up to "sixteen" in rating. Although certainty is impossible, most scholars accept his argument that the "twenty," "thirty," and "forty" were all built on the same pattern of two hulls.

38. Basch 1987, 353 remarks astutely that, even if we cannot understand it, there must be some underlying principle that explains why these largest galleys increased in size by "tens."

39. Hogarth et al. 1888, 255, no. 125; *OGIS* 39; Mitford 1961, 9, no. 17.

should consider the last of the extraordinary warships recorded by our sources.

The *Triarmenos* "Nine," the *Isthmia*, and the Dedicated Ship of Antigonus Gonatas

Although one additional ship is often discussed in the context of these extraordinary galleys, the evidence for it is not very compelling. Nevertheless, we should start with Tarn's argument regarding this vessel, published in 1910, which goes roughly as follows.[40] Following Antigonus's defeat in 281 at the hands of Ptolemy Ceraunus and *Leontophoros*, he built a fleet aimed at recovering his control of the Aegean. His desire to defeat the *Leontophoros* "eight" (originally built to defeat Demetrius's "thirteen"), drove him to follow its design principles (whatever they were) and build an extraordinary "nine." This vessel was his flagship, her name was *Isthmia*, she was termed *triarmenos* probably because of her size, and carried him to victory over Philadelphus's generals at Cos and Andros during the mid-third century. In thanks for his success in these two engagements, which gave him firm control of the Aegean, Antigonus dedicated to Delian Apollo his *triarmenos* flagship.

For some years following its publication, Tarn's hypothesis was accepted by many scholars as speculative, but convincing. Archaeologists at Delos even concluded that a long structure called "The Monument of the Bulls" was the building that housed Antigonus's dedicated flagship.[41] Although most scholars now see the flaws in Tarn's arguments, his 1910 article stands as a warning to the dangers of building an argument on unfounded suppositions. Admittedly, when dealing with third century events, the temptation exists to press the evidence that we have, but Tarn goes too far. I present below the sources that underlie his argument in order to establish clearly what we do and do not know about Antigonus's warship:

Plut. *Mor.* 545b: "Antigonus II among other things was sensible and moderate as in the naval battle around Cos [261?] when someone said

---

40. Tarn 1910.

41. Couchoud and Svoronos 1921, 276. Basch 1987, 347–50, points out the incorrect dimensions of the building (it is too narrow) and suggests that Antigonus's warship was located in the empty space to the east of the Monument of the Bulls.

to him: 'Do you not see how the enemy's ships outnumber ours?' To which he replied, 'Against how many of their ships do you set me?'"[42]

This same anecdote appears twice more in Plutarch's writings, once in relation to the same sea battle off Cos (Plut. *Mor.* 183c-d), and once in relation to another sea battle fought near Andros (in 246?) when Antigonus was an old man (Plut. *Pelop.* 2.4).

Poll. 1.82–83: In a long list of terms for ships that are organized according to their morphology, Pollux presents as a pair "the ship of Ptolemy, the 'fifteen,' and the *triarmenos* of Antigonus." Tarn argues that the monarchs are Ptolemy II Philadelphus and Antigonus II Gonatas and that the term *triarmenos* signifies that the ship was large because it was paired with Ptolemy's "fifteen" in Pollux's list.[43]

Moschion in Athen. *Deip.* 5.209e (*TLG*, 5.44.35–40): After explaining that Hiero II's (king of Syracuse, 270–15) monstrous grain carrier *Syrakosia* was built with wood sufficient to construct 60 "fours" (206f = *TLG*, 5.40.19), he says: "I purposefully omit the sacred *trieres* of Antigonus, with which he defeated Ptolemy off Leucolla in Cos, since [or perhaps where] he dedicated it to Apollo. This ship was not a third, not even a fourth the size of the ship called *Syrakosia*, or *Alexandris*."[44]

Paus. 1.29.1: "A ship is pointed out near the Areopagus [in Athens] which was built for the parade of the Panathenaic Festival. Some ship may have surpassed [or conquered—the word *hyperbaleto* is ambiguous] this vessel, but I know that no one ever vanquished the ship on Delos, which had as many as nine rowers from the decks."[45]

---

42. Plut. *Mor.* 545b: καὶ Ἀντίγονος ὁ δεύτερος τἆλλα μὲν ἦν ἄτυφος καὶ μέτριος, ἐν δὲ τῇ περὶ Κῶ ναυμαχίᾳ τῶν φίλων τινὸς εἰπόντος 'οὐχ ὁρᾷς, ὅσῳ πλείους εἰσὶν αἱ πολέμιαι νῆες;' 'ἐμὲ δέ γ' αὐτόν' εἶπε 'πρὸς πόσας ἀντιτάττετε;'

43. Tarn 1910, 209–12.

44. Athen. *Deip.* 5.209e (= *TLG*, 5.44.35–40): παρέλιπον δ' ἑκὼν ἐγὼ τὴν Ἀντιγόνου ἱερὰν τριήρη, ᾗ ἐνίκησε τοὺς Πτολεμαίου στρατηγοὺς περὶ Λεύκολλαν τῆς Κῴας, ἐπειδὴ καὶ τῷ Ἀπόλλωνι αὐτὴν ἀνέθηκεν· ἥτις οὐδὲ τὸ τρίτον, τάχα δὲ οὐδὲ τὸ τέταρτον εἶχε τῆς Συρακοσίας ἢ Ἀλεξανδρίδος ταύτης νεώς. Most editors accept the emendation of A. Meineke (Athenaeus 1858, 371 with Athenaeus 1859, 91) and substitute ὅπου δὴ ("where") for ἐπειδὴ ("since"): "where he dedicated it (i.e., the ship) to Apollo." Tarn 1910, 212, argues that the emendation is unnecessary and that the text simply means that the vessel was dedicated to the god prior to the battle. Hiero II, king of Syracuse (270–15), changed the vessel's name to *Alexandris* when he decided to give her to Ptolemy IV Philopator.

45. Paus. 1.29.1: τοῦ δὲ Ἀρείου πάγου πλησίον δείκνυται ναῦς ποιηθεῖσα ἐς τὴν τῶν Παναθηναίων πομπήν. καὶ ταύτην μὲν ἤδη πού τις ὑπερεβάλετο· τὸ δὲ ἐν Δήλῳ πλοῖον οὐδένα πω νικήσαντα οἶδα, καθῆκον ἐς ἐννέα ἐρέτας ἀπὸ τῶν καταστρωμάτων.

Plut. *Quaest. conv.* 5.3.2 (*TLG,* 676 D): "And moreover, Antigonus's flagship, whose stern spontaneously burst into leaf with celery, got the eponym *Isthmia.*"[46]

The problems begin with Tarn's fundamental premise that *Leontophoros* was responsible for Antigonus's defeat and therefore drove him to find a way to beat her.[47] It is a supposition that is unsupported by any ancient evidence. The truth is that we cannot conclude anything about the design of Antigonus's undefeated ship from *Leontophoros.* Nor can we conclude anything precise about the ship's characteristics from the obscure adjective *triarmenos* provided by Pollux. Since the term is used elsewhere to describe a merchant ship and should mean something like "three-masted," or "with three decks," it perhaps means something similar in regard to this warship.[48] We may assume, however, that the vessel was a midsized polyreme from the fact that she was considered to be around a quarter of the size of Hiero's massive freighter, which was itself constructed with the wood sufficient to build 60 "fours."

If all these references point to the same ship, Casson's assessment[49] is the best we can do: Antigonus built a noteworthy, probably large, ship that became associated with his naval victories over Ptolemy II. She apparently served as his flagship, perhaps had three masts (or decks), and was associated with a story that explained her name. *Isthmia* was probably one and the same with the invincible ship known to Pausanias as a dedication of Antigonus on Delos, and described by him in vague terms that suggest the ship was some kind of "nine."[50] Lacking details of the battles in which she fought, we cannot conclude anything about her performance characteristics beside the fact that she was deliberately taken into battle and, later,

---

46. Plut. *Quaest. Conv.* 5.3.2 (676 D): ἔτι τοίνυν ἡ Ἀντιγόνου ναυαρχὶς ἀναφύσασα περὶ πρύμναν αὐτομάτως σέλινον Ἰσθμία ἐπωνομάσθη.

47. Tarn 1910, 211: "In 280, this great octeres was largely responsible for the very important defeat at sea which Gonatas suffered at the hands of Ptolemy Ceraunus, then in possession of Lysimachus's navy. . . ."

48. LSJ[9], s.v. τριάρεμνος; and Casson 1995, 115 with n. 61.

49. Casson 1995, 115–16.

50. While Pausanias mentions the term "trieres" (in its various forms) on 28 separate occasions, he does not use the -*eres* term for any other size of warship. By the time he wrote, little was known about the *enneres* or "nine" and this may explain his difficulty in describing the vessel at 1.29.1.

deemed to be "invincible." Perhaps she was simply a "nine," like Pausanias implies, dedicated by Antigonus following a series of victories that left him in control of the Aegean Sea.

The Fleet of Ptolemy II Philadelphus: An Historical Perspective

[Ptolemy II] Philadelphus stood apart from all other kings in wealth and strove so zealously in regard to all his constructions that he surpassed everyone even in the number of his ships. Indeed, the largest of his ships included two "thirties," one "twenty," four "thirteens," two "twelves," 14 "elevens," 30 "nines," 37 "sevens," five "sixes," and 17 "fives." He had twice as many ships as these from "fours" to *triemioliai*; and the ships sent to the islands and to the other cities he ruled and to Libya numbered more than 4000.[51]

—ATHEN. *DEIP.* 5.203D (*TLG*, 5.36.11–21)

We are now in a position to revisit the quote presented first at the start of this book. It comes from Athenaeus's work "The Learned Banqueters" (*Deipnosophistai*) which we consulted for details from Callixenus regarding Philopator's "forty." And since we find this quote in the same section of his banqueters' discussion on marvels of shipbuilding, it has been thought to derive from Callixenus as well, although Athenaeus does not directly tell us so.[52]

Table 6.2 Large Ships in Ptolemy II's Fleet.

"thirty"	2	"nine"	30
"twenty"	1	"seven"	37
"thirteen"	4	"six"	5
"twelve"	2	"five"	17
"eleven"	14	"fours" and smaller	224

51. J. Grainger (personal communication, Nov. 24, 2010) correctly observes that the total of 17 "fives" seems rather low and suggests that Ptolemy should have had roughly 300 of this class, since "fives" had become the naval workhorses of the major fleets by his time. Grainger also suggests that these "fives" are hidden amongst the "more than 4000" ships left undetailed by our source.

52. Felix Jacoby included this section as a paraphrase from Callixenus's work and listed it at the end of *FGrH* 627 F2 (= Dritter Teil, Text, I. Aegypten, p. 177, lines 7–20); see also Rice 1983, 152–53.

Wherever he got this information, his reliability elsewhere suggests that he took care to quote his sources faithfully.[53] While certainty is impossible, the ultimate source of information may have been an official record made by the state during the reign of Philadelphus. Appian, a native of Alexandria and an older contemporary of Athenaeus, tells us (*Praef.* 10) that he consulted "royal records" (*basilikai anagraphai*), "produced and left behind" (*proagagon te kai katalipon*) by Philadelphus, for his estimation of the land and naval forces of Egypt during this time.[54]

However we wish to evaluate this list, its date, and precise origin, one thing is clear: at some point in his reign, Ptolemy II Philadelphus amassed an impressive number of large ships in his fleet at Alexandria. His possession of 72 vessels in the range of "six" to "nine" and 20 in the range of "eleven" to "thirteen" is difficult to place in perspective. Because we lack similar totals for Demetrius Poliorcetes or Antigonus Gonatas, the best we can do is compare these numbers with the armada brought to Actium by Antony and Cleopatra in 31. Based on evidence from Augustus's Victory Monument at Nikopolis, I estimate that the eastern fleet contained roughly 27–28 vessels in the range of "six" to "ten."[55] Philadelphus's fleet dwarfs that amassed by his distant relative and her ally to fight Octavian and "all Italy" for control of the Mediterranean.

The sums involved in building, maintaining, and deploying such a fleet on an annual basis must have been staggering. While we lack financial documents from Egypt allowing us to calculate this expenditure, we can gain a sense of its magnitude from the fleet finances of fourth century Athens. Here, a series of inscriptions preserve details of the financial administration of the fleet from the 370s to 320s. Working from this information, Vincent Gabrielsen figures that, during the fourth century, it cost an average annual amount of 3000–4000 drachmai to run a single Athenian "three." While this expense could be defrayed from the private sources of one or more citizen sponsors, called *syntrierarchoi*, the annual

---

53. On the general reliability of Athenaeus, see Rice 1983, 138–39.

54. Specifically, Appian says (*Praef.* 10) that the records were produced and left "by the king of Egypt second in succession after Alexander." Technically, if we count Alexander as the first king of Egypt, then Ptolemy I Soter would be the "second in succession." That Appian is referring to Philadelphus, however, is clear from his description of this king as "remarkable . . . for the lavishness of his expenditure and for the magnificence of his public works." Cf. Morrison and Coates 1996, 37.

55. Murray and Petsas 1989, 142; and chapter 7.

outlay *per ship* could total more than 10,000 drachmai when amounts for various extra expenses were included.[56] If only 60 ships were commissioned in a year, a number that we see frequently in our texts, then the total of private money financing the fleet could be as much as 100 talents per year (600,000 drachmai or roughly 2620 kg. of silver). By one estimate, this sum was equal to the entire annual budget for the Athenian democracy at the time.[57]

None of these calculations takes into account the considerable costs involved in building and maintaining the infrastructure for the fleet. First there were the costs involved with building the ships, and this required large stocks of timber of different kinds, miles of rope, oceans of pitch, tow, wax, copper, tin, iron, and all the other materials required for construction. Then there were the costs associated with the ships' gear: timber (for oars, masts, yards, gangplanks, ladders, and poles), more rope, side screens made of goat hair and canvas, sailcloth, sunshades, bailing buckets, ships' tools, anchors, chain, lead for brailing rings, and so forth. Additional expenses would include the cost of shipsheds in which the vessels were stored (an expenditure second only to the city's defensive circuit),[58] the foundries where the rams were produced, the arsenals where the catapults were constructed, the workshops where the engineers theorized and built models, and the shipyards where the vessels were built, fitted for service, and repaired. We must also include the warehouses filled with ships' gear, as well as the weapons and supplies signed out to individual trierarchs for use at sea. And finally, there were the annual salaries for all the personnel required to run this gigantic enterprise, which in Philadelphus's case included the 100 thousand (and more) oarsmen, skilled sailors, deck officers, and marines who were required to place his vessels in service. And none of these calculations

---

56. Gabrielsen 1995, 240.

57. Gabrielsen 1995, 240.

58. For the evidence, see J. Pakkanen in Blackman and Rankov (forthcoming). According to B. Rankov (email communication, Jan. 31, 2011), the working title of Pakkanen's chapter is "The Economics of Shed Complexes." In Zea Harbor at Athens, Rankov notes that the shipsheds were substantial buildings "with two-foot thick back walls, and side-walls between groups of sheds to act as fire breaks; sheds elsewhere were similar and often incorporated decorative elements to make them look impressive. Our impression, incidentally, is that quite a lot of the basic maintenance would have taken place within the sheds, with only major work being undertaken elsewhere."

account for the considerable expenses associated with the fleet of transports that usually accompanied the dispatch of a large war fleet. All these sums were annual, recurring expenditures that demanded annual, recurring revenues of equal or greater magnitude. As I said, the outlays required for building, maintaining, and deploying Philadelphus's fleet must have been staggering.

Even if the fleet remained in port, the high rate of annual expenditure associated with such a navy implies that the perceived needs were equally great. If my argument is sound regarding the reasons for building a polyreme navy of this magnitude, then we should be able to detect a period during Ptolemy's reign that explains his need to amass such a massive naval siege unit. The main problem standing in our way, however, is the nature of our source record, which is extremely meager. No single historical narrative exists to describe the reign of Philadelphus, or to detail his struggles with the other monarchs of his day.[59] As a result, we must piece together the picture as best we can from inscriptions, papyri, coins, and chance bits of information preserved in the works of authors whose attention is focused on other topics. In spite of this handicap, it is still possible to see that Philadelphus amassed an overwhelming collection of big ships in his Alexandrian fleet toward the end of his reign in response to specific strategic issues that faced both him and his designated successor. In order to demonstrate how this was so, we need to consider the nature of the Ptolemaic empire during the reigns of Ptolemy II Philadelphus and his son and successor Ptolemy III Euergetes.

The Nature of the Ptolemaic Empire

During the generation in which Alexander's successors fought over the remains of his empire, Ptolemy established a secure kingdom for himself in Egypt, aided by the region's geographical isolation and extreme fertility. Of all the Diadochoi (immediate successors of Alexander), the first Ptolemy was the least interested in territorial conquest, preferring to safeguard his kingdom by establishing a string of allied cities and garrisoned fortifications at strategic points around the shores of the eastern

---

59. See the remark by Tarn (1930), 123, quoted on p. 182.

MAP 6.1 Ptolemaic coastal dependencies during the third century BCE.

Mediterranean. These strategic points allowed him access to the raw materials needed to build and maintain a fleet, as they also allowed him to safely block the ambitions of his rivals far from the borders of Egypt.

The maintenance of such a network of allied cities and fortified strongholds took more than the reign of a single king to establish. We have seen how Demetrius destroyed Ptolemy's fleet of "fours" and "fives" off Cyprian Salamis in 306 and how, after Ipsus, he relied on his fleet to preserve a network of fortified coastal cities that, for a time, represented his power base. Although Ptolemy managed to recover his Cypriot possessions in the mid-290s, Demetrius remained a formidable naval adversary. When reports circulated that Demetrius was preparing to invade Asia Minor, his enemies united and drove him from Macedonia. During this same period, Ptolemy regained control of Sidon and Tyre, if he had not already done so in the 290s when he regained control of Cyprus (the evidence is unclear). In 285, the same year that Demetrius was captured by Seleucus in Cilicia, Ptolemy appointed his son Ptolemy Philadelphus as coruler and heir. So, when the old man died in late 283 (the same year in which Demetrius died), the transfer of power in Egypt had already taken place.

The period between 283 and 280 witnessed a great shake up of the kingdoms that had formed from Alexander's empire. In 282, Seleucus, the king of Syria, Mesopotamia, and Alexander's eastern satrapies, invaded Asia Minor and killed Lysimachus at the battle of Koroupedion in the following year. Shortly thereafter, as Seleucus prepared to cross to Macedonia, he was killed by Ptolemy Ceraunus, a half-brother of the new Egyptian king, to whom he had offered protection as a sort of high-class refugee. This Ceraunus was the man who took over control of *Leontophoros* and used it to gain control of Macedonia for a brief time.

In 280, when Seleucus's son Antiochus came from the east to claim his father's territories, Philadelphus's position was quite stable by comparison: he controlled Egypt, south and central Syria, Cyprus, and "a string of port cities in Asia Minor" from Korakesion in Pamphylia around to Miletus (Map 6.1).[60] His half-brother Ceraunus controlled Macedonia, at least temporarily, and another half-brother Magas served as viceroy in Cyrenaica (Cyrene and its neighboring cities). Although the evidence must be pieced together from inscriptions, coins, and other scraps of evidence, the picture is fairly clear. Philadelphus and his successors Ptolemy III and IV

---

60. Grainger 2010, 77.

all felt the need to secure their power by maintaining this overseas net-work of allies, dependents, and garrisoned positions, some of which served as naval stations.[61] Scholars characterize this complex network of allies and dependents as the Ptolemaic empire.

Importance of Cities and their Protection

Table 6.3 presents a list of those cities considered to form the so-called Ptolemaic empire during the third century, that is, during the reigns of Ptolemy II Philadelphus, Ptolemy III Euergetes, and Ptolemy IV Philopa-tor. Because wars during this period involved the capture and defense of cities, we can see two things from this list. First, the numerous entries and their geographical range explain why Philadelphus needed a large fleet. Second, the list's geographical spread also helps to explain why he amassed so many big ships in his Alexandrian fleet: presumably, he wanted to be able to respond to multiple areas of conflict at a single time.

Events that unfolded at Miletus in 262 provide a glimpse of the mutual expectations between the Egyptian king and his dependents, and show clearly how Ptolemaic "friendship" worked. The evidence appears in a letter written by Philadelphus to Miletus and a corresponding decree of thanks issued by the city in response.[62] It seems that sometime around 262, the city was attacked by an unnamed enemy who arrived by sea, but had chosen to remain firm in its alliance with Ptolemy. The Milesians had apparently contacted the Ptolemaic regional commander, which we learn was Ptolemy's son, and he and his advisers had informed the king by a written dispatch.[63] He, in turn, responded with an official letter of thanks for the city's steadfast loyalty and promised future benefactions and spe-cial treatment;[64] the letter was brought by a man named Hegestratus, who probably arrived by sea with some sort of naval force. Following this mechanism, the king could evaluate the threats facing his dependents and

---

61. I have lumped into the category "dependents" all cities whose precise legal relationship with Egypt is unknown but whose connection is attested by the presence of Ptolemaic offi-cials. For the complex administrative nature of the Ptolemaic empire, see Bagnall 1976, 213–51.

62. Both documents were inscribed on the walls of the Delphinion in the city's sanctuary of Apollo Delphinius. See Kawerau and Rehm 1914, no. 139; and Welles 1934, no. 14.

63. Welles 1934, no. 14, lines 8–10.

64. Ptolemy had once given a grant of land to the city: Welles 1934, no. 14.

Table 6.3 Ptolemaic Coastal Dependencies during the Third Century BCE (as defined by B. = Bagnall 1976, with additions from G. = Grainger 2010).[1]

REGION / ISLAND	CITY (Garrisoned cities are listed in **bold** type; naval bases are preceded by an asterisk)[2]
SYRIA & PHOENICIA (B. 11–24)	**Sidon** and **Tyre** (B. 11–13, 14–17, 22–24)
PALESTINE	**Ake-Ptolemais**, **Dor**, **Gaza** (G. 96–98)
CYRENAICA (B. 25–37)	Cyrene, Apollonia, **Ptolemais**, **Teucheira**, **Berenike** (B. 25–27, 29, 35)[3]
CYPRUS (B. 38–79)	Paphos, Old Paphos, **Kourion**, **Amathous**, **Kition**, *Salamis, Carpasia, Akanthou, **Kerynia**, **Lapethus**, Morphou, Soloi, Marion-Arsinoe (B. 38–57, 61–64, 79)
ASIA MINOR, S. COAST (B. 80–88)	*Samos (B. 80–82)
NORTHERN CARIA (B. 89–94)	Iasus (B. 91–92)
HALICARNASSUS PENINSULA (B. 94–98)	*Halicarnassus (B. 95–97), Myndos (B. 97–98)
SE CARIA, COS & CALYMNA (B. 98–105)	Cnidos, Caunus, Calynda (B. 98–99), Cos, Calymna (B. 103–105)[4]
LYCIA (B. 105–110)	Lissa, Araxa, Telmessus, **Xanthos** (B. 108), Patara, Andriake, Linyra
PAMPHYLIA & PISIDIA (B. 110–114)	Termessos, **Aspendos** (B. 111–12)[5], Ptolemais, Korakesion, Arsinoe
ROUGH CILICIA (B. 114–16)	**Charadrus** (B. 115), Selinus, Anemurion, Arsinoe, Berenike, Zephyrion, Aphrodisias, Corycus, **Soloi** (B. 115), Mallos[6]
CRETE (B. 117–23)	Gortyn, Matala, Lebena, Olous, Rithymna, *Itanus (B. 121)

CENTRAL AEGEAN (B. 123– 36)

LEAGUE OF ISLANDERS (B. 136–56)

NORTH AEGEAN (B. 159–68)

IONIA (B. 168–75)

IONIAN COAST (B. 169–75)

*Thera (B. 123–34), *Arsinoe–Methana (B. 135–36)

Ceos (B. 141–45)[7], Ios, Delos

Ainos, Maroneia (B. 162–63), Lesbos (B. 162–64, 165)[8], Parts of Thrace and the Hellespont (B. 164–65), Samothrace (B. 162, 164–65)[9]

Chios (B. 168–69)

Lebedus, *Ephesus, Colophon, Magnesia, Priene, Miletus, (B. 169, 170–75)

1. I have excluded inland communities or cities that lacked harbors; see Map 6.1 for locations.

2. The garrisons presented in this list are sometimes conjectural for the third century, being based on spotty historical references, literary sources, and inscriptional evidence, sometimes from the second century (as in the case of many cities on Cyprus). I assume that places garrisoned during the second century were also garrisoned during the third century except when surviving evidence indicates otherwise. As for naval bases, I also assume that places characterized by Bagnall as "way stations" (like Itanus on Crete) qualify.

3. The presence of garrisons in all the cities is assumed. For the evidence, see the references in the table.

4. Because of the sanctuary of Asclepius on Cos, we cannot infer direct control from Ptolemaic officials listed on the sanctuary's inscriptions. Whether under direct control or not, Cos, at least, had long and cordial relations with the Ptolemies, particularly in the reigns of Philadelphus and Philopator.

5. The evidence for a garrison at Aspendus is uncertain.

6. For a possible garrison at a place called Neapolis (unlocated), see B. 115–16.

7. Ceos includes the four cities of Ioulis, Carthaia, Coresia, and Poiessa.

8. For a possible garrison at Eresus on Lesbos, see B. 163–64.

9. The evidence regarding a third century garrison on Samothrace is uncertain.

then decide how to apportion his naval forces. The more resources at his disposal, the greater was his ability to influence the cities he wished to control.

When, therefore, did Philadelphus develop this system of defense based on a sizeable pool of big ships? The difficulty in answering this question derives, once again, from the meager nature of our sources. In the past, scholars studying this period have seized on three poorly known sea battles as important historical markers in the political landscape of this period. In general, we know that between the 260s and 240s, Antigonus II Gonatas defeated Ptolemaic fleets at Cos, Ephesus, and Andros.[65] The result was the eclipse of Ptolemaic influence in the Aegean among a loose federation of states called the League of Islanders. While these battles are clearly significant markers, and were thus remembered by our sources, they were not decisive engagements, like the battle off Salamis in 306. This battle coincided with a major effort by Ptolemy to break the equally major siege campaign of Demetrius and the losses sustained by Ptolemy were considerable. None of these third-century battles seem to have had this effect.[66] So, even if we knew precisely where to date them, these battles still fail to explain the need for either the super-galleys of the period or the large, harbor-busting, polyreme navy amassed by Ptolemy II during his reign. We must look elsewhere for evidence.

John Grainger has recently argued that Ptolemy may have expanded his fleet during the 270s when he seems to have sent one naval expedition into the Black Sea and another into the Western Mediterranean. According to Grainger, his buildup continued into the 260s when he began to fortify positions in Palestine like Ake-Ptolemais, Dora, and Gaza, and embarked on elephant hunts along the coasts of Sudan and Eritrea.[67] If this was the case, however, it is difficult to see why Philadelphus did not send a weightier naval force to assist his Athenian allies

65. There is a huge debate over the dates of the battles of Cos and Andros, with the current consensus favoring dates around 261 for Cos, 258 for Ephesus, and 246 for Andros; see Grainger 2010, 119 and 145 for a synopsis of the differing views.

66. See Reger 1994, 34 who argues that while these three battles were important, they were not by themselves decisive in determining the fate of the islands.

67. See Grainger 2010, 91–102. His statements regarding the Black Sea expedition require the following corrective. The ancient evidence behind Philadelphus's supposed Pontic Expedition is found in St. Byz. s.v. Ἄγκυρα; and Dion. Geogr. *Per Bosp.* 41; see Otto 1931, 408–409. The event has been dated ca. 271/0; see Will 1979, 147 and 149; who is followed by Hölbl 2001, 40–41. A large image of a Ptolemaic warship appearing in a cult building at Nymphaion in

during the Chremonidean war of 267–262 (or early 261).[68] In general, during the period from 267 to 258, Ptolemy's navy sustained repeated losses at the hands of Antigonus and this weakened his influence over the cities in the Aegean and along the coast of Ionia.[69] It is difficult, therefore, to see any hint that Philadelphus was adding ships to his fleet until we get to the mid-250s.

The financial preparations for this shipbuilding program can probably be detected during the early 250s, when Philadelphus conducted new tax surveys and drew up a set of bureaucratic guidelines aimed at increasing tax revenues. Grainger interprets these actions as his attempt to recoup losses from the previous decade, and I suspect that we can see in these tax reforms the foundation required for his planned expansion of military forces.[70] A program required to build so many large polyremes would have taken some years to effect and would have coincided with the latter stages of a war he was waging with the Seleucid monarch Antiochus II. Details of this war, which broke out around 260, are extremely sketchy, and we lack any reference to fighting after 257, or the reasons why peace was concluded in 253.[71] If I am correct that Philadelphus amassed his fleet of polyremes at this time, their increasing presence will have convinced his allies to remain firm as they also nudged Antiochus II into concluding peace. When peace was finally made, however, Ptolemy agreed to give up

---

the Tauric Chersonesus may represent a ship from this expedition, or give evidence of another event. The ship which bears the name *Isis* is probably not a "super-galley" as argued by Basch 1985 and accepted by Grainger 2010, 93–94, but rather a "three" with cultic imagery; see Murray 2001 and Murray 2002b. Although Grainger goes too far by suggesting (94) that this warship was part of a "demonstration cruise" intended to express Ptolemaic naval power, the image clearly reinforces the scrappy evidence provided by our literary sources of Ptolemaic contacts in the Black Sea region. For connections between Philadelphus and the western Mediterranean, see Fraser 1972, Vol. 1, 152 with notes 165–70 (= Vol. 2, 264–65).

68. For the Chremonidean War and the role of Patroclus and the Ptolemaic navy, see Habicht 1997, 142–49.

69. In the late 260s and early 250s, for example, he lost control over Miletus, Ephesus, and Samos, the location of one of his naval bases. A mercenary captain named Timarchus (who had recently made himself tyrant at Miletus) killed Ptolemy's general Charmides and, dressing in his clothes, slipped into and took the harbor of Samos, probably a Ptolemaic naval station; for the details, see Beloch 1925, 598 with n. 1; and Habicht 1957, 220 with n. 74. Ephesus remained in Ptolemy's hands until 258, when it was apparently lost following a naval battle. For a recent reconstruction of these events, see Grainger 2010, 126–27.

70. Grainger 2010, 127–28.

71. Grainger 2010 provides an excellent analysis of these series of wars. See his 117–36 for a discussion of the Second Syrian War.

those places he had lost at the start of the war, like Miletus, Ephesus, and some posts along the Cilician coast. He did this, perhaps, because he was already preparing for the next round of fighting. One of the terms of the peace treaty with Antiochus II required the king to divorce his wife Laodike and marry Philadelphus's daughter Berenike. Whatever the full range of motives behind this act, it successfully planted the seeds of discord that eventually allowed Philadelphus's son and successor to reopen the war on more favorable terms.[72]

The so-called Syrian Wars (Philadelphus's war with Antiochus II comprised the second in the series) formed a curious set of conflicts that tended to occur when a Seleucid or Lagid monarch died and his successor took over. Once peace had been achieved, however, war was never renewed until one of the two kings died, although this did not stop intrigue or adventurism in certain outlying regions, like Cyrene and the coasts of Asia Minor.[73] In the eight year period between 253 and Ptolemy's death, it seems that the king continued to bolster the perceived and real power of his naval siege unit. With each new vessel that slipped into the water, he projected an increasing image of strength and reliability to his friends, allies, and garrisoned cities around the eastern Mediterranean. During this same period, perhaps by 249, Philadelphus successfully reestablished his control over Cyrene and her neighboring cities and thus "shifted Cyrenaica out of the list of likely enemies of Egypt in the next war."[74] This addition of Cyrenaica to his possessions late in his reign nicely explains why Libya is mentioned in Athenaeus's list detailing the fleet strength of Philadelphus.

Philadelphus finally died in 246, and left his son, Ptolemy III Euergetes, well positioned to seize the offensive when the inevitable war came with his neighbor to the north. An occasion for conflict soon presented itself in the turmoil that enveloped the Seleucid court resulting from the marriage alliance sealing the peace that concluded the previous war. Antiochus II was reputedly poisoned by his former wife Laodike who then fought to secure the succession for her son Seleucus II. The specifics do not concern us here, but in the war that ensued, Ptolemy III Euergetes advanced with his fleet into Syria and gained control of Antioch and its

72. See Grainger 2010, 133–34, for the possible motives behind this marriage.

73. For this astute observation about the Syrian Wars, see Grainger 2010, 89–90.

74. Grainger 2010, 148.

port, Seleucia in Pieria, as well as much of northern Syria. Although he eventually chose to withdraw southward, he maintained control of Seleucia and managed to recover those areas lost by his father Philadelphus in the previous war, namely Miletus, Ephesus, and Samos, as well as positions in Cilicia, Lycia, the Aegean, Thrace, and the Hellespont.[75] When peace was made between Seleucus II and Euergetes in 241, Ptolemy's gains were spread from Thrace in the northern Aegean to Ionia, Caria, Lycia, Pamphylia, Cilicia, and Syria. Although virtually no details of these conquests survive, these gains make best sense as the result of his and his father's great outlay of money in order to build the largest collection of big ships ever amassed. If I am correct, then the list quoted by Athenaeus describes Ptolemy's fleet toward the end of his reign and helps to explain the great recovery experienced by Egypt during the Third Syrian War described here. In recognition of this recent increase in naval power, the Achaean League made an alliance with Ptolemy III Euergetes in 242/41 and accepted his leadership on land and sea (Plut. *Arat.* 24.4).

Philo's *Poliorketika*

Although Philo's preserved text lacks a clear statement concerning the date and context of its composition, I have followed the arguments of Marsden (who argues for the 240s) and Garlan (who argues for the 220s) as providing the range for the work's likely date of composition. If I have correctly read the evidence for the reigns of Philadelphus and Euergetes, Philo's siegecraft manual seems to fit more naturally in the reign of Euergetes than that of Philadelphus. I say this for the following reasons. First, the work, as a whole, is overwhelmingly defensive in its outlook, with the single section dealing with offensive siege warfare comprising less than a third of the total.[76] Second, the defensive parts of the work imply that Ariston, the general to whom it is addressed, is not the commander of a major naval station. This emerges from the resources at his disposal, which do not seem to include a squadron of warships (as at Ake-Ptolemais, Sidon, Samos, or Thera), which he could anchor across the harbor mouth, bows

---

75. We often learn of these changes in power from inscriptions dealing with unrelated matters, so it is difficult to determine the precise dates. In general, for the details of this war, see Grainger 2010, 153–70.

76. In Garlan's text, sections dealing with offense total only 11.75 out of a total of 36.5 columns: Garlan 1974, 291–327.

seaward, when threatened by attack. To the contrary, Philo assumes Ariston will have to rely on a chain suspended from buoys (C 52) or cobble together a pontoon barrier of different sized ships, including small open galleys and freighters armed with catapults and lead amphoras (C 54–55). Third, Philo's manual includes no advice regarding how Ariston should relieve a neighboring city undergoing siege, a further indication that Ariston could not be expected to have a squadron of warships under his command. On the other hand, when Philo gives him instructions on how to engage in naval siege warfare, he speaks to his patron as the commander of a respectable naval campaign with access to various sizes of warships, including big ships that might not be very serviceable for war.

This odd mixture of siege instructions paired with lengthy discussions of how to secure a city from attack makes sense if we place its composition during a period when war was contemplated, but not yet declared. While certainty is impossible, Marsden's suggestion that Philo's work dates to the period immediately following the death of Ptolemy II, when everyone knew that war was coming, has merit. When war broke out, commanders like Ariston led the forces of Euergetes against coastal cities throughout the eastern Mediterranean and then stayed on to secure them for the throne. This might explain the work's focus on rebuilding defensive fortifications and taking safeguards against the very tactics that won the city in the first place. The primary duty of a commander like Ariston would have been to fortify and secure the city under his command and to use the resources at his disposal to send for help and then wait for a relief force should trouble arise.

While this seems plausible enough as a context for Philo's siegecraft manual, it is odd that he fails to include specific references to different classes of big ships in the fleet of his patron. He assumes that his patron will not have access to warships, let alone big ships, if his job involved organizing a city's defenses. And yet, he assumes big ships will probably be present should Ariston find himself in charge of an offensive siege campaign.[77] Beyond this, he has little to say about the specifics of big ship warfare and advises the placement of one's "timber constructions" or siege machinery on freighters and small *lemboi* (D 21), not on big ships like "twenties" or "thirties." We might explain this lack of precision in a

---

77. He advises their use in breaking through harbor barriers (D 22–23) and carrying out ram strikes on sections of the city wall that run at sea level (D 29).

number of ways, although I admit that no one explanation is more persua-
sive than another. Perhaps Philo had no experience to impart either
because Ptolemy's big ships were not yet battle tested, or because he had
nothing specific to say about their different characteristics, or because regional commanders had no access to the largest ships in the Alexandrian
fleet. Or we might explain the problem by the known fact that Philo's text
was seriously abbreviated in antiquity, perhaps losing sections that were
considered irrelevant by later editors. Whatever the true reason (or reasons), our imperfect understanding of Philo and his context keeps us
from grasping a fully satisfying answer.[78]

Ptolemy IV Philopator's "Forty": An Historical Perspective

Events at the outbreak of the Fourth Syrian War (221–217) provide additional evidence for the nature of the Ptolemaic empire while the war and
its aftermath provide an excellent occasion for the construction of Ptolemy's "forty." The war, as described by Polybius, started with the attempt by
Antiochus III to recover those portions of northern Syria that his father
had lost during the previous war. Although most consider Antiochus III to
be the more competent military commander, the new king of Egypt, Ptolemy IV Philopator, managed to defeat Antiochus on the border of Egypt at
Raphia, recover his losses, and conclude the war on favorable terms.

Grainger's recent study of the war dates its start to 221 when Antiochus
III first advanced with an army into northern Syria after the death of Ptolemy III.[79] The war started in earnest, however, in 219 when Antiochus III
recovered Seleucia in Pieria as well as a number of other fortified positions
in Syria and northern Palestine.[80] His actions at Seleucia, as described by
Polybius (5.59.1–60.10), provide a textbook case for how to detach a fortified coastal city from Ptolemaic control. Because a major frontal attack
with a siege force was expected to initiate the dispatch of a relief force by
land and by sea, Antiochus determined to effect the capitulation of the city

---

78. It is even possible that Philo's text might date to the reign of Philopator, when the largest
big ships were no longer in service and his patron had little need of learning their specifics.

79. Grainger 2010, 187 with n. 51.

80. A decree of Egyptian priests written soon after the war's conclusion (see text below) dates
its outbreak to this second incursion; for a translation and commentary on the so-called
"Raphia decree," as well as references to further bibliography, see Austin 2006, #276.

before these forces could arrive. In the case of Seleucia, he cut the land routes to the south, camped his army in full sight before the city, secretly subverted junior officers of the garrison by bribery, and then attacked the city circuit from numerous directions, including its harbor walls. His plan worked to perfection and, once the commander realized his officers had no stomach for resistance, the city quickly capitulated.[81]

Following this success, Antiochus received Tyre and Ake-Ptolemais from mercenary commanders who decided to change sides, and thus gained control of the ships in the harbor of Ake-Ptolemais. These included 40 warships, 20 of them cataphract galleys, the smallest of which were "fours" (Polyb. 5.62.4–5). Later this same campaigning season (219), Antiochus attacked the coastal city of Dor (Polyb. 5.66.1 calls it *Doura*), but could not take it, owing to the strength of its position and the support provided by Philopator's general Nicolaus. Catapult balls in the Tantoura Lagoon to the south of the city may suggest that he mounted small caliber machines on his recently acquired cataphract galleys; nevertheless, the city seems to have held firm.[82]

Over the next year and a half, Antiochus steadily gained ground in Phoenicia and Palestine, defeating Ptolemy's forces in a battle north of Sidon at Porphyrion (218), and gaining control of numerous fortified positions and cities like Gaza (in spring 217?). The stubborn nature of some allies like Sidon and Dor, who never capitulated, reveals how difficult it was to capture a coastal city without overwhelming naval superiority. According to Grainger, Philopator's slow withdrawal in the face of Antiochus's advance toward Egypt bought him the necessary time to recruit and train his infantry, so that when he marched to Raphia, his forces outnumbered his enemy's by roughly 10%.[83] The result of the battle, fought on 22 June 217, was a resounding victory for Ptolemy, who followed up his success by a northern campaign into Syria aimed at recovering his positions and gathering booty. Peace was concluded a few months later, as revealed by a unique document.

Upon Ptolemy's return to Egypt, a synod of priests gathered at Memphis to vote a decree of thanks for Ptolemy's victory and subsequent benefactions; they published their text on a stone stele in hieroglyphic and

---

81. See Grainger 2010, 196–98 for an excellent description and analysis.

82. See chapter 5, Table 5.2.

83. For a useful discussion of this war, see Grainger 2010, 195–218, and 213, for his remarks about the forces at Raphia.

demotic Egyptian as well as in Greek. The demotic version is the best pre-served and presents a narrative of the recent campaign from a nationalis-tic perspective. Despite the obvious exaggeration and hyperbole, the decree (Austin 2006, #276, lines 14–15) describes the large amount of wealth brought back to Egypt by Philopator as well as his generous (and showy) religious dedications and donatives after his return (lines 29–30). "He caused much temple furniture and equipment to be made of gold and silver, although he had spent a vast sum for that campaign, and had given 300,000 pieces of gold as a reward to his army." In addition, the decree mentions (line 31) benefactions "upon the priests, the temple staff, and the rest of the people throughout Egypt."

As part of this euphoric mood of display and ostentation, I suggest that Philopator built his monstrous "forty." We have already seen from Callix-enus's description how the ship was "extremely well-proportioned" and "a marvel in its other decoration." Huge paintings of animals decorated its bow and stern while ivy leaves and *thyrsoi*—traditional symbols of the god Dionysus—were painted along its hull beneath the oarports. Such decora-tion is seen in both ceremonial ships and warships, attested from New Kingdom contexts, and the imagery accords well with Philopator's per-sonal identification with Dionysus. The animals at the bow were probably drawn from the normal Dionysiac menagerie of panthers, peacocks, and lions, and the ivy motif on the hull recalls ivy leaves tattooed on Philopator himself.[84]

Thus decorated, Philopator's "forty" represented an impressive display that broadcast a dual message of the king's awesome might in securing his cities as well as his devotion to the god Dionysus. As Plutarch observed, the ship was intended as a show piece, but we should not conclude from this that the vessel lacked a functional purpose. Just like Philopator's grand gestures to the priests, temple staff, Egyptian people, and army, this "warship" sent a message to all who witnessed its launch that Philopator was the worthy son and grandson of god kings who would protect their traditions of leadership. The display was intended to amaze and delight the crowds who packed the shore to see the launch and, at the same time,

---

84. Sculpted reliefs, plus models found in tombs provide evidence for ships decorated with religious symbols appropriate to the occupant. Some bear symbols of Montu, the falcon-headed god of war, and signify warships; see Landström 1970, 102–21 with figs. 326, 329, 336, 368, and 370. For Dionysiac fauna, see Fraser 1972, 206; for Philopator's identification with Dionysus, see Fraser 1972, 203–204. Philopator's ivy leaf tattoo is referred to in *Etym. Mag.* s.v. Γάλλος; cf. also Fraser 1972, Vol. 2, 347–48n118.

to honor the god Dionysus and secure his continued good favor. He seemed to be saying, "We still honor our foreign obligations, bring aid to those attacked, and defeat our enemies." Never mind that he could never send such a vessel on campaign, away from its special shipyard and dry dock.[85]

Conclusion

In the past, the so-called super-galleys of the Hellenistic period have been interpreted as "fives" on steroids, that is, warships that were intended for ship-against-ship combat in pitched naval battles. I have tried to show how these extraordinarily large warships fit naturally into a context involving naval siege warfare. I do not mean to imply that a ruler who possessed a number of large ships used these weapons for every siege opportunity that arose. Clearly, this was not the case. The career of Demetrius Poliorcetes demonstrates that big ships were best deployed in large fleets, when they could be surrounded and protected by smaller, more maneuverable galleys. Such a fleet must have accompanied *Leontophoros* or Ptolemy's "twenty" and "thirties" and brings to mind the Aircraft Carrier Battle Groups used by the United States following World War II as instruments of foreign policy. While this parallel has limitations, it is fair to say that both modern carriers and ancient big ships worked most effectively as part of a large combined force, with a host of specialized support ships providing logistical support and protection.[86] Polyreme navies were also attended by sizeable infantry and cavalry units carried along in transports. The entire force employed tens of thousands of men who required protection on shore as well as large supplies of food and drink, and this demanded a separate fleet of merchantmen and an army of stevedores and porters. When big ships were taken on campaign without adequate supporting

---

85. See also Rice 1983, 140–41 who arrives at a similar conclusion. I cannot accept her view, however, that we should dismiss Plutarch's assessment of the ship's performance characteristics as I have explained in the text and n. 35 above.

86. Carrier Battle Groups (CVBG) are formed on an ad hoc basis and thus differ one from another. Even so, they are comprised of similar types of ships, which normally include an aircraft carrier, two guided missile cruisers (for long-range strike capability), a guided missile destroyer and destroyer (for anti-submarine warfare), two attack submarines (to seek out and destroy hostile surface ships and submarines), and a combined ammunition, oiler, and supply ship (for logistical support). Source: Global Security Group, "Battle Group – Introduction," http://www.globalsecurity.org/military/agency/navy/batgru-intro.htm, accessed Feb. 10, 2011.

forces, the results could be disastrous, as Demetrius experienced when he hurriedly embarked on his last campaign into Asia Minor from Athens.

To state this in other terms, the kind of military operation that included large numbers of big ships was not the norm. It was simply too expensive, required too much planning, and involved the coordination of too many people. This said, it seems that a monarch like Philadelphus wanted to project the image that he was capable of such an operation if he felt the need. Thus, his possession of a larger stockpile of polyremes than anyone else served as a powerful deterrent. He might not choose or be able to use them in every instance, but his possession of such weapons tended to keep both his friends and enemies in line. Plutarch (*Demetr.* 20.6) seems to express this sentiment when he says that the "sheer size" of Demetrius's military constructions "alarmed even his friends, while their beauty delighted even his enemies."

The ability to inspire such awe and respect for power may help to explain why Philadelphus amassed so many polyremes toward the end of his reign. And if this is hard to comprehend, the reader might ponder the impossibly large arsenals of nuclear weapons we have amassed since the end of World War II. While the costs and risks associated with using such weapons (both ancient and modern) differ markedly in magnitude, their simple existence represent strong deterrents. This, at any rate, is the modern logic used to justify our continued maintenance of these stockpiles.[87] So, in a world without weapons of mass destruction, Ptolemy's polyremes represented serious power. And the memory of this power drove Philopator to build the largest warship ever constructed, proclaiming to all that he was still mindful of his family's naval tradition and that both his friends and enemies should act accordingly.

Although it was doubtless delivered with sincerity and conviction, Philopator's message was really an empty promise because the kind of navy evoked by the "forty" had ceased to exist by his reign. As we have seen, the massive fleets built between 315 and 245 were only as useful as a monarch's willingness to mount equally massive and expensive campaigns "by land and by sea." By the end of the third century, however, the

---

87. See, for example, Powaski 1987, who presents a useful summary, 222–31. The Cold War concept of mutual assured destruction (MAD) was thought to hold in check those who possessed the stockpiles (Powaski 1987, 234). Using the language of Defense Secretary Robert S. MacNamara, we might say that Philadelphus achieved, with his big ship navy, the image of assured destructive capability (Powaski 1987, 114).

sums required to sustain the big ship phenomenon were simply too great. As a result, the major powers found it difficult to build the size of naval force required to protect their largest galleys, particularly when Rome began to intervene in the affairs of the eastern Mediterranean. This story spells the end of the big ship phenomenon and thus forms the final chapter of our study.

7

The End of the Big Ship Phenomenon

FOUR SEPARATE BATTLE accounts involving midsized polyremes ("sixes" to "tens") allow us to complete our picture of the big ship phenomenon. The battles are not only important for the few rare details they provide of "sevens," "eights," and "tens" in action, they also clearly demonstrate the difficulties in deploying big ship navies and suggest the reasons behind their abandonment. The first conflict happened off Chios in 201 and was fought between Macedonia and the combined fleets of Pergamon and Rhodes. The second and third occurred 11 years later along the same stretch of coast. This time, the combatants were Rome, Rhodes, and Antiochus III of Syria. The fourth occurred in 31 BCE off Actium, the southern cape at the entrance to the Ambracian Gulf in western Greece. Here, the combatants are well known: the future emperor Augustus and his unsuccessful rival for power Mark Antony. Since details of this engagement are obscured behind a veil of Augustan propaganda, we might begin by reviewing the details of the first three engagements. Once we consider their implications for the challenges involved in using big ship navies, we can better address the Actian campaign of Antony and Cleopatra. What follows is not intended to be a detailed narrative of these battles, but rather an attempt to place each battle in a context that explains the uses to which big ship navies were put.[1]

---

1. The best detailed narrative of the battles off Side and Myonnesus is still found in Thiel 1946, 338–345 (Side) and 352–357 (Myonnesus). Morrison in Morrison and Coates 1996, 76–85 (Chios), 102–109 (Side and Myonnesus), 157–170 (Actium) also provides a detailed discussion with many useful observations, although his text is full of small errors and must be used with caution; see Murray 1998. On Actium see also Murray and Petsas 1989, 131–151 and Murray 2002a, 339–360 for the evidence and a discussion of the basic literature. The commentaries by Walbank, Briscoe, and Reinhold are indispensible: Walbank 1999, Vol. II; Briscoe 1981; and Reinhold 1988, 101–116. For a comprehensive treatment of the complex events leading up to and including the Battle of Actium, one can hardly do better than Carter 1970.

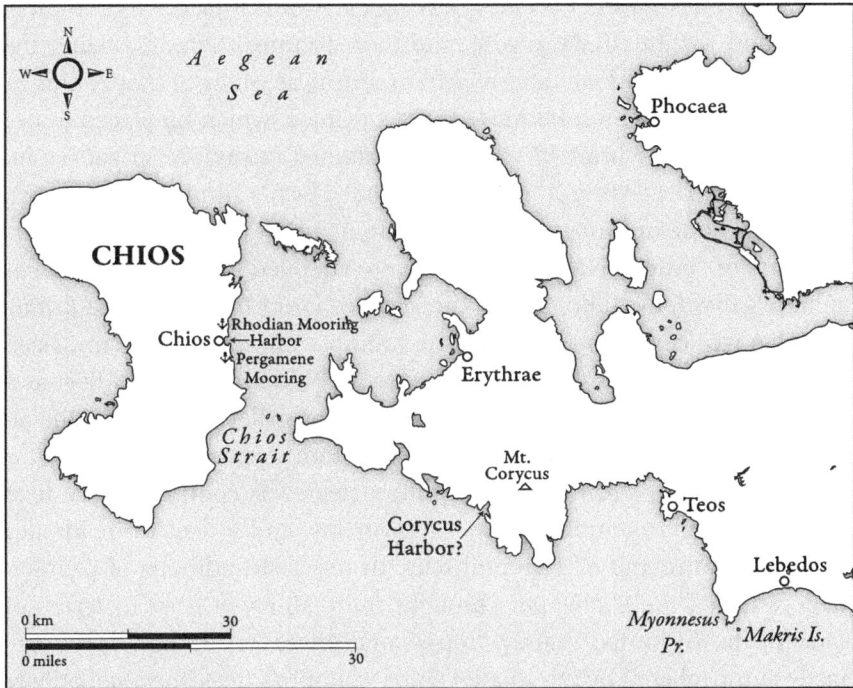

MAP 7.1 Chios Strait. Map adapted from Morrison and Coates 1996, 80, Map J.

The Battle off Chios (201)

Ptolemy IV Philopator, builder of the gargantuan "forty," died in 204, and his death sparked a flurry of activity when the news spread to the other major powers of the eastern Mediterranean. Syria was still ruled by Antiochus III and Macedonia by Philip V, the grandson of Antigonus Gonatas. Both kings saw in Ptolemy's death an excellent opportunity for expansion into Egyptian controlled regions, their hopes fueled by the expectation of another Syrian war (which tended to occur on the death of each Egyptian monarch), by the fact that Ptolemy's successor was a six year old child, and by the apparent disarray emanating from the Egyptian court.[2]

In this context, Philip V led a naval campaign to the coast of Asia Minor with the intention of ending Ptolemaic dominance in the Aegean. He first

---

2. A synopsis of these affairs contained in a fragment of Appian (*Mac.* 4) mentions an agreement between Antiochus III and Philip V to assist each other in their plans. For the chaos in the Ptolemaic court, see Grainger 2010, 235–243.

proceeded through the Cyclades, leaving garrisons at places like Andros, Paros, and Kythnos (Livy 31.15.8), and then occupied Samos, seizing the Ptolemaic ships stationed there.[3] After refitting as many of these ships as possible (Polyb. 16.2.9), he moved next to Chios, which he placed under siege. The fleet he brought with him contained 53 cataphract galleys including Philip's flagship, a "ten," commanded by his admiral Democrates, and at least one or more of the classes from "nine" to "six" plus multiple numbers of "fours." His larger ships were attended by a mass of smaller aphract galleys, including an unknown number of *triemioliai* and *hemioliai*, plus 150 *lemboi* and *pristeis*.[4] The multiple numbers of his midsized polyremes (i.e., "sixes" to "tens") underscore Philip's use of this fleet as a naval siege unit, and the large mass of smaller galleys represents his attempt to provide his larger units with protection, as events will show.

The allied force sent to break Philip's siege was comprised of a fleet from Pergamon, commanded by King Attalus, and a fleet from Rhodes under the command of Theophiliscus. In the best traditions of counter-siege warfare, the challengers brought more ships, at least in terms of cataphracts: 65 units, mainly "fours" and "fives." Although they were vastly outnumbered by the smaller ships in Philip's fleet (they had only 12 aphracts: nine *triemioliai* and three "threes"[5]), the speed with which Philip abandoned his siege in the face of their challenge implies that he felt he could not win a direct confrontation. So, he made haste to get to sea, persuading himself that he could outrun the enemy and proceed southward along the mainland to his base at Samos (Polyb. 16.2.4). Polybius, our main source for the battle, describes two combat zones: an engagement between Attalus and the right wing of Philip's fleeing ships, and another one between Theophiliscus and Philip's left. The first engagement was near the shore of Chios, while the second was more toward the mainland.[6]

---

3. See Walbank 1999, Vol. II, p. 503.

4. "Ten" (Polyb. 16.3.3), "nine" (16.7.1), at least two "eights" (16.3.2, 3.7–8), "seven" (16.3.7, 7.1), "six" (16.7.1), "fives" (16.6.4), "fours" (16.7.2), *triemioliai* (16.7.1), *hemioliai* (16.6.4), *lemboi* (16.4.2, 4.8, 4.10, 5.5, 6.4, 6.7), and *pristeis* (16.2.9). See Glossary for the definitions of *triemioliai*, *hemioliai*, and *pristeis*.

5. Fleet total (Polyb. 16.2.10), Pergamene flagship (large but size unstated: Polyb. 16.3.1, 6.10, 7.3, 8.2), "fives" and "fours" (16.5.1, 5.4, 6.2, 7.3).

6. Once the Macedonians turned about to face the enemy, their left was now close to Chios and their right toward the mainland, a fact that causes some confusion in Polybius's account; see Walbank 1999, Vol. 2, 504 at 16.2.7.

According to Polybius (16.2.5), as soon as Attalus and Theophiliscus saw Philip putting out to sea, they prepared to engage him. Philip signaled to his right wing to engage the enemy and then withdrew with a few *lemboi* to the islands in the middle of the strait to await the result of the battle. Attalus, sailing on a large ship, began the battle by ramming an "eight" bow-on. The ram strike occurred under the "eight's" waterline and proved fatal to the struck ship. She apparently took on water slowly because her deck troops fought for some time before the ship settled to the waterline (Polyb. 16.3.1–2). Elsewhere, Philip's "ten" rammed a *triemiolia* in the side. Considering the difference in speed and maneuverability between the two vessels, it makes sense that such an event occurred at the battle's outset when the lines first collided. Presumably sensing an easy kill, the "ten" struck the smaller vessel amidships but jammed a part of her bow structure (probably her "fore ram" or *proembolion*) under the struck vessel's top bank of oars. Stuck like this and unable to maneuver, the "ten" was attacked on both sides by two separate "fives" who managed to destroy the vessel and all aboard including the admiral Democrates (Polyb. 16.3.3–6).

Polybius also preserved the exploits of Dionysodorus and Deinocrates, two brothers who served as commodores (*nauarchoi*) for Attalus. Dionysodorus, probably on a "five," charged a "seven" head-on, swerved at the last moment to miss her bow, but suffered the loss of his starboard oars and tower supports as he slid along her starboard side (Polyb. 16.3.7, 12). Although the enemy completely surrounded him and destroyed both his ship and crew, he and two others dove overboard and swam to "the *triemiolia* giving support to him" (Polyb. 16.3.14). His brother Deinocrates charged an "eight," prow-to-prow, and as the enemy was high in the water, he struck her below the waterline but was unable to back away following the strike.[7] In the struggle between the marines that followed, Deinocrates, being on a smaller vessel, would have surely been overwhelmed, but was saved when Attalus rammed the "eight" and separated the two ships. After the marines aboard the "eight" were all killed, Attalus captured the vessel (Polyb. 16.3.8–11).

While Attalus attacked the right (leading) wing immediately south of the city, it took the Rhodian commander a bit longer to catch up with Philip's left (Polyb. 16.4.4). Perhaps this was because the Rhodian camp

---

7. I have translated the text "under the waterline" based on the overall sense of the passage. The actual word that describes where Deinocrates landed his blow "under the βίαχα" appears nowhere else in Greek; see Walbank 1999, Vol. 2, 507.

was located to the north of the city and was thus further removed from the enemy when Philip fled southward.[8] Whatever the explanation, when they finally caught up with the left wing, the Rhodians attacked their sterns and rear-most oars forcing Philip's ships to turn about and engage in prow-to-prow attacks. Hoping to hinder the Rhodians from carrying out their accustomed tactical maneuvers, the Macedonians had stationed *lemboi* between their cataphract galleys (Polyb. 16.4.8). After the first charge, when the lines became disordered, the Macedonian *lemboi* fouled their enemies' oars, attacked enemy prows and sterns, and thus hindered the helmsmen and rowers from doing their work (Polyb. 16.4.10).

On the other side, Polybius describes how the Rhodians avoided closing with the enemy's cataphracts because they feared the Macedonian marines. They therefore avoided prow-to-prow attacks if they could, but if not, they tried to depress their bows in order to strike below the waterline and receive enemy blows above it. Normally, they tried to cut through the enemy line, shearing off oars and turning back around to attack their enemies' sterns; and if a vessel turned to meet their attacks, they aimed their strikes at the enemy's exposed flank (Polyb. 16.4.11–15).

In describing the heroic exploits of a number of Rhodian "fives," Polybius reveals how ships in the line were expected to work in concert with one another. For example, one "five" piloted by Autolycus rammed an enemy vessel and put her out of action, but in so doing, broke off her ram in the enemy's hull. As the sea poured in from the bow, Autolycus and his men were surrounded by the enemy and all eventually perished.[9] Seeing Autolycus in trouble, the admiral Theophiliscus came up in support with three "fives," and, although he could not help the stricken vessel that was full of water, he rammed two nearby enemy ships and forced their deck soldiers overboard. He was quickly surrounded by a number of *lemboi* and cataphracts and, after losing most of his soldiers, just managed to save his own ship, partly through the help of Philostratus, who had arrived on another "five" to lend aid.

As the battle began to wind down, Attalus approached the islands where Philip was waiting and observed one of his own "fives" slowly sinking after being rammed by the enemy. Supported by two "fours," Attalus drove away the ship that had destroyed his vessel. Seeing that he was now separated from the other ships in his fleet, Philip took four "fives,"

---

8. The suggestion is that of Morrison and Coates 1996, 81.

9. It is noteworthy that Autolycus, a helmsman, wore armor; see Polyb. 16.5.2–3.

three *hemioliai*, and the *lemboi* that happened to be nearby him and forced Attalus "in great distress" to beach his flagship along with (presumably) the two "fours" that supported her. Attalus and his crew got away, but Philip gained control of the ships (Polyb. 16.6.1–5) and towed them back to his fleet. The casualty totals given by Polybius (16.7.1–6) are likely derived from a Rhodian source and therefore downplay Rhodian losses. Despite this fact, the battle was a serious setback for Philip, who lost 18 cataphracts, many of them quite large (see Table 7.1), and more than 9000

Table 7.1 Battle of Chios—Losses.

	Cataphract Galleys	Aphract Galleys
Philip's losses:		
to Attalus by sinking	"ten," "nine," "eight,"* (Polyb. 16.3.2), "seven," "six," 10 "fives" & "fours"	3 *triemioliai*, 25 *lemboi* with crews
to Attalus by capture	"eight"? (Polyb. 16.3.8–11)	none
to Rhodians by sinking	none	10 cataphracts and 40 *lemboi*
to Rhodians by capture	2 "fours"	7 *lemboi*
Attalus' losses to Philip:		
by sinking	2 "fives"	1 *triemiolia*
by capture	2 "fours" and the royal ship	none
Rhodian losses to Philip:		
by sinking	2 "fives"	1 "three"
by capture	none	none

Casualties	Killed	Captured
Philip	3000 soldiers, 6000 sailors/oarsmen	2000
Attalus	70	700 total for Attalus and Rhodians
Rhodians	60	–

men. Although he would win a battle near Lade in the days to come, this defeat demonstrated beyond any doubt that he lacked the naval dominance required to protect his naval siege unit. We will return to this point after considering the two other battles involving midsized polyremes that occurred in this same general region 11 years later.

The Syrian War between Rome and Antiochus III: Battles off Corycus (191), Side, and Myonnesus (190)

Following his defeat at Chios, Philip V was unable to realize his goals of expansion into Asia Minor and thus turned his attention back to Greece, where he became embroiled in a war with Rome that lasted from 200 to 197. His defeat in this war convinced him to side with Rome for what was to follow. After Philip's withdrawal from Asia Minor, the Seleucid king Antiochus III brought a land and sea force along the coast of Asia Minor to recover what he considered to be his ancestral lands (Livy 33.40.4–6). He first recovered a number of Ptolemaic possessions in Caria and Lycia, established a naval base at Ephesus (197), and then coordinated further

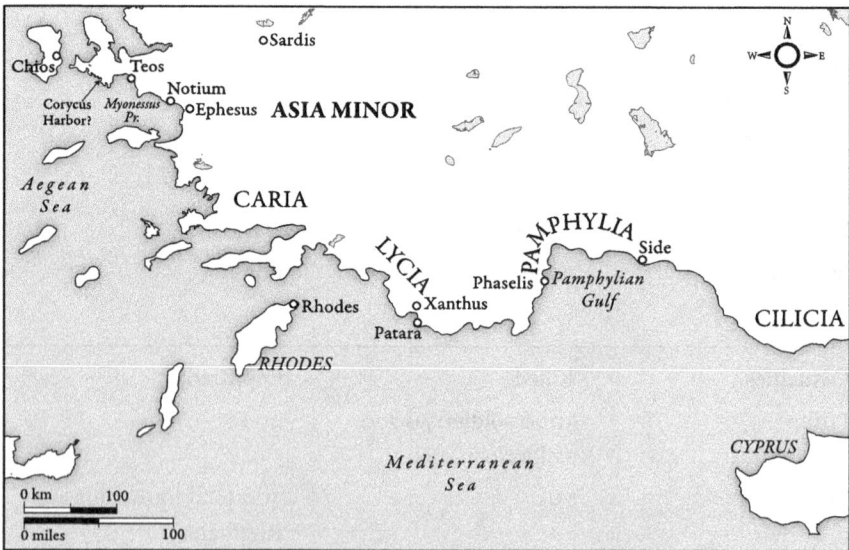

MAP 7.2 Coast of Asia Minor showing Corycus, Side, and Myonnesus.

attacks from here on the cities of the western coast.[10] In the spring of 196, he moved into the Hellespont, crossed to the Chersonesus, and brought a combined land and sea force to a city called Madytus (Livy 33.38.8). When he unpacked his siege machinery, the place surrendered in fear, causing a ripple effect throughout the region. Sestus soon followed, and then every other town in the Chersonesus surrendered voluntarily to his forces. Following this success, he proceeded to Lysimacheia, the old capital of Lysimachus, and resettled the place (Livy 33.38.10–14).

Between 196 and 192 a protracted series of negotiations took place between Antiochus and Rome that were designed to limit the king's ability to intervene in Greece. Political maneuvering by the Aetolian League forced the issue and Antiochus was convinced by them to invade Greece in 192. The war he fought there was short and he was defeated the following year at Thermopylae in a land battle (Livy 36.18–19). When he retreated back to Asia, the Romans made preparations to move their land army across the Hellespont to conclude the war. To this end, they sent a fleet under Gaius Livius to coordinate with their Rhodian and Pergamene allies with two main objectives: to secure the Hellespont for the army's crossing, and to prevent Antiochus from gaining naval superiority along the Aegean coast.[11]

The Battle off Corycus (191)

When Antiochus received news of the Roman fleet's approach along with a force from Pergamon, he decided to follow the advice of his admiral Polyxenidas to intercept them before they joined up with their Rhodian allies. Polyxenidas accordingly set out from Ephesus to meet the enemy with a fleet of 100 ships, 70 of which were "decked" (*tectae*) or cataphract galleys. Livy (36.43.8) further characterized the fleet as *minoris omnes formae erant*: "they were all of lighter build."[12] What he meant by this has stirred some debate which need not concern us here; what is striking, however,

---

10. For the precise cities Antiochus III captured, see Briscoe 1973, 321 at 33.38.1–3.

11. For the naval war in Asia, see Thiel 1946, 293–372.

12. The precise Syrian fleet total is uncertain. Some scholars prefer Appian's 200 (*Syr.* 5.22, 103) as it helps to explain why Polyxenidas was so eager for battle with the 81 cataphract galleys of the enemy. For the reasons for preferring Livy's total, see Briscoe 1973, 283 at 43.8. For the problems involved with Livy's terminology (including *naves minoris, maioris* and *maximae formae*), see McDonald and Walbank 1969, 31–34.

is his characterization of the Syrian fleet as "light."[13] We are told that the commander felt this would be an advantage against the enemy's heavier galleys that would be loaded with equipment and supplies (Livy 36.43.6–7).

On the Roman side, the commander Livius arrived at Phocaea with 81 cataphract galleys plus many smaller ships, some with rams, and some without (Livy 36.42.8). He was joined here by Eumenes of Pergamon with 24 cataphracts and about 50 open vessels. As the combined fleet made for Corycus harbor on the Erythraean Peninsula under sail, we are told that Polyxenidas was delighted to get this chance to meet them, and drew up his fleet off Corycus in battle formation. The allied fleet struck sails and adjusted their battle lines to meet the length of the enemy's formation. The battle began when two Punic ships from the Roman fleet were caught in front of the battle line by three Syrian warships (Livy 36.44.5).[14] The Syrians swept the oars of one galley and put her out of action through boarding. Enraged by this disgrace, the Roman commander attacked the victorious galleys with his flagship, ordered his marines to throw grappling irons, and turned the battle into an infantry contest, which his men won by their superior valor. When Polyxenidas saw that his men were "outmatched by the courage of the Romans," he ordered a retreat (Livy 36.45.1).[15]

The battle account, as presented by Livy, contains a number of problematic episodes. First, it is difficult to understand why Polyxenidas would be "delighted" to bring on a battle against 105 "fours" and "fives" with his own fleet of 70 light cataphracts (Livy 36.44.1: *Polyxenidas . . . occasione pugnandi laetus*). If he felt his open galleys gave him some advantage, Livy preserves no details of their fighting. Then we have the Syrians' use of boarding tactics

---

13. Although Livy does not record the classes involved, most assume that Polyxenidas would have wanted "fours" and "fives" among his cataphract galleys. Nowhere else, however, do we have evidence for "fours" and "fives" being classed among the lighter units in the fleet. Indeed, where Livy makes it clear, he places "fours" and "fives" among the ships "of heavier build." Some have therefore interpreted Livy's remark as evidence for light "fours" and "fives," while others believe that Livy had cataphract "threes" in mind; see McDonald and Walbank 1969, 31–34. The characterization of the fleet as light is also reflected in Appian's account (*Syr* 5.22, 103) and presumably derives from Polybius. With such evidence, we will never know the precise classes in this fleet, but we can be certain that the force lacked the midsized polyremes that appear in conflicts the following year.

14. Presumably these *Punicae naves* were either captured during the recent war with Carthage, or they represent an allied contingent. Their loss, the only ones sustained by the Romans, would thus underscore the excellence of the Roman marines.

15. Appian (*Syr.* 22) presents a few conflicting details: the Syrians captured both Punic ships and were the first to grapple the Roman commander's vessel.

at the beginning of a battle. Normally, vessels put out of action, like the Punic ship, were left in a disabled condition until later in the battle, when boarding posed fewer risks to the attacker. As described here, the boarding took place dangerously close to the Roman battle line. And finally, there is Livy's repeated emphasis on the superior valor and courage of the Roman marines as the decisive factor in the victory (Livy 36.44.9, 45.1). While the casualty totals tend to support his conclusion for this battle (Livy 36.45.3: 13 vessels captured vs. 10 "swamped"), he repeats the same observation for the battle off Myonnesus (37.30.6) where the casualty totals are less supportive (see Table 7.2). When combined with the other problems associated with this battle, Livy's narrative seems rather generic and lacking in useful detail other than that Polyxenidas relied on "light" ships.[16]

What is frequently overlooked by those who study the naval war between Rome and Antiochus III is the keen competition for coastal cities that developed during the brief period before the Roman army crossed into Asia. During this awkward period of waiting, and with each side roughly balanced in power, the willingness of a city to embrace or desert Antiochus or the allies often depended on their perceptions of whose naval force was stronger and where it was based. These perceptions, in turn, were impacted by battles and maneuvers that had nothing to do with naval sieges.[17] In the year following the Roman arrival in Ionia and defeat of Polyxenidas off Corycus, we encounter a number of midsized polyremes in the fleet of Antiochus III. Scholars have seen in this fact Antiochus's recognition that his fleet at Corycus was too light. They argue that he consciously decided to outclass the Roman "fives" by building larger galleys.[18]

I believe the evidence suggests something different. Antiochus had sent a fleet of light cataphracts to meet the Romans off Corycus because he felt it would be sufficient. When the outcome proved he had underestimated his enemies' abilities, he was left with an enemy along his western coast. In order to prevent a mass defection of his coastal cities, he needed

---

16. Livy's narrative is much more detailed in its description of the way the Roman fleet drew up into battle order; see Morrison and Coates 1996, 94–95.

17. Antiochus, for example, left his son Seleucus with an army in Aeolis with orders to hold the costal cities which Eumenes and the Romans were trying to win over (Livy 37.8.5). In the Hellespontine region, the Romans won over Sestus and placed Abydus under siege (Livy 37.9.9–11). Alarmed for their safety, the citizens of Abydus began to discuss terms of surrender, but broke off their talks when they heard that the Syrian fleet had defeated a Rhodian squadron at Panormus (Livy 37.12.1–4), far away on the north coast of Samos.

18. See Thiel 1946, 344–345 and McDonald and Walbank 1969, 34.

to amass a credible naval siege force as quickly as possible. During the winter of 192–191, he sent Hannibal to gather together in Cilicia as many ships from his Phoenician cities as possible.[19] He also ordered Polyxenidas to refit the fleet at Ephesus, which already included a number of mid-sized polyremes.[20]

Battle off Side (190)

The fleet gathered by Hannibal in Cilicia was ready during the summer of 190, and the Rhodians sent a squadron of 32 "fours" and four "threes" to intercept it as Hannibal progressed westward along the southern coast of Asia Minor. He had with him 37 "ships of larger build" (*maioris formae navium*), including three "sevens" and four "sixes" (Livy 37.23.4–5) as well as 10 "threes" and a number of smaller open vessels.[21] When the two forces met in the Pamphylian Gulf off the city of Side, Hannibal commanded the seaward end of his fleet's left wing and faced the Rhodian admiral Euda-mus. At the battle's start, the Rhodian fleet formed into line a bit haphaz-ardly and the fighting began on the seaward wings before the landward wings were fully in order.[22] Whatever confusion may have attended the start of the battle, the Rhodians quickly regained their poise and closed with the enemy in prow-to-prow charges (Livy 37.23.1–11).

As we saw at Chios in 201, Rhodian galleys preferred to avoid the prows of larger opponents and pass through the gaps between warships when possible, shearing off oars and turning about to attack their enemies' sterns. Livy preserves no specific details of the fighting except for the unexpected

---

19. Hannibal, the invader of Italy, had come to Antiochus's court in 193, prior to his invasion of Greece; see Livy 34.60.2.

20. Steinby 2007, 181 believes that Antiochus also ordered ships to be built; see Livy 37.8.3: *itaque et Hannibalem in Syriam miserat ad Phoenicum accersendas naues, et Polyxenidam, quo minus prospere res gesta erat, eo enixius et eas, quae erant, reficere et alias parare naues iussit.* "And so he sent Hannibal to Syria to summon Phoenician ships, and ordered Polyxenidas, since his previous efforts had been less than successful, to be that much more energetic in refitting those ships he had and in preparing others."

21. For various attempts to reconcile the Rhodian fleet numbers (two different totals are given in 37.22.2 and 23.4), see Briscoe 1981, 325 at 23.4 and Morrison and Coates 1996, 103. Briscoe's suggestion (p. 325) that two of the "fours" were *apertae* or "open" is unsupported by any other reference to open "fours" which were, by definition, *tectae* or "decked," i.e., cata-phract.

22. See Thiel 1946, 342, who attempts to make sense of the confusing process by which the Rhodians began the battle.

swamping of a Syrian "seven" by a single blow (*uno ictu demersa*) from a Rhodian "four" (Livy 37.24.3). The kill, apparently resulting from a prow-to-prow strike, greatly alarmed (*maxime exterruit*) the Syrian ships who observed it and caused the inshore wing to show signs of flight. On the seaward wing, as Hannibal was about to surround Eudamus, he raised a signal on his flagship (Livy 37.24.4) that called to his aid the ships from the victorious inshore wing; Hannibal was thus forced to withdraw.[23]

Because the Rhodian crews were a little sick, they were completely spent after the battle and were thus unable to pursue the enemy as they towed away their disabled ships.[24] Eudamus, observing this action from a deck tower (*turris*) on his command ship (surely a "four"), sent others in pursuit, although they accomplished nothing for their efforts (Livy 37.24.6–8). In the meantime, the Rhodians towed, with difficulty, the swamped "seven" back to Phaselis (Livy 37.24.9).[25]

Battle off Myonnesus (190)

Following their victory off Side, the Rhodians sent a fleet toward Patara in Lycia to watch for Hannibal, should he attempt another westward voyage, and sent Eudamus to Samos to convince the Romans to take Patara by force. Antiochus, meanwhile, resolved to bring about a naval battle with the Romans, thinking perhaps that a victory would free Hannibal to continue his westward journey. He therefore marched from Sardis to Ephesus to inspect his fleet and from there to Notium, which he placed under siege.[26] He figured that this action would provoke the Romans to leave their base on Samos and provide an opportunity for his admiral Polyxenidas to attack them somewhere. The plan worked in a round-about way. The Roman commander, Lucius Aemilius Regillus, was unwilling to abandon the defense of Ionia in order to besiege Patara and, so, sent his reply

---

23. Nepos *Hann.* 8.4 actually makes Hannibal victorious on his wing, although the Syrian fleet eventually lost the battle.

24. The fact that the Syrian ships were still intact, but unable to propel themselves, implies their damage resulted from Rhodian attacks on their oars and sterns.

25. Livy's expression here—*hepterem . . . aegre Phaselidem pertraxerunt*—"they towed the 'seven' to Phaselis with difficulty," makes sense when the reader recalls the vessel had been swamped (*demersa*) by a "four."

26. For the status of Notium, at this time called Colophon-on-the-sea, see Briscoe 1981, 329 at 37.26.5.

to the Rhodians with a few ships to support them. Livy (37.26.12–13) por-
trays Aemilius as a reluctant participant in the strategy of defense that had
kept him at Samos watching the coast while others moved north to help
the consular army across the Hellespont. But now, Eudamus and the other
generals urged Aemilius to action, stressing how satisfying it would be
either to lift the siege of Notium or defeat the fleet of Antiochus and gain
mastery of the seas. It is revealing that Livy (through Eudamus) frames the
developing conflict in the terms of siege and countersiege warfare.

Their stores consumed, the Roman fleet left Samos for Chios to get
supplies, but on the way, stopped at Teos where they expected to find a load
of wine prepared for Antiochus. In order to convince the Teians to cooperate, the Roman fleet anchored north of the city and began plundering
operations until the Teians agreed to make provisions and wine available
to the Roman fleet, which thereupon moved to the south side of the city to
take on supplies.[27] At this point, the news arrived that Polyxenidas and the
Syrian fleet were anchored nearby, and so the Romans and their allies
hastily embarked (in some confusion) and put to sea (Livy. 37.29.1–5).

Once at sea, the allied fleet proceeded southward in two lines, the Rhodians bringing up the rear. When they first saw the Syrian fleet, they were
"between Myonnesus and the promontory of Corycus" (Livy. 37.29.7). The
Roman fleet, consisting of 80 ships, including 22 from Rhodes, were
largely "fives" and "fours," while the Syrian fleet, numbering 89 units,
included five "of the largest build" (*maximae formae*), namely, three "sixes"
and two "sevens." According to Livy (37.30.2), the Roman ships were stronger and their soldiers more courageous (*robore navium et virtute militum
Romani longe praestabant*); the Rhodian ships were quicker and their pilots
and rowers more skillful, traits which were considered more important
than the five largest ships in the Syrian fleet.

The Syrian fleet was sailing up the coast in column, ships following
one another bow-to-stern. When they deployed from column into line
abreast (ships aligned side-by-side), their left overlapped the Roman right.
In response, Eudamus and his Rhodians extended the length of the
Roman right, with Eudamus taking the position opposite Polyxenidas at
the end of the line. In the prow-to-prow charge that started the battle, the
Syrians were upset by the Rhodian use of fire pots mounted on some of

---

27. There is a good deal more to this story (largely involving pirates and intrigue) than what
I present in the text, but none of it contributes to our understanding of the resulting battle;
see Livy 37.27–38.

their prows. These pots were filled with fire and coals and were rigged in such a way as to dump their contents into the bow of an attacking ship. Polyxenidas and his men had faced these devices once before and thus respected the damage they could cause and, so, they tried to avoid prow-to-prow collisions with the Rhodians which, of course, left them vulnerable to attacks on their oars, sterns, and sides (Livy 37.30.3–5).[28]

Although Livy (37.30.6) credits the victory to the excellence of Roman deck soldiers, he describes how the Roman galleys broke through the enemy center and worked around to the rear of the ships engaged with the Rhodians; in a short time the Syrian center and left were surrounded and put out of action. When the ships on the right saw what was happening elsewhere, they hoisted sail and fled toward Ephesus. Other than the fire pots, the most memorable event of the battle involved the loss of a Rhodian ship during a prow-to-prow ramming contest with a galley from Sidon. The force of the collision knocked loose the Rhodian ship's anchor, which became fouled in the prow structure of the Sidonian vessel. As the Rhodians backed away and the anchor line payed out from the bow, it eventually fouled and then broke their entire starboard set of oars. Unable to move away, the ship fell captive to the Sidonian vessel she had struck (Livy 37.30.9–10). Aside from this piece of good fortune, however, the royal fleet suffered terrible losses, amounting to more than half their force. The totals in Table 7.2 make it clear that ramming tactics, aided by the Rhodian fire pots, played more of a role in the battle's final outcome than the excellence of Roman soldiers in grapple-and-board warfare.

Following the battle, the Roman fleet sailed to Chios, where Aemilius repaired his damaged ships, gave a share of the battle spoils to the Rhodians and dismissed them. He then proceeded with his fleet to Phocaea where he threatened the town with a siege if they did not surrender to him. Their continued opposition forced him to unpack his ladders and rams and begin operations against the city walls and towers (Livy 37.32.1–2). After a period of stout resistance, the townspeople negotiated an armistice, and sent to Antiochus for aid, but when none was forthcoming, they

---

28. For these fire pots, see Livy's description of a naval encounter at Panormus in Samos (37.11) when they were first used. Polybius (21.7.1–4) describes them, as does Appian (*Syr.* 24); see Walbank 1999, Vol. III, 97–99. An image of such a device survives in a graffito from Alexandria of second century BCE date (Basch 1987, 386 ill. 807; and Casson 1995, ill. 115), although we never hear of it used again in battle—why, we do not know. Perhaps the Rhodians found it too dangerous to use safely.

Table 7.2 Losses in the Battle off Myonnesus.

Losses	by capture	by ramming / burning	Total
Antiochus	13	29	42
Romans	0	2	2
Rhodians	1	0	1

opened their gates to the Romans who plundered the town. Roman dominance at sea thus secured, Antiochus had no further room to utilize his
siege forces and that included his navy of big ships. He withdrew his garrison from Lysimacheia, broke off the siege of Notium, and returned to
Sardis (Livy 37.31.1–3) to await the Roman consular army, the agent of his
final defeat.

Observations on the Battles off Chios, Side, and Myonnesus

Except for the battle off Corycus, each of the battles described above
involved naval forces that were intended to capture and retain coastal
cities by force and persuasion. In other words, the fleets containing midsized polyremes were amassed by Philip V and Antiochus III for the purpose of naval siege operations. Considering the nature of these forces, the
absence of transports or freighters is striking. They may have been present, although merchant ships do not figure in any of the battle accounts.
Certainly the Romans did not have them, as we can see from the fact that
their warships secured provisions at Teos before the battle off Myonnesus.
If this was the case generally, then it seems that all the siege equipment
and supplies were carried aboard the galleys and smaller vessels. Such a
feature is markedly different from the naval siege operations carried out
by Demetrius at Salamis or Rhodes and reflects a different scale of operations as well as a general lack of naval dominance. If there were no transports, as seems likely, then this also explains the curious absence of
catapults in our battle accounts. This is because catapults were usually
kept out of the elements when not in use and, without transports, there
was simply no place to stow them aboard warships in active service. If
catapults had been present, surely our sources would have preserved some
mention of their use. If they were not present, as seems likely, then this

represents a departure from the tactics of Demetrius's day, and removes from the big ships an effective antipersonnel weapon that could have been used against Roman deck soldiers.

These battles also demonstrate clearly that naval superiority across all classes was required for the safe and effective use of midsized polyremes. Without this superiority, one's big ships were vulnerable when the fleet moved from harbor to harbor. This is presumably why Philo advised an attacker, when faced with a relieving force, to prepare one's defenses in the environment of the harbor under siege. In none of these battles, however, do we find such a condition; indeed, each battle was fought outside the confines of a fortified harbor, when the fleets were moving from one anchorage to another.

At Chios, when Philip chose to break off his siege and flee southward toward Ephesus, he placed his fleet at a disadvantage because he did not possess a sufficient number of "fours" and "fives" to protect his larger galleys. A similar situation existed off Side, where Hannibal's big ships were caught at sea where they could be surrounded by the more agile Rhodians. At Myonnesus, the big ships in Polyxenidas' fleet were ill-suited for the search-and-destroy mission assigned to them by Antiochus. For this reason, Polyxenidas hoped to catch the Roman fleet at Teos within a restricted anchorage where his big ships could be used to prevent a break out, but when this did not happen, his ships were caught at sea, and were put out of action by the more maneuverable "fours" and "fives" of his opponents.

In battles fought at sea, the lesser speed and maneuverability of midsized polyremes was a potential liability. From the battle descriptions, we see that big ships were prone to being outmaneuvered by smaller vessels like "fives" and "fours." They needed, therefore, to be surrounded by more than one protective "support" ship. At Chios, Philip V employed scores of *lemboi* and smaller galleys for this purpose, and they had some effect against the *diekplous* attempts of the Rhodians. They did not possess the ability to inflict fatal blows, however, and thus the Rhodians lost only two "fives" and a "three" out of their total fleet of 77.

When single midsized polyremes got separated from their support vessels, or were attended by too few of them, they were vulnerable, as shown by the capture of Attalus's flagship at Chios. This is because "tens," "nines," "eights," and "sevens" were vulnerable to ramming strikes from smaller cataphracts. A well placed strike from a "four" could sink a "seven," although this was clearly not expected as we saw from the reaction of the Syrian fleet off Side. If a big ship was immobilized, however, as was the "ten" at Chios, a pair of "fives" attacking from both sides (presumably splitting the attention of their marines) could put it out of action. It is worth restating the obvious one more time: the possession of naval superiority across all classes was key to protecting one's larger ships from being surrounded and put out of action. Without this level of naval superiority, one's big ships were vulnerable when the fleet was moved from harbor to harbor. This reality explains the Romans' generosity in allowing Philip to retain his "sixteen" along with five cataphracts when peace was struck between the two in 197 (Polyb. 18.44.6–7). Five cataphracts were not enough.

Once a naval commander possessed sufficient "fours" and "fives" to protect his larger units in the open sea, then he could use with impunity the brute force of his larger galleys to crack cities' defenses. Naval sieges, indeed all sieges, required a lengthy period of uninterrupted time and such a condition only existed with the establishment of naval superiority in the region of the siege. Once this was achieved, a single victorious outcome often negated the need for additional sieges.[29] The events that unfolded in 201 and 190 reveal that both Philip and Antiochus lacked the naval dominance to insure their unhindered use of a naval siege force. When they were challenged and forced to withdraw, their lack of naval dominance left their midsized polyremes vulnerable in the open sea. In sum, they built multiple numbers of midsized polyremes in pursuit of objectives clear to them from their dynastic histories, but failed to achieve dominance with their "fours" and "fives." This was so, presumably, because they lacked the resources to build, man, and maintain such fleets. In simple terms, both Philip V and Antiochus III lacked the resources to follow in the footsteps of their grandfathers.

In 1946, J. H. Thiel concluded that Antiochus built his "dreadnoughts" in a vain attempt to adopt the Roman style of fighting, namely grapple-and-board warfare. His efforts "bore bitter fruit," however, as proved by the battle off Side when his heavier ships were defeated by the quicker, more nimble Rhodian "fours."[30] By viewing the "dreadnoughts" primarily as galleys intended for pitched naval battles, Thiel and others have ignored the historical development of these classes. In so doing, they

---

29. The terms of surrender were more lenient when agreed to before the besieger started a siege in the first place, or carried it to completion.

30. See Thiel's summation of the battles off Side and Myonnesus: Thiel 1946, 344–345.

have overlooked their frontal ramming characteristics and the strategic objectives for which they were designed by Demetrius Poliorcetes and built in great numbers by Ptolemy II Philadelphus. I will not dispute the conclusion that the battles in 201 and 190 show these big ships as ineffective relics of a bygone age, but I believe that these battles also reveal the conditions necessary for their successful use—conditions that Philip V and Antiochus III failed to meet.

From Myonnesus to Actium

Between 190 and the build-up to Actium in the latter half of the 30s, warships larger than "sixes" disappeared from the fleets of the Mediterranean powers. Rome had methodically destroyed her major rivals at sea and emerged from the war with Antiochus as the undisputed naval power of the Mediterranean.[31] One might reasonably ask why the Romans never developed an interest in midsized polyremes, except for their occasional use of "sixes" for flagships. The commonly accepted answer is derived from authors like Polybius and Livy, who chronicled the development of Roman naval power during the Punic Wars. The answer goes like this: the Romans perfected the art of grapple-and-board warfare in order to offset the nautical skill of their adversaries. Their first "fives" were of sturdy build, and although they did not handle as well as the Carthaginian "fives" they faced, they carried the Romans to victory thanks to a special boarding bridge called a "raven" (*corax*) with a spike on the outboard end that firmly gripped the deck of the attacked ship. The Romans soon dispensed with the cumbersome raven, but continued their preference for grappling their enemies—this time with iron hooks attached to ropes (*ferreae manus*)—dragging them alongside so their marines could decide the battle. They so perfected the use of "fives" for this purpose that they did not need or want to build larger ships. When faced with larger ships in battle, they simply grappled them and let their marines do the rest. During the first century, they sometimes employed naval artillery to soften up their enemies from a distance before closing with

31. Carthage surrendered her fleet to Rome in 202 except for 10 "threes"; see Livy 30.37.3, 43.11–12. Philip V did the same in 197, keeping only his flagship, a "sixteen," plus five cataphracts (i.e., a small contingent of support ships); see Livy 33.24.7 and Polyb. 18.44.6; Plut. *Aem.* 30.2–3. Antiochus III surrendered his fleet in 188, retaining only a token force. Although the texts of Polybius (21.42.13) and Livy (38.38.8) are both faulty at this point, Walbank 1999, Vol. III, 159–160 suggests that he kept 10 aphract galleys.

them, throwing grapnels, and letting their marines finish them off. By this means, for example, Octavian defeated Antony's larger vessels at Actium.[32]

I have already discussed in chapter 5 the distortions stemming from preserved battle narratives that focus on the experiences of the marines. A similar view emerges from the recent study of the Roman navy (up to 167 BCE) by Christa Steinby. She demonstrates convincingly how our sources routinely minimize the nautical expertise of Roman naval personnel and downplay the full measure of the navy's effectiveness.[33] A more defensible answer to our question (i.e., why the Romans avoided midsized polyremes) will be found in the strategic objectives they built their naval forces to achieve.

We should start with the most obvious reason, namely, that the Romans avoided the desire to build bigger and bigger warships because their primary enemies lacked *effective* naval siege units populated by midsized polyremes. These enemies included, first and foremost, the Carthaginians, but also the Sicilians, the Macedonians, the Syrians, and the Egyptians. As a result, the Romans were not driven, like the enemies of Demetrius, to compete in this arena to achieve their foreign policy objectives. When they began to build a fleet of any size, we see from Polybius that they matched the Carthaginians' largest vessels, i.e., their "fives," and worked to achieve naval dominance with this class.[34] During the course of the first Punic War, they built hundreds of "fives," and when these were lost in storms or in battle, they resolutely built hundreds more, making sure to surpass their enemy in numbers of units.[35]

During the decade of the 240s, we might have expected Rome, with Syracusan help, to develop a naval siege unit as they struggled to gain control of Drepanum and Lilybaeum in western Sicily (250–41), but

---

32. A few examples demonstrate this widely held view: Köster 1923, 224–34; Tarn (1930) 1960, 152; Thiel 1946, 25–26; Casson 1995, 120–21; and Casson 1991, 143–56; Pitassi 2009, 121. For a few examples of opposing views, see Wallinga 1956, 26–57; and more recently Steinby 2007, 87–104.

33. See Steinby 2007.

34. Although we know of a single "seven" that was captured from Agathocles and used by the Carthaginians as a flagship at Mylae (see Appendix C), it seems that neither "sevens" nor "sixes" were routinely built and maintained by the Carthaginian navy.

35. Cf. Polyb. 1.63.4–8 with Walbank 1999, Vol. 1, 128 at 1.63.5–6.

they chose not to do so. It seems that the Roman ruling class was simply unwilling to assume the staggering costs such a navy would require on an annually recurring basis. The demands asked of them were already high; in 243, for example, the wealthiest Romans were asked to loan the capital required to prepare a fleet of 200 "fives" (Polyb. 1.59.6–8), which eventually won them the war. Prior to their victory over the Carthaginians at the Aegates Islands in 241, they also lacked the naval superiority required to safeguard a siege unit from attack and insure their unhindered application of force against the besieged Carthaginian garrisons.

In general, the strength of Roman naval power depended upon the superior manpower and timber reserves of the Italian peninsula. Drawing from these considerable resources, the Romans produced fleets that achieved naval dominance over their enemies and allowed them to transport superior land forces to the region of conflict. They then counted on their armies to defeat their enemies, rather than relying on city-by-city campaigns waged with military transports and naval siege units. They did indeed wage some campaigns against individual cities such as Lilybaeum, but their overall preference in their major wars seems to have been to establish naval dominance over the seas between Italy and the area of conflict, and then import a land force from Italy. For example, when fighting Antiochus III in the Syrian War (192–88), the Romans transported an army to Apollonia in Illyria and then marched it through Greece to Asia Minor for the crucial battle at Magnesia in Lydia that resulted in peace.

Their naval battles principally resulted from attempts to intercept enemy supplies and reinforcements before they came to specific land bases, generally outside the confines of a harbor. Quite simply, in this kind of warfare, medium-sized polyremes were a liability rather than an asset. There are a few exceptions during the Second Punic War when Roman commanders developed skills in naval siege warfare, but they never felt the need to build midsized polyremes, that is, until the Actian campaign of Antony and Cleopatra almost two centuries later. In order to appreciate the reasons behind Antony's construction of multiple ships in the range of "sixes" to "tens," we should first review the Roman accomplishments in naval siege warfare that occurred during the third century. Two main episodes document their learning curve and are thus worth examining in detail.

Roman Naval Sieges at New Carthage, Syracuse, and Utica

Surprisingly, prior to their capture of Syracuse in 211, it seems that the Romans did not regularly use catapults *on their warships*. A review of prior siege operations shows their use of catapults in their siege of Lilybaeum in 250 (Diod. 24.1.1–4) and on a beach near Cape Pachynus in 249 (Polyb. 1.53.11–13), but in both instances, the weapons were set up on land and were never carried aboard the warships. They apparently lacked naval catapults when they besieged Syracuse in 213 and suffered terribly as a result.[36] For their attacks on the wall of the city, they lined up archers, slingers, and javelineers on the decks of their warships, but used no catapults (Livy 24.34.5–6; Polyb. 8.4.1). As a result, their killing range was less than that of the defenders on the walls, who wounded many on the decks with their artillery (Polyb. 8.5.2–5). Again, when the Romans yoked "fives" together to carry towers of several stories "and other devices for breaching defenses" (Livy 24.34.6–7), like their deck-mounted siege ladders called *sambucae* (Polyb. 8.4.2–11), they apparently lacked catapults.[37]

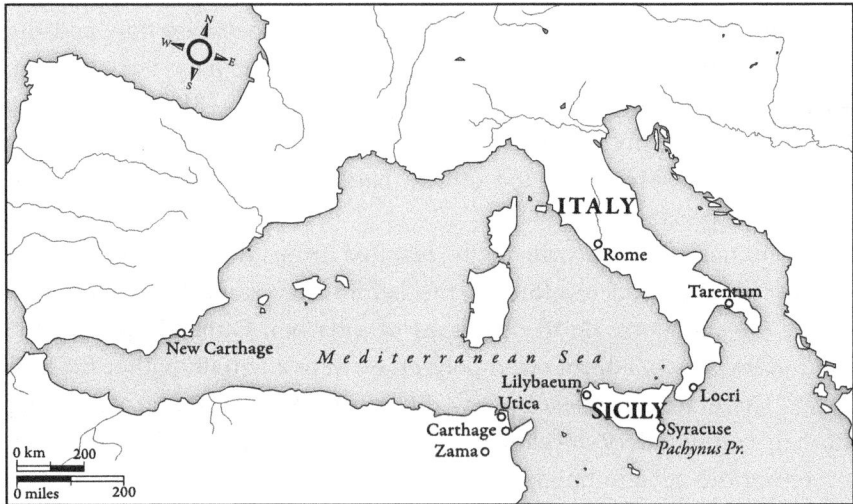

MAP 7.3 Western Mediterranean.

36. Although Livy dates this event under the year 214, it is likely that it occurred in 213; see Walbank 1999, Vol. 2, 6–8.

37. Polybius describes four *sambucae*, each mounted on a pair of "fives" that had been lashed together with the inner oars removed. Plutarch (*Marc.* 14.3) describes a single device

The defenders, however, were advised by Archimedes to set up catapults everywhere (Livy 24.34.13); they used them from atop the wall to attack the ships lying offshore (Livy 24.34.8) and through loopholes to wound those who approached the wall at its base (Livy 24.34.9). Each new Roman attempt was repulsed, sometimes in spectacular fashion. In one case the defenders used grappling hooks attached to large beams and heavy counter-weights to grab the bows of enemy warships, lift them out of the water, drop them, and thus cause the ships to swamp (Livy 24.34.10–11).[38]

Aside from their lack of catapults, a situation that would have made Philo shudder, the Roman navy also failed to block or close off the city's harbor. Marcellus, the Roman commander, simply lacked the naval power to carry out an effective blockade and, as a result, the Carthaginians made regular visits to the city with warships and supplies, establishing a camp before the city in the area of the Great Harbor.[39] By spring 212, Marcellus successfully attempted an escalade near the Hexapylon Gate, sending 1000 picked troops over the wall during a festival (Philo would have approved). Although the Romans managed to secure the section of the city walls called Epipolai, the siege continued into the autumn. At this point, following an outbreak of plague, the commander Bomilcar sailed from Syracuse to Carthage for more warships and supplies. After gathering 130 warships and 700 transports, he departed the city for Syracuse, but was met off Cape Pachynus by Marcellus who had decided to intercept the Carthaginian before he could return to Syracuse (Livy 25.27.9–10). His strategy worked, because when the two fleets approached one another, the Carthaginian commander disliked his position in relation to the enemy, sent a message to the transports to return to Carthage, raised sails, and steered a course toward the coast of Italy (Livy 25.27.12).[40]

---

mounted on the decks of eight warships lashed together. For illustrations of these devices, see Lendle 1983, Abb. 48–49 on pp. 171–172.

38. Plutarch (*Marc.* 14.5–15.7) describes many of the same details provided by Livy and Polybius. See Lendle 1983, Abb. 34 on pp. 123–124 for a set of four illustrations that show the lifting device in action.

39. During the summer of 213, the Carthagninian Bomilcar sailed into the Great Harbor with 35 warships (Livy 24.36.3) and Marcellus laments in the spring of 212 how he cannot stop supplies from reaching the besieged city (Livy 25.23.2–3). By the summer of 212, there seem to be 90 Carthaginian ships in the Great Harbor when Bomilcar sails for Carthage with 35 vessels, leaving 55 behind (Livy 25.25.11–13). He returns shortly thereafter with 100 additional warships and no doubt additional men and supplies.

40. Bomilcar was dubious about his chances, not because of his fleet strength, but because of the unfavorable east winds that were blowing and his downwind position from the enemy fleet (Livy 25.27.11).

Soon thereafter, when the Romans finally gained control of Syracuse, they captured considerable stocks of artillery as well as, no doubt, the technical personnel required to tune them and keep them in working order.[41] This, and their dismal performance during their naval attack on Syracuse, convinced the Romans to begin using these weapons on naval campaigns in the years immediately following. For example, Livy describes a string of sieges at which the Romans use both naval artillery and siege machinery from their warships: at Anticyra in 210 (Livy 26.26.3), at Tarentum in 209 (Livy 27.15.5–7), and at Locri in 208. At the siege of Locri, we learn that the general Tiberius Quinctius Crispinus, mindful of the recent success at Tarentum, had sent to Sicily for artillery and siege engines (Livy 27.25.11). He had also collected a number of ships from which to attack the seaside parts of the city, although as events turned out, Hannibal approached and the siege was abandoned. We see naval artillery again at the siege of Oreus on Euboea in 207 or, rather, artillery brought by sea and then set up on land (Livy 28.6.3).

By the end of the century, more than one Roman commander clearly possessed an ability to deploy naval artillery and utilize naval siege techniques. None, however, was more proficient than Publius Cornelius Scipio, the man called "Africanus" following his defeat of Carthage at Zama in 201. Although the details of his learning curve are not recorded, it seems that he and his men lacked naval artillery when they attacked New Carthage "by land and sea" in 210.[42] By 204, however, when he placed Utica under siege, they had successfully learned some important naval siegecraft techniques. First of all, he made sure he had the benefit of artillery, which he ordered to be brought by sea from Sicily (Livy 29.35.8). In 203, when he wished to divert attention from his goal of burning the enemy camp, he placed catapults on his naval ships as if he intended to attack Utica by sea (Livy 30.4.10). A little later, when Scipio renewed siege operations against Utica (he had besieged the place for 40 days the previous year—Livy 29.35.12), the Carthaginian fleet unexpectedly sailed in relief. Faced with this threat, he brilliantly adopted, on very short notice, a

41. In Marcellus's victory parade, he proudly displayed examples of the catapults and other engines of war that had fallen into his hands (Livy 26.21.7).

42. Although Livy (26.43.6 and 47.5–6) mentions catapults among the defender's weaponry (see also App. *Hisp.* 20), it seems clear from his description of the siege that Scipio did not place artillery on his warships (Livy 26.44–45).

defensive plan outlined by Philo in his *Poliorketika*. At the time of the attack, Scipio's warships were lying bow-on to the shore to facilitate their siege operations and were thus not ready for naval action (Livy 30.10.3–8):

> (3) Ships cluttered up with artillery and siege engines, and either turned over to transport work or lying close enough to the town walls to be a sort of equivalent to the earthwork and bridge used in land-operations for scaling the walls—ships in that condition could hardly have been expected to stand up to a fleet properly equipped with sea-going gear and capable of rapid manoeuver. (4) In these circumstances Scipio on his arrival reversed the ordinary procedure in a sea-fight, sent the warships which might have been used to protect the other vessels to a position in the rear close to shore, (5) and drew up the transports in line four deep in front of the town wall, to receive the enemy's attack. To prevent their regular formation from going to pieces in the heat of the battle, he had the masts and yards laid across from one ship to another and the whole lashed together with stout ropes to form, as it were, a single unit; (6) planks were then laid on top to enable men to pass right along the line, and gaps left underneath between one vessel and the next through which small assault craft could pass for a rapid attack, and return again in safety. (7) All this was hurriedly completed, and as adequately as lack of time allowed, 1000 selected fighting men were ordered aboard the transports. An immense quantity of weapons, mostly missiles, were amassed, enough to suffice for the most protracted engagement, (8) and thus equipped all kept a sharp look-out for the enemy's approach.[43]

The Carthaginians did not immediately attack, but held back until the following day, when they formed a battle line expecting the Romans to respond. When they did not, they attacked the transports. Livy likened the scene to ships attacking walls, in other words, it was anything but a regular sea fight. The Romans fought from higher positions and the Carthaginian marines found it difficult to throw their weapons upward. The Romans' assault craft stationed under the floating barrier were not deployed effectively because they were frequently sunk and generally in the way, causing the Romans to hold their fire. Eventually, the Carthaginians grappled the

---

43. Livy 30.10.3–8; translation by de Sélincourt 1972, 629.

first line of transports with hooks attached to poles called *harpagones* and pulled the first line of transports away from the others. The rest of the defensive line held, and the Carthaginians broke off their attack, towing some 60 transports back to Carthage (Livy 30.10.9–20). As this was the sum total of their success, Scipio's siege remained unbroken and his warships preserved intact. This strange battle is often referred to as a Roman defeat, but it should be viewed as a victory of sorts: Scipio adopted a siege tactic well known to Philo and his readers that successfully preserved his naval force and maintained his siege.

We began this discussion of Roman naval sieges to see not only what they learned, but also why they avoided adding midsized polyremes to their fleets. Simply stated, their "fives" effectively achieved their strategic objectives, which only rarely involved direct attacks on coastal cities. On the few occasions when they were engaged in this kind of warfare, their enemies possessed nothing larger than "fives" with which to challenge them. A second reason can be found in the Roman preference for fighting overseas wars with large land armies rather than relying on the slow capture of coastal cities by naval siege units. As a result, their fleets were often used to intercept enemy supplies and reinforcements before they made it to the region of conflict, and such actions generally took place outside the confines of fortified harbors. When a commander like Scipio adapted Hellenistic naval siege tactics for his own use, it was not to execute a systematic capture of the enemy's coastal cities but, rather, to provide the Roman invasion force with a safe port for receiving supplies and reinforcements. The land army, not the fleet, was the main offensive arm of the invasion force, as was proved by Scipio's final victory over Hannibal at Zama in 201. For this reason, Scipio's "fives" and transport ships were sufficient for the task that faced him. Any benefits resulting from the use of larger vessels were simply not worth the increased infrastructure required to deploy them, nor the additional expense involved, nor the concern over their protection. And when the Carthaginians rejoiced in their capture of 60 transports, Scipio surely looked at his warships, still safely moored behind the last line of transports, and breathed a sigh of relief.

The Actian Campaign (32–31)

Considering the Romans' well-established preference for "fives," the fact that Antony built multiple numbers of midsized polyremes for his final confrontation with Octavian requires explanation. In order to understand the issues that were involved, we need to place the event into a proper context. The conflict in question was the well known Battle of Actium fought in 31 off the entrance to the Ambracian Gulf on Greece's western coast. On the one side there was Gaius Iulius Caesar Octavianus, known to most as Octavian or Augustus (after 27 BCE), and on the other there was Marcus Antonius—Antony—and his wife and chief ally Cleopatra VII, the last of the Ptolemies. The narrative of this battle and the war it concluded came to form an important part of the "creation myth" of the

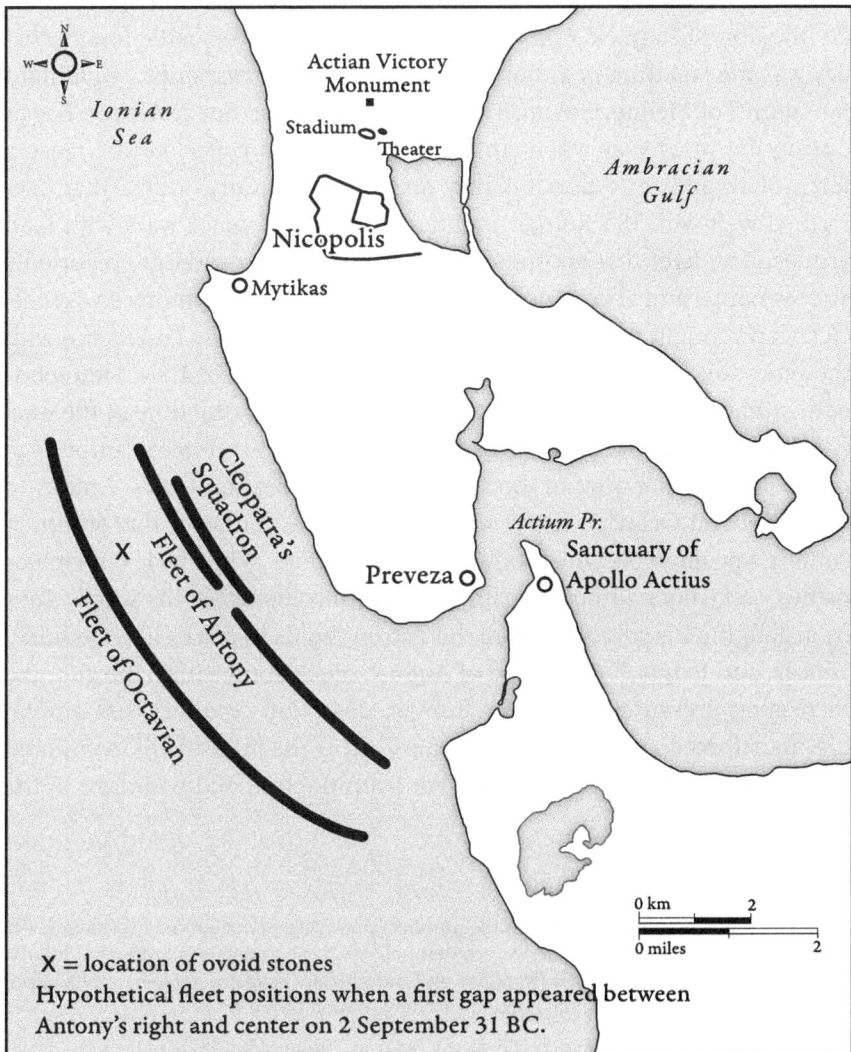

MAP 7.4 Actium battle zone.

Augustan principate. It was so important that Augustus himself published a version of what happened in his *Memoirs*, and the authority of his voice influenced all surviving battle accounts. Knowing well the importance of public perceptions, Augustus chose to present the war as a struggle between Rome and the Egyptian queen instead of what it was, a power struggle between two Roman autocrats. Thanks to his account and the subsequent success of his regime, alternate views were not encouraged and thus we will never fully know Antony's side of the story. Accounts of this battle, then, must be used with care if we hope to extract anything useful regarding Antony's big ships and their intended use.

On September 2nd, 31 BCE, Octavian extinguished Antony's hopes for an invasion of Italy. No one knew it at the time, but the battle fought that day was the last time in antiquity that large fleets of warships would fight for control of Mediterranean. The campaign snuffed out at Actium began during the prior year when Antony and Cleopatra collected in Greece a force of roughly 100,000 infantry and 12,000 cavalry, a size that conformed well with the Roman tradition of fighting major wars with land armies. The fleet that accompanied this force was also large, reportedly 500 warships and 300 transports. Rather than wait for Antony's advance, Octavian brought to Greece in the spring of 31 an equally large force with the intention of stopping Antony far from the shores of Italy. He reportedly gathered 80,000 infantry, 12,000 cavalry and, by the time of the final naval battle, 400 warships.[44] By midsummer, the two forces camped opposite one another around the shores of the Ambracian Gulf—Antony to the south and Octavian to the north. During the course of that summer, Antony's position became progressively untenable. While he lost no major battles, Octavian's admiral Agrippa successfully disrupted his supply lines by dislodging his garrisons from their strongholds in places like Methone, Leucas, and Patras.[45] By the end of August, blocked up within the gulf, the increasing pressures caused by hunger, desertion, and sickness among his men forced Antony to action. He held a meeting of his command officers at which he decided to retreat from the gulf and withdraw to the

---

44. There has been much debate over the numbers preserved in our surviving accounts. For a convenient synopsis of the evidence, see Reinhold 1988, 99 and 113. According to Plutarch (*Ant.* 56.1), of the 800 ship total (warships and transports) Cleopatra herself supplied 200, plus 20,000 talents (for pay) and supplies for the duration of the war.

45. See Vell. 2.84.2; Florus 2.21.4; Dio 50.13.5, 30.1; and Reinhold 1988, 103 at 13.5.

Peloponnesus. This meant he would have to abandon the preferred strategy of relying on his land forces and trust in his fleet to salvage the situation. He burned those warships he was unable to man and loaded some 20,000 soldiers and 2000 archers on his remaining 230 ships, moving them on the morning of September 2nd to the seaward exit of the Actium Straits. In response, Octavian manned some 400 ships with 35,000–40,000 deck troops and stationed them in a long line to block his enemy's seaward escape.[46]

Composition of the Battle Fleets

All attempts to understand the composition of the respective battle fleets are confounded by a distortion in the way our sources characterize the two sides—one as a heavy fleet and the other as a light one. This distortion surely derives from Augustus's *Memoirs* and has affected all surviving versions of the battle.[47] On the one hand, we read that Antony amassed a heavy fleet composed mainly of large galleys between the range of "sixes" and "tens." On the other, we are told that Octavian possessed ships that were light and maneuverable, including numerous two-level *liburnae*, a type of vessel developed from speedy pirate craft.[48]

Let us take both fleets in turn, starting with Octavian's. Its characterization as light cannot be accurate because Octavian's fleet was essentially unchanged from the one prepared by Agrippa in 37 to fight Sextus Pompey off Sicily. At the time, this fleet was described by Appian as "heavy" and capable of giving and receiving crushing blows.[49] Furthermore, the emphasis on liburnian galleys, known to be favored by Octavian, is a transparent attempt to associate Octavian with the victory and downplay the role of Agrippa's wing in defeating the heavier units in Antony's fleet.

---

46. For the numbers, see n. 44.

47. This work, now lost and surviving only in fragments, was published sometime between 25 and 22 BCE; see Murray and Petsas 1989, 143–51.

48. Specific numbers are recorded by Florus (2.21.5), Orosius (6.19.9, 11), and Plutarch (*Ant.* 61.1–2; 68.1). Livy (*Per.* 133) and Velleius (2.84.1) record the moderate size and speed of Octavian's fleet when compared to Antony's massive ships which were more terrifying than their capabilities warranted. Dio (50.18.5; 23.2–3; 29.1–4) mentions the height of Antony's ships, their thick timbers and great weight. The numbers and distribution of classes in Octavian's fleet are difficult to reconstruct with precision; for references to the appropriate literature, see Reinhold 1988, 113 and Murray and Petsas 1989, 133–134.

49. See App. *BC* 5.11.98–99, 106; with Murray and Petsas 1989, 144.

The characterization of Antony's fleet is also misleading. The best estimate of the range of warships he had comes from the so-called *dekanaia* or
"ten-ship monument" dedicated by Octavian after the battle, which included
one of each of the classes in Antony's fleet, from a "one" to a "ten" (Strabo
7.7.6). More information can be gathered from the Actian Victory Monument Octavian built at the site of his personal camp. Here the sizes of the
preserved ram sockets provide a guide to the minimum class distributions
in Antony's fleet. I have argued elsewhere that the victor displayed on his
monument *all* the large warship rams that fell into his hands in order to
make the dedication as grand as possible. Considering that there are some
rams from "fives" and perhaps even a "four" displayed on the monument, it
seems likely that Octavian used all the big rams that fell into his hands after
the battle. From this evidence, it seems likely that there were at least four to
five "tens," four "nines," five "eights," six "sevens," and perhaps eight
"sixes," a total of 27–28 units.[50] This would represent roughly 6% of Antony's total fleet strength of 500 warships.[51] We have good reason, therefore,
to conclude that Antony's fleet was not dominated by midsized polyremes.
He also took care to avoid the mistakes that destroyed the campaigns of
Philip V and Antiochus III by including a generous number of "fours" and
"fives" in his fleet.[52] These were the vessels that would ensure the safe passage of his larger warships. And these larger warships would give Antony
the capability of conducting naval siege operations if he so desired.

The Battle

The details of the final battle fought off Actium are beyond recovery except
for the bare outlines, and even these provoke disagreement. Dio, who presents our longest narrative, is rhetorical, ill-informed where we can check

---

50. Ironically, Augustus's Victory Monument allows us to detect the distorted view of Antony's fleet broadcast by his *Memoirs*. A final analysis of the monument is currently in progress; although I expect these numbers will change slightly as a result, this will not
significantly change the impressions expressed in the text.

51. To the total from the memorial, I have added an additional "ten," "nine", "eight,"
"seven," and "six" from the "ten ship" monument that was dedicated at the sanctuary of
Actian Apollo on Cape Actium. See Murray and Petsas 1989, 142.

52. We are told by Plutarch (*Ant.* 64.1) that Antony embarked 22,000 men on his warships
for the battle. If the average size of his vessels were "fives," then this allows roughly 130
marines per ship on the 170 warships that comprised his front line (not counting the 60
ships in Cleopatra's squadron). These numbers imply that the majority of his ships were
"fours" and "fives" and not "sevens" to "tens."

him, and short on specifics.[53] Plutarch's account is somewhat better, but is much shorter, and still reflects the distortions of the official versions produced following the publication of Augustus's *Memoirs*. Contemporary sources, like Horace, whose Ninth Epode mentions some details, are cryptic and subject to multiple interpretations. Since good reasons exist to question everything we are told, it is impossible to construct a convincing battle reconstruction. Despite these misgivings, we must work with what we have to explore the reasonable possibilities. What appears below represents my attempt to understand the role of Antony's big ships in the battle, a subject on which we are particularly ill informed. I feel this approach is worthwhile because we have the physical evidence from the nearby trophy monument to provide a corrective to what we are told by the written record.[54]

On the morning of September 2nd, a few days after a storm front had passed, Antony drew up his fleet at the seaward exit from the Actium straits in two unequal lines. He and Lucius Gellius Publicola commanded the right wing, Marcus Octavius and Marcus Instaeus held the center, and Gaius Sosius the left. A second line of 60 ships was formed by Cleopatra's Egyptian squadron. As they lay motionless in the calm narrows, Octavian positioned his fleet directly in their path arrayed in a long line from north to south. Agrippa took a position on the (northern) left wing opposite Antony, Lucius Arruntius the center, and Octavian and Marcus Lurus the right.[55]

Although we are not told the precise layout of Antony's battle line, Octavian may have represented it for us on the ram display of his victory monument. If so, then Antony's big ships were on the right wing, while the center and left were held by "fives" and "fours" with a single large ship, probably for Sosius, at the southern end of the line.[56] The second

---

53. See Reinhold 1988, 113.

54. Long ago, when I tried to reconstruct the main phases of the battle with a seminar class using individual scaled warships on a large-scale map (16.75 m. × 22.15 m.) of the battle zone, I concluded that we know too little about too many factors to produce a convincing reconstruction. My published views concerning the battle can be found in Murray and Petsas 1989, 131–51; and Murray 2002a. For an extremely readable version, see Carter 1970, 215–27.

55. For the commanders involved in the battle, see Reinhold 1988, 113.

56. There are other reasons for locating the big ships on Antony's right wing. During the course of the battle when a gap developed between Antony's right and center, Plutarch (*Ant.* 66.3) states that Cleopatra's squadron hoisted sail and made their way through the midst of the combatants. As they had previously been posted "behind the large ships" (ὀπίσω . . . τῶν μεγάλων) these larger galleys must have been either on the right end of the center, or the left end of the right wing. For the tactical advantages of placing the heavy ships in the right wing, see Murray 2002a, 348.

line formed by Cleopatra's squadron was tasked with preventing *diekplous* attacks on the heaviest ships in the right wing, where the fleet was most vulnerable. Although our sources imply that Antony tried to conceal his intentions to withdraw southward, he made these crystal clear when he burned those ships he could not man and ordered that sails and masts be carried aboard all warships (Dio 50.15.3–4; Plut. *Ant.* 64.2). These public decisions show that he intended to cut his losses in the gulf, break through the enemy blockade, and regroup his forces elsewhere, probably in the Peloponnesus.[57] I personally feel that he hoped for victory, but if this was not secured by the frontal charge that opened the battle, he planned to break free from the enemy, hoist sails, and flee southward on the sea breeze. For this plan to work, Antony's fleet needed to move toward the north and west so that when the breeze began to blow, the ships would be able to carry the wind in their sails and still miss Leucas Island to the south. Antony's chance for victory, as I said above, lay in the battle's opening prow-to-prow charge when his heavy ships had their best opportunity for crushing the enemies' bows. With luck, his heavy units could inflict serious damage on the enemy if he could find a way to protect their flanks and sterns from enemy attacks. On the morning in question, however, matters did not develop following this best-case scenario. At first, Antony's fleet adopted a defensive position with their bows outward, marines at the ready, and troops drawn up along the shore—as if at a harbor entrance.[58] Knowing Antony's plan from deserters, Agrippa (whose greater experience at sea implies that he coordinated the battle strategy for Octavian) ordered the men to wait about eight stades (1.5 km.) distant from the enemy and force them to abandon their tightly packed formation. Finally, around mid-day—Plutarch (*Ant.* 65.5) says at the sixth

57. The statement (Dio 50.15.1) that Cleopatra prevailed in her advice to withdraw to Egypt is unconvincing. Nothing of the deliberations in this war council can be known for certain, and this applies especially to the opinions attributed to Cleopatra. Prior to his defeat on September 2nd, his departure from Greece would have been premature. The fact that some of his transport ships met up with him in the Peloponnesus (?) following the battle implies the existence of a pre-agreed rendezvous point; see Plut. *Ant.* 67.5.

58. Both Dio (50.31.4–5) and Plutarch (*Ant.* 65.4) mention this curious formation adopted by Antony's fleet. Plutarch (*Ant.* 65.2–3) says that Antony even advised his men to receive the enemies' attacks as if they were fighting on land. If there is a kernel of truth to these descriptions, Antony's defensive posture recalls Philo's advice to those resisting a relieving force (*Polor.*D 103–106).

hour—when he was unable to bring about a fight with his big ships packed side-by-side, the sea breeze forced Antony's hand.

Every day, during the summer months and into the early autumn, a breeze blows from the sea into the Ambracian Gulf. It starts offshore between 8 and 10 AM and then progressively spills in toward the shore, increasing in speed until it reaches its maximum velocity (approx. 10–25 mph) between 3 and 6 in the afternoon. By 7 it has started to drop, and by sunset, or shortly thereafter, a condition of calm is restored.[59] Since Antony knew from daily experience that it would become increasingly difficult to row into this freshening breeze, he ordered his fleet to advance toward the enemy, hoping to incite a prow-to-prow charge. But Agrippa had also anticipated this move and forewarned his men to resist charging Antony's advancing line. Octavian reportedly ordered his right wing to back water so as to draw the enemy further and further from the shore (Plut. *Ant* 65.5). As Agrippa kept his distance on the left, he also extended his line and threatened to surround the wing opposite him, which kept close contact with the shore to prevent this from occurring. By the time Antony's ships had narrowed the mile between themselves and Agrippa, they were starting to tire and a gap had developed between Antony's right and center (Plut. *Ant.* 66.3). In order to cover this gap, Cleopatra presumably positioned her squadron to discourage an enemy *periplous* while Antony ordered a charge at the enemy.

One can imagine the trumpet blasts, the battle songs, the volleys of arrows, stones, and other missiles launched at the enemy as the lines approached. Antony's men shot from wooden towers mounted on the decks while both sides used catapults of various sizes to discharge bolts, fire arrows, and river cobbles gathered nearby. If the small ovoid stones photographed on the sea floor in 1997 originally came from this barrage, Antony's right wing had advanced more than halfway toward Mytikas Point as the oarsmen struggled against the freshening breeze, hoping to gain a weather advantage on their enemies. This exertion took a toll, however, and by the time the order came to engage, the men below decks were unable to sprint toward their enemies' prows. Sensing that this worrisome threat had been frustrated, Agrippa proceeded to decide the

59. For the best description of this wind and its affect on the position of Antony's fleet, see Carter 1970, 218–20. Personal experience in the battle zone shows that wind speeds can vary from Force 3–5 on the Beaufort scale, or between approximately 10 and 25 mph.

battle on terms more favorable to his better conditioned fleet—by further catapult barrages, by gang attacks on individual ships, and by the use of fire.[60]

Unlike the other battles discussed in this chapter, our sources describe no specific details involving midsized polyremes. Antony's ships are generally described as motionless, too heavy to move, and the object of attacks from Octavian's smaller vessels working in twos or threes (Dio 50.32.6). Once a victory seemed unlikely, Cleopatra and her squadron made for the gap separating Antony's left and center, broke free from the enemy, and raised sails. Predictably, the victors described her move as the ultimate betrayal of a jittery female or the treachery of a poisonous queen; just as predictably, some modern scholars defend the act as one of a level-headed commander.[61] However we interpret the action, her departure precipitated a general flight among Antony's men with the predictable result of chaos and confusion. Unfavorably positioned downwind from their enemies' fleet, Antony's commanders had two choices: stay and fight in a broken formation against superior numbers, or turn and flee back to the gulf. Scholars have argued for both outcomes. The surviving battle accounts, however, describe the former option, with many of Antony's ships being destroyed by incendiary missiles. Either way, the defeat of Antony's fleet was total.

Analysis

If we hope to extract anything useful from the battle concerning the role of Antony's midsized polyremes, we must consciously move past the "heavy fleet vs. light fleet" theme permeating our sources. Otherwise, we are forced to accept that Antony's ships were simply too large to be useable and that their heavy hulls, armored with thick timbers and iron fasteners, made them easy prey for Octavian's nimble liburnians. Assuming that my arguments concerning the composition of Antony's fleet are even partially correct, we must recognize this theme for what it is and consider other reasons for Antony's defeat—reasons that are unrelated to the performance

---

60. It seems that both sides used artillery and flaming missiles (Dio 50.32.5; 34.2; and Plut. *Ant.* 66.2). Plutarch (*Ant.* 66.2) describes gang attacks in groups of two or three. For fighting towers on Antony's ships, see Dio 50.23.3, 33.4; and Plut. *Ant.* 66.2.

61. See Murray and Petsas 1989, 132–33, for the references.

of his midsized polyremes on September 2nd. There are plenty of other explanations.

For example, the sources make it clear that Antony's oarcrews had degraded seriously during the course of the summer-long war. Sickness (Dio 50.12.8, 15.3), hunger (Dio 50.14.4), and defeats had taken their toll and, as a result, the men were utterly demoralized (Dio 50.15.3). So many had died, deserted, or were otherwise unfit for service that Antony was forced to burn a number of ships he could not man with crews (Plut. *Ant.* 64.1; Dio 50.15.4). At the time of the final battle, Antony's ships were thus undermanned, a factor that hindered their attempts to charge prow-to-prow (Plut. *Ant.* 65.5). Cleopatra's presence on this campaign also caused Antony serious problems that resulted in a continuous stream of desertions. The most damaging were men like Gnaeus Domitius Ahenobarbus, whose grievance against Cleopatra caused others to follow his example (Plut. *Ant.* 63.2–3; Dio 50.13.6), and Quintus Dellius, who deserted shortly before the final battle and may have communicated Antony's plans to Octavian.[62] Plutarch (*Ant.* 63.3) also mentions the desertion of non-Romans to Octavian, as well as the blunt advice of Antony's field commander Canidius: "Send Cleopatra away."[63]

Another of Antony's serious problems involved his inability to assert naval dominance over his enemy. By the time of the final battle, he had lost his garrisons at Methone, Leucas, and Patras, solely through the actions of Agrippa and his naval raiding.[64] The implications of this progressive, summer-long demonstration of naval inferiority would have been obvious to everyone who understood the dynamics of a major campaign. At the end of August when he held his war council, Antony should have known that his chances for gaining a victory during his breakout were poor. Every possible parallel from the previous two centuries led to the same conclusion: he would be hard pressed to protect his big ships without naval superiority. And worse, the local conditions at Actium would require his degraded oarcrews to row upwind to engage the enemy, something that

---

62. Dio (50 23.1) mentions the desertion of Dellius after his description of Antony's war council but before the battle.

63. Canidius had previously supported Cleopatra, but recognized the deleterious effect her presence was having on the officers. For the reasons why Antony could not send her away, see Carter 1970, 188–189; for additional details, see Southern 1998, 140–141.

64. It seems that Corinth had come under attack as well; see Reinhold 1988, 103.

competent commanders tried to avoid like the plague. Because Antony should have known his big galleys would be more of a liability than an asset in the final battle, why did he man them? Surly he believed they gave him some sort of strategic advantage. But what was it?

To detect what this may have been, we must consider the military traditions behind Antony's campaign strategy. Romans preferred to fight their wars primarily with their armies, not with their fleets and Antony was no different, bringing with him to Greece a large infantry and cavalry force. He had amassed a large fleet to secure his transports and to maintain naval superiority in the regions through which he marched. Surely, when he gathered this force in 32, he had an invasion of Italy in mind. Dio (50.9.2) says this was his intention and I see no reason to doubt him. Antony was a hard-nosed soldier who had fought alongside Caesar for control of Italy and would have no qualms about transferring his forces to Italy if events required it.[65] For this to occur, he would have to land his forces at one or more of the ports in the south of the peninsula—at Brundisium, or at Tarentum, both of which were controlled by Octavian's men.

The difficulty in forcing access to these ports was something well known to Antony through two personal experiences. The first occurred in 48 when Pompey the Great held Brundisium and forced Caesar to attack the fortified harbor by building a pontoon barrier out of large floats on which he erected defensive works. Pompey resisted for nine days by attacking the works with merchant ships fitted with catapults and three story towers, but when Caesar had closed off nearly half the entrance, he decided to abandon the city.[66] Antony's second experience occurred in 36 when Brundisium refused to admit his considerable force of 300 ships and forced him to sail to Tarentum. As a result, it was from Tarentum that he dispatched his wife Octavia to bring about a strained meeting of reconciliation with her brother Octavian. Now, five years later, he could expect both ports to be tightly shut against him and he knew well what kind of fight that would mean. Surely he brought these midsized polyremes to

---

65. Reinhold 1988, 100 at 9.2 argues against accepting Dio's statement, but I find his arguments less compelling than the presence of Antony's midsized polyremes which only make sense if he intended to invade Italy.

66. Caes. *BC* 1.25–28: Alerted by the townspeople, Caesar managed to scale the walls of the city, reach the harbor from the land side, and capture two shiploads of men who had run afoul of his floats.

force his way into southern Italy and not to square off with Agrippa in pitched naval battles on the open sea.

Despite these best laid plans, by September 2nd, conditions had changed and Antony should have realized that his biggest ships were ill-suited for a break-out attempt when the enemy had disciplined squadrons of "fours" and "fives." Nevertheless, he chose to man his largest ships and station them in the line. The question is often asked whether Antony intended to fight for victory or escape on the day of the battle and scholars have persuasively argued both sides of the issue.[67] Antony's decision to save his largest ships, however, implies that he was unwilling to concede the ultimate objective of his campaign, the battle for Italy. However he evaluated his precise odds for success, when he advanced into battle on the morning of the 2nd, he had not yet abandoned hope for a successful outcome to the campaign.[68] And yet, to an impartial observer, he had already lost the battle for Italy by conceding to Agrippa naval dominance along the west coast of Greece. He should have known he was doomed. Whatever hopes he may have had at the battle's start, by mid-afternoon the disciplined oarcrews of Octavian's fleet had negated Antony's frontal charge, and began their group attacks on his ships. Better conditioning, higher morale, and superior numbers produced the victory for Octavian, not the inherent superiority of light over heavy warships.

Who can deny, however, that Octavian's victory firmly ended the big ship phenomenon? According to his own account, his small liburnians defeated the monstrous ships of Antony, thus demonstrating the folly of eastern monarchs whose addiction to empty grandeur produced warships too big to be effective. We now know the faults with such a view. The big ships of Antony were effective, just not in pitched sea battles with superior numbers of "fours" and "fives" armed with fire-throwing artillery. Had Antony fared better against Agrippa during the summer of 31, had more of his "fives" and "fours" been present for the final battle, and had he won against his rival, forcing him back to Italy, I suspect the big ships

---

67. See Murray and Petsas 1989, 132–133.

68. I find Dio's explanation (50.15.1–3) less compelling. He says that Cleopatra was convinced by terrible portents that the campaign was doomed, and so advised Antony to leave garrisons at important places and return to Egypt. Conceivably, Antony could be saving his big galleys for a defense of Alexandria, but such a plan seems unlikely prior to the decisive outcome of the September 2nd battle. Dio's explanation, therefore, sounds like an attempt to foreshadow Cleopatra's treachery and further brand her as a womanly coward.

would have proved their value at Brundisium or Tarentum. Like Demetrius returning to Greece after his failed siege of Rhodes, Antony would have awed these coastal cities into opening their gates, or forced them to do so. But history did not turn out this way, and subsequent ages tended to side with Augustus and view big ship navies as a failed relic from an age of extravagance.[69]

69. See, for example, Warry 1995, 187: "Octavian's slender vessels . . . were able to manoeuvre in groups of three or four around single galleys of Antony's ponderous fleet . . . although fear of being grappled and boarded by the swarms of marines which these leviathans carried deterred them from coming too close." Meijer 1986, 207–208, suggested (based on Plut. *Ant.* 66.2) that Antony protected his ships against ramming by covering their hulls with iron plates, and observed that Antony "wrongly expected to be confronted by a fleet of heavy ships, which he intended to fight with even heavier ones. Instead, Octavian brought into action light ships manned with capable seamen." A similar sentiment is reflected in the battle's summation by Casson 1995, 141. Such is the influence of Augustus's version, even today.

Conclusion

THE COURSE OF this study was determined more than three decades ago by the discovery of the Athlit ram and its relationship to the sockets on Augustus's Actian Victory Monument at Nikopolis. Although smaller than the sockets currently *in situ* and, thus, probably from a "four," the quality of the ram's cast revealed how its makers took extra pains to increase the strength of their weapon. They carefully purified the copper and tin, strictly regulated the temperature of the melt, and followed exacting procedures designed to produce a superior cast that resisted cracking under impact. The timbers inside the weapon revealed an equal attention to detail, with a design developed after thousands of ram strikes aimed at producing a bow that would survive the bone-jarring forces of deliberate prow-to-prow collisions. If this ram comes from a "four," judged by Livy to be among warships of larger build, what about the larger "eights," "nines," and "tens"? The Actian sockets suggest that such warships, that is, polyremes of medium size, generated tremendous power from their heavy hulls, multi-ton rams, and massive bow timbers. A growing body of evidence makes us unavoidably conclude that such big ships were built to excel in frontal ramming and, thus, played a critical role in naval siege warfare.

Such a conclusion emerges clearly from the historical development and use of ships larger than "threes." At the beginning of the fourth century, "fours" and "fives" were built by Carthage and Syracuse to excel in harbor fights where their superiority over "threes" in prow-to-prow contests was desirable. Then, in 332, Alexander drew upon the skill of his father's engineering corps to produce the first naval siege unit for his siege of Tyre. He used it with such astounding success, against a city widely thought to be impregnable, that he changed the way in which navies were built and used in subsequent years. Remembering the lesson of Tyre, Antigonus and his son Demetrius built increasingly large galleys for the wars they waged with Ptolemy, Lysimachus, and Seleucus. Their success in numerous sieges, and even their failure at Rhodes, demonstrated the awesome power they were able to wield, and so eased their dealings with other cities they controlled or wished to control. Even after the battle of Ipsus and the death of his father in 301, Demetrius managed to retain his key Greek possessions owing to the strength of his naval force, and recovered his fortunes for a time.

Demetrius's rivals responded in different ways. Lysimachus witnessed the awesome power of Demetrius's siege unit at Soloi in 298 (or 297), and thereafter built a double-hull "eight" that he used with a siege unit to recover his Asiatic possessions from Demetrius in 294. Although we lack evidence for anything larger than "fives" in Ptolemy's fleet, his son and successor Ptolemy II Philadelphus built the largest collection of medium-to-large polyremes ever assembled. His big ship navy represented serious power and contributed to the recovery of numerous cities upon the accession of Ptolemy III Euergetes after his father's death. The largest working warships constructed in antiquity were built at this time. While their descriptions allow for varied interpretations of their designs, they make best sense as floating platforms for naval siege towers and other kinds of siege machinery.

Unfortunately, we lack descriptions of Ptolemy's big ship navy in action. Nevertheless, we can still recover a sense of its use from the siege-craft manual written by Philo the Byzantine during the reign of Euergetes. A military engineer who worked for one of Ptolemy's generals, Philo described in detail how best to utilize various kinds of water craft, catapults, and skilled fighting personnel to attack and defend the harbors of coastal cities. If a commander had access to big ships, he might use them to break through harbor barriers and attack walls whose foundations were placed in the sea. Because the fighting at harbor barriers was often quite fierce, big ships could be useful by providing stable platforms for catapults that targeted enemy marines, machinery, and fortification walls. Philo also explained that sea battles, no matter where they were fought, required skilled marines with the discipline to resist boarding enemy warships, men who knew to rely on the rams of their warships.

For all its information about the use of big ships in naval siege warfare, Philo's text also reveals that big ships might not be available to the general for whom he wrote, implying that even Ptolemy's commanders might not have access to big ships. This advice underscores the limitations of big ship navies that required squadrons of smaller classes to provide protection and support. While the massive collection of ships in Ptolemy's Alexandrian fleet represented real power, it was a power that was not used for every foreign war or conflict. The costs and logistical preparations involved in dispatching a fleet with the largest big ships were simply too great. We catch a glimpse of these limitations regarding the use and protection of big ship fleets during the late third and early second centuries with the fleets of Philip V and Antiochus III. Neither monarch possessed the naval resources to establish superiority over their enemies and, as a result, their big ships became vulnerable to attacks from smaller vessels.

For various reasons related to their wars with Carthage, the Romans never developed and maintained a naval siege unit, and when faced with the need for one, as at Syracuse and Utica during the Second Punic War, they made do with their "fives." In their naval war with Antiochus III, they limited their siege operations to the use of ladders and rams and focused their energy on denying naval superiority to their enemy. As a result, the Romans and their Rhodian allies were able to catch Antiochus's big ships in unprotected environments during a number of sea battles. Antony suffered a similar fate at Actium and so lost his big ships to his rival. Following Actium, Augustus stripped off their rams, built monuments and memorials to glorify his achievement, and thereafter commissioned nothing larger than "sixes."

Augustus lived for almost a half century following his Actian victory and during this period, as his preferred version of the battle account became firmly established, popular knowledge regarding polyremes and their uses began to fade. In the generation following his death, during the reign of Tiberius (14–32 CE), artists in southern France were still able to render correctly the rams from the great naval battle on their arch at Arausio (modern Orange; cf. Fig. 2.20). During the reign of Claudius (41–54 CE), however, those who carved a large scene of the great battle for an imperial cult center in Italy revealed a surprising disinterest in such

---

1. This scene, occupying three separate marble slabs, forms part of a series of images related to the "Actian Cycle," which presumably come from a single monument. Other images relate to a triumphal procession in Rome; see Schäfer 2007, Vol. 1, 471-81, with Vol. 2, 353-56. Many details of the naval battle scene have been so altered since antiquity that other interpretations are possible. T. Schäfer, who is preparing a complete study of these sculptures, suspects that the two rams on the left side of the upper register are not carved on the original surface of the stone (personal communication, 8/5/11), and thus represent modern additions as well. See Trunk 2010 for the modern history of these pieces; and for excellent color photographs of the slabs showing the naval battle, see Schnapp et al. 2008, especially 2-3 and 158-59.

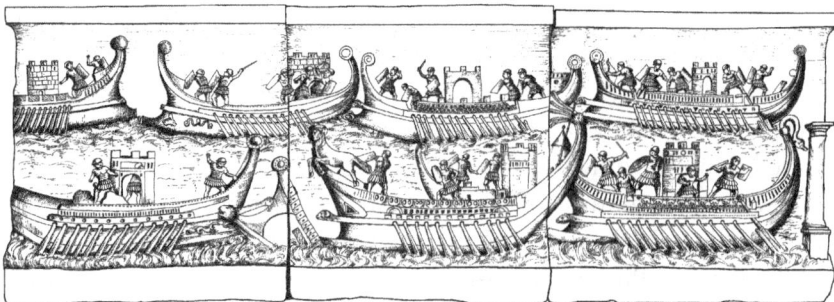

A

B

FIGURE C.1 Marble relief from Cordoba thought to depict the battle of Actium. Line drawing by TNQ Books and Journals. Photo by Peter Witte, courtesy of the German Archaeological Institute, Madrid.

details (Fig. C.1)[1]. If the surviving image can be trusted (the animal-headed rams are modern additions), the sculptors fashioned the rams as simple chisel-shaped extensions of the hulls. Examples of proper warship rams could still be found on numerous monuments, but such detail was apparently deemed unnecessary. In like manner, naval architects ignored, and then forgot, the old designs, writers began to use nouns like *triereis* or *liburnae* to signify warships in general (e.g., Veg. *Mil.* 4.33), and a clear understanding of the differences between "threes," "sevens," and "tens" was lost. General interest in the techniques of naval warfare diminished to such an extent that naval sections were cut from tactical manuals and excluded from theoretical discussions of military science. Still later, by the ninth century, all that remained from this genre of military science was

Philo's siegecraft manual. And when modern scholars began to wrestle with the problems of polyreme navies, Philo's evidence was ignored because the first editions of his text were based on manuscripts that were virtually unreadable.

Faced with this situation, naval historians judged the evidence surviving from the big ship era according to the modes of fighting from better known periods and the result was a misunderstanding of the evidence. Scholars focused their main attention on explaining the oarsystems of the big galleys and assumed incorrectly that they were designed to defeat other big ships in set naval battles. Furthermore, they explained the big ship phenomenon as a race to build increasingly large platforms for gangs of marines and batteries of catapults, and they interpreted the victors of such contests as those with the best marines. Such views corresponded to what authors like Livy had to say about the quality of Roman deck soldiers and ultimately explained the victories of Rome over Macedonia, Syria, and Egypt. But then, Yehoshua Ramon discovered the Athlit ram and the more we learned about this amazing weapon, the more we had reason to question the old theories about the big ship era.

The time has now come to propose a new model or style of naval power that recognizes the unique qualities of the big ship phenomenon. This model, whose evidence appears in the preceding pages, might be called "Macedonian" after those who invented it. It was first defined by Alexander at Tyre in 332, and thereafter embellished and expanded by Demetrius Poliorcetes and Ptolemy II and III. It defined the kind of naval war assumed by Philo when he explained to his patron the different ways to attack and defend coastal cities. If one had them, big ships or cataphract galleys were used with a variety of smaller aphract galleys, boats, and freighters for attacks on fortified harbors. In such contexts, they excelled in attacks on harbor barriers where the fighting was often fierce and always crucial to the siege's success. This Macedonian style of naval war produced ships of staggering size that excelled in frontal ramming but were also vulnerable to attacks by smaller warships in wide-open settings, like battles at sea. For this reason, naval siege units comprised of medium to large polyremes were vulnerable when moved from harbor to harbor and thus required a sizeable escort of smaller classes to protect them. Although Demetrius's "sevens" fared well against Ptolemy's "fours" and "fives" off Salamis in 306, the classes preferred for most naval battles were "fours" and "fives." Those few times that we see ships larger than "sixes" in battle, they do not fare well, particularly when they were separated from the line and attacked from both sides by smaller warships operating in unison.

As with the elephant and chariot corps found in Hellenistic armies, the naval siege unit was developed to achieve specific goals that were unique to the eastern Mediterranean and Aegean. They were also unique to the late fourth and third centuries BCE when monarchs could still afford the staggering costs and desired the kind of power that Alexander displayed at Tyre or Demetrius displayed at Rhodes. The Romans did not come from such a tradition, and never felt the need to maintain a large navy with a collection of big ships designed primarily for attacking coastal cities. This makes Antony's alliance with Cleopatra so interesting because it shows how he adopted this Macedonian model for the fleet he took to Greece and suggests that his ultimate goal was Italy. Do we see the hand of Cleopatra behind these decisions as Octavian's propaganda proclaimed? Perhaps, but what we know for sure is the finality of Antony's failure. In the words of Lionel Casson, "Actium wrote finis to the formal sea battle for over 300 years."[2] We might add that Actium also wrote finis to the need for naval sieges and, with them, the need for midsized polyremes. With the removal of the last great Hellenistic naval power other than Rome herself, no one cared to deliver a proper eulogy and the details of this mode of naval war were quietly forgotten.

2. Casson 1995, 141.

Testimonia for "FOURS"

Note: The references here point to where the class is mentioned in the text and do not refer to the entire historical episode. All dates are BCE unless noted otherwise.

Historical Development

Invention (end of fifth century).

Pliny *NH* 7.208: The Carthaginians were the first to build "fours."

Clem. Al. *Strom.* 1.16.75.10: In a list of various "firsts": the Carthaginians were the first to build a "four"; Bosporus built it from what was at hand (*autoschedion*).

See Diod. 14.41.3 and 14.42.2 (at "Fourth Century: *Syracuse*").

Fourth Century.

Syracuse (beginning of fourth century).

Diod. 14.41.3 and 14.42.2: In the preparations for war with Carthage (dated to 399), Dionysius I built "fours"[1] and "fives"—"fives" never having been built before. He gathered skilled workers from Greece, Italy, and even from the Carthaginian realm.

Diod. 14.44.7: The prototype "five" is sent in Spring 397 to pick up a woman betrothed to Dionysius from Locri.

Tyre, Phoenicia, and Cyprus (prior to 332).

---

1. The mss. read "threes" instead of "fours" in both passages, but this conflicts with Diod. 2.5.7; as a result, P. Wesseling (Diodorus 1746) long ago substituted "*tetrereis*" for "*te triereis*" in both passages. Morrison 1990 argues, unconvincingly to my mind, that we should keep the original text.

Arr. *Anab.* 2.21.9: There were "fours" in the Tyrian fleet at the siege of Tyre in 332. Curt. 4.3.14 reveals that the Macedonians also had "fours" in their fleet at Tyre, but because they do not figure before this point in any source, the Macedonians had certainly received these ships from their new Cyprian and/or Phoenician allies (e.g., Sidon, Byblos or Arados).

Macedonia, reign of Alexander III (332).

See above, *"Tyre, Phoenicia, and Cyprus."*

Athens (332/31–325/4).

IG II² 1628.81–85 (326/5): The "four" (restored) *Hegemonia*, built in the archonship of Niketes (332/31) was assigned to grain convoy duty: lines 37–42. The class seems certain from a similar formula used at line 10, from other mentions of "fours" in the surrounding text, and from line lengths.

IG II² 1627.275–8 (330/29): 18 "fours" are listed among the Athenian fleet. [Note: "Fives" are not added to the fleet until 328/27 at the earliest, see App. B.]

IG II² 1629.808–10, 812 (325/24): The number of "fours" is listed at 50, seven of which were at sea.

Diod. 18.10.2 (323, upon the death of Alexander): The orators gave shape to the wishes of the people and wrote a decree that the people should assume responsibility for the common freedom of the Greeks and liberate the garrisoned cities and prepare 40 "threes" and 200 "fours," and that all men up to the age of 40 should be enrolled for this purpose.[2]

Wars of the Diadochoi.

Diod. 19.62.8: The fleet of Antigonus in 315 numbered 240: of these 90 were "fours," 10 "fives," three "nines," 10 "tens" and 30 aphracts (open galleys).

Diod. 20.49.2 (in a sea battle off Cyprian Salamis in 306): Ptolemy had 140 ships, the largest were "fives" and the smallest were "fours."

Diod. 20.50.3 (in the same battle): Demetrius had 30 Athenian "fours" with him.

Diod. 20.93.4 (during the siege of Rhodes in 304): A Cilician "four" was captured that had on board purple clothes and other gear that Phila, the wife of Demetrius had prepared for him.

Third to First Centuries.

Fleet of Ptolemy II (282–46).

Athen. *Deip.* 5.203d (*TLG*, 5.36): In this major fleet with "big ships" it was thought proper to have twice as many "fours" to *triemioliai* as the larger units. See above, p. 188 with n.51.

Diod. 3.43.5: "Fours" were used by the Ptolemies to go after pirates in the Gulf of Aqaba.

---

2. Morrison (in Gardiner and Morrison 1995, 67) accepts this somewhat surprising number. The editor Wesseling (see n. 1) suggests that the text originally read 200 "threes" and 40 "fours." Justin 13.5.8 estimates the force as 200 ships in all.

Carthage and Rome during the Punic Wars.

Livy 21.22.4: The Carthaginians used a few "fours" and "fives" against the Romans in Spain. The commander Hasdrubal was given 50 "fives," two "fours," and five "threes," although of these only 32 "fives" and five "threes" were outfitted and manned.

Livy 28.45.21: In 205, P. Cornelius Scipio (the future Africanus) has to fight to be given the province of Sicily/Africa. Upon his selection, he raises a fleet of 30 ships from contributions from allied communities. The keels of 20 "fives" and 10 "fours" were laid and work pressed so that the ships were launched fully equipped and rigged just 45 days after the timber was felled. The 30 ships carried some 7000 volunteers.

Rhodian navy: a preferred ship class.

For examples, see Polyb. 16.31.3; 27.7.14; 33.13.2; Livy 31.16.7, 37.16; and 37.23–24.

Roman Civil Wars: Julius Caesar (48).

B. *Alex.* 13.4: The Egyptians pressed into service some old ships, producing 22 "fours" and five "fives" to which they added a considerable number of smaller, open craft. Caesar had 10 "fives" and "fours" and a number of smaller open ships.

Caes. *BC* 3.111.3: When Caesar held the harbor area of Alexandria, a fight developed over 50 warships that had been sent to Pompey and had now returned from Thessaly, all of them "fours" and "fives"; there were 22 besides, all decked ships (*constratae omnes*), normally assigned to guard the port at Alexandria.

Roman Civil Wars: Octavian and Agrippa (36).

App. *BC* 5.11.107: Near Mylae, the Pompeian commander Papias (probably in a "four") suffers a fatal ram strike from Agrippa, in a "five" or "six." See below at "Physical Characteristics. Oarsystem."

Roman Civil Wars: Marcus Antonius (31, 29?).

Dio 50.23.2: "Fours" among classes in Antony's fleet at Actium.

Dio 51.1.2: Octavian dedicated on Cape Actium a "three," a "four," and one of every class up to "ten" from captured enemy vessels.

Physical Characteristics

Note: These testimonia apply only to the period and region from which they derive. Both regional and chronological variations in design should be expected.

Size and Appearance.

Classed among cataphract galleys.

Polyb. 5.62.3: Antiochus III took possession of Tyre and Ptolemais in 219 and received 40 ships, 20 of them cataphracts, "of these none smaller than 'fours,' and the rest were 'threes,' *dikrota* and *keletes* (two-level and single-level open craft).[3]

---

3. Although we possess evidence for cataphract "threes" and even smaller vessels in most Hellenistic fleets, "fours" were at the lower end of those classed as cataphracts; see Morrison and Coates 1996, 113 and 257.

Livy 37.23.5: In the Syrian fleet of Antiochus III (190), there were 37 ships "of larger build" and, aside from these, 10 "threes," implying that "fours" were among the ships "of larger build."

Cic. *Ver.* 2.5.86–91 (delivered in 70): A "four" is decked (*constrata*), fast when supplied with a full crew, and looks "like a city" amongst a bunch of pirate craft (*myoparones*).

"Fours" are the primary ship of the line for the Rhodians in the battles off Side and Myonnesus in 190.

Livy 37.23.4–5: At Side, the Rhodian fleet had 32 "fours" and four "threes." The fleet at Myonnesus (22 vessels; Livy 37.30.2) must have had roughly the same composition.

"Fours" were fitted with turrets or deck towers for fighting; the turrets were also used as lookout positions.

Livy 37.24.6: During a sea battle off Side (190), the admiral Eudamus watched the enemy from a turret (*e turri praetoriae navis*) on his ship.

"Fours" (both Ptolemaic and Roman) are two level (bireme) galleys that can accommodate deck towers at bow and stern. See "Oarsystem" (below).

Lightly ballasted.

"Fours" were lightly ballasted (as were "fives") and floated when "sunk."

Diod. 20.52.6: In a sea battle off Cyprian Salamis (306), Ptolemy's "destroyed" ships (80 in number) were towed, full of sea water, to the camp before the city. The same might be said of Demetrius's destroyed ships (20 in number) which were towed to shore, repaired, and used again. He had "fours" and "fives" in his fleet (Diod. 20.49.2).

Speed.

"Fours" are slightly faster than "fives" and lower in the water (Third Century?, First Century).[4]

Polyb. 1.47.5: At the siege of Lilybaeum (250), the Romans tried to block up the harbor, but were unable to do so. There was a shallow area that they managed to place a mole on, and one night, an enemy "four" of fine build grounded on it. The Romans used this vessel to catch a blockade runner called "the Rhodian" who used a "five." He was unable to outrun the "four" and had to put about and fight. The Romans had more deck soldiers, captured the "five," and then used both ships to intercept other blockade runners.

Livy 30.25.1–8: Three Roman envoys were sent by P. Cornelius Scipio to Carthage in 204 to deliver a protest, accomplished nothing, and were sent away. Fearing for their safe return, the Romans, on a "five," were escorted by two Carthaginian "threes" to the

---

4. See Morrison 1980, 40: ". . . whichever account we prefer [i.e., that of Livy, Polybius or Appian], the important thing is what Livy in the first century knew about the relative heights of 'fours' and 'fives'." The same holds true for the hull speeds of "fours" and "fives."

Bagradas River, from which the Roman camp could be seen. As soon as the escort broke off and returned to Carthage, three "fours" from the Carthaginian fleet lying off Utica (30.25.5) attacked the Roman "five" from the seaward side. The attacking vessels failed to ram the Roman "five" because of her speedy avoiding tactics, and her higher freeboard prevented her from being boarded, so long as the supply of missiles held out. When these ran out, however, the "fours" drove the "five" ashore. The envoys escaped harm. [Note: Although the "fours" were not fast enough, relative to the "five," to damage her steering oars or stern by ramming (as they sailed on the same course), they were able to harass her as she continued on her way and this implies superior speed.]

Polyb. 15.2.12: Describing the same incident as the previous text, Polybius calls the hostile Punic ships "threes" and does not say anything about the relative heights of the vessels.

App. *Pun.* 34: (*TLG, Lib.* 143–146): Describing the same incident as the previous two texts, Appian calls the escort vessels "threes" but does not give any details about the envoys' ship or the ones who pursued and overtook it.

Livy 37.29.9: When the fleets lined up for battle off Myonnesus (190), Rhodian "fours" are described as quickest in the fleet. They are more agile and their pilots and rowers more skillful than the Romans whose ships were stronger and manned by more courageous soldiers (37.30.2). While Livy does not explicitly describe the Rhodian ships as "fours," most were surely from this class; see above, "Size and Appearance. *'Fours' are the primary ship of the line for the Rhodians in the battles off Side and Myonnesus in 190."*

Oarsystem.

"Fours" (both Ptolemaic and Roman) are two level (bireme) galleys that can accommodate deck towers at bow and stern.

B. *Alex.* 13.1, 4; 16.6: During the winter of 48/47, while Caesar was in Alexandria, the Egyptians pressed old hulls into service to fight him: 22 "fours," five "fives," and a number of small open ships (on which we would not expect a difference between rowers and combat crews). From this force, Caesar captured in battle one "five" and a bireme with their combat crews and rowers. Conclusion: Ptolemaic "fives" *were not* biremes, and "fours" *were* biremes.[5]

App. *BC* 5.11.107: Near Mylae in 36, the Pompeian commander Papias (probably in a "four")[6] suffers a fatal ram strike from Agrippa, in a "five" or "six."[7] Agrippa

---

5. This is the *only* occasion on which this author uses the term *biremis*, so we can be certain that he is not using it as a synonym for *aperta navis* (open or small ship) which he uses three times (B. *Alex.* 11.2, 13.4, 13.6).

6. Papias, a Pompeian commander, would have been on one of the larger units in the fleet, which Appian stresses was composed of ships that were lighter and smaller than those of Octavian. Although Appian does not record its class, Papias's ship held towers, so it was likely no smaller than a "four."

7. Were the two men on flagships opposite one another?

struck Papias's ship beneath the *epotis*, or cathead, broke into the hull and the collision ejected the men in the towers into the sea (there were towers at bow and stern; see App. *BC* 5.11.106), which began to flood the ship. The *thalamian* (i.e., lower) oarsmen were cut off, and the other oarsmen (= i.e., the other of two groupings, *heteroi* not *alloi*) broke through the canopy deck and swam away.[8]

A "four" has double-manned oars.[9]

IG II[2] 1629.695 (325/4): The curators receive 415 drachmai for a set of oars from a "four," characterized as "*tarrou argou*" (unfinished oar set).[10] In 411 (during the Peloponnesian War) a rough hewn spar for a trireme oar (*kopeus*) was apparently worth 5 drachmai.[11] Although we must use prices that are separated by almost nine decades for two different commodities (oar spars for "threes" and for "fours"), we can still get a general idea of the relative numbers involved. The money received for the unworked oars of a "four" would purchase roughly 83 units if they cost 5 drachmai a piece. Even if we are off by a variance of 25% to account for the imprecise nature of our evidence, our calculations still indicate a relatively low number of oars for a "four" (roughly 40 to 50 per side) when compared to a "three," whose *tarros* numbered 170 (roughly 85 per side), and this implies that the oars were double manned.[12]

Ship's Gear.

The following gear is assigned to each "four" at Athens. It is roughly the same as that assigned to a "three."

IG II[2] 1627.138–91, 457–72 (330/29):

Wooden gear: set of oars, steering oars, boarding ladders, boat poles, mast, yard arms.

Hanging gear: undergirds, sail, white screen (*pararrhymata leuka*), hair screen (*pararrhymata trichinia*), *katablema* (side curtain), lines [4 sets each of 8 daktyl and 6

---

8. See Morrison and Coates 1996, 269.

9. Morrison (in Gardiner and Morrison 1995, 71) lists a "four's" oar numbers at 70 (35 per side), on what evidence, I am not sure. In Morrison and Coates 1996, 269, he concludes that a *tarros* or full set equals roughly 88 oars. Since he works from the price for a finished set of oars for a "four" (*IG* II[2] 1629.685–86 = 665 drachmai) his calculations are less exact than those I have adopted.

10. Theophrastus (*Lap.* 27) uses the adjective *argos* to describe unpolished gemstones, and a later technical writer named Athenaeus Mechanicus (Athen. Mech. 12) uses the term to mean "unworked," "raw" or "unfinished" when describing hide coverings for siege machinery; see Whitehead 2004, 98.

11. Andocides (2.11) claims that when he provided oars for the fleet at Samos (in 411), he could have sold the rough oar spars for five drachmai a piece.

12. For the number 170, see Morrison and Williams 1968, 256 with 272n16. The *tarros* of a "three" did not include the 30 spare oars commonly assigned to each "three" (see *IG* II[2] 1614.30), so we can leave them out of our calculations.

daktyl lines = 470–72; coils of lines = *merymata kaloidion* = lines 149–50 in the inscription], leather straps, double halyards, sheets, braces (*hyperai*), strap (*chalinos*).

Anchors: 2 iron anchors.

IG II² 1629.1050–85 (325/24): Standard issue for a "three" includes side screens called *hypoblemata* and sometimes a light sail (lines 581–82 in the inscription).

In Athens, the total cost for a complete set of gear on a "four" is roughly 50% more than a full set for a "three."[13]

IG II² 1631.446–48, 517 ff. (323/2): The total cost of ship's gear (wooden and hanging) on a "three" is roughly 4100 drachmai on average.

IG II² 1629.636–56 (324/3): The total cost of ship's gear (wooden and hanging) on a "four" is 6105.5 drachmai on the *Aktis* built by Epigenes; and 6000 drachmai on the *Homonoia* built by Archineus.

Ramming Characteristics.

"Fours" are used in the front line of battle and routinely participate in prow-to-prow attacks.

Diod. 20.50.3: For a sea battle off Cyprian Salamis in 306, Demetrius places in his left wing's front line seven Phoenician "sevens" with 30 Athenian "fours"; these are supported by 10 "sixes" and 10 "fives" in a second line behind them. Ptolemy's fleet was made up of 140 "fives" and "fours" (Diod. 20.49.2).

*A Rhodian "four" unexpectedly sank a "seven" with a single blow (*uno ictu*) in a battle off Side in 190.*

Livy (37.24.3): The fate of the "seven" was unexpected and greatly frightened the enemy.

"Fours" are expected to defeat "threes" which can be used to lure "fours" into a trap.

Caes. *BC* 3.24.1–3: Antonius, at Brundisium in 48, laid a trap with a number of small vessels inside the harbor and then sent out two "threes" to the mouth of the harbor; Libo saw them come out recklessly and sent five "fours" to intercept them. One "four" was captured by Antony's small boats.

A "four" is bested by a "five" in a prow-to-prow encounter.

B. Alex. 46.1.4: During the war between Caesar and Pompey in 48, a sea battle was fought off Tauris Island (N. Illyricum = Barrington Atlas, Map 20, D-6) in which a "four" is destroyed by a "five" in a prow-to-prow encounter (*ut navis Octaviana rostro discusso ligno contineretur* = "so that the ship of Octavius is held fast by its ram, the wood having been shattered"). The "four" eventually sinks to the waterline.

"Fours" (and "fives") can be defeated by smaller vessels through entanglement and subsequent boarding.

Polyb. 2.10.5: During an Illyrian naval attack on Greece in 230, the Illyrians lashed four of their smaller craft together and let them be rammed by their enemies

---

13. Gabrielsen 1994, 152–53.

the Achaeans. Once the attackers became entangled at the bows with the smaller vessels, marines swarmed onto the Achaean ships and captured them. In this way, four "fours" were captured and a "five" was destroyed along with her crew.

The Rhodian "fours" used bow-mounted fire pots to punish larger vessels that attacked their bows.

Livy 37.30.3–5 (Battle off Side in 190): In order to avoid the fire, the larger ships of Antiochus avoided prow-to-prow encounters with the Rhodians.[14] This did not prevent Rhodian prow-to-prow attacks, as revealed by Livy 37.30.9–10: a Rhodian ship (no doubt a "four") was captured when its anchor fouled a Sidonian prow following a prow strike.

Additional Characteristics of Usage.

Used to convoy grain shipment to Athens (326/5).

IG II² 1628.37–42 (326/5).

Used as support ships for "sixes" and "royal ships."

Polyb. 16.6.2 (Battle off Chios in 201): Attalus hastened in his royal ship with two "fours" to come to the aid of a stricken "five." When the "royal ship" was eventually captured, the two "fours" were captured as well (Polyb. 16.7.2).

"Fours" used for reconnaissance.

Pliny *Ep.* 6.16.9: "Fours" were used by Pliny the Elder, as Prefect of the Fleet at Misenum, to investigate effects of the Vesuvius eruption in 79 CE with the intention of assisting seaside towns along the Bay of Naples.

Less Certain or Doubtful Characteristics.

"Four" similar in design to a "five"?

Polyb. 1.59.7–8: During the First Punic War (243–42), there being no state funds for the navy, wealthy citizens at Rome undertook to underwrite the expenses of a new fleet of "fives" and in this way built a fleet of 200 "fives." These "fives" were all built on the superior model of Hannibal "the Rhodian's" ship that had been captured at Lilybaeum in 249 (Polyb. 1.47.5–9). Despite Morrison's argument (Morrison 1980, 39) that "the Rhodian's ship" was a "four," Polybius's account makes much more sense if it was a "five." As he tells it, the Romans first captured a "four" that was slightly faster than a "five," and then used this ship with a select crew of deck soldiers to capture Hannibal's vessel. That the latter ship was a "five" is made all but certain by its use as the model on which the Roman fleet of "fives" was thereafter based.

Single-level "four" with four men to an oar?

---

14. Cf. Livy's description of a naval encounter at Panormus in Samos (37.11) when fire pots were first used. Polyb. 21.7.1–4 describes them, as does App. *Syr.* 24. See Walbank 1999, Vol. III, 97–99. This device was not in regular use in later times—why, we do not know.

Casson 1995, 105: Once multiple man sweeps were introduced, "there is no reason for their not designing a 'five' which simply put five men on each oar—even a 'four' with four men on each. We have almost certain evidence that 'fours' and 'fives' were oared in this fashion from 100 B.C. on. . . ." His view is based on an interpretation of images on coins,[15] and does not correspond to the surviving testimonia, which show that "fours" were two-level galleys and were lower in the water than "fives."

---

15. Casson 1995, Appendix to Ch. 7: "Coin Evidence for Single-Banked 'Fours,' 'Fives,' and Larger Units," pp. 155–56.

APPENDIX B

Testimonia for "FIVES"

Note: The references here point to where the class is mentioned in the text and do not refer to the entire historical episode. All dates are BCE unless noted otherwise.

Historical Development

Invention at Syracuse (399).

Diod. 14.41.3 and 14.42.2: Dionysius was the first to build "fives" in 399.

Diod. 14.44.7: Dionysius sent the prototype "five" to pick up his betrothed from Locri in spring 397.

Fourth Century.

Sidon (351/50).

Diod. 16.44.6: Sidon possessed more than 100 "threes" and "fives" when the Persian king attacked the city in 351/50.

Tyre and Cyprus (prior to 332) and Alexander (332).

Curt. 4.3.11: Alexander chose a Cyprian royal "five" for his flagship at Tyre.

Arr. *Anab.* 2.21–22: "Fives" were used by both Alexander and the Tyrians for skirmishes at harbor mouths and by the Tyrians for attacks on blockade ships.

Curt. 4.4.7–8: During a surprise Tyrian raid at the siege of Tyre, a Macedonian "five" engaged two Tyrian ships, striking the prow of one, as a "three" from Alexander's fleet intercepted the other. The "three" hit the Tyrian "five" with such force that it ejected the helmsman into the sea.

Athens (between 329/28 and 326/25).

IG II² 1629.808–11: In 325/4, 7 "fives" are listed among the warships in the Athenian inventories. "Fives" are not listed among the fleet totals preserved in the inventory lists for 330/29 (*IG* II² 1627.266–78).

Alexander's Euphrates Fleet (323).

Arr. *Anab.* 7.19.3: In 323, a number of ships were carted overland from Phoenicia to Thapsacus on the Euphrates before sailing to Babylon: two "fives," three "fours," 12 "threes," and 30 triacontors.

Olympias (mother of Alexander III) at Pydna (316).

Diod. 19.50.4–5: In 316 at Pydna, Olympias intended to escape from Cassander on a "five." When he captured the ship, Olympias surrendered.

Antigonus's fleet following his successful siege of Tyre (313).

Diod. 19.62.8: Antigonus gathered 240 fully equipped ships: 90 "fours," 10 "fives," 3 "nines," 10 "tens," and 30 aphracts.[1]

Invasion fleet of Demetrius and relieving fleet of Ptolemy (Cyprus, 306).

Diod. 20.49.2: In 306, Ptolemy's relief fleet totaled 140 warships and was comprised of "fives" and "fours." He also had more than 200 troop transports carrying at least 10,000 soldiers.

Diod. 20.50.2–3: In the battle against Ptolemy off Salamis, Demetrius had more "fives" than any other ships. He also had seven "sevens," 10 "sixes," and 30 Athenian "fours."

Third to First Centuries.

Fleet of Ptolemy II Philadelphus (282–246).

Athen. *Deip.* 5.203d (*TLG*, 5.36.11–21): In his Alexandrian fleet, Philadelphus had 17 "fives" out of a big ship total ("fives" and larger) of 112. Surprisingly, he had many more "sevens" (37) and "nines" (30) and almost as many "elevens" (14). J. Grainger suggests that more "fives" are hidden among the more than 4000 ships left undefined by our source; see above, p. 188 with n. 51.

First Punic War (264–41).

Polyb. 1.20.9–16: In 261, the Romans decided to build a fleet of 120 "fives" and 20 "threes." The Romans used a captured Carthaginian "five" for a model since "fives" were not in use in Italy at that time.

Polyb. 1.47.5–10: At Lilybaeum (243–42), the Romans first captured a "four," and with this vessel managed to capture an elusive "five" commanded by Hannibal "the Rhodian" that routinely ran their blockade.

Polyb. 1.59.6–8: In 243–42, the Romans built a fleet of 200 "fives," on the model of a "five" captured from Hannibal "the Rhodian"; their new ships were financed by wealthy Roman citizens who would be repaid if the war proceeded favorably.

Polyb. 1.63.5–8: In a summary of the war, Polybius lists the total naval forces engaged on one occasion as more than 500 "fives," and on another, as a little less

---

1. Tarn 1939, 127, suggested that the text originally read 3 "sevens" and 10 "sixes" instead of 3 "nines" and 10 "tens."

than 700. The losses were also great, as the Romans lost about 700 "fives" and the Carthaginians about 500. This war surpassed all previous naval wars in scale.

Second Punic War (218–201).

Livy 21.17.3, 5, and 8: In 218, the Romans commissioned a fleet of 220 "fives."

Polyb. 3.75.4: The Romans outfitted 60 "fives" after their defeat at the Trebia River (218) by Hannibal.

Livy 21.22.4: In 218, Hasdrubal, the Carthaginian commander in Spain, received 50 "fives," two "fours," and five "threes," although only 37 of the vessels (32 "fives" and all of the "threes") were battle ready with crews and equipment.

Livy 21.49: In 218, the Carthaginians sent "fives" to Sicily and the islands off the Italian coast to conduct raids.

Polyb. 3.96.8–10: In 217, the Romans launched 120 "fives," responding to the arrival of a Carthaginian fleet of 70 ships that had sailed to Italy.

Livy 22.37.13: In 216, after Hiero had sent some gifts to Rome to help the war effort, he urged the Romans to send a force to Africa. As part of this force, the Senate added 25 "fives" to T. Otacilius's fleet of 50 "fives."

Livy 24.34.4–12: The Roman fleet at the Siege of Syracuse (213–11) relied on "fives." In 213, Marcellus attacked the seaside walls of the Achradina district with 60 "fives." In the assault, he used archers, slingers, and javelin throwers on board his ships; he also used pairs of "fives" lashed side-by-side for carrying siege towers and engines (like the *sambuca*).

Polyb. 8.4.2–11: Four pairs of "fives" were lashed side-by-side with their inner oars removed to serve as bases for *sambucae.*

Plut. *Marc.* 14.5–6: At Syracuse (213) Marcellus had a fleet of 60 "fives" together with a large machine supported by eight ships yoked together.[2]

Livy 25.31.12–15: In 211, a few days before the Romans captured Syracuse, T. Otacilius with 80 "fives" crossed from Lilybaeum to Utica, captured some grain ships, and sent the grain to Syracuse.

Livy 26.19.11: In 210, P. Cornelius Scipio, the future Africanus, set out for Spain with a fleet of 30 "fives."

Livy 26.24.10–11: In 210, in the treaty of mutual alliance between Rome and Aetolia, the Romans agreed to send a fleet of at least 25 "fives."

Livy 27.7.15: In 209, at the distribution of commands for this year, 30 "fives" from Sicily were sent to the consul Fabius at Tarentum.

Livy 28.5.1: In 207, the proconsul P. Sulpicius, with 25 "fives," and King Attalus, with 35 warships (presumably "fives"), combined their fleets and sailed from Aegina to Lemnos.

---

2. From Plut. *Marc.* 15, we see that this was a *sambuca*, which Archimedes destroyed by dropping large stones on it.

Livy 28.17.12–15: In 206, P. Cornelius Scipio sailed to Africa for a meeting with Scyphax on two "fives" to conclude a treaty. Upon his arrival, he encountered Hasdrubal and seven Carthaginian "threes" that were at anchor and, therefore, unable to intercept him before he docked.

Second Macedonian War (200–197).

Livy 32.9.7: In 198, T. Quinctius Flamininus crossed to Epirus in a "five" and from there made a rapid journey to the Roman camp.

Livy 32.16.2–7: The Senate had assigned the consul's brother, L. Quinctius, command of the fleet and the coast. In 198, he crossed to Corcyra with two "fives" and then continued south to Malea (the southeast tip of the Peloponnesus), the journey being slow because the supply ships needed to be towed. From Malea, he sailed ahead to Piraeus with three stripped down "fives" (*quinqueremibus expeditis*), and took over the Roman fleet at Athens. At this point, a fleet of 24 "fives" under Attalus and a Rhodian fleet of 20 decked ships sailed out from Asia and made its way to Euboea.

Livy 32.39.4–6: In 197, T. Quinctius crossed from Anticyra to Sicyon with 10 "fives," brought by his brother from their winter fleet station at Corcyra. He was going to a meeting with Nabis and Attalus near Argos.

Second Century.

Livy 37.14.2–3: In 190, the Roman commander L. Aemilius Regillus arrived off Asia Minor in a "five" to take over command of the fleet from C. Livius. En route to Samos, where he formally took command, additional ships joined Aemilius, including two more "fives" from King Eumenes.

Livy 41.9.2: For putting down a revolt in Sardinia (177–76), the consul Ti. Sempronius Gracchus had 10 "fives" at his disposal if he wanted them from the dockyards in Rome.

Livy 42.27.1: At the start of the Third Macedonian War in 172, the Romans raised a fleet of 50 "fives" from old ships stored in Rome and Sicily, of which 38 were launched from the docks near Rome and 12 from Sicily (42.27.6–7).

App. *Pun.* 75 (*TLG, Lib.* 350.1–4): In 149, during the Third Punic War, the Senate dispatched M. Manilius and L. Marcius Censorinus to be in command. They went to Utica with 50 "fives," 100 *hemioliai*, and numerous aphract galleys and *kerkouroi* and transports.

First Century.[3]

B. *Alex.* 13.4–6: In 48, the Alexandrians used guardships posted at the mouths of the Nile and old ships in secret royal dockyards to fight against Caesar. In a few days, they had surprisingly prepared 22 "fours" and five "fives." These engaged Caesar's fleet of 10 "fives" and "fours," with numerous smaller ships on each side. In the battle, Caesar's fleet captured one "five" and a bireme with their combat crews and rowers and sank three others with no losses.

---

3. See also Appendix A: "Historical Development. Third to First Centuries. *Roman Civil Wars: Julius Caesar (48)*" on p. 253.

Caesar *BC* 3.111.3–6: In 48, Achillas (the commander of Ptolemy XIII's army) attempted to take control of an arsenal of 50 warships in the harbor of Alexandria that included fully-equipped "fours" and "fives," in addition to 22 decked ships that normally guarded the port. Taking these ships was crucial to maintaining naval superiority and Caesar managed to seize the ships and set them and the docks on fire.

Physical Characteristics

Number of Oarsmen.

Polyb. 1.26.7: For the battle off Cape Ecnomus in 256, each Roman "five" carried 300 oarsmen and 120 marines.

Pliny *NH* 32.4: Pliny says that the efforts of 400 rowers on Caligula's (37–41 CE) "five" were insufficient to overcome the power of the *echeneis* ("ship detaining") fish. Although Pliny calls Caligula's ship a "five," it was more likely a "six." Not only was the vessel the emperor's flagship, it also carried 400 oarsmen.

Similar in design to a "four"?

See Appendix A: "Physical Characteristics. Less Certain or Doubtful Characteristics" on p. 258.

Seaworthiness of a "five."

"Fives" are more seaworthy than "threes".

Diod. 14.100.4–5: In 390, Dionysius I, sailing on a "five," managed to weather a storm off Rhegium that drove seven of his ships ashore, with a loss of 1500 men (the lost ships were probably "threes" since the average was 214 men per ship).

A "five" is slower than a "three," but more seaworthy.

See "Speed" below.

"Fives," like "fours," do not sink when put out of action.

See Appendix A: "Physical Characteristics. Lightly ballasted" on p. 254.

Use in fights at harbor entrances.

Arr. *Anab.* 2.21–22.5: In 332, during Alexander's siege of Tyre, the Tyrians manned three "fives," three "fours," and seven "threes" with picked crews who knew how to fight at sea and engaged Alexander's blockade ships, rammed and swamped a Cyprian royal "five" along with some others, and drove the rest ashore. Alexander led a counterattack with the "fives" in his contingent plus five to six "threes" and drove the Tyrians back to the northern harbor, capturing a "five" and "four" from them at the harbor entrance.

Diod. 20.52.5: In 306, Demetrius left 10 "fives" to blockade 60 ships inside the harbor at Salamis. When these ships forced their way out, Demetrius's "fives" fled back to the camp.

Use in Siege Warfare.

Livy 24.34.4–12: The Roman fleet at the Siege of Syracuse (213–11) relied on "fives." In 213, M. Claudius Marcellus attacked the seaside walls of the Achradina district with 60 "fives." In the assault, he used archers, slingers, and javelin throwers on board his ships; he also used pairs of "fives" lashed side-by-side for carrying siege towers and engines (like the *sambuca*).

Polyb. 8.4.2–11: Four pairs of "fives" were lashed side-by-side with their inner oars removed to serve as bases for *sambucae*.

Plut. *Marc.* 14.5–6: At Syracuse (213) Marcellus had a fleet of 60 "fives" together with a large machine supported by eight ships yoked together.

App. *Pun.* 16 (*TLG, Lib.* 66.1–4): In his siege of Utica (203), P. Cornelius Scipio placed a tower on two "fives" yoked together from which he shot 3 cubit bolts and large stones against the enemy.

App. *Mith.* 73–74 (*TLG*, 313.1–319.2): During the siege of Cyzicus in 74, Mithridates encircled the harbor with a double wall and lashed together two "fives" to carry a siege tower with an assault bridge. In the attack against the port, he was only able to get four men onto the walls before the defenders repelled the ships with burning pitch.

Speed.

"Fives" can be called "fast sailers" or "stripped down," presumably for speed.

Polyb. 1.27.5: At Ecnomus (256), Hanno commanded the right wing of the Carthaginians with the fast sailing "fives" used for outflanking the Romans.

Livy 32.16.2–5: In 198, L. Quinctius crossed to Corcyra in two "fives" and then continued south to Malea (the southest tip of the Peloponnesus), the journey being slow because the supply ships needed to be towed. From Malea, he sailed ahead to Piraeus with 3 stripped down "fives" (*quinqueremibus expeditis*), no doubt to increase his speed.

"Fives" are fast enough to "avoid the strikes" of "threes" (or "fours").

Polyb. 15.2.12–15: In 203 (or 202), when the Carthaginians escorted a Roman "five" carrying envoys back to the Roman camp from Carthage, the escort broke off and three Carthaginian "threes" attacked (Livy 30.25.5 makes the attacking ships "fours"). They were unable to ram the "five" because it "avoided the attacks," nor could they board it due to the crew's resistance. The "threes" instead circled the "five," shooting at the marines onboard until the "five" ran ashore.

A fleet of "fours" and "fives" overtakes a fleet of mixed warships, where the midsized polyremes set the speed for the entire fleet.

Polyb. 16.4.4–15: In the Battle of Chios (201), the Rhodians caught up with the Macedonian fleet and broke the oars of the rear-most ships, forcing the rest of the fleet to turn about and face the attacking force. The Macedonian fleet employed numerous *lemboi* and placed them in between their ships to foil the Rhodians from maneuvering effectively.

A "five" is slower than a "three," but more seaworthy.

Livy 28.30.4–12: In 207, at Gades, a plot to betray the city to the Romans was detected, and Mago arrested the conspirators and handed them to Adherbal for transport to Carthage. He put the prisoners in a "five" and, since it was the slower vessel, sent it ahead of the eight "threes" he commanded. C. Laelius moved to intercept with a Roman "five" and seven "threes" just as the Carthaginian "five" entered the Strait of Gibraltar. In the ensuing battle, the current affected every ship, but the "fives" had it better than the "threes." The Roman "five" sank two "threes" and disabled a third before Adherbal escaped with his "five" and remaining "threes."

"Fives" are slower than "fours" and have a higher freeboard.

See Appendix A: "Physical Characteristics. Speed" on pp. 254–55.

Ramming Characteristics.

Two "fives" can destroy a "ten" when she is immobilized.

Polyb. 16.3.3–6: At the Battle of Chios in 201, Philip V's "ten" became stuck under the thranite thole of a *triemiolia* she had just rammed. Two "fives" took the opportunity to destroy the "ten" by ramming her on both sides.

When a "five" and "four" collide at the prows, it is expected that the "five" will prevail.

See Appendix A: "Physical Characteristics. Ramming Characteristics" on pp. 257–58.

Use of fire pots.

Livy 37.11.10–13: In 190, the Rhodian Pausistratus attempted a breakout from the narrow harbor entrance at Panormus on Samos. The attempt largely failed as Polyxenidas's forces surrounded Pausistratus and captured or destroyed most of his ships. The only ships that escaped were five Rhodian and two Coan ships that deployed fire pots on their bows.

Rhodian "fives" (?) are special and even when outnumbered can defeat their enemies.

App. *Mith.* 24–25 (*TLG*, 94–101): For his attack on Rhodes in 88, Mithridates used a "five" as his flagship. On two separate occasions, the Rhodians won victories although outnumbered by the enemy; on one of these occasions, six Rhodian "fast sailers" (*tachynautousais*) sent to search for a lost "five" defeated a superior Mithridatic force through their superior seamanship. [Note: See "Speed" (above) for fast sailing "fives."]

Additional Characteristics of Usage.

The Romans prefer "fives" for missions requiring special authority.

Polyb. 10.19.8: In 209, P. Cornelius Scipio sent C. Laelius back to Rome on a "five" to report his victory in Spain.

Livy 28.17.11–15: In 206, P. Cornelius Scipio sailed with two "fives" to Africa for a meeting with Scyphax to conclude a treaty; see also Zonar. 9.10 (*TLG*, 2.277.24–26), who speaks in similar terms, drawing his information from the lost account of Dio Cassius.

Polyb. 33.11.6: In 155–54, the Romans dispatched five legates commanded by Cn. Merula and L. Thermus, each with a "five," in response to a dispute that had developed between Ptolemy VIII and Ptolemy VI over Cyprus.

Livy 26.51.2: In 210, P. Cornelius Scipio sent Laelius, his second in command, back to Rome in a "five" to report the capture of New Carthage and to transport prisoners.

Livy 29.11.4: In 204, the Romans sent five "fives" on a religious mission to Attalus, the ships being suitable for displaying the dignity and greatness of Rome.

Livy 30.13.4: In 203, Syphax is brought in chains to the Roman camp and Livy remarks on the former power of this king that had induced P. Cornelius Scipio to travel on two "fives" to seek his friendship.

Livy 30.26.4: The Romans sent three envoys, each in a "five," to Philip in Greece to complain about his support of Carthage.

Livy 31.11.18: In 200, the Romans sent three legates, each in a "five," to Africa with various messages.

Livy 44.29.1: In 168, three ambassadors of Rome each sailed in a "five" from Chalcis to Delos, and found 40 *lemboi* and five "fives" that belonged to Eumenes.

Misc. Information

Use as command ships.

App. *Mith.* 24 (*TLG*, 96.1–2): For his attack on Rhodes in 88, Mithridates used a "five" as his flagship.

Appian's use of term "trieres" signifies "warship" and applies to "fives" (among other classes).

App. *Praef.* 10 (*TLG*, 39.1–40.1–4): In describing Egypt's forces after Alexander, Appian states that they had 1500 "triereis" that included ships from *hemioliai* to "fives."[4]

App. *Pun.* 121 (*TLG, Lib.* 575.2–577.1): During the Third Punic War (149–46), P. Cornelius Scipio Aemilianus closed up the harbor entrance at Carthage. The people inside the city secretly excavated a new exit, and at the same time built "fives" and "threes" using old materials. When they completed the new opening, they sailed out with 50 "trieritic ships" (perhaps implying both "fives" and "threes") and other smaller vessels.

Shortest time to build and outfit 20 "fives" and 10 "fours" = 45 days.

See Appendix A: "Historical Development. Third Century. *Carthage and Rome during Punic Wars*" on p. 253.

Hephaistion's funeral pyre may provide general dimensions for the prow.

Diod. 17.115.2: 240 golden prows of "fives" were used on the *krepidoma* or foundation course (which was square and measured 1 stade per side) of the funeral pyre for Hephaistion. On the *epotides* (catheads) were two kneeling archers that were 4 cubits tall.[5]

---

4. Appian says that his information comes from Ptolemy II's royal records.

5. See Morrison 1996, 270, who calculates from this reference that 240 prows would fit into a linear space of 784 m. (196 m. × 4) with a space of 3.26 m. for each prow. He interprets this to mean from *epotis* to *epotis* (cathead to cathead).

Testimonia for "SIXES" to "TENS"

Note: The references here point to where the class is mentioned in the text and do not refer to the entire historical episode. All dates are BCE unless noted otherwise.

"Sixes"

Invention (367–44).

Ael. *VH* 6.12.3: Reports "no less than 400 warships, sixes and fives" in the fleet of Dionysius II at Syracuse (367–57, 346–44).

Pliny *NH* 7.208: According to Xenagoras, the Syracusans invented the "six."

Fourth Century.

Demetrius Poliorcetes (306).

Diod. 20.50.3: Demetrius possessed 10 "sixes" in his fleet at Salamis in 306; these, along with seven "sevens" and a number of "fives" and 30 "fours," anchored his left wing. There are problems with the fleet totals as presented by Diodorus, but no one has questioned the class totals.

Third Century.

Agathocles of Sicily (289).

Diod. 21.16.1: In 289, the navy of Agathocles included 200 "fours" and "sixes."

Ptolemy Ceraunus (281).

Phot. *Bibl.* 224.226b 14–26: In 281, "sixes" were among a contingent sent from Herakleia (presumably they were part of Lysimachus's fleet) to supplement the force of Ptolemy Ceraunus for his invasion of Macedonia. This contingent also included "fives," aphracts, and the *Leontophoros* "eight."

Ptolemy II Philadelphus (283–245).

Athen. *Deip.* 5.203d (*TLG* 5.36): Philadelphus's fleet had 5 "sixes" out of a big ship total ("fives" and larger) of 112. See Appendix B: "Historical Development. Third to First Centuries. Fleet of Ptolemy II Philadelphus" (p. 262) for the likelihood that the "fives" are reported incorrectly.

Battle of Chios (201).

Polyb. 16.7.1: In the sea battle off Chios, Philip V lost a "ten," a "nine," a "six," 10 "decked ships" (cataphracts), and other smaller vessels.

Second Century.

Battle off Side (190).

Livy 37.23.5: In the Syrian fleet of Antiochus III, there were four "sixes" and three "sevens" among a total of 37 ships "of larger build" (i.e., "fours" and above).

Battle off Myonnesus (190).

Livy 37.30: The Syrian fleet (of Antiochus III) had 89 ships, including five ships "of the largest build," namely, three "sixes" and two "sevens." See below, "Performance Characteristics."

Use as Flagships or Admirals' Ships: Third to First Centuries.

Flagships at Battle off Ecnomus (256).

Polyb. 1.26.11: Two "sixes" served as Roman flagships in the battle off Ecnomus in 256. They led the column into battle and were maneuverable enough to rush from one region of the fight to another; there were three major areas of fighting.

Ship for Special Embassy of Roman Consul (205.)

Livy 29.9.8: P. Cornelius Scipio (consul 205 and the future Africanus) sailed in a "six" to Locri to judge a case between Q. Pleminius and the military tribunes.

Philip V (196).

App. *Mac.* 9.3: In the settlement following his defeat by Rome, Philip V was allowed to keep one "six" and five cataphracts; the rest were to be handed over to T. Quinctius Flamininus.

Flagship for Cato the Younger (58–56).

Plut. *Cat. Mi.* 39.2: Cato returned to Rome from Cyprus (in March 56) on a royal "six." The ship must have belonged to Ptolemy, the king of Cyprus, whose property fell to Rome after his suicide and Rome's annexation of the island; Cato oversaw the process as Rome's representative (*quaestor pro praetore*).[1]

Sextus Pompey (39).

Plut. *Ant.* 32.4; App. *BC* 5.8.71, 73: When Octavian, Antony and Pompey met at Puteoli in 39 to resolve their differences, the first banquet was held on Pompey's "six" tied up alongside the mole. This "six" had presumably been his father's ship (Cn. Pompeius Magnus).

---

1. See Hölbl 2001, 226, for the circumstances.

Octavian (36)

App. *BC* 5.11.98: Octavian lost one "six" among other vessels in a storm before crossing to Sicily to confront Sextus Pompey in the summer of 36. The ship was apparently not his flagship, thus implying that he possessed more than one "six."

First Century.

Battle of Actium (31).

Both Antony and Octavian had "sixes" in their fleets at Actium. The "six" was Octavian's largest class. See entry at "Tens."

Performance Characteristics.

In prow-to-prow contests, "sixes" and "sevens" defeated "fives" and "fours".

Diod. 20.51–52: In the battle off Cyprian Salamis in 306, "sixes" and "sevens" provided the extra weight that gave Demetrius a crushing victory over Ptolemy. See below, "Oarsystem of a Six" (App. *BC* 5.11.107).

Maneuverability and Speed of a "Six" (256).

Polyb. 1.26.11, 28.3, 7: The Battle off Ecnomus in 256 involved three separate regions of fighting separated by some distance. The Roman commanders rushed from one region to another in their "sixes" in order to bring aid.

Crew Capacity of a "Six" (302).

Diod. 20.112.4: One "six" that was part of a fleet transporting troops in 302 was lost in a storm and only 33 survived "from the more than 500 men who sailed on her."[2]

Oarsystem of a "Six" (49 and 36).

Two or Three Levels?

Luc. *BC* 3.525–37: In a sea battle fought at Massilia in 49, Brutus's "six" may have had three levels of oars (but the evidence could also be interpreted as signifying two levels).[3]

App. *BC* 5.11.107: In the naval battle off Mylae in 36, the flagship of Papias, the Pompeian commander, was struck and shattered by Agrippa's ship with a frontal

---

2. Morrison in Morrison and Coates 1996, 271, argues that the "six" might have carried 90–100 troops, a *hyperesia* of 50–40 men, and 12 files of oarsmen with an average of 30 men per file, i.e., 360 oarsmen + 140 troops and *hyperesia*.

3. Morrison 1980, 36 and 39, argues that Brutus's "six" was rowed at three levels based on Lucan's line 537, "and seeks the water from afar with its highest oars" (*invehit et summis longe petit aequora remis*) thus implying that there was a "highest" bank of oars. While this seems to be a sound observation, we find in Silius Italicus's *Punica*, 14.425, the word *summis* used in a similar context to mean the "top" level of oars (it is paired with *ad imos*, which seems to mean "bottom"). So perhaps Lucan's phrase simply means "uppermost oars" and does not necessarily indicate three levels.

ram strike: the men in the deck towers were ejected into the sea, water rushed into the ship, and all the oarsmen on the thalamian (lower-most) bench were cut off. "The others" (*hoi heteroi*, a word that implies only two levels of oarsmen) broke through the covering deck and escaped by swimming. Papias may have sailed on a "six," but more likely on a "four" or "five" (see Appendix A, n. 6 on p. 255). It is likely that Agrippa fought on a "six" as these were the largest ships in Octavian's fleet at the time.

Freeboard of a "Six."

V. Max. 1.8 ext. 11 (early first century CE): A sailor, hauling up bilge water from a "six," was knocked overboard by a wave and then brought back on board by another wave coming from the other direction. Precisely where the sailor was standing is not stated, but wherever it was, the position was close enough to the sea's surface to make this "memorable occurrence" plausible.

"Sevens"

Invention.

Reign of Alexander III (336–23)?

Pliny *NH* 7.208: According to Mnesigiton, Alexander III was the first to build "sevens" to "tens."

Curt. 10.1.19: Just before his death, Alexander ordered wood to be cut on Mt. Libanus for building 700 "sevens" at Thapsacus (on the Euphrates). These vessels were to be transported to Babylon.

Diod. 18.4.1–4: Alexander's last plans were deemed too expensive to carry out and the army decided not to authorize their completion after his death. One plan called for building warships larger than "threes" in Phoenicia, Cilicia, and Cyprus for an expedition against the Carthaginians and the others who lived along the coast of Libya and Iberia, and the coasts of Italy to Sicily.

Plut. *Alex.* 68.1–2: After meeting up with Nearchus and hearing of his voyage back from India (December 325), Alexander "suddenly had the impulse" to lead a large fleet down the Euphrates, circumnavigate Arabia and Africa, and enter the Mediterranean by way of the pillars of Heracles. He accordingly built vessels of every sort at Thapsacus, and assembled sailors and pilots from all parts.

Arr. *Anab.* 7.1.1–4: Arrian says that he had no data from which to confirm or reject the claims of some writers about Alexander's plans for future expeditions.

Note: Despite the evidence cited above, we have no evidence for anything larger than "fives" in actual use during Alexander's reign. Still, he was the kind of ruler who might have urged his naval architects to build larger galleys. If so, this would imply that ships larger than "fives" were valued by him for how they might contribute to future expeditions, i.e., with their greater transport capabilities, their increased stability in rough seas, and their ability to serve as frontal ramming weapons and as siege platforms.

Fourth Century.

Fleet of Antigonus Monophthalmus (314–313)?

Diod. 19.62.7–9: Three "nines" and 10 "tens" are said to have been in the fleet that Antigonus built at the time he besieged Tyre (314–313). Many scholars would follow W. W. Tarn and emend the text to read "sevens" and "sixes" instead of "nines" and "tens." See below at "Nines, Invention."

Demetrius Poliorcetes (306).

Diod. 20.50.3: Demetrius possessed seven "sevens" in his fleet at Cyprian Salamis in 306; these along with 10 "sixes," a number of "fives," and 30 "fours" comprised his left wing in the sea battle with Ptolemy.

Third Century, Fleet and Battle Evidence.

Ptolemy II Philadelphus (283–245).

Athen. *Deip.* 5.203d (*TLG*, 5.36.17): Philadelphus's fleet had 37 "sevens" out of a big ship total ("fives" and larger) of 112. See Appendix B: "Historical Development. Third to First Centuries. *Fleet of Ptolemy II Philadelphus*" (p. 262) for the likelihood that the "fives" are reported incorrectly.

Pyrrhus and Carthage (276 and 260).

Polyb. 1.23.1–10: C. Duillius captured a "seven" from the Carthaginians off Mylae in 260; this vessel served as the commander's flagship and originally belonged to Pyrrhus, who presumably lost the ship while departing from Sicily in 276 (Plut. *Pyr.* 24.1).

Battle off Mylae (260).

Polyb. 1.23.4–7: Hannibal's flagship (Pyrrhus's "seven") presumably engaged a Roman "five" in a prow attack and was impaled by a Roman corax (boarding bridge); the commander escaped in the ship's launch.[4]

Battle of Chios (201).

Polyb. 16.3.7: In the sea battle off Chios in 201 between Philip V and the allied force of Attalus and Rhodes, a Macedonian "seven" attacked an Attalid "five," which swerved at the last moment, but lost her starboard oars and deck towers.[5] Thereafter the "five" was surrounded, and the marines and ship destroyed. Her commander Dionysodorus escaped with two others to the *triemiolia* giving support. It seems (16.7.1) that Philip lost a "seven" in this battle, perhaps this same vessel.

Battle off Side (190).

---

4. In the account written by Zonaras (8.11 = Loeb Dio, Vol. 1, 408–11 = *TLG*, 2.203.13–204.7), drawn from the lost books of Dio Cassius, Hannibal's "seven" became entangled with a "three." Polybius's version is generally to be preferred.

5. Polybius, drawing from a source with a Rhodian perspective, describes the "five" attacking the "seven," but veering at the last moment and then sustaining its damage; the outcome is the same regardless of who initiated the attack. The casualty totals (Polyb. 16.7.3) demonstrate that Dionysodorus was aboard a "five."

Livy 37.23.3–5, 9: For the sea battle off Side between the fleet of Antiochus III and the Rhodians, the Syrian fleet had 37 ships "of larger build" including three "sevens" and four "sixes." The battle opened with a prow-to-prow charge and a Rhodian "four" unexpectedly destroyed a Syrian "seven" with one bow strike. This act caused "great alarm" (*maxime exterruit*) on the Syrian side.[6] After the battle, the "seven" that had been destroyed was towed back to Phaselis by the victors with difficulty.

Battle off Myonnesus (190).

Livy 37.30 (also 37.23.5): In the sea battle off Myonnesus between the fleet of Antiochus III and the allied forces of Rome and Rhodes, the Syrians had three "sixes" and two "sevens" among five ships "of the largest size."[7] While the Syrian weight advantage was nullified by the Rhodians' use of bow-mounted fire pots (cf. Livy 37.11.13), the Romans broke through to the rear of the Syrian fleet and attacked from astern or from the side.

First Century.

Battle of Actium (31).

Antony had "sevens" in his fleet at Actium. See entry under "Tens."

Performance Characteristics.

In prow-to-prow contests, "sixes" and "sevens" defeated "fives" and "fours".

Diod. 20.51–52: In the battle off Cyprian Salamis in 306 between Ptolemy I and Demetrius Poliorcetes, "sixes" and "sevens" provided the extra weight that gave Demetrius a crushing victory. See remarks at Appendix A: "Physical Characteristics. Ramming Characteristics" (p. 257).

Performance of a "Seven" at the Battle of Chios (201).

Polyb. 16.3.7: In the sea battle off Chios between Philip V and the allied force of Attalus and the Rhodians, a Macedonian "seven" attacked an Attalid "five," which swerved at the last moment but lost her starboard oars and deck towers as a result of the collision. See above, "Third Century. Fleet and Battle Evidence."

"Eights"

Invention.

Reign of Alexander III (336–23)?

Pliny *NH* 7.208: According to Mnesigiton, Alexander III was the first to build "sevens" to "tens." See entry at "Sevens."

---

6. Since the Rhodian fleet had 32 "fours," and four "threes," it is all but certain that the victorious Rhodian vessel was a "four."

7. Livy 37.23.5: The Romans had 80 ships (22 were Rhodian); the Syrian fleet had 89 ships, including five ships of exceptional size, three "sixes" and two "sevens." The Rhodian fleet had "fours" and "threes."

The Extraordinary "Eight" *Leontophoros.*

Reign of Lysimachus (ca. 295?)

Phot. *Bibl.* 224.226b.14–33: See chapter 6. This extraordinary "eight" does not tell us anything useful about the characteristics of typical "eights."

Performance Characteristics in Battle.

Battle of Chios (201).

Polyb. 16.3.2: In the sea battle off Chios between Philip V and the allied force of Attalus and the Rhodians, Attalus's royal ship (size unknown) began the battle by attacking an "eight" and striking her with a blow of the ram "below the waterline." After a good deal of resistance by the deck troops, Attalus destroyed the "eight." One wonders how big Attalus's ship was. Surely she was at least a "six."[8]

Polyb. 16.3.8–11: Deinocrates (an admiral of Attalus), probably in a "five" (like his brother Dionysodoros), struck an "eight" that was high at the bow and got stuck under some part of its superstructure. He could not free himself by backing astern (all of which implies this entanglement was the result of a prow strike). Attalus came up and rammed the "eight" with his ship (clearly a large vessel) and knocked the two ships apart. This "eight" was later captured by Attalus after its crew was destroyed.

Fleet of Antony (32–31).

Plut. *Ant.* 61: Antony had many "eights" and "tens" in the fleet he gathered in 32. See entry under "Tens."

"Nines"

Invention.

Reign of Alexander III (336–23)?

Pliny *NH* 7.208: According to Mnesigiton, Alexander III was the first to build "sevens" to "tens." See entry at "Sevens."

Fleet of Antigonus Monophthalmus (314–313)?

Diod. 19.62.7–9: Three "nines" and 10 "tens" are said to have been in the fleet that Antigonus built at the time he besieged Tyre (314–313).[9] Many scholars would follow W. W. Tarn and emend the text to read "sevens" and "sixes" instead of "nines" and "tens."[10]

---

8. Polybius (16.6.2–8) describes Attalus's ship as surrounded by two "fours" (16.6.2) and then by four "fours" and three *hemioliai* when she separates herself from the fleet. He also describes the magnificence of the "royal furniture" on board the vessel.

9. According to Diodorus, among the 240 warships he gathered, there were 90 "fours," 10 "fives," three "nines," 10 "tens, and 30 open vessels. Since this makes a total of 143, did "threes" make up the rest?

10. Tarn 1939, 127. If present in Antigonus's fleet in 315, the vessels do not take part in the campaigns against Cyprus in 306 or Rhodes in 305.

Third Century.

Fleet of Antigonus Gonatas (mid-third century).

Paus. 1.29.1: In referring to the Panathenaic ship, Pausanias makes a brief allusion to a ship at Delos. "I know of no one who ever beat the ship on Delos, the one reaching to nine oarsmen from the decks." It would seem that the vessel was built with wood sufficient to build roughly 15 "fours."[11]

Fleet of Ptolemy II Philadelphus (283–245).

Athen. *Deip.* 5.203d (*TLG*, 5.36.16–17): Philadelphus's fleet had 30 "nines" out of a big ship total ("fives" and larger) of 112. See Appendix B: "Historical Development. Third to First Centuries. *Fleet of Ptolemy II Philadelphus*" (p. 262) for the likelihood that the "fives" are reported incorrectly.

PCair.Zen. 59036, lines 4–5, 11, 21 (= Loeb *Select Papyri*, Vol. II, #410) (257): A series of letters that mention the disbursement of various sums to Antipater acting as *epiplous* (captain of the marines?) for Xanthippus, the trierarch of a "nine."[12]

Sammelb. 8, 9780 (= *BGU* 10, 1995) (mid-third century): Paus writes to Zenon seeking the job of *skeuophylax* (guard of ship stores and equipment) aboard the "nine" for which Amynandrus serves as trierarch.

Syracusan Fleet (278).

Diod. 22.8.5: Pyrrhus took over 120 cataphracts when he gained control of Syracuse in 278; the largest was the "royal" nine.

Battle of Chios (201).

In the sea battle off Chios between Philip V and the allied force of Attalus and the Rhodians, Philip lost one "nine" in this battle.

First Century.

Battle of Actium (31).

Antony had "nines" in his fleet at Actium. See entry under "Tens."

"Tens"

Invention.

Reign of Alexander III (336–23)?

---

11. According to Moschion in Athen. *Deip.* 5.209e (*TLG*, 5.44.38–40), the vessel was "not even a quarter of the size" of Hiero's monstrous grain carrier *Syrakosia*, which was constructed with the wood of 60 "fours" (*Deip.* 5.206f; *TLG*, 5.40.18–20). Antigonus's greatest naval might should have coincided with his victories over Ptolemy II in the Aegean during the mid-third century; see chapter 6.

12. See Casson 1995, 140n17 with 307n29, who suggests that as *epiplous*, Antipater is the captain of the marines aboard the "nine." The word *enneres* is represented by the numeral *theta* (= 9) at the end of line 12. An image of the text can been found at http://ipap.csad.ox.ac.uk/4DLink4/4DACTION/IPAPwebquery?vPub=P.Cair.Zen.&vVol=1&vNum=59036.

Pliny *NH* 7.208: According to Mnesigiton, Alexander III was the first to build "sevens" to "tens." See entry at "Sevens."

Fleet of Antigonus Monophthalmus (314–313)?

Diod. 19.62.7–9: Three "nines" and 10 "tens" are said to have been in the fleet that Antigonus built at the time he besieged Tyre (314–313). Many scholars would follow W. W. Tarn and emend the text to read "sevens" and "sixes" instead of "nines" and "tens." See note 10.

Third Century.

Fleet of Ptolemy II Philadelphus (283–245).

PCol. 4.63 (after 23 Feb 257): An account of miscellaneous expenditures from the Zenon archive records (recto, col. 2, lines 2–3) a loan of 20 drachmai to Themistos the pilot of a "ten."[13]

Battle of Chios (201).

Polyb. 16.3.3–6: Philip's "ten," his flagship, struck a *triemiolia* amidships, got stuck under the vessel's thranite bench of oars, and was subsequently destroyed by two "fives" who also killed the entire crew and the admiral Democrates.

First Century.

Antony's fleet (32–31).

Strabo 7.7.6–10: In describing the Acarnanian side of the entrance to the Ambracian Gulf, he mentions a "ten ship dedication" (*dekanaia*) made by Augustus after the battle. It contained one of each class captured from Antony's fleet, from a "one" (*monokrotos*) up to a "ten."[14]

Plut. *Ant.* 61: Antony had many "eights" and "tens" in the fleet he gathered in 32.

Dio 50.23.2–3: Antony's fleet contained few "threes" but many in the range of "fours" to "tens." He intended his ships to hold lofty towers and large numbers of men, so that it would be as if his troops were fighting from fortresses.

Dio 50.29.1–4: Octavian, in a highly rhetorical speech written by Dio, notes the enemy's ships as having large dimensions, great weight, and thick timbers. Since they are too heavy to move properly, his men can rip them open with their rams, damage them with catapults from a distance, and burn them to the water's edge with incendiary missiles.

---

13. See Westermann et al. 1940, # 63 (pp. 10–12). There is no comment on the pilot of the *dekeres* by the editors. A text and illustration can be found at http://papyri.info/apis/columbia.apis.p5/.

14. Dio mentions this monument, but says he dedicated ships in size from "threes" to "tens." Although this is in keeping with his statement (50.23.2) that Antony's fleet contained ships in size from "threes" to "tens," it fails to account for the dedication's nickname *dekanaia*.

Dio 50.32–34: The battle description gives the impression that Antony's ships did not move at all, but just sat there as they were attacked by Octavian's vessels. Antony's fleet did not engage in prow-to-prow ramming.

Florus 2.21.5: Antony had from "sixes" to "nines" in his fleet at Actium while Caesar (Octavian) had "twos" to "sixes."

Orosius 6.19.9: Antony possessed 170 ships, and made up in size for what he lacked in numbers (Octavian had 230 "with rams" and 30 "without rams"), "for his ships stood 10 feet above the sea in height."[15]

---

15. Orosius 6.19.9: "... *nam decem pedum altitudine a mari aberant.*" Cf. Morrison and Coates 1996, 163–64, who argue from this statement that a "ten" is 2.957 m. (9 feet 3 ½ inches) above the waterline when the height of their reconstructed "three" *Olympias* is only 8 ft. 2 ½ in. above the waterline. This difference of a foot in height between a "three" and a "ten" seems too small to explain numerous ancient references that stress the lofty height of these larger classes. Considering how poets like Lucan (*BC* 3.529–37) describe the "building up" of files of oarsmen (see his use of *crevisse* in *BC* 3.534), it seems more likely that the idea of 10 feet above the waterline originates somehow in the class number of the "tens" in the fleet; see Murray 1998, 82.

Testimonia for "ELEVENS" to "FORTY"

Note: The references here point to where the class is mentioned in the text and do not refer to the entire historical episode. All dates are BCE unless noted otherwise.

"Elevens"

Ptolemy I Soter (306–283)?

Pliny *NH* 7.208: According to Philostephanus, "elevens" were first built by Ptolemy Soter. Considering the naval dominance of Demetrius, this statement is generally dismissed as unlikely.

Fleet of Demetrius Poliorcetes (306–301).

Theophr. *Hist. pl.* 5.8.1: In the context of talking about the trees on Cyprus, Theophrastus says that the timbers cut for Demetrius's "eleven" were 13 *orguia* (52 cubits = approx. 24 m.) in length, and were amazing for being smooth and free of knots.

Fleet of Ptolemy II Philadelphus (283–245).

Athen. *Deip.* 5.203d (*TLG*, 5.36.11–21): Philadelphus's fleet had 14 "elevens" out of a big ship total ("fives" and larger) of 112. See Appendix B: "Historical Development. Third to First Centuries. *Fleet of Ptolemy II Philadelphus*" (p. 262) for the likelihood that the "fives" are reported incorrectly.

"Twelves"

Ptolemy I Soter (306–283)?

Pliny *NH* 7.208: According to Philostephanus, "twelves" were first built by Ptolemy Soter. Considering the naval dominance of Demetrius, this statement is generally dismissed as unlikely.

Fleet of Ptolemy II Philadelphus (283–245).

Athen. *Deip.* 5.203d (*TLG*, 5.36.11–21): Philadelphus's fleet had two "twelves" out of a big ship total ("fives" and larger) of 112. See Appendix B: "Historical Development. Third to First Centuries. *Fleet of Ptolemy II Philadelphus*" (p. 262) for the likelihood that the "fives" are reported incorrectly.

"Thirteens"

Ptolemy I Soter (306–283)?

Pliny *NH* 7.208: According to Philostephanus, "thirteens" were first built by Ptolemy Soter. Considering the naval dominance of Demetrius, this statement is generally dismissed as unlikely.

Demetrius Poliorcetes (301–298).

Plut. *Demetr.* 31.1–3: Following the Battle of Ipsus (301), when Demetrius returned to Athens and the people refused him entrance to the city, he asked them to return the ships he had left in Piraeus, among which was a "thirteen." After this, he left Pyrrhus as his lieutenant in Greece and sailed to the Thracian Chersonesus to plunder the territory of Lysimachus. No details of the "thirteen" are given.

Plut. *Demetr.* 31.5–32.4: Demetrius accepted the marriage alliance proposed by Seleucus and sailed with his wife and daughter to Syria. Along the way, he paused to march inland to Cynda to recover 1200 talents left by his father. He then proceeded to Rhossus where he hosted a banquet on the deck of his "thirteen." Thereafter he seized control of Cilicia.

Fleet of Ptolemy II Philadelphus (283–245).

Athen. *Deip.* 5.203d (*TLG*, 5.36.11–21): Philadelphus's fleet had four "thirteens" out of a big ship total ("fives" and larger) of 112. See Appendix B: "Historical Development. Third to First Centuries. *Fleet of Ptolemy II Philadelphus*" (p. 262) for the likelihood that the "fives" are reported incorrectly.

"Fifteen" and "Sixteen"

Ptolemy I Soter (306–283)?

Pliny *NH* 7.208: According to Philostephanus, "fifteens" were first built by Ptolemy Soter. Considering the well-known connection of Demetrius with this class (see below), this statement is generally dismissed. Interestingly, Philostephanus did not ascribe the "sixteen" to Ptolemy I (he ascribes it to Ptolemy II Philadelphus; see below, "Twenty" and "Thirties").

Demetrius Poliorcetes (289?).

Plut. *Demetr.* 20.5–9: Demetrius did everything in a grand style and personally took part in the design of his military hardware. His constructions were so grand that they alarmed his friends and delighted his enemies. His enemies would stand on the shore and admire his "fifteens" and "sixteens" and his mobile siege towers (*helepoleis*) "were a spectacle to those whom he was besieging." Plutarch's use of plural nouns here seems purely rhetorical; there is no solid evidence that Demetrius built more than one each of these vessels.

Plut. *Demetr.* 43.4–7: When describing Demetrius's preparations for his last campaign into Asia Minor (289?), Plutarch remarks on the scale of his undertaking: he laid the keels for 500 warships, some at Piraeus, some at Corinth, some at Chalcis, and some around Pella. Prior to this time, no one had ever seen a "fifteen" or a "sixteen." Philopator's "forty" was larger, but barely functional. On the other hand, Demetrius's ships were as remarkable for their speed as for their size. Cf. also Phot. *Bibl.* 245.397b.15–28 for a brief synopsis.

Philip V (196).

Polyb. 18.44.6–7: The peace treaty between Rome and Philip V called for, among other things, Philip to surrender all his cataphracts, except for five units and his "sixteen."

Zonar. 9.16: (= Loeb Dio, Vol. II, p. 294; *TLG*, 2.298.20–31). This epitome of Dio Cassius mentions that the terms of the peace agreement with Philip called for his surrender of all his warships except for five "threes" and his flagship, a "sixteen."

Perseus (167).

Plut. *Aem.* 30.1–3: Upon his return to Italy from Greece, after defeating Perseus at Pydna (in 168), L. Aemilius Paullus brought back the royal "sixteen," which rowed up the Tiber to Rome. This was the "sixteen" of Philip V, thought by some to be the ship originally built by Demetrius. If so, the vessel was more than 120 years old, four times older than the oldest galleys attested by epigraphical records.

Polyb. 36.5.9: In 150, 300 hostages were sent from Carthage to Rome as part of the terms for peace demanded by the Romans. The hostages were confined in the shipshed (*neorion*) for the "sixteen." No further details are given.

"Twenty" and "Thirties"

Fleet of Ptolemy II Philadelphus (283–245).

Athen. *Deip.* 5.203d (*TLG*, 5.36.11–21): Philadelphus's fleet had one "twenty" and two "thirties" out of a big ship total ("fives" and larger) of 112. See Appendix B: "Historical Development. Third to First Centuries. *Fleet of Ptolemy II Philadelphus*" (p. 262) for the likelihood ... that the "fives" are reported incorrectly.

OGIS 39: A statue base found in the sanctuary of Aphrodite at Paphos records that Ptolemy II Philadelphus set up a statue of Pyrgoteles, son of Zoes, as the architect of his "thirty" and "twenty." Apparently, by the end of his reign, Ptolemy built another "thirty" (see previous reference).

Pliny *NH* 7.208: According to Philostephanus, ships "up to 'thirty'" (i.e., larger than the class "fifteen") were first built by Ptolemy II Philadelphus.

"Forty"

Ptolemy IV Philopator (221–204).

Callixenus in Athen. *Deip.* 5.203e–204b (*TLG*, 5.37.5–48): Callixenus provides a detailed description of this large double-hull vessel. For a translation and discussion, see chapter 6, pp. 178-85.

Plut. *Demetr.* 43.6: According to Plutarch, Philopator's "forty" was only intended for show. She was like a stationary building on land, and could only be moved with great difficulty and danger. Cf. also Photius *Bibl.* 245.397b.18–28 for a brief synopsis.

Pliny *NH* 7.208: According to Philostephanus, ships "up to 'forty'" were first built by Ptolemy IV Philopator.

BOOK V of Philo's *Compendium of Mechanics*—The Naval Sections

Ancient Military Writers and Naval Warfare

Philo's *Poliorketika* stems from a genre of ancient literature, which today might be called military science. The genre developed from didactic works like Xenophon's "The Cavalry Commander" (*Hipparchikos*) and was first fully expressed in a series of treatises written by Aeneas Tacticus (Aeneas the Tactician) during the mid-fourth century BCE. On the basis of comments in Aeneas' surviving work, we can see that he wrote separate discussions or "books" on various aspects of warfare from preparing for conflict, to procuring supplies and equipment, to techniques of encampment, tactical deployment, and siege warfare. Other possible books included a collection of plots to advise commanders against treachery, and a collection of pronouncements or appropriate things to say on various occasions. And finally, we have Aeneas' surviving book discussing how to survive under siege, its precise title being unknown.[1] These subjects, as well as the design and use of military hardware such as catapults, siege towers and so forth, appear in subsequent ages as favored topics.

Writers from this genre produced a steady stream of works from the Hellenistic Age onward, which were copied and adapted by later authors up through late antiquity. The works that survived this process of transmission were then collected,

---

1. For the likely subjects of the "military books" ($\sigma\tau\rho\alpha\tau\eta\gamma\iota\kappa\grave{\alpha}$ $\beta\iota\beta\lambda\acute{\iota}\alpha$) written by Aeneas (Aen. Tact. 1.2) see the translation by Whitehead 1990, 13–15: 1) preparation for conflict or $\pi\alpha\rho\alpha\sigma\kappa\epsilon\upsilon\alpha\sigma\tau\iota\kappa\acute{\eta}$, 2) procurement or $\pi\circ\rho\iota\sigma\tau\iota\kappa\acute{\eta}$, 3) encampment techniques or $\sigma\tau\rho\alpha\tau\circ\pi\epsilon\delta\epsilon\upsilon\tau\iota\kappa\acute{\eta}$, 4) tactics or $\tau\alpha\kappa\tau\iota\kappa\acute{\eta}$, 5) siege warfare or $\pi\circ\lambda\iota\circ\rho\kappa\eta\tau\iota\kappa\acute{\eta}$; the book on pronouncements was referred to as 6) $\alpha\kappa\circ\acute{\upsilon}\sigma\mu\alpha\tau\alpha$ or "things heard."

recopied, and adapted for military manuals written by Byzantine authors from the ninth to the early eleventh centuries CE, during an active period of warfare and revived interest in military science.[2] The earliest surviving manuscripts to preserve ancient works from this genre of military science date from this period of revived interest.

Since the genre embraced military works of all kinds, we find that its authors addressed a range of different audiences. Some, like Aeneas, wrote for young men aspiring to leadership positions or for city officials. Others, like Philo, addressed military commanders. Still others, and particularly those who composed discussions of theory like Asclepiodotus (first century BCE) and Aelian (first century CE), aimed their works at a more academic audience.[3] While surviving works from this genre preserve much that is useful for the study of ancient war, the discussions almost always concern aspects of land warfare, and where discussions of naval war once existed, they are now missing from the preserved texts. As a result, we are quite fortunate that Philo's discussion of siege warfare still preserves its naval sections. This is presumably because subsequent ages continued to assault seaside cities from watercraft and considered these sections useful.[4] Most every other work, however, fell victim to a process whereby discussions of naval theory and practice were either selectively abbreviated or cut from existing manuscripts and purposefully left out of new copies.

A number of texts provide evidence for this process. Aeneas Tacticus (40.8), Asclepiodotus (*Tact.* 1.1), and Aelian (*Tact.* 2.1) all wrote tactical works promising naval sections that do not appear in the surviving manuscripts. Although the evidence is complicated, the conclusion is undeniable. Already by the second century CE, many works of military science were being selectively edited to reflect contemporary tastes and needs. By the late fourth or fifth century CE, when we encounter

---

2. A useful review of ancient Greek and Roman military authors can be found in Campbell 2004, 13–20. For the revived militarism of the Byzantine army from the 9th to 11th centuries, see Treadgold 1995, 32–39, and 211–19; and for the impact this had on the compilation of military authors, see Trombley 1997.

3. In contrast to military men like Aeneas and Philo, Asclepiodotus wrote at a time when "the discussion of tactics [had] become the subject matter for lectures by philosophers and theorists" and, therefore, he "outlined the organisation and tactical evolutions of a hypothetical and idealised army." For the quotes, see Illinois Greek Club 1923, 231; and Rance 2007, 718.

4. A continuing interest in using ships to attack seaside city walls can be seen in at least two additional surviving works. Athenaeus (Athen. Mech. 32), writing in the late first century BCE, describes a device called "the little ape" (*pithakion*) to steady machines (i.e., timber constructions) mounted on the decks of two freighters brought up to attack seaside walls. Later, perhaps in the ninth century, Syrianus Magister (*Strat.* 11.10–12) advises those planning cities along the coast to avoid building at the sea's edge or else risk attack from ships who will either "undermine the walls from below or overthrow them, attacking from above" (καὶ κατενεγκεῖν κάτωθεν ὑπορύττοντας καὶ καταβαλεῖν ἄνωθεν ἐπιτρέχοντας).

Vegetius's "Epitome of Military Science" (*Epitoma Rei Militaris*), we can see further results of this process.[5] As Vegetius himself explained (*Mil.* 4.31), the fleet had long ceased to be an important arm of the state's military force and, as a result, the subject of naval warfare required less discussion.[6] So, he compiled his remarks by selecting those details from past naval traditions that he considered appropriate for the needs of his audience. And since his interests focused squarely on Rome, his description of naval matters draws mainly from Roman traditions and from sources (where we can detect them) writing in Latin.[7]

After Vegetius, the first surviving discussion of naval tactics is found in a Byzantine text titled the *Naumachiai* or "Naval Warfare" of Syrianus Magister. This text, originally considered a 6th century work, has been convincingly connected with two other parts of a treatise on strategy, written most likely during the ninth century, and ascribed until recently to the "anonymous" Byzantine (Anonymus Byzantinus). It is now clear that all three works were written by the same author whose name, "Syrianos Magistros," is faintly preserved in the manuscript containing the *Naumachiai*.[8]

Two things are worth noting about Syrianus's naval discussion. First, it represents the kind of naval section that was amputated from military discussions of earlier authors. This seems certain from a statement in Syrianus's treatise "On Strategy" (*Strat.* 14.3–4) that echoes similar statements in Aeneas Tacticus (40.8), Asclepiodotus (*Tact.* 1.1) and Aelian (*Tact.* 2.1): "There are two kinds of war, at sea and on land.

---

5. Vegetius's work, written somewhere between 380 and 450 CE, is the first to treat naval matters in any detail; for a recent discussion of the work's date, see Charles 2007.

6. See Milner 1993, 132; and Stelten 1990. This situation did not apply to ancient descriptions of infantry warfare because the elites of the landed military class still regarded this knowledge as useful; see Veg. *Mil.* 1.28 and Syr. *Strat.* 15.1–3.

7. Vegetius describes Roman fleets and fleet officers (*Mil.* 4.32); he uses the noun *liburna* as a generic term for "warship" (this type was preferred by Roman commanders after Actium; see *Mil.* 4.33); his remarks about weather signs cite Virgil's *Georgics* and Varro's *Libri navales* (*Mil.* 4.41) as authorities; etc. Vegetius does include a few Greek terms and loan words in his discussion of storms and weather signs (*Mil.* 4.40), but uses the wrong forms when inserting the Greek into his text: Charles 2007, 43–44. On the likely sources used by Vegetius for his sections on winds and weather, see Milner 1993, 136–139 with notes. In general on the subject of Vegetius's intended audience as well as his sources, see Charles 2007, 39–50, who includes a thorough review of the relevant bibliography.

8. See Rance 2007 for a concise description (with extensive bibliography) outlining the process of recognition that Syrianus wrote the works assigned to Anonymus Byzantinus. For a Greek text and English translation of his *Naumachiai*, see Pryor and Jeffreys 2006, 455–81. "Magistros" (Latin *magister*) can denote a "master," in the sense of a teacher or instructor, or in the sense of a ship's helmsman or captain; it is also a military title during the Middle Byzantine period. For an excellent discussion of the problems involved with Syrianus's date, including an extensive bibliography, see in general Rance 2007. A concise discussion of the relationship between the texts and manuscripts of Aeneas, Philo, Asclepiodotus, Aelian, Vegetius, and Syrianus can be found conveniently in Pryor and Jeffreys 2006, 176–78.

The tactics appropriate to each must be examined separately. We do not get organized in the same way for fighting on foot and fighting in ships. We do not use the same formations or the same disposition of troops. The officers and their titles are different. These two forms of warfare are so different that completely different tactical methods have to be employed. To avoid confusion, then, we shall discuss each form of warfare by itself, taking the land warfare first."[9] Prior to recognizing Syrianus as the author of both texts, it appeared as if another naval section had been lost. Now, however, we see that a useful naval discussion involved much more than a paragraph or two. In fact, Syrianus devoted 10 manuscript pages to the subject.[10] The second noteworthy fact about Syrianus's *Naumachiai* is its content, which makes no reference to ramming tactics and describes naval warfare in terms of ship size, strength, crew numbers, and soldiers (Syr. *Naum.* 9.2–4). In other words, by the time Syrianus compiled his section on naval warfare, ramming tactics had become irrelevant and his advice reflected different tactical objectives.

A similar trend can be seen in Syrianus's description of elephant and chariot forces. By the time he wrote. (perhaps in the 9th century), he felt the need to mention these forces among the ways that armies had historically fought with one another, but says nothing more because, as he puts it, "Why talk about them when even the terminology for their tactics has become obsolete?"[11] In mentioning this process of selective editing, I do not mean to over-simplify the complex relationships between these authors and the way these texts were transmitted.[12] Nor do I wish to ignore the differences between theoretical discussions of military science (like the works by Asclepiodotus, Aelian, and Arrian) and the practical manuals that informed some of their content. My point is simply this: developments in "real world" armies and navies progressively influenced the content of works by tactical authors, regardless of their intended audience. Some elements, like the infantry phalanx, remained topics of interest long after the Spartan or Macedonian style of fighting had passed from active use. This was because the techniques of marshaling men into square,

9. Both Greek text and English translation can be found in Dennis 1985, 44–45.

10. The *Naumachiai* occupies 10 pages (folios 333r–338v) in the tenth century manuscript that preserves the text, and 12 ½ pages in the edition of Pryor and Jeffreys 2006, 455–81.

11. Syr. *Strat.* 14.20–23: . . . ὁ μὲν περὶ ἐλεφάντων καὶ ἁρμάτων τρόπος ἐν τῷ παρόντι ἀφείσθω· τί γὰρ ἂν καὶ περὶ τούτων ἐροῦμεν, ὁπότε μηδὲ μέχρι ῥημάτων τὰ τῆς τακτικῆς σώζεται; "In these pages we shall not bother to discuss fighting with elephants and chariots. Why talk about them when even the terminology for their tactics has become obsolete?" Text and translation: Dennis 1985, 44–45.

12. We can see from the *Codex Ambrosianus graecus* 139 (B 119 sup.) a clear example of the Byzantine practice of separating sections of a single work and placing them in different thematic sections of the codex. Syrianus's work, for example, was split into three sections, thus confusing their single authorship: Rance 2007, 734. How this practice impacted the transmission of naval sections from other authors' texts (if at all) remains unknowable.

rectangular, or rhomboid formations were still considered useful (Syr. *Strat.* 15.1–17 and Veg. *Mil.* 1.28).

The sections on naval war, however, were different. Warships represented specialized hardware that required specialized skills from those who fought aboard them. As technology or the resources of the combatants changed, so too did naval hardware. And with these changes came further changes in tactics, training, fleet organization, and terminology. The specialized details of these topics were irrelevant to subsequent modes of war and, thus, whole sections of tactical handbooks were left out when new copies were made, or when new compilations were constructed from old sources.

This same tendency was noted in the nineteenth century by Captain Alfred Thayer Mahan, when he lectured at the Naval War College in Rhode Island, and then published these lectures in a book titled "The Influence of Sea Power upon History." As he astutely observed, "The unresting progress of mankind causes continual change in the weapons; and with that must come a continual change in the manner of fighting,— in the handling and disposition of troops or ships on the battlefield. Hence arises a tendency on the part of many connected with maritime matters to think that no advantage can be gained from the study of former experiences; that time so used is wasted."[13] Considering this pervasive tendency of military men and the general absence of naval sections from ancient writers of military science, we are fortunate that Philo's text survives to give us a taste of what we have lost (see esp. Philo *Polior.* D 101–110). As noted before, the text was saved, presumably, because its advice was still considered useful (see n. 4). And while the naval hardware changed over time, Philo's practical advice remained relevant enough to insure the survival of the entire text.

Naval Historians and Philo's *Poliorketika*

Considering Philo's central importance to our present discussion of Hellenistic naval developments, it is surprising that Philo's text is not better known. The reason seems to stem from two interrelated factors. First and foremost there was the poor quality of the late manuscript (*Parisinus* 2435) used for the first modern edition, published in 1693. This sixteenth century copy bore the worst effects of a clumsy editor who so abridged the text at some point before the mid-ninth century that its meaning had become obscured in many places.[14] The text's poor condition partly explains why the work was considered "unreadable" by many modern scholars, and accounts for its exclusion from an important collection of military texts edited by

---

13. Mahan (1918) 1928, 9. The first edition of Mahan's influential work was published in 1890.

14. The first modern edition is Thévenot et al. 1693. Garlan 1974, 286–87, argued that the work's main problems can be explained by the intervention of a learned Byzantine from the high empire (perhaps during Justinian's reign, a time of renewed fortification building), who abridged the text clumsily, but without introducing his own ignorance.

H. Köchly and W. Rüstow in the mid-nineteenth century.[15] The second factor was a tendency among ancient historians to ignore siege warfare as a meaningful part of naval war. In other words, most ancient historians felt that proper naval history involved sea battles, not sieges, and there was no easily available text of Philo to suggest otherwise. Furthermore, the naval traditions of the countries that produced many of the maritime scholars tended to reinforce this view.[16]

Despite the fact that new modern editions, based on older manuscripts with better readings, appeared in the late nineteenth and early twentieth centuries, scholars interested in naval history took no notice of Philo's text.[17] W. W. Tarn provides an excellent example: his influential *Hellenistic Military & Naval Developments*, published in 1930, ignored Philo's *Poliorketika* and described naval developments solely in terms of sea battles between fleets of warships.[18] Tarn's predilection for equating naval history with sea battles typifies the general view of most scholars through the end of the 20th century. As a result, those scholars interested in ancient naval warfare remained largely unaffected by Y. Garlan's *Recherches de poliorcétique grecque*, published in 1974, which included an improved critical text of Philo's *Poliorketika*, along with a French translation and detailed commentary.[19] The situation remained largely unchanged by 1979 when the first English translation of Philo's work appeared as a section of A. W. Lawrence's *Greek Aims in Fortification*.[20] While Lawrence finally made Philo accessible to many interested in the history of Greek fortifications, he considered the sections on naval warfare as partly irrelevant to his subject, choosing to exclude certain important sections.[21]

In conclusion, a three-step process has affected our knowledge of naval theory and with it, the text of Philo regarding naval siege warfare. First off, discussions of ancient military science were whittled down by a process that edited naval discus-

---

15. Köchly and Rüstow (1853–55) 1969, 198–99, declared Philo's *Poliorketika* to be "virtually unreadable" (*äusserst unlesbar*), like "bad notes from a college lecture" (*nachgeschriebenes Collegienheft*), and thus chose to put off its publication. According to the introduction of their third volume (Vol 2.2, vi–vi), the editors intended to include Philo's *Poliorketika* in a final volume, but due to problems at the press, the work was never published.

16. The so-called "classic age of sail" involved seven major wars between Britain and France over a century and a quarter (1689–1815). These wars were characterized by battles between fleets of warships of increasing size where victory often turned on issues like capital-ship superiority (i.e., who had the most big ships): see Baugh 2007.

17. On the various "éditions moderns," see Garlan 1974, 286–88, who describes the process by which a number of French and German scholars improved the text during the course of the nineteenth and twentieth centuries.

18. Tarn (1930) 1960, 123.

19. Garlan 1974, 279–404.

20. Lawrence 1979, 67–107.

21. Lawrence's most notable omission was D 101–11. The recent collection of military texts edited by Brian Campbell continues this trend (Campbell 2004). Eight different selections are presented from Philo's *Poliorketika*, none dealing with naval siege warfare.

sions from the texts. Luckily, Philo's advice concerning naval siege warfare survived this process because later ages saw value in his instructions for attacking coastal positions from watercraft. That said, the first manuscripts containing Philo's text included a terribly corrupt version of his manual on siegecraft. This, in turn, prevented the text from being more widely read until the latter half of the nineteenth century. Finally, scholars of the nineteenth and twentieth centuries who studied antiquity were predisposed to view changes in warship design as the result of contests between warships in set naval battles, such as were waged during the fifth century BCE. They did not notice, therefore, how Philo's text clearly outlined the strategic goals behind the naval arms race of the Hellenistic period—an arms race that produced the largest fleets and largest warships of the ancient period.

Considering the central importance of Philo's text for Hellenistic naval history, I present in this appendix a translation of Philo's *Poliorketika* where it is relevant to the subject of naval warfare. As my translation consists of excerpts and not the whole text, I have indicated the proper context of each section where appropriate. My translation is based on the Greek text as established by Y. Garlan, and owes much to the translation by A. W. Lawrence mentioned above.

Conventions Used in the Translation

In rendering the Greek into English, I have attempted to follow the original as closely as possible, preserving the flavor of the Greek and choosing to leave certain ambiguities intact. Philo wrote his manual for readers who knew far more about the subject than we do and, as a result, employed a terse style, brevity of expression, and technical vocabulary. Because of the nature of the text we possess, surely an abbreviated form of the original, I have often resorted to amplifications for the sake of clarity, indicating these additions by placing them within parentheses (). Upon occasion, I also place inside parentheses references to figures in the text as well as Greek words in *italics* to indicate the original on which the English translation is based. Words that have been supplied by the editor are placed within angled brackets < >, while summarized sections at C 1–51 and D 2–4 are printed in italicized text. Throughout the translation, I have also added subject headings to help clarify Philo's organization. These are not original to the text and are printed in capital letters to signify this fact. Where corruptions in the manuscript tradition have resulted in emendations, I have accepted the ones adopted for grammatical reasons without comment, but signify in a note if a proposed emendation changes the meaning of the received text.

Following the conventions adopted by Lawrence, I signify the difference between two terms used by Philo for "stone projector," *petrobolos* and *lithobolos*, by writing an initial capital for the first term (Stone projector), but not for the second (stone projector).[22] In like manner, I translate *katapeltes* as "bolt projector," and *mechanema* as "timber construction." This latter term is frequently applied to various kinds of constructions that served as siege towers (both mobile and stationary) and other devices. English speakers often use the cognate "machine" to translate *mechanema*, which is fine, so long as the reader understands that these ancient machines were largely made of wood and not metal. Wishing to avoid this confusion, I have followed the example of Garlan, who uses a similar periphrasis, "ouvrages de charpente" ("framed wooden constructions"). Numbers inside square brackets indicate page and line numbers of the first modern edition (Thévenot et al. 1693) and allow for easy reference to the text presented in the Online *TLG* (= Diels and Schramm 1920).

Chapter C: THE DEFENSE AGAINST A BESIEGER

1–51 *[90.46–94.35]: Philo describes the precautions one must take both before and during a siege (***1–7** *[90.46–91.24]), how one can destroy the enemy's equipment from your own wall (***8–13** *[91.25–47]), techniques for counter ramming the enemy's siege towers (***14–17** *[91.47–92.22]), how to build improvised fortifications in case your wall is breached (***18–27** *[92.22–93.4]), how guard duties should be carried out on such an improvised wall (***28–29** *[93.5–11]), and defensive measures that must be taken should the enemy enter your city (***30–33** *[93.12–32]). Following this advice, Philo discusses precautions one must take for guard duties in general (***34–38** *[93.32–52]), he describes additional ways to destroy enemy equipment (***39–44** *[94.1–20]), he explains how to promote morale (***45–48** *[94.20–31]) and how objects might be rolled against the enemy to disrupt their operations (***49–50** *[94.32–35]).*

51–62 *[94.36–95.32]: How One Defends Against Attacks from the Sea.*

(**51** [94.36]) If the (enemy) approach is performed from the sea, it is necessary to place doors (studded) with nails in concealment at the landing places, to disperse caltrops of iron and boxwood, and to enclose the more accessible places with stockades.[23] (**52** [94.40]) And it is necessary to secure the mouths of the harbors with strung-out barriers (*kleithrois*), in which there are round rolling <buoys> with iron hollows[24] (Fig. E.1); (**53** [94.43]) or to put platform constructions in position (on the seabed) and to put on them a mound of large stones, in which you insert crossing stakes joined together with iron in alternating directions, and tied together (where the stakes cross); they

---

22. Although Lawrence 1979, 72 felt that Philo tended to favor the use of *petrobolos* over *lithobolos* for larger stone projectors, D 31 shows that he specifically used *petrobolos* to describe a two mina weapon, the smallest known of the stone projectors. As there may be some significant reason for his choice of nouns that is currently unknown to me, I have chosen to retain Lawrence's distinction.

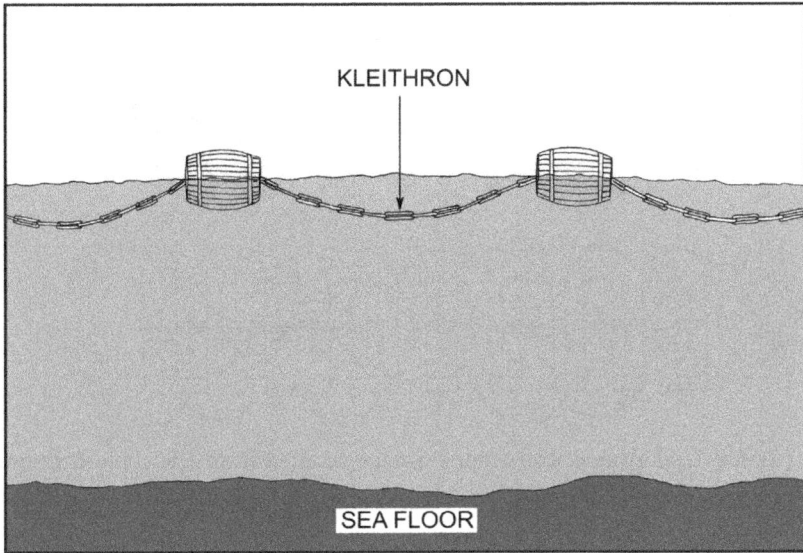

KLEITHRON

SEA FLOOR

FIGURE E.I *Kleithron* consisting of a chain and floats. Line drawing by Niki Holmes Kantzios and W. M. Murray.

should not protrude above the sea but should be an interval of a palm's breadth (8 cm.) below the surface (Fig. E.2). (54 [94.49]) Or ships having military weaponry—or else *lemboi* and light boats of what sort you have—should be anchored opposite (the harbor mouth) and closely connected to one another, and constructions prepared for them of thick squared beams placed in front of (each) prow, pegged and bound together into a unit, with a ram fitted on the outward end around the beams.[25] (55 [95.5]) Rowing boats should be anchored beside all the aforesaid barriers and pontoon bridges, having (in them a supply of) pitch and brimstone and caltrops wrapped in tow (Fig. E.3).[26]

---

23. Caltrops are devices made of metal or wood with four projecting spikes so arranged that when three of the spikes are on the ground, the fourth projects upward. Caltrops are frequently strewn over the ground to pierce the feet of the enemy and their animals (cf. Fig. E.3).

24. H. Diels (Diels and Schramm 1920, 62) supplied the noun χῶναι here which he translated as "buoys" (Bojen). While the context of this passage demands a noun meaning buoys or floats, I remain uncertain that χῶναι is the word we seek; cf. D 53 where it denotes a protective sheath for anchor lines in shallow water, and B 29 where it denotes chutes built into granaries. I envision something like a large version of the floats used on lane markers in a swimming pool. If this is what Philo intended, the hollow could be defined as the iron tube through which the barrier or κλεῖθρον—in this case, a chain—was led, much as the line for the swim lane is passed through the center of the float. The float itself might be constructed out of wood in the manner of a large barrel, and thus require a pitch sealant (as in Aen Tact. 11.3). The entire contraption with chain and floats was often referred to by the plural form κλεῖθρα. For futher possibilities, see above, p. 135 n. 21 with Garlan 1974, 388–89.

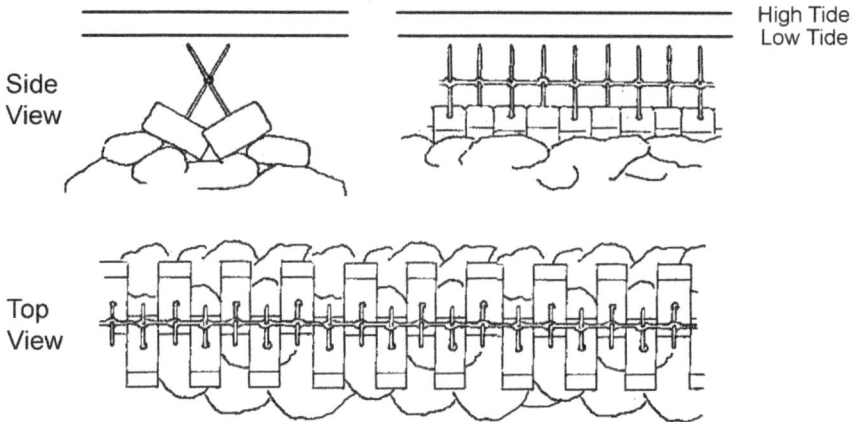

FIGURE E.2 Underwater obstructions. Image adapted from Diels and Schramm 1920, 62, Bild 29.

And on the cargo-vessels (that compose a pontoon bridge), these (materials) and such like them should also be present.

(56 [95.9]) And on either side of the harbor mouth, a 20 mina (c. 8.7 kg.) stone projector should stand so that whenever some of the enemy's small boats attack the harbor, they will be set afire[27] or, stuck around the rams, they will be destroyed or swamped, being hit by both lead amphoras and the Stone projectors.[28] (57 [95.15]) But if the distance across (the harbor-mouth) is somewhat great, a tower should also stand in the middle, and there should be a 30 mina (c. 13.1 kg.) stone projector in it.[29] (58 [95.17]) Against <timber constructions> brought forward (by the enemy) and attacking ships, it is most necessary to use Stone projectors, incendiary missiles[30] (*pyrphoroi*: Fig. E.4), and spear-projectors.[31]

---

25. In nautical shipbuilding terminology, γόμφοι are the trenails that firmly fix mortise and tenon joinery. Rather than translate this sentence as "nailed together and bound together into a unit" (as does Lawrence 1979, 97), the specialist nature of Philo's work allows for a more technical translation: Orlandos 1966, 47 with n. 2. The timbers inside the Athlit ram give us a good example of what was involved when skilled craftsmen did such work. We should note that only a major naval power would have had access to a supply of unused rams for the purpose Philo suggests here.

26. Pitch and brimstone (sulfur) are highly flammable, and thus desirable in this context. Pitch is a dark viscous substance obtained as a residue in the distillation of tars or other organic materials (like pine sap) and is used in shipbuilding as a sealant. Tow is a fiber which can be woven into a twine and when soaked in pitch and wrapped around a caltrop burns steadily after the caltrop is thrown at the enemy vessel.

27. The setting on fire of the ships goes with the incendiary materials of the previous sentence, not with the two stone projectors discussed at the beginning of this sentence.

FIGURE E.3 The placement of caltrops with a rake. Line drawing adapted by C. Wescher from Codex B, folio 163 of the *Parangelmata Poliorketika*.

(59 [95.20]) If there are ever sectors of the city walls beside deep water, always make deposits (of stones offshore) so that there may be no bringing up (of siege machinery on ships), nor (the chance for) a ram of one of the large ships to attack the

---

28. Philo provides the conditions under which a ship can be destroyed (literally, driven down into the water) by a stone projector: 1) the ship must be small; 2) it must be unable to move freely; 3) it must be hit, presumably more than once, by both (τε . . . καὶ) lead amphoras and 20 mina stone shot. A *mina* (or μνᾶ in Greek) is roughly equivalent to 0.4366 kg.: see Marsden 1969, xix.

29. The best manuscripts present 4 minae as the weight of the stone projector in the middle tower. H. Diels suggested that a Δ (= 4) slipped into the text in place of the Λ (= 30) originally written by Philo, and that this explains why our manuscripts read τετράμνους instead of the more obvious τριακοντάμνους. On the other hand, an argument might be made for a light weapon with the ability to discharge numerous projectiles over a wider range as opposed to a 30 mina weapon with the limitations its size placed on it. Nevertheless, considering what Philo says at C 67–78 about the usefulness of the 30 mina weapon against siege machinery, we might suspect that he would advise its placement in such an important middle tower.

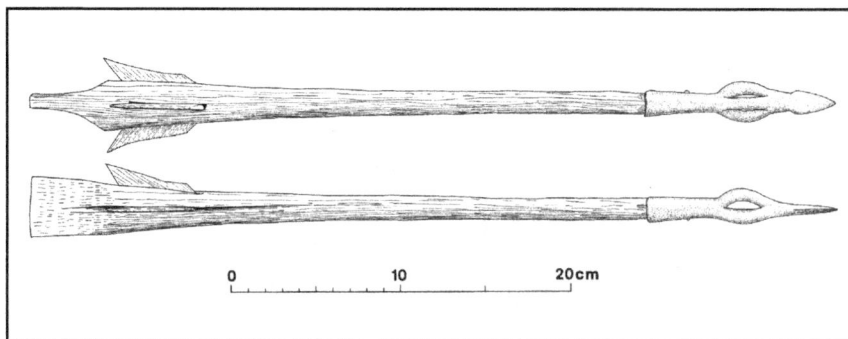

FIGURE E.4 Reconstruction of a catapult incendiary bolt (*pyrphoros*). Third century CE. Line drawing from James 1983, 143 Fig. 4.

wall, otherwise (the enemy) may capture some tower by putting out gangways.[32] (**60** [95.25]) And it is necessary also during the night, when it is stormy, to order the divers to cut the anchors of ships blockading your harbor and to drill through their hulls. (**61** [95.28]) This is the best way to thwart your enemies who anchor opposite your harbor.[33] (**62** [95.29]) All the other things which are useful in such attacks are also useful against attacks carried out by land.

---

30. The Greek term used by Philo for incendiary missiles is πυρφόροι or "fire bearers." They are made from catapult bolts fitted with special tips that include looped projections at their sides for the attachment of flammable materials, such as tow soaked in pitch. The archaeological evidence that we currently have for these projectiles is later than the Hellenistic period, but the preserved tips must closely represent what Philo describes here. See James 1983; and Bishop and Coulston 1993, 113, nos. 12–13.

31. Spear projectors are also mentioned by Josephus (*AJ* 9.221) along with other types of gear appropriate for conducting a siege.

32. At D 29, where Philo repeats the possibility of ships ramming the walls (this time, from the attacker's perspective), he makes it clear that ramming attacks were intended to make the wall collapse. In this passage, Philo is less explicit. According to him, the defender should not allow the enemy to get close to the walls with their large ships because: 1) they might ram the walls with their ships, and 2) they might attempt to make a landing from the ships themselves. Precisely how such a landing would be made must have depended on the height of the wall and the degree to which it had been battered down, as well as the design of the *epibathra*, the gangway used for the landing process. Since Philo uses the term *klimakas* (C65 and D4) to define a scaling ladder, and *diabathra* (C65 and 66) to signify a gangway with planks that could be dragged or "run out" horizontally (τὰς ῥυτὰς σανίδας), *epibathrai* might be interpreted as gangways that would allow soldiers to ascend to the wall at a slight incline.

63–66 [95.32–49]: How One Defends Against Attacks by Land

(63 [95.32]) If some part of the wall of a long city is liable to be shot at from both sides, it must be partitioned by a wall or by hides or by cloth hangings, in order that the men on the wall will not be wounded from the rear. (64 [95.36]) Whenever a track is made for the (enemy) mobile tower that is being advanced, throw forward from your Stone projectors stones of the largest possible size—but not round ones—in order that they (the enemy) may not be able to move the city taker (i.e., mobile siege tower) onward. (65 [95.39]) Heavy linen throws, made beforehand, are useful against those coming up the wall by ladders or across landing-gangways, for the enemy become easily overpowered when (these throws) are cast upon them since they hold them together. (66 [95.44]) Barbed harpoons also (are useful in these circumstances); for if they are well thrown out on their ropes and thrown from above, when they stick in protective padding and the extended planks of the gangways, and (are) pull(ed) back, it will be possible to drag many things away from them (i.e., the enemy).[34]

67–71 [95.49–96.14]: The Defensive Use of Artillery[35]

(67 [95.49]) Care must be taken above all to make the best possible arrangements for 30 mina (c. 13.1 kg.) Stone projectors and for the operators and emplacements of these instruments. (68 [96.2]) For when the stone projectors are well made, their emplacements set up in suitable positions and rightly prepared, and their operators skilled, then no timber construction or covered way or mantlet will easily be brought forward. (69 [96.8]) But if one does approach its goal, it will not move onward at all (as a result of) being hit by these (30 mina Stone projectors). (70 [96.10]) These (weapons) are proportionate (to the timber constructions or covered ways or mantlets being brought up) and are most violent in regard to the impact of their projectiles. (71 [96.12]) The result is, with these in action, the city will suffer no disaster during the assaults that are being made.

---

33. Strictly: "Thus you will best thwart those opposed to you who come to anchor." Philo relies on the close relationship between two slightly different verbs: ἐφορμέω (to anchor against a place, or blockade) and ἐφορμίζω (to reach port or come to anchor). Their meanings, as determined by the context of C 60–61, seem almost to overlap here. I therefore translate "those opposed to you" as "your enemies" and "come to anchor" as "anchor opposite your harbor."

34. Although the text is defective at this point, the general meaning is clear.

35. The translation of C 67–71 is largely derived from Lawrence 1979, 99.

Chapter D: HOW TO LAY SIEGE.

1–5 *[96.27–42]: HOW TO PREPARE FOR A SIEGE*

(**1** [96.27]) It is necessary to prepare for a siege as follows. (**2–4** [96.28–37]): *The would-be taker of a city should make his attacks during a festival, or during some other occasion when men are off their guard or out of the city. He should approach the wall secretly with ladders and seize some of the towers.* (**5** [96.37]) But should this miscarry, if the city is beside the sea, build a stockade around it from sea to sea and, if you have warships, anchor them at the (entrance to the) harbor so that nothing can sail in.

6–20 *[96.43–98.24]: PRELIMINARIES TO A FULL-SCALE ATTACK BY LAND.*[36]

21–23 *[98.24–34]: PRELIMINARIES TO A FULL-SCALE ATTACK BY SEA.*

(**21** [98.24]) In like manner, if you make the attack from the sea, bring forward your timber constructions, placing them on both the merchant ships and the *lemboi*. (**22** [98.27]) And breaching the harbor boom (*kleithron*) with your largest ships if you have cataphracts,[37] make the attack with those who are the most experienced and, above everything else, who are able to fight at sea.[38] (**23** [98.31]) Let it be done—the breaking of the boom and the barriers—with the rams of the ships or with the anchors, hauling them up from the merchant ships that are loaded (with assault gear?) out front.

---

36. For a translation of sections 6–11 and 17–19, see Lawrence 1979, 99–101.

37. Cataphract (κατάφρακτοι) warships possess a full deck that covers and protects the oarcrew and provides a fighting surface for deck soldiers and artillery. During the Hellenistic period, this term usually applies to classes larger than "three" in the size.

38. This sentence clearly implies that it takes a certain kind of skill for a marine to fight a battle from ships, and that this skill comes from experience. The ones doing the fighting here are the marines on the decks of the cataphracts. This passage and the next (D 23) suggest the role of the increasingly large cataphract warships (the "eleven," "thirteen," "fifteen," and "sixteen") that appear in the fleet of Demetrius after the siege of Rhodes.

24–29 [98.34–99.10]: GENERAL INSTRUCTIONS
REGARDING THE ATTACK BY LAND AND BY SEA.

(24 [98.34]) When the timber constructions are brought up, after having exhorted the soldiers and having made the same proclamation as you made earlier (D 6: not to loot or damage anything; D 9: rewards will be given to the first three men who mount the wall), make the attack on the city from all sides, both by land and by sea, if a section of the wall is in the sea. Do this in order to inspire as much fear as possible in those besieged inside and to divide their forces. (25 [98.42]) Employ all your projectiles and rams and borers[39] and hooks and gangways both by land and by sea at the suitable places. (26 [98.45]) And make the attack with successive waves of your soldiers, never slacking off, so that fresh troops are always engaged and the fight is vigorous and continuous. (27 [98.48]) And (it is necessary) to make lots of noise and sound the trumpets along the strongest sectors of the city, so that, thinking the wall has been taken there, (the enemy) might flee from the section between the towers with the others. And you might divert (from there) as many as possible of those inside, and so take the city by conquest. (28 [99.3]) You, yourself, must not take any undue risks; for, in regard to all your plans, you could not accomplish anything as great with your own body as you would damage by suffering harm.

(29 [99.6]) One must also make ramming attacks against the curtains with the vessel least serviceable (for war) among the big ships; (do this) if there is deep water along extensions of the wall where (the curtain) is weak and can be captured if it should collapse.[40]

---

39. Borers were drills of various sizes that were used to bore through mud brick walls; for examples, see Nossov 2006, color plate 14; Lendle 1983, 149 Abb. 44; and Schneider 1908a, Tafel 2, Fig. 7; and Tafel 3, Fig. 8.

40. Although it may surprise the reader to learn that warship rams were sufficiently strong to be used against city walls, this was clearly the case. When Diodorus describes the massive rams used by Demetrius on land against the city wall at Rhodes, he uses a naval parallel (20.95.1): "For each shed held a ram with a length of 120 cubits (55.5 m.), sheathed with iron and striking a blow like that of a ship's ram." The high quality of the Athlit ram's casting explains how rams from much larger vessels could be brought to bear against a heavy stone wall with a reasonable expectation of survival.

30–33 *[99.11–20]*: MINING OPERATIONS

(30 [99.11]) It is necessary to engage in secret tunneling under the walls just as, even now, miners for ore do it. (31 [99.13]) And if those within (the city) are countermining and their passage breaks through or almost meets your own, it is necessary to use ox-goads, javelins, hunting spears, three-span bolt projectors,[41] and 2 mina Stone projectors.[42] (32 [99.18]) And use smoke against those men who are inside the (counter-)mines.[43] (33 [99.19]) These (methods) are available to besieged and besiegers alike.

34–40 *[99.21–47]*: CONSTRUCTION OF VARIOUS KINDS OF EQUIPMENT

(38 [99.37]) Mantlets (*chelonai*) (for use) on *lemboi* are made rounded above, constructed of strong planks, having a small opening below, through which the stone projectors discharge (their missiles).[44]

41–55 *[99.48–100.44]*: PREVENTIVE ACTIONS AGAINST VARIOUS DEFENSIVE COUNTER-MEASURES

(53 [100.33]) Against the cutting of the anchor lines, one uses chains, if the place is deep, and if it is shallow, "funnels"[45] to hold the anchors of the boats. (54 [100.36]) Against the enemy's drilling of your ships' hulls, one must set out guards all around

---

41. A three-span catapult shot a bolt that was about 69 cm. (27 in.) in length. This weapon was prized for its long range (Diod. 20.85.3) and was utilized by Demetrius on the bows of his warships for the sea battle off Salamis in 306 (Diod. 20.49.4) and for his crossing to Rhodes in 305 (Diod. 20.83.1).

42. It is important to note how small stone projectors are used in the confined space of a mine to inspire fear among the enemy's forces. Two small (6–8 cm. diameter) white stone projectiles were found in one of the mines in the siege ramp zone at Dura Europus dating to the Persian siege of 256 CE; see du Buisson 1944, 34.

43. See James 2011 for a recent analysis of approximately 20 Roman soldiers found in the Tower 19 counter-mine at Dura Europus, along with associated bituminous materials and sulphur crystals. James suggests that the soldiers were killed by toxic fumes purposefully released into the mine by a smoke-emitting device. For additional ancient examples of combat inside mines, see Garlan 1974, at 32 a) on p. 398.

44. What is described here seems to serve both as a frame or base (Hero Mech. *Bel.* 3.1) and a protective covering for small stone projectors (λιθοβόλοι) on *lemboi*. We should envision the smallest caliber of stone projectors being placed on ships like *lemboi*, weapons like the small *lithoboloi* used inside mines (see D 31 and n. 44).

45. Although the term used here, χῶναι, literally means "funnels," the context demands that we envision some sort of covering which protects the anchor line, perhaps flaring toward the upper or lower end in the shape of a funnel.

and anchor rafts beside (your ships) from which men with tridents keep watch for underwater divers.[46] (55 [100.39]) Against underwater mounds and for clearing, on land, of stones thrown from the walls and wall extensions, it is good to use, from the sea, <scoops>, such as they clear harbors with, and iron grapnels.[47]

56–71 [100.44–102.8]: DETAILS OF A LAND SIEGE AND THE FINAL TAKING OF A CITY

72–86 [102.9–103.16]: ALTERNATIVES TO A FULL-SCALE ASSAULT

87–110 [103.16–104.42]: WHAT TO DO IF A RELIEVING FORCE ARRIVES

(**101** [104.1]) If you are about to undergo danger from the sea, fill up, if possible, the mouth of the harbor (with rocks and earth). And if this is not possible, fortify the harbor mouth with the merchant ships, or with such boats you have that are suitable for these things, and join them side-by-side, constructing a pontoon bridge (*schedia*) out of the wood you have around. (**102** [104.6]) And take care of your watch fires especially during the night, lest relief troops elude you, creeping in along the part of the city away from the sea. (**103** [104.9]) If you should chance to have a naval force that is slightly inferior to that of the enemy,[48] take on your fighting decks your best and most experienced soldiers.[49] Order them neither to climb out,[50] nor to board any enemy ship, but to use the bronze ram.[51]

---

46. I translate τοὺς ὑποδενδρυάζοντας as "underwater divers," but the Greek is less explicit: "those slipping in underneath under cover," in this case, by being submerged.

47. Garlan accepts the word ὑποχώσεις, "underwater mounds," suggested by de Rochas d'Aiglun, for ὑποχωρήσεις, "excrements," which appears in the manuscripts, and I have followed him here. If this was indeed what Philo originally wrote, the idea is not expressed very clearly. He seems to say that one can clear submerged mounds and stone piles along the shore by the use of dredging scoops and grapnels operated from ship-platforms (i.e., from the sea).

48. If the relieving force had any hope of breaking the siege, it should be at least slightly superior to the besieging force and that is why Philo phrases his sentence in this way. If the relieving force was significantly weaker than the besieging force, it would not attempt to relieve the siege. Such a case can be seen in 298 when Lysimachus came to break Demetrius's siege of Cilician Soloi, but had to back down in the face of his enemy's superior force (Plut. *Demetr.* 20.8–9).

Offer battle to the enemy making a crescent-shaped formation, placing the attack ships, the maneuverable ships and fastest ships on the wings, and both the aphracts and the support ships in the middle toward the pontoon bridge (at the harbor entrance). (**104** [104.19]) Then, when (the enemy) gets close, set them afire with incendiary missiles, with burning caltrops, with torches and with pitch, if you have them. (**105** [104.21]) And using as many stone projectors and bolt projectors and other missiles as possible, it is necessary to harm the marines, and to crush and burn the hulls of your opponents, striking them from the land and from the timber constructions and from the other boats, smashing them into pieces as much as possible, if they make an attack somewhere.[52] (**106** [104.28]) And if they remain on the defensive, take the combat forward gathering together your force from both wings.[53]

---

49. The noun τὰ καταστρώματα (which I have translated loosely as "fighting decks") reveals that Philo is speaking about the larger ships in one's fleet—the cataphracts. The *katastroma* is first and foremost a protective deck that closes in the oarcrew and protects them from incoming missiles and the disruption of enemy boarding parties.

50. According to LSJ[9], 58, the verb ἀκρωτηριάζειν can mean "to cut off *akroteria* of ships," or of persons, "to cut off hands and feet, mutilate." Here, the meaning must be something like "to climb out on an extremity" (as you would when collecting an enemy prow or stern ornament) or "to make an *akroterion* of yourself." Although LSJ[9] does not report this particular meaning of the verb, its general sense comes from what follows: "order the men . . . not to board any enemy ship. . . ."

51. Although the word used here for ram, χάλκωμα, can apply to anything made of copper or bronze, the context makes its meaning clear. The word is used in a similar manner by both Diodorus (20.9.2, 15.2) and Plutarch (*Them.* 14.4; *Ant.* 64.3) to signify the bronze ram of a warship.

52. Philo advises a cautious, defensive posture with one's most vulnerable ships placed within the protective range of projectiles launched from the city walls and pontoon bridge. When the enemy comes within range, the main goal is to attack his forces with projectile weapons and incendiary missiles. The primary targets of both stone and bolt projectors are the marines. When the enemy approaches even closer, the marines are not to cross over to the enemy ships, but are to let the oar crews do their jobs with the rams. This involves "crushing the hulls of your opponents" (συντρίβειν . . . τὰ τῶν ἐναντίων σκάφη). It would seem from Philo's description that these marines are aboard those ships most suitable for offensive action, i.e., those stationed on the wings.

53. Garlan 1974, 327 translates the sentence thusly: "S'ils restent sur la défensive, il faut mener le combat à l'extérieur et, à partir de chacune des ailes, se rabattre vers le centre." "And if they remain on the defensive, it is necessary to take the combat forward, and from each of the wings, turn toward the center." According to Philo's advice, the naval force was originally ordered with the attack ships on the two wings and with the center anchored by the pontoon barrier. If you now wanted to move the battle forward, then you would have to gather your ships *in front of the pontoon barrier* in a line-abreast formation. Such an action must be envisioned, however we choose to word this abbreviated sentence.

(**107** [104.30]) It is necessary to fight the sea battle in this way. Some of their ships you will sink, taking them on their sides, while others, fighting prow-to-prow, you will crush and set on fire as was stated before. (**108** [104.33]) And if you should catch them in disorder or fleeing under sail, attack them in formation with the entire fleet, and try to swamp them and burn them to ashes when they are defending against you.[54] (**109** [104.36]) And when you catch up to those fleeing, shatter the steering oars, sheer off the rowers' oars, and so bring them to land.[55] (**110** [104.39]) If you do not have naval ships, use fire and missiles to hinder them from making a landing.

(**111** [104.40]) Anyone who besieges cities after this fashion is very likely to take them without himself suffering anything irremediable.

---

54. A fleet that is being overtaken by a pursuing force must turn and defend against the types of attack that are described in the next section. It is at this point that Philo advises one to crush and burn the enemy.

55. One would shatter the steering oars with attacks of the ram, and thus it makes sense for Philo to use the verb συντρίβων which was used for other attacks of the ram. The expression τὸν ταρσὸν παρασύρων refers to a maneuver by which you pass your vessel close to the side of the enemy and snap off their oars. With an approach from the stern, you would not be able to sheer all the oars because your own would become fouled. Presumably the attack would be made on the steering oar, and then the fleeing ship would turn to defend against you or try to escape shoreward, and you might get a chance to sweep the oars along one of its sides. If they were unable to turn and face you (either because they waited too long, or because you had support ships that could attack the enemy's sides as they turned about), the enemy vessel would have to flee towards the shore. The attacker would have to defend itself from boarding if it followed without support. This is why Philo specifically said that one pursues fleeing ships "in formation with the entire fleet" (D 108).

Testimonia for Naval Artillery

Note: This list is intended to demonstrate the many applications of naval artillery during the Hellenistic period. In the interest of space and simplicity of presentation, examples have been limited to one or two per category; many other examples can be cited in almost every category. All dates are BCE.

General Information

Sizes and Weights.

5 mina (2.2 kg.) *petrobolos*: length = 3.7 m.; width = 1.94 m.; height= 2.7 m.

        Space needed (incl. clearance): length= 5.05 m.; width = 2.5 m.

        Calculations based on Marsden 1969, 25, 34, 46–47 and Fig. 1.22.

Weight of a "small" *petrobolos* (5 *mina?*) = approx. 1820 kg. (Marsden 1969, 171).

1 talent (26.2 kg.) *petrobolos*: length= 7.75 m.; width = 5 m.; height = approx. 6.35 m. (Garlan 1984, 358).

Three-span (0.694 m.) *oxybeles*: length = 2.74 m.; width = 1.08 m.; height = 1.47 m. (Marsden 1969, 25 and Fig. 1.21).

Weight of a 3 span *oxybeles*: approx. 50 kg. (Marsden 1969, 171).

A "five" might carry (in place of 120 marines = 18,000 lbs. = 8164.7 kg.): 10 three-span *oxybeleis* (1000 lbs. = 453.6 kg.), 2 "comparatively small" *lithoboloi* (4 tons = 3628.7 kg.), artillerymen and ammunition (1.5 tons = 1360.8 kg.) and 40 marines (3 tons = 2721.6 kg.) (Marsden 1969, 171).

Artillery Used Against Ships

Naval Battles and Campaigns.

The damaging effects of moisture.

> Philo *Bel.* 48 [72.15–25]: Bronze spring catapults are stronger and less liable to damage than sinew springs and are thus better for field and naval campaigns because they remain unaffected by breakage or wetting. "For when the sinew of the springs are wet or snapping, it is impossible that the machines are not harmed." Even machines stored in a covered place can be harmed by changes in the atmosphere.

Petroboloi as offensive weapons for sea battles.

> Salamis (306): Diod. 20.49.4, 51.2.
>
> Actium (31): Dio 50.32.5; 34.2 (used to hurl pots of coal and pitch against Antony's ships).

Oxybeleis as offensive weapons for sea battles (positioned on the prow and in towers).

> Salamis (306): Diod. 20.49.4 (3 span machines mounted at the prow in preparation for action).
>
> Actium (31): Plut. *Ant.* 66.2 (placed in wooden towers); see also Dio 50.23.3, 33.4.
>
> Naulochus (36): App. *BC* 5.12.118 (used to launch a harpoon-like device).

Land Based Artillery against Ships.

Land based catapults against ships attacking your city.

> 20 mina (= 20 lb.) *petroboloi* used in conjunction with lead-filled amphoras at the harbor mouth (third century): Philo *Polior.* C 56 [95.9–11].
>
> Syracusans use *petroboloi* and *oxybeleis* to attack Marcellus's fleet (213–12): Livy 24.34.8–9; Polyb. 8.7.2 (marines targeted).
>
> People of Thessalonike use *petroboloi* to attack both skirmishers and marines on Roman warships (169): Livy 44.10.6.

Artillery Used in Naval Siege Warfare

Petroboloi *(either deployed from ships or brought by ship to be used against a coastal position).*

Use:

> to shear off battlements (Salamis, 306): Diod. 20.48.4.
>
> to attack a "light and low" harbor fortification (Rhodes, 305–4): Diod. 20.86.2.

to damage siege engines and fortification wall (Rhodes, 305–4): Diod. 20.87.1.

to clear defenders from the battlements (Mounychia, 307): Diod. 20.45.7.

Placement:

on yoked warships (Tyre, 332): Diod. 17.43.4, 46.1–2; see 17.45.2.

on single freighters anchored at the harbor mouth (Rhodes, 305–4): Diod. 20.85.4.

in covered penthouses (*chelonai*) on yoked freighters (Rhodes, 305–4): Diod. 20.85.1.

on *lemboi* for sieges (third century): Philo *Polior.* D 38 [99.37–40].

Oxybeleis *(either deployed from ships or brought by sea to be used against a coastal position).*

Use:

to hit men on the battlements of a city wall (Tyre, 332): Diod. 17.42.7.

to hit crews at work on a harbor fortification (Rhodes, 305–4): Diod. 20.85.3, 86.2, 88.2.

to secure a shore position (Alexandria, 48): *B. Alex.* 19.

Placement:

on light craft for siege and counter-siege warfare (Tyre, 332): Diod. 17.42.1.

in a penthouse (*chelone*) on yoked cargo vessels (Rhodes, 305–4): Diod. 20.85.1.

on shipboard wooden towers (Tyre, 332): Diod. 17.45.2.

Ship-Based Artillery Used to Attack Land Forces
Oxybeleis *and Scorpions.*

Use:

to attack besiegers at Tyre by the Tyrians (332/1): Diod. 17.42.1.

to attack an army on the march in Lucania (282?): Fron. *Str.* 1.4.1.

to neutralize a hostile shore in Britain and thus enable a marine landing (55): Caes. *BG* 4.25.

to drive away an Egyptian garrison on the mole at Alexandria (48): *B. Alex.* 19.

Artillery Brought by Sea but Set Up on Land
Petroboloi, Oxybeleis, Ballistae, Catapultae *and* Tormentae *(not a complete listing).*

Dionysius of Syracuse besieges Motya (397): Diod. 14.51.1 (*gastraphetai*—belly bows—employed; see Marsden 1969, 54–56).

Agathocles besieges Croton (approx. 295): Diod. 21.4.1.

Agathocles besieges Hipponium in Bruttium (approx. 294): Diod. 21.8.1.

Pyrrhus's Sicilian campaign (278–76): Diod. 22.8.1–6.

Roman siege of Lilybaeum (250): Diod. 24.1.1–4 (note that Polyb. 1.41–48. describes no clear use of catapults).

Philip V's siege of Pale on Kephallenia (218): Polyb. 5.4.6 (cf. 5.2.4).

Philip V's siege of Apollonia, (214): Livy 24.40.15.

Roman attack on Locri (208): Livy 27.28.13.

Roman siege of Oreus in Euboea (207): Livy 28.6.3.

Roman/allied siege of Oreus on Euboea (200): Livy 31.46.6-47.1.

Roman/allied assault (under L. Quinctius) on Eretria (198): Livy 32.16.10.

Roman siege of Leucas (197): Livy 33.17.3.

Antiochus dislodges a Roman position at the Euripus (192): Livy 35.51.9.

Roman siege of Same on Kephallenia (189): Livy 38.28.10.

Glossary

al scaloccio: "on the staircase," a system of rowing.

alla sensile: "in the simple fashion," a system of rowing.

anastrophe: "turn about," a tactical maneuver.

antiproiros: "prow opposed," describing the position of opposing warships or fleets before a prow-to-prow charge.

aphract: "open" or "undecked" warship.

auletes: timekeeper.

batten: extra handles attached to the shaft of a large oar to aid the oarsmen in gripping it.

cataphract: "armored," "fenced," or "decked," in the sense of having reinforced decks and sides to protect the oarcrew from deck fighting.

catheads: the lateral ends of the outriggers, which were made from heavy timbers on cataphract galleys and used, along with the ram, as offensive ramming weapons in prow-to-prow collisions.

chelone,-ai: a "turtle," "penthouse," "mantlet" or protective covering for military machinery and personnel.

class: a particular constructional design that marks one kind of vessel as different from another.

corax: "raven," a Roman boarding device.

cutwater: forward edge of the stem at the waterline.

dekeres: a "ten."

diaphragma: defensive barrier across harbor entrance.

diekplous: "sailing through and out," or "cutting the line," a tactical maneuver.

dodekeres: a "twelve."

dolphin: a weight suspended from a yard or crane that could be released to plummet down on a warship that passed underneath.

doryboloi: spear projectors.

drachma: unit of weight, frequently representing a coin comprised of 6 obols; 6000 silver drachmai equaled 1 talent.

eikoseres: a "twenty."

endekeres: an "eleven."

enneres: a "nine."

epibatai: marines or deck soldiers.

epimeletai ton neorion: "Curators of the Naval Yards," a board of 10 officials who were in charge of the naval yards at Athens.

epotis,-des: thick beam at the forward end of an outrigger or oarbox, cathead.

forefoot: the area of a ship's hull where the keel and stem are joined.

freeboard: the vertical distance between the water and the upper watertight portion of the hull, frequently located at a gunwale or deck.

gastraphetes: belly bow.

gunwale (also wale): the upper course of planking on a vessel's side (on which the guns rested in sixteenth century vessels); in ancient vessels the term defines a horizontal line of thicker than normal hull planking; warships had a primary gunwale that ran from bow to stern at the waterline that terminated in the ram, and a secondary gunwale above that terminated in the *proembolion*.

harpax: "grip," a device that was shot onto an enemy warship so that its trailing line could be hauled back aboard, hopefully dragging the struck ship alongside for boarding.

hekkaidekeres: a "sixteen."

helepolis: large siege tower mounted on a moveable base.

hemiolia,-ai: class of fast galley that was smaller than both a "three" and *triemiolia*.

hepteres: a "seven."

hexeres: a "six."

holkas,-des: a "towed ship," or merchant ship that often had to be towed into and out of port.

hyperesia: support staff.

hypozomata: undergirds.

interscalmium: the linear distance between thole pins (*skalmoi*) at the same level.

katapeltes oxybeles: "sharp shooter" or catapult that shoots bolts.

katapeltes petrobolos / lithobolos: stone throwing catapult.

katastroma: protective deck covering the oarsmen on which deck soldiers fight.

keleustes: boatswain.

kleithron,-a: barrier, sometimes comprised of a chain suspended from floats, strung across the entrance to a harbor; the plural form *kleithra* is frequently used.

kopeus: "oar spar" or raw timber from which a trireme oar is made.

krios,-oi: a "ram" (like the animal of the same name) or battering device, which consisted of a long beam reinforced with a metal cap at its end that was used for battering down walls or breaking through wooden constructions like gates.

kybernetes: helmsman.

kyklos: "circle," or defensive tactical maneuver in which warships are aligned in a circle with their sterns toward a central point and bows outward.

lembos,-oi: a type of open warship, smaller than a "three," that was used for a variety of purposes.

liburna,-ae: a type of open warship developed from pirate craft that were smaller than "threes."

line-abreast: battle formation with ships aligned side-by-side, bows toward the enemy.

line-ahead: formation, often used for traveling from place to place, with ships arranged in a line, bow-to-stern.

lithobolos,-oi: see *katapeltes*.

mechanema: "timber construction"; a term frequently applied to various kinds of constructions that served as siege towers (both mobile and stationary) and other devices; often translated by the noun "machine."

mechane,-ai: "machine"; often used as a synonym for *mechanema* in the context of siege warfare.

megala skaphe / megalai nees: "big hulls," or large ships, denoting cataphract galleys larger than "threes."

mina: unit of weight equal to 436.6 gr. or 0.96 pound (British).

mantlet: see *chelone,-ai*.

mortise and tenon joinery: joined wooden timbers, like the planks of a ship's hull, held together by tenons or rectangular pieces of wood seated in regularly spaced cavities or mortises cut into the adjacent edges of each plank to be joined; after the planks are firmly positioned edge-to-edge with all tenons securely seated in their mortises, the joints are usually locked in place with wooden pegs that are driven into holes drilled through both plank and tenon from the exterior; a common Mediterranean shipbuilding technique used in warship hulls during antiquity.

nauarchos,-oi: nauarch, commodore, or officer in grade between a captain and an admiral.

naupegos: shipwright.

nautai: oarsmen.

oarbox: the portion of the ship's structure through which the oars projected; a straight oarbox allowed the oars at bow and stern to be the same length as those amidships.

oarport: the opening in the side of the hull or oarbox (depending on the design) through which the oar projects.

okteres: an "eight."

parodos,-oi: gangways.

pentecontor (Gk. *pentekontoros*): fifty-oared galley.

pentekaidekeres: a "fifteen."

pentekontarchos: purser.

penteres: a "five" (Lat. *quinqueremis*).

periplous: a tactical maneuver in which ships sailed around the end of the enemy line.

petrobolos: see *katapeltes*.

phragma: harbor barrier; see *kleithron,-a*.

pithakion: "little ape," or device described by Athenaeus Mechanicus to reduce the effect of two hulls rocking in opposite directions.

polyremes: ships with an *-eres* classification that are larger than "threes."

pristis,-eis: type of small war galley.

proembolion: fore ram or subsidiary ram that projects forward above the waterline ram, whose purpose is to prevent entanglement, as well as damage to the ship's superstructure at the bow, during ram strikes.

protome: a decorative element, often adorning utilitarian artifacts like pitchers or pottery, in the form of an animal head or human bust.

ram: reinforced projection of the bow, comprised of a bronze sheath protecting the timbers that connect the ram to the bow, designed to act as an offensive and defensive weapon.

sambuca,-ae: large siege ladder mounted on pairs of yoked warships.

stoichos: file.

syntrierarchos,-oi: one of two or more trierarchs who are financially responsible for a warship.

tarros: full set of oars.

tesserakonteres: a "forty."

tetreres: a "four" (Lat. *quadriremis*).

thalamian: the lowermost oarsman on a three-level warship.

thole pins (Gk. *skalmoi*): vertical wooden pins (i.e., dowels) against which the oars were worked.

thranite: the uppermost oarsman on a three-level warship.

torsion catapults: catapults whose propulsive power is generated by twisted skeins of sinew-rope.

tortoise: see *chelone,-ai*.

triacontor (Gk. *triakontoros*): thirty-oared galley.

triakonteres: a "thirty."

triemiolia,-ai: type of warship frequently called a "three and one-half"; the vessel was aphract and used as a cheaper alternative to a "three."

trierarch: the one financially responsible for a warship; often sailed aboard as the captain of the warship.

trieres: a "three."

trireme: see *trieres*.

triskaidekeres: a "thirteen."

wale: see gunwale.

wale pockets: space inside the ram which receives the forward ends of the wales; there are two wale pockets: one for the starboard wale and one for the port wale.

vogavante: in sixteenth century galleys, the innermost man on a multi-man oar who served as a foreman of the others on his oar and was responsible for their timing during the stroke.

zeugma: pontoon barrier made of watercraft that are yoked together.

zygian: the middle oarsman on a three-level warship.

Chronology

Chapter 1

480   First account of *antiproiros* maneuver recorded at Artemision.

440   Athenians utilize siege machinery at Samos.

433   Corcyreans and Corinthians utilize "old fashioned" tactics in a naval battle off Sybota (near Corcyra).

431–404   Peloponnesian War.

429   Phormio employs the best of Athenian naval tactics to defeat a larger Peloponnesian force off Naupactus in the Gulf of Corinth.

425   Athenians use *antiproiros* maneuver to defeat a Spartan force off Pylos.

414–413   Athenians besiege Syracuse and employ naval siege tactics; Syracusans employ countersiege tactics.

409   Athenians attack the harbor of Byzantium.

407   Peloponnesians attack the harbor of Mytilene, which the Athenians have attempted to close.

410–409   Carthaginian Invasion of Sicily; Hannibal utilizes superior siege techniques for sieges of Selinus and Himera.

406–405   Second Carthaginian Invasion of Sicily; Acragas, Gela and Camarina besieged; Dionysius I of Syracuse attacks Carthaginian camp at Gela with his fleet.

399   Dionysius I begins preparations for war with Carthage and initiates an arms program that includes "fours," "fives," and catapults, probably *gastraphetai*.

397   Dionysius I sends a "five" to Epizephyrian Locri (Italy) on a diplomatic mission to fetch his bride Doris.

397   Dionysius I's siege of Motya.

396   Leptines, a commander of Dionysius I, tries to block the Carthaginian advance toward Syracuse off Taurus (Sicily) and places his 30 "best ships" ("fives"?) in the front line; after defeating Leptines, the Carthaginian commander Himilco enters the Great Harbor at Syracuse and besieges the city.

Chapter 3

367–344	Reign of Dionysius II of Syracuse; his fleet possessed the first mentioned "six."
359	Accession of Philip II of Macedonia.
340–339	Philip II conducts sieges of Perinthus, Selymbria, and Byzantium; displays an inability to block the besieged from the sea and, as a result, the sieges fail.
336	Upon assassination of Philip II, his son Alexander III (the Great) takes the Macedonian throne.
334	Alexander III crosses the Hellespont and begins the Persian campaign; his men display knowledge of naval siege warfare techniques at Miletus; after capturing Miletus, Alexander disbands his fleet but retains some ships to transport and protect his siege machinery.
332	Alexander III besieges Tyre and, in so doing, creates the first naval siege unit.
323	Alexander returns to Babylon, dies in June; his plans to gather a sizeable fleet in Babylon and to build ships larger than "fives" are abandoned.
314–13	Antigonus Monophthalmus besieges Tyre for 18 months and is forced, as a result, to initiate a major shipbuilding program.
307	Demetrius Poliorcetes, son of Antigonus Monophthalmus, captures Mounychia (one of Athens' harbors) by siege.
306	Demetrius leads a major invasion force to Cyprus and defeats Ptolemy's relief force off Cyprian Salamis; "sixes" and "sevens" appear as the largest ships in Demetrius's fleet and engage in *antiproiros* ramming attacks; after gaining control of Cyprus, Demetrius attempts an invasion of Egypt during the autumn, which fails.
305–304	Demetrius's famous siege of Rhodes; his failure stems from his inability to gain control of the Rhodian harbors.
304–303	Departing from Rhodes by early summer, Demetrius experiences numerous successes in Greece.
303	Demetrius gains control of Sicyon and Corinth by siege; both sieges involved surprise attacks on the cities' harbors; these victories led to further gains in the northern and central Peloponnesus.
301	Antigonus Monophthalmus and Demetrius Poliorcetes are defeated at Ipsus in central Asia Minor; Antigonus is killed, but Demetrius manages to keep hold of Corinth, the Cyclades, Cyprus, the chief cities of western Asia Minor, Sidon, and Tyre, thanks to his fleet; Demetrius retrieves his ships from Athens, including a "thirteen."
299 or 298	Demetrius married his daughter to Seleucus and hosts a banquet on this "thirteen"; soon thereafter, he besieges Soloi, Lysimachus arrives with a relief force, but then withdraws when he sees the size and

magnificence of Demetrius's siege unit; Demetrius recovers Cilician cities from Cassander's brother Pleistarchus.

296–295   Demetrius besieges Athens and gains control of the city in 295; at this time, there was a coordinated attack on Demetrius's possessions by the other Diadochoi: Lysimachus attacks Demetrius's cities in Asia Minor, Ptolemy takes Cyprus, and Seleucus invades Cilicia.

294   Demetrius regains control of the Macedonian throne; Lysimachus controls Demetrius's cities in Asia Minor.

287   Ptolemy, Lysimachus, Seleucus and Pyrrhus combine to attack Demetrius's possessions; Demetrius, forced from Macedonia, besieges Athens; premature departure of Demetrius for Asia Minor.
Winter 286/5 Seleucus takes Demetrius Poliorcetes into custody.

282   Deaths of Demetrius Poliorcetes and Ptolemy I Soter; each king is succeeded by his son: Antigonus Gonatas and Ptolemy II Philadelphus.

Chapter 6

281   Ptolemy Ceraunus defeats Antigonus Gonatas and takes control of Macedonia; the *Leontophoros* "eight" is in his fleet.

277   Antigonus Gonatas is recognized as the Macedonian king.

267–262/61 Chremonidean War between Athens (supported by Ptolemy II Philadelphus) and Antigonus Gonatas.

264–241   First Punic War between Rome and Carthage.

261?   Antigonus Gonatas defeats Ptolemaic fleet in a sea battle off Cos.

260–253   Second Syrian War between Antiochus II and Ptolemy II Philadelphus; big ships progressively added to the fleet of Ptolemy II Philadelphus until his death (246).

250   Roman siege of Lilybaeum.

by 249?   Ptolemaic recovery of Cyrenaica.

246?   Antigonus Gonatas defeats the Ptolemaic fleet in a sea battle off Andros.

246   Deaths of Ptolemy II Philadelphus and Antiochus II; both kings are succeeded by their sons, Ptolemy III Euergetes and Seleucus II.

245–241   Third Syrian War between Ptolemy III Euergetes and Seleucus II; big ship fleet partly responsible for Ptolemy's recovery of cities from Thrace in the northern Aegean to Ionia, Caria, Lycia, Pamphylia, Cilicia, and Syria.

226   Death of Seleucus II, who is succeeded by his son Seleucus III.

223   Assassination of Seleucus III, who is succeeded by Antiochus III.

221   Death of Ptolemy III Euergetes, who is succeeded by his son Ptolemy IV Philopator; Philip V becomes king of Macedonia.

221–217	Fourth Syrian War between Ptolemy IV Philopator and Antiochus III.
219	Antiochus III recovers Seleucia.
218	Antiochus III defeats Ptolemy IV Philopator at Porphyrion.
217	Ptolemy IV defeats Antiochus III at Raphia (June 22, 217); thereafter, he builds his giant "forty."

Chapter 7

218–201	Second Punic War between Rome and Carthage.
213–211	Roman siege of Syracuse.
210	Roman siege of Anticyra (Greece).
209	Roman siege of Tarentum.
208	Roman siege of Locri (Italy).
207	Roman siege of Oreus (Greece).
204	Roman siege of Utica (unsuccessful); Death of Ptolemy IV Philopator.
203	Roman siege of Utica; P. Cornelius Scipio displays knowledge of naval siege warfare tactics.
201	P. Cornelius Scipio defeats Hannibal in battle at Zama.
201	King Attalus of Pergamum and the Rhodians defeat Philip V of Macedonia in a sea battle off Chios; big ships up to "ten" in size engage in *antiproiros* ramming maneuvers.
200–197	Second Macedonian War; Antiochus III attempts to recover territory in Asia Minor.
192	Antiochus III invades Greece.
192–188	Syrian War between Rome and Antiochus III.
191	Allied force of Romans and Rhodians defeat Antiochus III in sea battle off Corycus (Asia Minor).
190	The Rhodians fight a sea battle off Side (Asia Minor), thus preventing a contingent of big ships gathered by Hannibal from joining the fleet of Antiochus III near Chios; Hannibal's fleet included a few "sixes" and "sevens."
190	An allied force of Romans and Rhodians defeat the commanders of Antiochus III in a sea battle off Myonnesus (Asia Minor); Antiochus's fleet included a few "sixes" and "sevens."
48	Julius Caesar besieges Pompey at Brundisium; Caesar defeats Pompey at Pharsalus.
36	Marcus Agrippa defeats Sextus Pompey in a sea battle off Naulochus (Sicily).
31	Octavian defeats Mark Antony and Cleopatra in a sea battle off Actium (Greece); the Battle of Actium is the last ancient sea battle in which a fleet of big ships takes part.

Bibliography

Adams, J. J. R., A. Antoniadou, P. Bennett, I. W. Croudace, G. P. Earl, N. C. Flemming, C. O. Hunt, J. Moggeridge, K. Oliver, A. J. Parker, and T. Whiteside. "The Belgammel Ram: A Hellenistic-Roman Bronze Proembolion Found Off The Coast of Libya, Test Analysis of Function, Date, and Metallurgy, with a Digital Reference Archive." *International Journal of Nautical Archaeology*. Forthcoming.

Alertz, Ulrich. 1995. "The Naval Architecture and Oar Systems of Medieval and Later Galleys." In *The Age of the Galley: Mediterranean Oared Vessels Since Pre-Classical Times*, edited by John Morrison and Robert Gardner, 142–62. London: Conway Maritime Press.

Amy, R., P.-M. Duval, J. Formigé, J.-J. Hatt, A. Piganiol, Ch. Picard, and G.-Ch. Picard. 1962. *L'Arc d'Orange, Gallia, 15th Supplement*. Paris: Centre National de la Recherche Scientifique.

Anderson, R.C. 1976. *Oared Fighting Ships From Classical Times to the Coming of Steam*. New ed. Herts, England: Argus.

Athenaeus. 1858. *Athenaei Deipnosophistae*, e recognitione Augusti Meineke. Vol. 1. Lipsiae: Teubneri.

Athenaeus. 1859. *Athenaei Deipnosophistae*, e recognitione Augusti Meineke. Vol. 3. Lipsiae: Teubneri.

Austin, Michel. 2006. *The Hellenistic World from Alexander to the Roman Conquest: A Selection of Ancient Sources in Translation*. 2nd ed. Cambridge: Cambridge University Press.

Avilia, Filippo and Luciana Jacobelli. 1989. "Le naumachie nella pitture pompeiane." *Revista di studi pompeiani* 3: 131–54.

Baatz, Dietwulf. 1994. *Bauten und Katapulte des Römischen Heeres*. Edited by M. P. Speidel, Mavors Roman Army Researches. Stuttgart: Franz Steiner.

Bagnall, Roger S. 1976. *The Administration of the Ptolemaic Possessions Outside Egypt*. Columbia Studies in the Classical Tradition 4. Leiden: Brill.

Basch, Lucien. 1979. "Roman Triremes and the Outriggerless Phoenician Trireme."
    Mariner's Mirror 65, no. 4: 289–326.

———. 1982. "The Athlit Ram: A Preliminary Introduction and Report." *Mariner's
    Mirror* 68, no. 1: 3–7.

———. 1985. "The *Isis* of Ptolemy II Philadelphus." *Mariner's Mirror* 71, no. 2: 129–51.

———. 1987. *Le musée imaginaire de la marine antique*. Athens: Institut hellénique
    pour la préservation de la tradition nautique.

Baugh, Daniel A. 2007. "Anglo-French Wars." In *The Oxford Encyclopedia of Maritime
    History*, edited by John B. Hattendorf, 329–40. Oxford: Oxford University Press.

Beloch, Karl Julius. 1925. *Griechische Geschichte*. 2nd ed. Vol. 4.1. Berlin: de Gruyter.

Berkowitz, Luci and Karl A. Squitier. 1990. *Thesaurus Linguae Graecae Canon of Greek
    Authors and Works*. 3rd ed. Oxford: Oxford University Press.

Berthold, Richard M. 1984. *Rhodes in the Hellenistic Age*. Ithaca, New York: Cornell
    University Press.

Berve, Helmut. (1926) 1988. *Das Alexanderreich auf Prosopographischer Grundlage*. 2
    vols. Munich: Beck. Reprint, 2 vols. in 1, Salem, N.H.: Ayer.

Billows, R. 1990. *Antigonos the One-Eye and the Creation of the Hellenistic State*. Berke-
    ley: University of California Press.

Bishop, M. C., and J. C. N. Coulston. 1993. *Roman Military Equipment: From the
    Punic Wars to the Fall of Rome*. London: Batsford.

Blackman, D. J. 1997–98. "Archaeology in Greece 1997–98." *Archaeological Reports*
    44: 1–128.

Blackman, D. J. and N. B. Rankov et al. forthcoming. *Shipsheds of the Ancient Mediter-
    ranean*. Cambridge: Cambridge University Press, forthcoming.

Bockius, Ronald. 2001. "A Roman Depiction of a War Ship Equipped with Two Cata-
    pults?" In *Tropis VI: 6th International Symposium on Ship Construction in Antiq-
    uity, Lamia 1996*, edited by Harry Tzalas, 89–97. Athens: Hellenic Institute for
    the Preservation of Nautical Tradition.

Bosworth, A. B. 1980. *A Historical Commentary on Arrian's History of Alexander*. Vol.
    1, *Commentary on Books I-III*. Oxford: Oxford University Press.

———. 1988. *Conquest and Empire. The Reign of Alexander the Great*. Cambridge:
    Cambridge University Press.

Bragantini, Irene, and Valeria Sampaolo. 2009. *La Pittura Pompeiana*. Naples: Electa
    Napoli.

Breitman, Beny, Moshe Doron, Emanuel Yellin, Henry Feldman, and Yoram Nir-El.
    1991. "Appendix: Radiographic Examination of the Athlit Ram." In *The Athlit
    Ram*, edited by Lionel Casson and J. Richard Steffy, 83–86. College Station, Tex.:
    Texas A&M University Press.

Briscoe, John. 1973. *A Commentary on Livy, Books XXXI–XXXIII*. Oxford: Oxford Uni-
    versity Press.

———. 1981. *A Commentary on Livy, Books XXXIV–XXXVII*. Oxford: Oxford University
    Press.

Burstein, Stanley Mayer. 1976. *Outpost of Hellenism: The Emergence of Heraclea on the Black Sea*. University of California Publications in Classical Studies. Berkeley: University of California Press.

Burstein, S. M. 1980. "Lysimachus and the Greek Cities of Asia Minor: the Case of Miletus." *Ancient World* 3: 73–79.

Cameron, Alan. 1993. *The Greek Anthology: From Meleager to Planudes*. Oxford: Clarendon.

Campbell, Brian. 2004. *Greek and Roman Military Writers*. Routledge Classical Translations. London: Routledge.

Carter, John. 1970. *The Battle of Actium: The Rise and Triumph of Augustus Caesar*. Edited by Sir Denis Brogan, Turning Points in History. New York: Weybright and Talley.

Casson, Lionel. 1969. "The Super-Galleys of the Hellenistic Age." *Mariner's Mirror* 55, no. 2: 185–93.

———. 1991. *The Ancient Mariners. Seafarers and Sea Fighters of the Mediterranean in Ancient Times*. 2nd ed. Princeton: Princeton University Press.

———. 1995. *Ships and Seamanship in the Ancient World*. Revised ed. Baltimore: The Johns Hopkins University Press.

Casson, Lionel, and J. Richard Steffy, eds. 1991. *The Athlit Ram*. College Station, Tex.: Texas A&M University Press.

Cavanagh, Paul K. 1990. "Practical Considerations and Problems of Bronze Casting." In *Small Bronze Sculpture from the Ancient World: Papers Delivered at a Symposium Organized by the Departments of Antiquities Conservation and Held at the J. Paul Getty Museum, March 16–19, 1989*, 145–60. J. Paul Getty Museum. Malibu, Calif.: The Museum.

Caven, Brian. 1990. *Dionysius I: War-Lord of Sicily*. New Haven: Yale University Press.

Charles, Michael B. 2007. *Vegetius in Context: Establishing the Date of the Epitoma Rei Militaris*. Historia Einzelschriften 194. Stuttgart: Fritz Steiner.

Couchoud, P.L., and J. Svoronos. 1921. "Le monument dit 'des Taureaux' et le culte du navire sacré." *Bulletin de Correspondance Hellénique*, Supplément 1, no. 45: 270–94.

Crawford, Michael H. 1974. *Roman Republican Coinage*. 2 vols. Cambridge: Cambridge University Press.

De Sélincourt, Aubrey, trans. 1971. *Arrian. The Campaigns of Alexander*. Revised, with a new introduction and notes by J. R. Hamilton. Penguin Classics. Harmondsworth: Penguin.

———, trans. 1972. *Livy. The War with Hannibal: Books XXI–XXX of The History of Rome from its Foundation*. Edited with an introduction by Betty Radice. Penguin Classics. Harmondsworth: Penguin.

De Souza, Philip. 1999. *Piracy in the Graeco-Roman World*. Cambridge: Cambridge University Press.

———. 2007. "Naval Battles and Sieges." In *Greece, the Hellenistic world and the rise of Rome*, Vol. 1 of *The Cambridge History of Greek and Roman Warfare*, edited by Philip Sabin, Hans van Wees and Michael Whitby, 434–60. Cambridge: Cambridge University Press.

Dennis, George T. 1985. *Three Byzantine Military Treatises*. Dumbarton Oaks Texts 9. Washington, DC: Dumbarton Oaks, Research Library and Collection.

DeVoto, James G. 1996. *Philon and Heron: Artillery and Siegecraft in Antiquity*. Chicago: Ares.

Diels, H. 1904. "Laterculi Alexandrini: aus einem Papyrus ptolemäischer Zeit." *Abhandlungen der Königlich Preussischen Akademie der Wissenschaften zu Berlin, Philosophisch-Historische Klasse*. Berlin: Verlag der Königlichen Akademie der Wissenschaften 2: 1–16.

Diels, H, and E. Schramm. 1920. "Exzerpte aus Philons Mechanik B. VII und VIII." *Abhandlungen der Preussischen Akademie der Wissenschaften Philosophisch-Historische Klasse*. Berlin: Verlag der Akademie der Wissenschaften. 12: 1–84.

Diodorus. 1746. Diodori Siculi Bibliothecae historicae, libri qui supersunt, interprete Laurentio Rhodomano. Ad fidem mss. recensuit Petrus Wesselingius, atque Henr. Stephani, Fulvii Ursini, Henr. Valesii, Jacobi Palmerii & suas adnotationes, cum indicibus locupletissimis, adjecit. Amstelodami: J. Wetstenii.

Diodorus. 1831. *Diodori Bibliotheca Historica*. Ex recensione Ludovici Dindorfii. Vol. 2, Pars 1. Lipsiae: Hartmanni.

Diodorus. 1844. *Diodori Siculi. Bibliothecae Historicae Quae Supersunt*. Ex nova recensione Ludovici Dindorfii. Vol. 2. Parisiis: Didot.

Dittenberger, Guilelmus. 1915. *Sylloge Inscriptionum Graecarum*. 3rd ed. Vol. 1. Leipzig: S. Herzel.

Dittenberger, Wilhelmus. 1903. *Orientis Graeci Inscriptiones Selectae. Supplementum Sylloges Inscriptionum Graecarum*. Vol. 1. Leipzig: S. Hirzel.

Du Buisson, R. du Mesnil. 1944. "Les ouvrages du siège à Doura-Europos." *Mémoires de la société nationale des antiquaires de France* 81 [n.s. 1]: 5–60.

Dueck, Daniela. 2006. "Memnon of Herakleia on Rome and the Romans." In *Rome and the Black Sea Region: Domination, Romanisation and Resistance*, edited by Tønnes Bekker-Nielsen, 43–61. Aarhus, Denmark: Aarhus University Press.

Eisenberg, Shlomo. 1991. "Metallurgical Analysis of the Ram." In *The Athlit Ram*, edited by Lionel Casson and J. Richard Steffy. College Station, Tex.: Texas A&M University Press.

Ellis, J. R. 1986. *Philip II and Macedonian Imperialism*. 1st Princeton paperback ed. with corrections. Princeton: Princeton University Press, 1986.

Ermeti, Anna Lia. 1981. *L'Agorà di Cirene III,1. Il Monumento Navale. Testo e Tavole, Monografie di Archeologia Libica*, Vol. 16. Rome: "L'Erma" di Bretschneider.

Errington, R. Malcolm. 2008. *A History of the Hellenistic World*. Malden, Mass.: Blackwell.

Foley, Vernard, and Werner Soedel. 1981. "Ancient Oared Warships." *Scientific American* 244, no. 4 (April): 148–63.

Fraser, P. M. 1972. *Ptolemaic Alexandria.* 3 vols. Oxford: Oxford University Press.

French, E. B. 1993–94. "Archaeology in Greece 1993–94." *Archaeological Reports* 40: 1–84.

Frost, Honor. 1982. "The Athlit ram. A round table conference at the Centre of Maritime Studies, Haifa University, December 2–5, 1981." *International Journal of Nautical Archaeology* 11: 59–60.

Gabrielsen, Vincent. 1994. *Financing the Athenian Fleet: Public Taxation and Social Relations.* Baltimore: The Johns Hopkins University Press.

———. 1995. "The Athenian Navy in the Fourth Century." In *The Age of the Galley: Mediterranean Oared Vessels Since Pre-Classical Times*, edited by John Morrison and Robert Gardner, 234–40. London: Conway Maritime Press.

Gardiner, Robert, and J. S. Morrison, eds. 1995. *The Age of the Galley: Mediterranean Oared Vessels Since Pre-Classical Times.* Conway's History of the Ship. Annapolis, Md.: Naval Institute Press.

Garlan, Yvon. 1974. *Recherches de poliorcétique grecque, Bibliothèque des Écoles Françaises d'Athènes et de Rome.* Paris: Bibliothèque des Écoles Françaises d'Athènes et de Rome.

———. 1984. "Hellenistic Science: Its Application in Peace and War. 9b War and Siegecraft." In *The Hellenistic World*, Vol. 7.1 of *The Cambridge Ancient History*, edited by F.W. Walbank, A.E. Austin, M.W. Frederiksen, and R.M. Ogilvie, 353–62. 2nd ed. Cambridge: Cambridge University Press.

Geer, Russel M., trans. 1954. *Diodorus of Sicily.* Loeb Classical Library. 12 vols. Cambridge, Mass.: Harvard University Press.

Global Security Group. "Battle Group – Introduction." http://www.globalsecurity.org/military/agency/navy/batgru-intro.htm. Accessed Feb. 10, 2011.

Gomme, A. W., A. Andrewes, and K. J. Dover. 1970. *A Historical Commentary on Thucydides.* Vol. 4, *Books V 25-VII.* Oxford: Oxford, Clarendon.

Göttlicher, Arvid. 1978. *Materialien für ein Corpus der Schiffsmodelle im Altertum* Mainz: Philipp von Zabern.

Grač, Nonna. 1987. "Ein neu entdecketes Fresko aus hellenistischer Zeit in Nymphaion bei Kertsch." In *Skythika. Vorträge zur Enstehung des skytho-iranischen Tierstils und zu Denkmälern des Bosporanischen Reichs anlässlich einer Ausstellung der Leningrader Ermitage in München 1984*, edited by Herbert Franke, 87–95 with Taf. 26–39. Munich: Verlag der Bayerischen Akademie der Wissenschaften.

Grainger, John D. 2010. *The Syrian Wars.* Mnemosyne Supplements: History and Archaeology of Classical Antiquity. Leiden: Brill.

Granger, Frank, trans. (1934) 1999. *Vitruvius. On Architecture. Books VI-X.* Loeb Classical Library. Cambridge, Mass.: Harvard Univ. Press.

Green, Peter. 1991. *Alexander of Macedon, 356–323 B.C. A Historical Biography.* Berkeley: University of California Press.

————. 2006. *Diodorus Siculus Books 11–12.37.1. Greek History 480–431 BC The Alternative Version.* Austin, Tex.: University of Texas Press.

Griffith, G.T. 1979. "Part Two: The Reign of Philip the Second." In *A History of Macedonia*, Vol. 2, edited by N. G. L. and G. T. Griffith Hammond, 201–726. Oxford: Oxford, Clarendon.

Guilmartin Jr, John Francis. 1974. *Gunpowder and Galleys: Changing Technology and Mediterranean Warfare at Sea in the Sixteenth Century.* London: Cambridge University Press.

Habicht, Chistian. 1957. "Samische Volksbeschlüsse der Hellenistischen Zeit." *Mitteilungen des Deutschen Archäologischen Instituts, Athenische Abteilung* 72: 152–274.

————. 1979. *Untersuchungen zur politischen Geschichte Athens im 3 Jahrhundert v. Chr.* Munich: Beck.

————. 1997. *Athens from Alexander to Antony.* Translated by Deborah Lucas Schneider. Cambridge, Mass.: Harvard University Press.

Harding, Phillip, trans. 2006. *Didymos: On Demosthenes.* Clarendon Ancient History Series. Oxford: Clarendon.

Hauben, Hans. 1975–76. "Antigonos' Invasion Plan for his Attack on Egypt in 306 B.C." *Orientalia Lovaniensia Periodica* 6–7: 267–271.

————. 1976a. "The Expansion of Macedonian Sea Power under Alexander the Great." *Ancient Society* 7: 79–105.

————. 1976b. "Fleet Strength at the Battle of Salamis, 306 B.C." *Chiron* 6: 1–5.

————. 1977. "Rhodes, Alexander and the Diadochi from 333/332 to 304 B.C." *Historia* 26: 307–39.

————. 1987. "Onesicritus and the Hellenistic 'Archikybernesis'." In *Zu Alexander d. Gr. Festschrift G. Wirth*, edited by W. Will and J. Heinrichs, 569–93. Amsterdam: Hakkert.

Hogarth, D. G., M. R. James, R. Elsey Smith, and E. A. Gardner. 1888. "Excavations in Cyprus, 1887–88. Paphos, Leontari, Amargetti." *Journal of Hellenic Studies* 9: 147–271.

Hölbl, Günther. 2001. *A History of the Ptolemaic Empire.* Translated by Tina Saavedra. London: Routledge.

Holley, Andrew E. 1994. "Ballista Balls." In *Masada IV. The Yigael Yadin Excavations 1963–1965 Final Reports*, 349–65. Jerusalem: Israel Exploration Society; The Hebrew University of Jerusalem.

Hölscher, Tonio. 1988. "Historische Reliefs." In *Kaiser Augustus und die verlorene Republik: eine Ausstellung im Martin-Gropius-Bau, Berlin, 7. Juni–14. August 1988*, edited by Mathias René Hofter. Mainz: von Zabern.

Hoepfner, Wolfram and Ernst-Ludwig Schwandner. 1994. *Haus und Stadt im Klassischen Griechenland.* Revised ed. Munich: Deutscher Kunstverlag.

Hultsch, Friedrich. 1882. *Griechische und Römische Metrologie.* 2nd ed. Berlin: Weidmannschen Buchhandlung.

Huys, Marc & Collaborators. "Catalog of Paraliterary Papyri." http://cpp.arts.kuleuven.be/index.php?page=closeup&id=0273. Accessed June 12, 2011.

Illinois Greek Club, trans. 1923. *Aeneas Tacticus, Asclepiodotus, Onasander.* Loeb Classical Library. Cambridge, Mass.: Harvard University Press.

Jacoby, Felix. 1954. *Die Fragmente der griechischen Historiker.* 15 Vols. in 3 Parts. Leiden: Brill.

James, Simon. 1983. "Archaeological evidence for Roman incendiary projectiles." *Saalburg-Jahrbuch* 39: 142–43.

James, S.T. 2011. "Stratagems, Combat and 'Chemical Warfare' in the Siege-Mines of Dura-Europos," *American Journal of Archaeology* 115, no. 1: 69–101.

Jones, H. Stuart, ed. 1912. *A Catalogue of the Ancient Sculptures Preserved in the Municipal Collections of Rome: Sculptures of the Museo Capitolino.* Oxford: Clarendon.

Kawerau, Georg, and Albert Rehm. 1914. *Das Delphinion in Milet.* Berlin: Georg Reimer.

Kern, Paul Bentley. 1999. *Ancient Siege Warfare.* Bloomington, Ind.: Indiana University Press.

Köchly, H., and U. W. Rüstow. (1853–55) 1969. *Griechische Kriegsschriftsteller.* 3 vols. Leipzig: Engelmann. Reprint, Osnabrück: Biblio Verlag.

Köster, August. 1923. *Das Antike Seewesen.* Berlin: Schoetz & Parrhysius.

Krauss, Friedrich. 1944. "Die Prora an der Tiberinsel in Rom." *Mitteilungen des Deutschen Archaeologischen Instituts Roemische Abteilung* 59: 159–72 with 6 Plans.

Kyriacopoulos, Constantinos. 1992. "Boulets en pierre de Pirée: colonettes funéraires remployées." *Bulletin de Correspondence Hellénique* 116: 217–28.

Landels, J.G. 1978. *Engineering in the Ancient World.* Berkeley: University of California Press.

Landström, Björn. 1970. *Ships of the Pharaohs: 4000 Years of Egyptian Shipbuilding.* Garden City, N.Y.: Doubleday.

Laurenzi, L. 1938–46. "Projettili dell' artigliera antica scoperti a Rodi." In *Memorie,* 33–36 with Tav. XXVII-XXXI. Rhodes: Istituto Storico-Archeologico, Rhodes.

Lawrence, A.W. 1979. *Greek Aims in Fortification.* Oxford: Oxford University Press.

Lehmann, L. Th. 1995. *The Polyeric Quest. Renaissance and Baroque Theories about Ancient Men-of-War (Academisch Proefschrift, University of Amsterdam, June 28, 1995).* Amsterdam: De Gouden Reaal.

Lehmann-Hartleben, Karl. 1923. *Die antiken Hafenanlagen des Mittelmeeres.* Beiträge zur Geschichte des Städtebaues im Altertum. Neue Folge. Klio, Beiheft 14.1. Leipzig: Dieterich'sche Verlagsbuchhandlung.

Lendle, Otto. 1983. *Texte und Untersuchungen zum technischen Bereich der antiken Poliorketik.* Palingenesia: Band 19. Wiesbaden: Fritz Steiner.

Lewis, D.M. 1994. "Sicily, 413–368 B.C." In *The Fourth Century.* Vol. 6 of *The Cambridge Ancient History,* edited by John Boardman, Simon Hornblower, and M. Ostwald, 120–55. 2nd ed. Cambridge: Cambridge University Press.

Linder, Elisha. 1991. "The Discovery." In *The Athlit Ram*, edited by Lionel Casson and J. Richard Steffy. College Station, Tex.: Texas A&M University Press.

Lund, Helen S. 1992. *Lysimachus: A Study in Early Hellenistic Kingship*. London: Routledge.

Mahan, A.T. (1918) 1928. *The Influence of Sea Power Upon History 1660–1783*. 12th ed. Reprint. Boston: Little, Brown.

Mark, Samuel. 2008. "The Earliest Naval Ram." *International Journal of Nautical Archaeology* 37: 253–72.

Marriner, Nick and Christophe Morhange. 2005. "Save Tyre." *Méditerranée* 104 [online], placed on line Feb. 2, 2009. http://mediterranee.revues.org/index2002. html. Accessed April 23, 2011.

Marsden, E.W. 1969. *Greek and Roman Artillery; Historical Development*. Oxford: Oxford University Press.

———. 1971. *Greek and Roman Artillery; Technical Treatises*. Oxford: Oxford University Press.

———. 1977. "Macedonian Military Machinery and its Designers under Philip and Alexander." In *Ancient Macedonia II. Papers Read at the Second International Symposium Held in Thessaloniki, August 19–24, 1973*, 211–23. Thessaloniki: Institute for Balkan Sudies.

Maryon, Herbert. 1957. "Fine Metal-Work." In *A History of Technology*. Vol. 2:, *The Mediterranean Civilizations and the Middle Ages c. 700 B.C. to c. A.D. 1500*, edited by Charles Singer, E. J. Holmyard, A. R. Hall and Trevor I. Williams, 449–92. Reprint with corrections. Oxford: Clarendon, 1956.

Maryon, Herbert, and H. J. Penderleith. 1954. "Fine Metal-Work." In *A History of Technology*. Vol. 1. *From Early Times to Fall of Ancient Empires*, edited by Charles Singer, E. J. Holmyard and A. R. Hall, 623–62. Oxford: Clarendon.

Mattusch, Carol C. 1988. *Greek Bronze Statuary from the Beginnings through the Fifth Century B.C.* Ithaca: Cornell University Press.

———. 1996. *The Fire of Hephaistos: Large Classical Bronzes from North American Collections*. Cambridge: Harvard University Art Museums.

McDonald, A. H., and F. W. Walbank. 1969. "The Treaty of Apamea (188 B.C.): The Naval Clauses." *Journal of Roman Studies* 59: 30–39.

Meer, L. B. van der. 2005. "Domus fulminata. The House of the Thunderbolt at Ostia (III, VII, 3–5)." *Bulletin antieke beschaving: BABESCH* 80: 91–111.

Meiggs, Russell. (1982) 1998. *Trees and Timber in the Ancient Mediterranean World*. Oxford: Oxford University Press. Reprint, London: Sandpiper Books.

Meijer, Fik. 1986. *A History of Seafaring in the Classical World*. London: Croom Helm.

Merker, Irwin L. 1958. "Studies in Sea-Power in the Eastern Mediterranean in the Century Following the Death of Alexander." PhD diss., Princeton University.

Milner, N. P. 1993, ed. and trans. *Vegetius: Epitome of Military Science*. Translated Texts for Historians 16. Liverpool: Liverpool University Press.

Miltner, Franz. 1929. "Das praenestische Biremenrelief." *Jahresheft des Österrichischen Archäologishen Instituts in Wien* 24: 88–111.

Mitford, T.B. 1961. "The Hellenistic Inscriptions of Old Paphos." *Annual of the British School at Athens* 56: 1–41.

Modica, M. 2008. "Il Settimo Rostro." *Centonove: Settimanale Regionale di Politica, Cultura ed Economia* 16, no. 34 (September 12, 2008): 28–29.

Moll, Friedrich. 1929. *Das Schiff in der bildenden Kunst*. Bonn: K. Schroeder.

Morrison, John. 1980. *The Ship. Long Ships and Round Ships*. London: National Maritime Museum; Her Majesty's Stationary Office.

———. 1990. "Tetrereis in the Fleets of Dionysius I of Syracuse." *Classica et Medievalia* 41: 33–41.

Morrison, John, and John F. Coates. 1996. *Greek and Roman Oared Warships*. Oxford: David Brown.

Morrison, J. S. 1941. "The Greek Trireme." *Mariner's Mirror* 37, no. 1: 14–44.

———. 1972. "Review of Lionel Casson, *Ships and Seamanship in the Ancient World*." *International Journal of Nautical Archaeology* 1: 230–233.

Morrison, J. S. 1984. "Some problems in trireme construction." *International Journal of Nautical Archaeology* 13: 215–222.

Morrison, J. S., J. F. Coates, and N. B. Rankov. 2000. *The Athenian Trireme. The History and Reconstruction of an Ancient Greek Warship*. 2nd ed. Cambridge: Cambridge University Press.

Morrison, J.S., and R.T. Williams. 1968. *Greek Oared Ships 900–322 B.C.* Cambridge: Cambridge University Press.

Murray, William M. 1985. "The Weight of Trireme Rams and the Price of Bronze in Fourth Century Athens." *Greek, Roman, and Byzantine Studies* 26: 141–50.

———. 1991. "The Provenance and Date: The Evidence of the Symbols." In *The Athlit Ram*, edited by Lionel Casson and J. Richard Steffy, 51–66. College Station, Tex.: Texas A&M University Press.

———. 1996. "Polyremes from the Battle of Actium: Some Construction Details." In *Tropis IV: Proceedings of the 4th International Symposium on Ship Construction in Antiquity, Athens 1991*, edited by Harry Tzalas, 135–50. Athens: Hellenic Institute for the Preservation of Nautical Tradition.

———. 1998. "Review of J.S. Morrison, *Greek and Roman Oared Warships*." *International Journal of Nautical Archaeology* 27: 81–83.

———. 2001. "A trireme named Isis: the Sgraffito from Nymphaion." *International Journal of Nautical Archaeology* 30: 250–56.

———. 2002a. "Reconsidering the Battle of Actium—Again." In *Oikistes: Studies in Constitutions, Colonies, and Military Power in the Ancient World. Offered in Honor of A.J. Graham*, edited by Vanessa B. Gorman and Eric W. Robinson, 339–60. Mnemosyne, bibliotheca classica Batava Supplements 234. Leiden: Brill.

———. 2002b. "Observations on the 'Isis' Fresco at Nymphaion." In *Tropis VII.2, Proceedings of the 7th International Symposium on Ship Construction in Antiquity, Pylos 1999*, edited by Harry Tzalas, 539–61 Athens: Hellenic Institute for the Preservation of Nautical Tradition.

———. 2007. "Recovering rams from the Battle of Actium." In *Nikopolis B: Proceedings of the Second International Nicopolis Symposium (September 11–15, 2002)*, edited by Konstantinos L. Zachos, Vol. 1, 445–51 and Vol. 2, 333–41. Preveza: Actia Nikopolis Foundation.

———. 2008. "The Development of a Naval Siege Unit Under Philip II and Alexander III." In *Macedonian Legacies. Studies in Ancient Macedonian History and Culture in Honor of Eugene N. Borza*, edited by Timothy Howe and Jeanne Reames, 31–55. Claremont, Calif.: Regina.

Murray, William M., and Photios M. Petsas. 1989. "Octavian's Campsite Memorial for the Actian War." *Transactions of the American Philosophical Society.* 79, no. 4: 1989, vol. 79, no. 4: i-xi, 1–172.

Nichols, R. V. 1970–71. "The Trinity College Collection and Other Recent Loans at the Fitzwilliam Museum." *Archaeological Reports* 17: 77–85.

Nossov, Konstantin. 2006. *Ancient and Medieval Siege Weapons: A Fully Illustrated Guide to Siege Weapons and Tactics.* Guilford, Conn.: Lyons.

Oldfather, C.H. 1950. *Diodorus of Sicily.* Loeb Classical Library. Vol. 5. London: Heineman.

———. 1954. *Diodorus of Sicily.* Loeb Classical Library. Vol. 6. London: Heineman.

Oleson, John Peter. 2008. *Oxford Handbook of Engineering and Technology in the Classical World.* Oxford: Oxford University Press.

Orlandos, A. 1966. *Les matériaux de construction et la technique architecturale des anciens Grecs.* Translated by Vanna Hadjimichali and Krista Laumonier. Vol. 1. Paris: E. de Boccard.

Oron, Asaf. 2006. "The Athlit Ram Bronze Casting Reconsidered: Scientific and Technical Re-examination." *Journal of Archaeological Science* 33: 63–76.

———. 2001. "The Athlit Ram: Classical and Hellenistic Bronze Casting Technology." Master's thesis, Texas A&M University.

Otto, Walter. 1931. "Zu den syrischen Kriegen der Ptolemäer." *Philologus* 40: 400–418.

Papademetriou, Ioannis. 1941. "Ἀνασκαφή Νικοπόλεως." *Praktika tes Archaiologikes Hetaireias*, 1940 (1941): 28–31.

Piranesi, Giovanni Battista, and Francesco Piranesi. 1756. *Le Antichità Romane.* 4 vols. Rome: Angelo Rotilj.

Piranesi, Ioanni Baptista [Giovanni Battista]. 1762. *Il Campo Marzio dell' antica Roma.* Rome.

Pitassi, Michael. 2009. *The Navies of Rome.* Woodbridge, England: Boydell.

Pomey, Patrice. 1983. "Remarques à propos de l'épiron d'Athlit." *Mariner's Mirror* 69: 247–48.

Powaski, Ronald E. 1987. *March to Armageddon: The United States and the Nuclear Arms Race, 1939 to the Present.* New York: Oxford University Press.

Prager, Frank David. 1974. *Philo of Byzantium, Pneumatica.* Wiesbaden: Ludwig Reichert.

Pridemore, Matthew Garnett. 1996. "The Form, Function, and Interrelationships of Naval Rams: A Study of Naval Rams from Antiquity." Master's thesis, Texas A & M University.

Pryor, John H., and Elizabeth M. Jeffreys. 2006. *The Age of the ΔΡΟΜΩΝ: The Byzantine Navy ca. 500–1204*. Leiden: Brill.

Rance, Philip. 2007. "The Date of the Military Compendium of Syrianus Magister (Formerly the Sixth-Century Anonymus Byzantinus)." *Byzantinische Zeitschrift* 100: 701–37.

Rathgen, Bernhard. 1909–11. "Die Punischen Geschosse des Arsenals von Karthago und die Geschosse von Lambaesis." *Zeitschrift für historische Waffen-und Kostümkunde* Band 5, Heft 8: 236–44.

Reger, Gary. 1994. "The Political History of the Kyklades 260–200 BC." *Historia* 43: 32–69.

Reinhold, Meyer. 1988. *From Republic to Principate: An Historical Commentary on Cassius Dio's Roman History Books 49–52 (36–29 B.C.)*. American Philological Association Monograph Series. Atlanta: Scholars Press.

Rice, E. E. 1983. *The Grand Procession of Ptolemy Philadelphus*. Oxford: Oxford University Press.

Richardson, L., Jr. 1992. *A New Topographical Dictionary of Ancient Rome*. Baltimore: Johns Hopkins University Press.

Robert, Louis. 1960. *Hellenica. Recueil d'épigraphie de numismatique et d'antiquitiés grecques. Publié par Louis Robert*. Vols. 9–12. Paris: Adrien-Maisonneuve.

Rodgers, W.L. (1937) 1964. *Greek and Roman Naval Warfare*. Annapolis, Md.: United States Naval Institute.

Romeo, Ilaria. 1998. *Ingenuus Leo: L'immagine di Agrippa*. Xenia Antiqua: Monografie 6. Rome: "L'Erma" di Bretschneider.

Romm, James, ed. 2010. *The Landmark Arrian*. New York: Pantheon Books.

Rougé, Jean. 1981. *Ships and Fleets of the Ancient Mediterranean*. Translated by Susan Frazer. Middletown, Conn.: Wesleyan University Press.

Schaeffer, Arnold. 1885–87. *Demosthenes und seine Zeit*. 3 vols. Leipzig: Teubner.

Schäfer, Thomas. 2007. "Ein Frühkaiserzeitliches Relief mit Pompa Triumphalis." In *Nicopolis B. Proceedings of the Second International Nicopolis Symposium (September 11–15, 2002)*, Vol. 1, 471–81, with Vol. 2, 353–56. Preveza: Actia Nicopolis Foundation.

Schnapp, Alain, Fundación Fondo de Cultura de Sevilla, et al. 2008. *El rescate de la Antiguedad clásica en Andalucía: Fundación Focus-Abengoa, Hospital de los Venerables, Sevilla, 24 de Noviembre de 2008–28 de Febrero de 2009*. Seville: Fundación Focus-Abengoa.

Schneider, Rudolf. 1908a. "Griechische Poliorketiker." *Abhandlungen der Königlichen Gesellschaft der Wissenschaften zu Göttingen (Philologisch-Historische Klasse)* Neue Folge 10, no. 1: 1–65 and Tafeln 1–14.

———. 1908b. "Griecische Poliorketiker II." *Abhandlungen der Königlichen Gesellschaft der Wissenschaften zu Göttingen Philologisch-Historische Klasse* Neue Folge 11, no. 1: 1–109 and Tafeln 1–11.

Schramm, Erwin. 1918. *Die antiken Geschütze der Saalburg. Bemerkungen zu ihrer Rekonstruktion*. Berlin: Weidmannsiche Buchhandlung.

Schulten, Adolf. 1927. *Die Lager des Scipio, Band III of Numantia. Die Ergebnisse der Ausgrabungen 1905–1912.* Munich: Bruckmann.

———. 1933. *Geschichte von Numantia.* Munich: Piloty & Loehle.

Seibert, Jakob. 1969. *Untersuchungen zur Geschichte Ptolemaios' I., Münchener Beiträge zur Papyrusforschung und antiken Rechtsgeschichte.* Munich: Beck'sche.

Serbeti, Eleftheria. 2001. Οινιάδες, Οικοδομήματα από την Αρχαία Αγορά. Athens: A. Kardamitsa.

Shatzman, Israel. 1995. "Stone-Balls from Tell Dor and the Artillery of the Hellenistic World." *Scripta Classica Israelica* 14: 52–72.

Shear, T. Leslie, Jr. 1978. *Kallias of Sphettos and the Revolt of Athens in 286 B.C.,* Hesperia Supplements 17. Princeton: American School of Classical Studies at Athens.

Sleeswyk, André Wegener. 1996. "Ramming Trim of Ships." In *Tropis IV: Proceedings of the 4th International Symposium on Ship Construction in Antiquity, Athens 1991,* edited by Harry Tzalas, 429–49. Athens: Hellenic Institute for the Preservation of Nautical Tradition.

Sleeswyk, André Wegener, and Fik Meijer. 1994. "Launching Philopator's 'Forty'." *International Journal of Nautical Archaeology* 23: 115–18.

Southern, Pat. 1998. *Mark Antony.* Stroud, Gloucestershire: Tempus.

Squarciapino, Maria Floriani, Italo Gismondi, Guido Barbieri, Herbert Bloch, and Raissa Calza. 1958. *Scavi di Ostia: Le Necropoli. Parte I. Le Tombe di Età Repubblicana e Augustea.* Vol. 2, 1, Scavi de Ostia. Rome: Libreria dello Stato, 1958.

Steffy, J. Richard. 1991. "The Ram and Bow Timbers: A Structural Interpretation." In *The Athlit Ram,* edited by Lionel Casson and J. Richard. College Station, Tex.: Texas A&M University Press.

———. 1994. *Wooden Ship Building and the Interpretation of Shipwrecks.* College Station, Tex.: Texas A&M University Press.

Steinby, Christa. 2007. *The Roman Republican Navy.* Commentationes Humanarum Littarum 123. Helsinki: Societas Scientiarum Fennica.

Steinhauer, Georges. 2002. "L'épiron du Musée du Pirée." In *Tropis VII: Proceedings of the 7th International Symposium on Ship Construction in Antiquity, Pylos 1999,* edited by Harry Tzalas, 709–24. Athens: Hellenic Institute for the Preservation of Nautical Tradition.

Stern, Ephraim. 1994. *Dor, Ruler of the Seas.* Jerusalem: Israel Exploration Society.

Strauss, Barry S. 2007. "Classical Naval Battles and Sieges." In *Greece, the Hellenistic World and the Rise of Rome,* Vol. 1 of *The Cambridge History of Greek and Roman Warfare,* edited by Philip Sabin, Hans van Wees, Michael Whitby, 223–47. Cambridge: Cambridge University Press.

Sutherland, C. H.V. 1984. *The Roman Imperial Coinage.* Vol. 1, *From 31 B.C. to A.D. 69.* Edited by C. H. V. Sutherland and R. A. G. Carson. Revised ed. London: Spink.

Tarn, W.W. 1910. "The Dedicated Ship of Antigonus Gonatas." *Journal of Hellenic Studies* 30: 209–22.

———. 1913. *Antigonos Gonatas.* Oxford: Clarendon.

―――. (1930) [1966?]. *Hellenistic Military and Naval Developments.* Cambridge: Cambridge University Press. Reprint, New York: Biblo and Tannen.

―――. 1939. "Alexander's Plans." *Journal of Hellenic Studies* 59: 124–35.

Thesaurus Linguae Graecae: A Digital Library of Greek Literature. TLG Project, University of California: Irvine, Calif., 2001–. http://www.tlg.uci.edu/.

Thévenot, M., J. Boivin, and P. de La Hire, eds. 1693. *Veterum mathematicorum Athenaei, Apollodori, Philonis, Bitonis, Heronis et aliorum opera Graeca et Latinae ex manuscriptis codicibus Bibliothecae Regiae pleraque nunc primum edita.* Paris: Pariis, ex Typographia Regia.

Thiel, J. H. 1946. *Studies on the History of Roman Sea-power in Republican Times.* Amsterdam: New-Holland.

Tomlinson, R. A. 1994–95. "Archaeology in Greece 1994–95." *Archaeological Reports* 41: 1–74.

Torelli, Mario. 1982. *Typology and Structure of Roman Historical Reliefs.* Ann Arbor: University of Michigan Press.

Treadgold, Warren. 1995. *Byzantium and Its Army 284–1081.* Stanford: Stanford University Press.

Trombley, Frank. 1997. "The Taktika of Nikephoros Ouranos and Military Encyclopaedism." In *Pre-modern Encyclopaedic Texts: Proceedings of the Second COMERS Congress Groningen, July 1–4, 1996* edited by Peter Binkley. Leiden: Brill.

Trunk, Markus. 2010. "Battala y triunfo: Los relieves históricos de la colección del premier Duque de Alcalá." In *Escultra Romana en Hispania VI: Homenajae a Eva Koppel. Actas de la Reunion international de escultra romana en Hispania, celebrada en el Parque Arqeológico de Segobriga los días 21 y 22 de octubre de 2008,* edited by Juan Manuel Abascal and Rosario Cebrian, 27–44. Murcia: Tabuliarium.

Varoufakis, G. 2007. "Το ἐμβολο τῆς Νικόπολης: Μία νέα γενιά ναυτικού ὁπλου του 1ου αιώνα π.Χ." ("The Ram of Nikopolis: A New Authentic Naval Weapon from the 1st century BC"). In *Nikopolis B: Proceedings of the Second International Nicopolis Symposium (September 11–15, 2002),* edited by Konstantinos L. Zachos, Vol. 1, 453–60 and Vol. 2, 343–45. Preveza: Actia Nikopolis Foundation.

Vermeule III, Cornelius C., and Mary B. Comstock. 1988. *Sculpture in Stone and Bronze: Additions to the Collections of Greek, Etruscan, and Roman Art 1971–1988 in the Museum of Fine Arts, Boston.* Boston: Museum of Fine Arts.

Von Szalay, Akos, and Erich Boehringer. 1937. "D. Die Artillerie von Pergamon." In *Die Hellenistischen Arsenale "Garten der Königen",* 48–56 with Taf. 31–32. Berlin: Walter de Gruyter.

Walbank, F.W. 1988. "From the Battle of Ipsus to the Death of Antigonus Doson." In N. G. L. Hammond and F. W. Walbank, eds. *A History of Macedonia.* Vol. 2, *336–167 BC.* Oxford: Oxford University Press.

―――. (1956–79) 1999. *A Historical Commentary on Polybius.* 3 vols. Oxford: Oxford University Press. Special Sandpiper Books edition. Reprint, London: Sandpiper.

Wallinga, H.T. 1956. *The Boarding Bridge of the Romans.* Groningen: Wolters.

Warner, Rex., trans. 1972. *The History of the Peloponnesian War*. With an introduction and notes by M.I. Finley. Penguin Classics. Harmondsworth: Penguin.

Warry, John. 1995. *Warfare in the Classical World: An Illustrated Encyclopedia of Weapons, Warriors and Warfare in the Ancient Civilizations of Greece and Rome*. Oklahoma Paperbacks edition. Norman, Okla.: University of Oklahoma Press.

Watts, Alan. 1975. *Wind Pilot. Eastern Mediterranean Coasts*. Supplement 4. Lymington, Hampshire: Nautical Publishing Company.

Welles, C. Bradford. 1934. *Royal Correspondence in the Hellenistic Period*. Newhaven: Yale University Press.

Wescher, Carle. 1867. ΠΟΛΙΟΡΚΗΤΙΚΑ ΚΑΙ ΠΟΛΙΟΡΚΙΑΙ ΔΙΑΦΟΡΩΝ ΠΟΛΕΩΝ. *Poliorcétique des Grecs. Traités théoriques.—Récits historiques*. Paris: Imprimerie Impériale.

Westermann, W. L., C. W. Keyes and H. Liebesny, eds. 1940. *Zenon Papyri*. Vol. 2, *Business Papers of the Third Century B.C. Dealing with Palestine and Egypt*. Columbia Papyri Greek Series 4. New York: Columbia University Press.

Wheatley, P.V. 1997. "The Lifespan of Demetrius Poliorcetes." *Historia* 46: 19–27.

Whitehead, David, trans. 1990. *Aineias the Tactician: How to Survive Under Siege*. Clarendon Ancient History Series. Oxford: Oxford University Press.

Whitehead, David, and P. H. Blyth. 2004. *Athenaeus Mechanicus, On Machines (Περί Μηχανημάτων)*. Historia Einzelschriften 182. Stuttgart: Steiner.

Wickander, Charlotte. 2008. "Technologies of Calculation. Part I: Weights and Measures." In *Oxford Handbook of Engineering and Technology in the Classical World*, edited by John P. Oleson. Oxford: Oxford University Press.

Will, Édouard. 1979. *Histoire Politique du Monde Hellénistique (323–330 av JC)*. 2nd ed. Vol. 1. Nancy: Presses Universitaires de Nancy.

———. 1984. "The Succession to Alexander." In *The Hellenistic World*, Vol. 7.1. *The Cambridge Ancient History*, edited by F. W. Walbank, A. E. Astin, M. W. Frederiksen and R. M. Ogilvie, 23–61. Cambridge: Cambridge University Press.

Yadin, Y. 1965. "The Excavation of Masada—1963/64. Preliminary Report." *Israel Exploration Journal* 15: 1–120.

Zachos, Konstantinos L. 2001a. "Excavations at the Actian Tropaeum at Nikopolis. A Preliminary Report." In *Foundation and Destruction: Nikopolis and Northwestern Greece*, edited by Jacob Isager, 29–41. Athens: Danish Institute at Athens; distributed by Aarhus University Press.

———. 2001b. *Το Μνημείο του Οκταβιανού Αυγούστου στη Νικόπολη*. Athens: Ministry of Culture: Scientific Committee for Nikopolis 2001.

———. 2003. "The Tropaeum of the Sea-battle of Actium at Nikopolis: Interim Report." *Journal of Roman Archaeology* 16: 64–92.

Zachos, K.L., D. Kalapakis, H. Kappa, and T. Kyrkou. 2008. *Νικόπολη: Ανακαλύπτοντας την πόλη της νίκης του Αυγούστου*. Athens: Ministry of Culture—Scientific Committee of Nicopolis, 2008.

Zhmud, Leonid. 2006. *The Origin of the History of Science in Classical Antiquity*. Translated by Alexander Chernoglazov. Berlin: de Gruyter.

Index of Citations from Ancient Authors

Parentheses following authors' names contain the abbreviation used in the text; parentheses following text references contain the numbering systems of alternate editions, most notably those utilized by *TLG* and *FGrH*.

1.100.2: 69n1
1.101.1–3: 69n1
1.116–117: 69n1
1.117: 69–70
2.69: 96n58
2.89.1–11: 15
2.89.8: 15
2.90–92: 15n6
3.88: 96n58
4.4.1–3: 70n2
4.8.5–7: 137n26
4.10.5: 140n31
4.14.1: 17n12
4.50: 96n58
6.66.2: 69n2
6.75.1: 71
6.97.1: 71
6.99.2–4: 69–70n2
6.102.1–4: 69–70n2
7.3.5: 72n5
7.7: 20
7.7.1: 70n2, 72n5
7.8.1: 70
7.11.1: 70
7.12.3–5: 72
7.12.4: 72
7.13.1: 70, 72
7.13.2: 72
7.21.3: 18–19
7.21.3–4: 21n18
7.22–24: 21n18
7.23–24: 72
7.25.5: 71
7.25.6–9: 72
7.34.1: 70
7.34.5: 20
7.34.6–8: 21
7.36: 72
7.36.2–5: 21–22
7.36.2–6: 28
7.36.3–4: 17–18
7.36.5: 18n13

7.37–38: 72
7.38.3: 72
7.40.5: 22, 28, 73
7.41.1–2: 72
7.41.1–4: 73
7.41.4: 28
7.42: 73
7.50: 73
7.52.2: 73
7.53: 73
7.53.4: 22, 73
7.56.1: 23
7.59.3: 23, 74, 136n23, 137n26
7.60.3: 74n7, 75
7.62.1–3: 29
7.62.2–63.3: 75
7.62.3: 75
7.65.2: 74n7, 75
7.67.2–3: 74n7, 79
7.69.4: 74, 136n23
7.70.1: 75
7.70.2: 75, 136n23, 137n26
7.70.4–7: 75–76
Valerius Maximus (V. Max.)
  1.8 ext. 11: 272
Vegetius (Veg.)
  Mil.
    1.28: 285n6, 287
    3.24: 138n28
    4.31: 285
    4.32: 285n7
    4.33: 248, 285n7
    4.40: 285n7
    4.41: 285n7
Velleius (Vell.)
  2.84.1: 235n48
  2.84.2: 234n45
Vitruvius (Vitr.)
  1.2.4: 6
  10.13.3: 87n33, 88, 90, 97n62

Inscriptions and Fragmentary Authors

General Index